GONE TO PITCHIPOÏ

A BOY'S DESPERATE FIGHT FOR
SURVIVAL IN WARTIME

JEWS OF POLAND

Series Editor:

Antony POLONSKY—*Brandeis University*

GONE TO PITCHIPOÏ

A BOY'S DESPERATE FIGHT FOR
SURVIVAL IN WARTIME

Rubin KATZ

Boston 2013

Library of Congress Cataloging-in-Publication Data:
A catalog record for this book is available from the Library of Congress.

ISBN 978-1-61811-274-3

Book design by Adell Medovoy

Published by Academic Studies Press in 2013
28 Montfern Avenue
Brighton, MA 02135, USA
press@academicstudiespress.com
www. academicstudiespress.com

To the memory of my loving parents and brothers
whose total commitment to our family
made survival possible
and my sister Fela, to whom I owe my life.

I Shall Not Submit

A child sojourns in solitude.
His eyes at the zenith,
Of not misery, not fear.
Raking and combing the bleak sky,
With a glaring countenance.
A countenance that speaks to the heavens themselves:
"I shall not submit."

A shadow upon the edge of the fog,
A memory – a forbidden childhood.
Never resting, never sleeping,
A ghostly wanderer,
With a penchant for Cain.
With those who housed him saying:
"He shall not submit."

Beneath the love that alters not,
A love not of softness, but of harsh spite.
A caress not of kindness,
But of hatred unending,
With a hunger to swallow the world,
A regime that despises those not of its children
"Who shall not submit."

So why does this child sojourn in solitude?
Why does this ghost wander resolutely?
Why does this love despise those not of its children?
Because of the voice.
The voice inside that shouts,
Not a shout, but a whisper:
"We shall not submit."

> For my grandfather:
> A man of courage like I have never known.
> *Alexander Nico-Katz – Age 14*

CONTENTS

I have endeavoured to recount my wartime experiences through the eyes and emotions of the young boy I was at the time of the Nazi Holocaust against the Jewish people—*my* people.

The only way I could do this was to present it in the form of a chronicle of events and recollections, not necessarily in strict chronological order, augmented here and there with background information. When I first began to commit my memories to paper, I found the process laboriously slow, but gradually my observations, experiences and incidents, all of them factual, came flooding back.

The resulting narrative may at times read like a diary, but in fact I did not keep one. As I was forced by circumstances to be frequently on the move, this would have been impossible, as well as potentially incriminating.

The memories of the traumatic events described here have hardly diminished over the years. So vivid do they remain that even with the passage of decades I did not have to delve deeply to retrieve them: they are always there, and I was able to recall virtually everything.

Apart from fond recollections of an idyllic early childhood, any reference to my birthplace only evokes sadness. Thus for a long time I saw no reason to go back and thereby rekindle unhappy memories. Indeed, it took me forty-six years to return to Poland and my birthplace in 1992. I did so at the behest of my children, who wanted me to retrace my steps and recount my story lest, with the passage of time, my memory of those harrowing years would fade.

Yet, despite my initial hesitation, there was an element of curiosity involved in returning to the scene one last time. Moreover, doing so it enabled me to acquire additional material, as well as photographs of some of the places featured in the narrative.

Though I always intended to record my eyewitness account, I kept putting it off, considering the story, spanning a number of years, too involved, and the task all too daunting. But now I am beholden to my children for having urged me to do so. I had been carrying these memories inside me for all of those years, and committing them to paper unburdened me and gave me a sense of achievement.

First and foremost, I remain deeply indebted to my late mother Gila, for relating the anecdotes and fables of a vanished world she recounted to me, which I attempt to describe in the Prologue. I would also like to thank my dedicated children, David, Simon and Juliette, for going over the original typescript.

Special thanks to Lillian Boraks-Nemetz of Vancouver BC for all her expert advice and invaluable suggestions. My gratitude also goes to Margaret Body for her opinion and constructive comments. I am also grateful to my friend, Dr. Stephen Smith, OBE, Executive Director, USC Shoah Foundation Institute. Formerly of Beth Shalom Holocaust Educational Centre, Laxton, UK for all his help and guidance.

I am deeply indebted to Professor Antony Polonsky of Brandeis University for writing the Introduction to this work, and for introducing me to Sharona Vedol of Academic Studies Press, who was instrumental in bringing this work to fruition. It was a pleasure working with her and Kira Nemirovsky.

Finally, I owe a huge debt to Michèle, my devoted wife of forty-seven years. My deep love and gratitude goes to her for all of her encouragement, patience, and countless hours spent typing and retyping the drafts, which began life in handwritten form many years ago. Without her tireless devotion, this project would not have become a reality.

—Rubin Katz

London 2011

When the Nazis embarked upon their ferocious attempt to murder every Jewish man, woman, and child within their territory, they left no stone unturned. They were persistent in their efforts to make sure no one escaped their clutches. They had a tightly guarded system of ghettos and camps, supported by an eager network of collaborators and inform- ants, making it virtually impossible to be Jewish and to live outside of the system without being denounced, caught, or handed in.

To live alone and to survive against these huge odds required courage, skill, ingenuity, quick thinking and some luck. Constantly assessing who could be trusted and who could not meant moving from place to place, assuming a new identity or a new story to fit the new circumstances. Few, if any, could be trusted—and yet from time to time the only way to survive was to rely on the goodwill of others. Lack of food, lack of clothing, no access to shelter or accommodation, the ever present pang of hunger, adverse weather, and the constant fear of being caught meant that day–to-day living was living life right on the edge of existence. Sur- viving the enemy was one thing; surviving the elements another. It was never safe. Death was only one wrong move away.

Rubin Katz was just eight years old when the Nazis invaded his home town of Ostrowiec. As a mere child, he managed to slip through the net of destruction and evade the system of camps and ghettos, and survived almost the entire period of the Nazi occupation of Poland living alone. It sounds impossible, and yet this young boy demonstrated that it was in fact possible to outlive the Nazis. He tells his story through the lens of a child, describing his survival as an "adventure." His story is compelling, drawing you into each twist of fate and ingenuity as he defies detec- tion and death time and time again. Beautifully and insightfully told, his story takes us behind the scenes. We see the normality of life for those who were not under threat and simultaneously the hostility and treachery that threatened those who were marked for death.

When his journey of survival started, only instinct could have told him what to do: he was living day-by-day in an animal existence. By the time the war ended, survival had become a finely honed skill. The

13-year-old Rubin Katz had been in hiding in the open air for almost half of his life, so on the day he rode into Warsaw atop a Russian tank feeling as if he personally were liberating the city, his sense of victory was entirely well deserved. He had outsmarted the Nazis, he had outwitted their collaborators, and he had outlived his death sentence again and again. He survived, but he was more than a survivor—he had won his battle with the system of death, and was the *victor* in his own war against the Nazis.

—Dr. Stephen D. Smith, OBE

Executive Director, USC Shoah Foundation Institute
February 2011

This vivid and moving memoir, like a number of other accounts which have appeared in recent years,[1] describes the survival of a Jewish child in the hell of Nazi-occupied Poland. Its author, Rubin Katz, was born in Ostrowiec Świętokrzyski in 1931. This town, located in the picturesque countryside of central Poland 42 miles south of Radom, had in 1931 a population of nearly 30,000 people, of whom more than a third were Jews. In the nineteenth century a local Jewish entrepreneur, Leopold Frankel, had established a metallurgical works making use of the iron ore in the surrounding hills, and by the end of the century this factory had become the second largest in Congress Poland, the area whose autonomy, granted at the Congress of Vienna, was almost entirely done away with after the unsuccessful 1863 revolt against tsarist Russia. Modern politics had penetrated the town, and during the revolution of 1905-07 it was the scene of considerable unrest and strikes.

Nevertheless, Ostrowiec Świętokrzyski retained many of the characteristics of the traditional Polish market town—the Jewish *shtetl*—that was still a major focus of Jewish life in the interwar period. In these towns, the social hierarchy was very different from that in the big towns, or in the country as a whole. Here the Jews constituted a significant part of the social and economic elite, and the non-Jewish inhabitants were, to a considerable degree, their clients or employees. Most Jews lived in the centre of the town, around the market-place, often in quite poor conditions, while non-Jews lived in the outskirts. These towns were also linked with the surrounding countryside. The two populations lived in what has been described as a "pattern of 'distant proximity" based on continued economic exchange and mutual disdain. Most Jews were economic middlemen—'pariah capitalists' filling a necessary but unpopular position between what had been the two major *strata* in the Polish lands, the peasantry and the landowners.[2] Jews and peasants mostly interacted in the economic sphere. On market days in the *shtetlakh*, and during the week as travellers in the countryside, Jews purchased agricultural produce from peasants and sold them goods produced in the towns. The weekly market in Ostrowiec is vividly described in the following pages. There were also closer contacts, with country people working as servants in Jewish homes and consulting Jews on medical matters. The folk music of the two groups also reflected their mutual interaction.

At the same time, the views which the two groups held of each other were marked by deeply entrenched prejudices. The peasants and the Gentile populations of these smaller towns despised the Jews for their lack of connection to the land, and distrusted them as cunning and untrustworthy trading partners, although their business skills were sometimes admired. The attitude of the Jews toward their Christian neighbours was equally contemptuous. In their eyes, the peasants were uncivilized and uncultured. This contempt was mitigaged by a feeling of pity resulting from their awareness that the peasants were even poorer than they were themselves.

The religious divide reinforced the wide gap between the two groups. The peasants saw the Jews as adherents of a religion which was not only false but deicidal, and found Jewish religious practices bizarre and in-comprehensible. To the Jews, Christianity was both idolatrous and hy-pocritical, since in their eyes it combined a call to "turn the other cheek" with encouragement of violent antisemitism. The relationship between the two groups was also at odds with the larger political environment, in which the Jews were at best second-class citizens. The two groups had very few close social relations: as Rubin points out, he had virtually no non-Jewish friends.

Although it remained a stronghold of tradition, the Jewish small town was not unaffected by developments in the country as a whole, and this was certainly the case in Ostrowiec Świętokrzyski. The traditional communal institutions—the town rabbinate, the burial society, the *bes medresh* (prayer hall) and the *mikve*—remained the focus of communal life. The persistence of traditional ways of life and the importance of the local hasidic rebbe in Ostrowiec, Yechiel-Meier (Halevi) Halsztok, as well as the introduction of such modernities as bubble gum, are effectively described in this memoir. So too are the deep political divi-sions between the Orthodox Jews, the Zionists, and the socialist Bund members. Ostrowiec seems to have been less affected by anti-Jewish violence after 1935 than some other towns of the Kielce province, such as Przytyk and Odrzywół. Rubin describes his childhood as "idyllic." His family was traditional—his father was a supporter of the religious

Zionist grouping Mizrachi—and prosperous. His mother's family had long been confectioners, and in the 1930s their sweet factory, located on the outskirts of the town, was the third-largest in Poland. Rubin's family lived on the fringe of the city, where he developed a strong feeling for nature and a solitary temperament. His main companion was his beloved dog Dynguś. The youngest of six children, he grew up in a loving and protected environment. Like his siblings, he began to adopt the Polish language and not only attended a heder but also completed the first year of Polish primary school, which he describes in somewhat equivocal terms. Although Jewish children felt their isolation, they were able to defend themselves and, in Rubin's view, were viewed with some sympathy by their female fellow students.

This secure and happy childhood was brutally interrupted by the Nazi occupation of western and central Poland.[3] The Germans entered Ostrowiec on September 7, 1939, and almost immediately began to persecute the local Jewish population, demanding a "contribution" of 200,000 zloty and killing ten Jews. Forced labour was imposed on the Jewish male population, at the end of September a Judenrat was established to facilitate German control, and by the end of the year Jews were required to wear an armband with a Star of David. Jewish property, including the Katz family's factory, was confiscated, and the factory was placed under two *Treuhänder, Volksdeutsche* from Poznań. In April 1941, a ghetto was established. Its population, swelled by refugees from nearby towns, numbered nearly 16,000. It was unfenced, and although the penalty for leaving it was death, a number of Jews were able to find shelter outside. Many of those confined in the ghetto worked in nearby labour camps or armament factories. The first deportation of Jews from the ghetto began on October 10, 1942, and resulted in ten to twelve thousand Jews being sent to their deaths in Treblinka. Some of those who had found hiding places were induced to come into the open with the promise of work in the armaments factory of Starachowice, but these were also then murdered. A second deportation began on January 10, 1943, following which only about 1,000 Jews were left in Ostrowiec. Some of thems were able to join the local Home Army (Armia Krajowa) detachment, but others were murdered by their supposed colleagues when they tried to enter this force. Among those who died in this way was Rubin's cousin Meier Berman, along with a number of his friends. The ghetto was fully liquidated at the end of March 1943, with most of its remaining inhabitants murdered, while around a thousand were sent to a forced labour camp in town. The labour camp, to which people were also sent from Piotrków Trybunalski, Starachowice, and Płaszów, was liquidated in August 1944.

Initially the impact of the war on the Katz family was relatively limited, but soon it was forced to move to the ghetto, and as conditions worsened Rubin's father, a very enterprising and dynamic individual, was able to obtain false papers for his wife, for Rubin's sister Fela, who used them to flee to Warsaw, where she would pass for a Gentile, and for Rubin. During the October 1942 deportation, five members of the family, including Rubin, hid in a bunker that had been prepared earlier. Rubin's two eldest brothers, Moniek and Izak, who had earlier decided to stay with the family rather than flee to the Soviet Union, remained in the ghetto to provide them with food. The hiding place was discovered by German troops, but miraculously the fugitives were not executed. Eventually, they were returned to the small ghetto which was created after the deportation. Moniek, however, now contracted a blood disorder and died. As the situation declined further, and Rubin, as a young child, was in increasing danger, his brother Leizer arranged for him to shelter with a Polish acquaintance, an engine driver named Radzik. When Rubin arrived, however, Radzik's wife would not take the risk. Willing though she was to risk herself in assisting the Katz family through its ordeal—as she would continue to do later—she could not endanger the safety of her own child, and Rubin was forced to return to the ghetto.

Through Izak's initiative, the family was able to find a new hiding place during the second major deportation, in January of 1943. When the ghetto was liquidated, Rubin escaped, and hid in the brick factory where two of his brothers worked and where he had several close brushes with death. He then hid in the Labour Camp where his brothers and the rest of his family were housed and finally, in December 1943, found shelter with his sister in Warsaw. Here he again had a number of close brushes with death, several of which he survived because he was able cleverly to conceal his circumcision. He and Fela witnessed the devastation of the Warsaw Uprising and were finally liberated by Soviet troops in mid-January 1945. The return to Ostrowiec, of whose Jews nearly none survived, was to prove a great disappointment. On the night that Fela returned to the town looking for her parents in mid-March 1945, the house in which the few surviving Jews were living was attacked, and four of the survivors were killed. Fortunately Fela had decided to stay elsewhere. She subsequently returned to the town with Rubin, as did their mother, who had been sent to Auschwitz and Ravensbrück after the liquidation of the labour camp in Ostrowiec and who had finally been liberated by the Russians at Neustadt-Glöwen. Rubin's father and three remaining brothers, unable to find shelter in Ostrowiec with their non-Jewish acquaintances, had been sent to Auschwitz and then Mauthausen, and only two brothers, Leizer and Abram, survived. These two moved immediately to Palestine. The combination of a desire to participate in the development of the emerging Jewish state, the persistent anti-Jewish violence in Poland, and the difficulty of living in a town where so many of their relatives and friends had died led Rubin's mother and sister, who had married Benjamin Majerczak, an officer in the Polish army created by the new authorities, to leave Poland for Israel. Rubin himself moved to England, where he had an uncle, under the sponsorship of Rabbi Solomon Shonfeld. The memoir concludes with an account of Rubin's adaptation to life in England in spite of his desire to participate in the Israeli War of Independence.

Although completed more than sixty years after the events it describes, the memoir is remarkable for the ability of its author to recall so many events in detail and for the way he is able to be fair to all those caught up in the tragic dilemmas of those years. It is a major contribution to our understanding of the fate of Jews in smaller Polish towns during the Second World War and the conditions which made it possible for some of them, like Rubin, his sister Fela, two of his brothers, and his mother to survive, though they led to the deaths of his father and his remaining two brothers. It also explains why most of those who survived, including Rubin and his remaining family, fled Poland in the immediate post-war period.

—Antony Polonsky

Brandeis University,
Albert Abramson Professor of Holocaust Studies

Endnotes

1 Henryk Grynberg, Żydowska wojna (second ed., Warsaw, 1989); *Zwycięstwo* (Paris, 1989); English translation, *The Jewish War* and *The Victory* (translated by Richard Lourie, Evanston, IL, 2001); Bogdan Wojdowski, *Chleb rzucony umarłym* (seventh ed., Warsaw, 1990); English translation *Bread for the Departed* (translated by Madeline Levine, Evanston, IL, 1997); Michał Głowiński, *Czarny sezony* (3rd ed., Kraków, 2002); English translation, *The Black Seasons,* (translated by Marci Shore, Evanston, IL, 2005); Wilhelm Dichter, *Kon Pana Boga* (Kraków, 1996); *Szkoła bezbożników* (Kraków, 1999); English translation *God's horse* and *The atheists' school* (translated by Madeline Levine, Evanston, IL, 2012).

2 Ewa Morawska, "Polish Jewish Relations in America, 18801940: Old Elements, New Configurations," *Polin: Studies in Polish Jewry*, vol. 19, 72-5.

3 On the fate of the Jews in Ostrowiec Świętokrzyski during the Second World War, see the article by Caterina Crisci in Geoffrey Megargee, and Martin Dean, eds., *The United States Holocaust Memorial Museum Encyclopedia of Camps and Ghettos, 1933-1945*, Volume II: *Ghettos in German-Occupied Eastern Europe* (Bloomington and Indianapolis, IN, 2012); Abraham Wein, Bracha Freundlich, and Wila Orbach, eds., *Pinkas hakehilot: Encyclopedia of Jewish Communities in Poland,* vol. 7, *Lublin and Kielce* (Jerusalem, 1999) 55-8; J. Rosenberg, *Nazywam się Józef Nowak* (Warsaw, 2004); M. Geshuri, ed., *Sefer Ostrovtse: lezikaron uleadut* (Tel Aviv, 1971), and M. Jacobs, *Holocaust Survivor: Mike Jacobs' Triumph over Tragedy, a Memoir* (ed. G. Jacobs, Austin,TX, 2001).

A Carefree Childhood

I was born into a traditional Jewish family in 1931, in a small town in the Kielce province of south-central Poland with a long, unpronounceable name: Ostrowiec-Świętokrzyski, to give it its full due. The second part of the name is to differentiate it from one or two other, similar-sounding places. Świętokrzyski stands for Holy Cross, after the range of low-lying hills in the province. The town had also been referred to as Ostrowiec-on-Kamienna, the river that runs through the town, which makes more sense. However, during the Occupation, the Germans did away with the Holy Cross designation altogether and referred to it as Ostrowitz (Radom District). Perhaps the original name was too long and too difficult for any German to pronounce! After the war, the place reverted back to its original double-barrelled name, the name it had when I spent an idyllic early childhood there, in lovely pastoral surroundings.

I was the youngest of six siblings, and my family owned a substantial chocolate factory—surely every child's dream! Once, as an inquiring young boy, I realized I simply had to know how my birthplace came to acquire its unusually long name. If anyone should know, I reasoned, it would be my mother Gila, as she and her parents before her were natives of Ostrowiec-Świętokrzyski. My mother came up with an amusing tale, involving the *szlachta*, or gentry, no less. This type of storytelling was characteristic of her; she was well-versed in folklore and loved telling tales, and had quite a repertoire. Mama went on to explain that way back in time, before roads were paved, the deep swamps in our area were legendary. One day, the local *hrabia* (count) is said to have toured the estates within his domain, which included the marshlands where Ostrowiec-Świętokrzyski stands today. As the vast bog-lands of the Kamienna valley were not easy to traverse, the nobleman's carriage-and-pair got stuck and began to sink ever deeper into the mud. The horses reared up and began to neigh wildly, refusing to go any further. Consequently, the count got ruffled and charged his coachman to urge the horses on, yelling at him sternly: "*Ostro-wić!*," to press on sharply and extricate the carriage forthwith. Thereafter, this stretch of bog-land came to be known as Ostrowiec, to mark the very spot where our noble count had almost met his demise. Presumably the town had to later adopt the Holy Cross designation to avoid any confusion with other places bearing the same name. One may safely deduce from this that the other lordships must have undergone much the same ordeal in the deep mire!

During my childhood, Ostrowiec-Świętokrzyski was a small indus-trial town and yet an important metallurgical centre in Poland. While the place itself may have been rather drab and polluted by heavy in-dustry, the surrounding area was wooded and pastoral, like most of Poland. It is situated in the valley of the Kamienna River, which flows into the nearby Wisła, or Vistula, the main river in Poland. This in turn empties into the Baltic Sea, way up to the north. The local Zakłady smelting plant employed several thousand people from the surround-ing area, producing pig-iron as well as rolling stock. From where we lived, we could look down on the town and beyond, toward an array of tall chimney-stacks that dominated the skyline, with a mix of black and white smoke billowing out of them. A separate pall of smoke always hung in the sky over the northern edge of town, where the steel furnace was first established in the nineteenth century by the Jewish banker and industrialist Baron Leopold Frankel. The existence of this heavy industry would prove to be a godsend, if you can call it that; it provided a lifeline for its Jewish inhabitants during the war. As a result of the Nazi policy of exploitation of Jewish labour, they maintained a slave labour camp for 2,000 inmates, mostly employed at the steelworks. This resulted in staving off, at least for a time, their total destruction, unlike the inhabitants of many other communities that were wiped out without trace.

Ostrowiec-Św. had a Jewish population of about ten thousand be-fore the war, forming roughly one-third of the town's inhabitants. This really qualified it as a *shtoht,* or town in Yiddish, as opposed to a *shtetl,* which is the diminutive of the former, but the dwellers felt more com-fortable with the latter designation, as it signified communal warmth and cohesion in times of both happiness and sorrow. The Polish *shtetl* was typically a small market town where the Jewish inhabitants led a traditional lifestyle, usually in grinding poverty but nevertheless happy in their quaint way of life, or so I'm led to believe. The tightly-knit community dated back to the middle of the seventeenth century when the place was first founded, and the main synagogue in the centre of town was built in that period. In fact, the old wooden synagogue was the most historically interesting structure in town, though sadly it was burnt to the ground by the Nazis during the war. There was also an ancient Jewish cemetery situated right in the middle of town, in use since 1657. That site dated back to the time of Jan Sobieski, the legendary Polish king who led the allied army that stopped the Ottoman Turks at the gates of Vienna, thereby saving European Christendom from the infidels.

Reverence for the dead plays an important part in Jewish tradition. And wherever Jews set down roots, contrary to what one would think, the first thing they do is not build a synagogue, but purchase a piece of land for a burial ground, so they can lay their dead to rest. It's not obligatory to pray in a synagogue; a modest room in a private house will suffice. Over the years, most Jews tended to gravitate towards the Rynek or market square and the streets and alleyways leading off it, as well as in the proximity of the synagogue on Starakunowska. This street was referred to within the community as Schwamegass, for the story that an entire Jewish family who lived there had died as a result of having eaten poisonous *schwammen,* mushrooms, that they had gathered in a nearby wood. This heavily-Jewish neighborhood was the oldest and poorest part of town, where everyone knew everyone else, and people led a lowly existence, toiling hard to eke out a bare living.

Though small, our town boasted an acclaimed *rebbe*; communities vied with each other for the honour of hosting such a great scholar. A *rebbe*, as opposed to a rabbi, is a Hasidic spiritual leader and guide. Our crowning glory was Rabbi Yechiel-Meier (Halevi) Halsztok, who fasted for no less than forty years—or at least was never seen eating in public. This was in an effort to hasten *geulah,* the redemption, when the Messiah would come. People said he was more a *tzaddik,* a saintly man, than a mere rabbi. Although there is no cult of saints in Judaism, some of these mystic holy men were reputedly endowed with the authority to act as intermediaries between Man and God, like the legendary Levi-Yitzhok of Berdichev, who with utmost respect and humility boldly dared to question his Maker for allowing so much suffering to afflict His people. The much-loved figure passed on during the early nineteenth century, but during my time there was an intense song dedicated to the revered rabbi, "*Und der Rebbe fun Berdichev zohgt*," "The Rabbi of Berdichev says." The song was immortalised in the 1930s by the acclaimed black American singer Paul Robeson, who sang it in faultless Yiddish. It was in the form of a remonstration with the Almighty by Rabbi Levi-Yitzhok of Berdichev.

Our own beloved *rebbe* was a pious and humble man, but unlike other famous sages he didn't encourage or foster a cult following. He preferred to be remembered as the author of essays and commentaries on the Halakha (Jewish Law). A man of ascetic habits, he lived an austere life of utmost piety. After fathering a son and daughter early in his married life, he distanced himself from the physical world and led the life of a celibate. It was even rumoured that his wife, the *rebbetzin*, had summoned him before the town's rabbinical court to account for his neglectful connubial conduct. Thereafter the *rebbe* withdrew into intense study for the rest of his life. After his death in 1928, his more temporal son, Yehezkel, known affectionately as "Hezkele," succeeded him, to become the spiritual head of the community during my own childhood. As a young boy, I wasn't so much impressed by his father's scholarly accomplishments as by his ability to get by without eating! As I got older, I became rather disillusioned when I discovered that our esteemed *rebbe* did not in fact subsist entirely without sustenance, and apparently survived on a diet of figs and milk at night, before retiring.

The hasidic movement which galvanized Eastern-European Jewry began in the eighteenth century. Its founder was a legendary "wonder-rabbi" known as the Baal Shem-Tov. Hasidism was a pietistic spiritual movement that attracted a large following within the Jewish masses of Poland and Eastern Europe. The quaint Hasidim dressed in distinctive garb, particularly on the Sabbath. This comprised a silky black caftan, which was tied round the waist with a plaited cord when immersed in prayer. The cord symbolically separated the upper from the lower, unchaste, part of the body. The headgear consisted of a *shtreimel*—a large fur hat trimmed with sable tails—and knee-high white or black socks, depending on the sect, completed the outfit. As the majority of shtetl dwellers were humble folk who had to struggle to make a bare living, the idea of hasidism appealed to them. It came to be known as the religion of the poor, and advocated that the destitute and downtrodden could serve God by whatever means with joy in their hearts in their humdrum everyday lives.

The hasidim had their fierce opponents in the misnagdim, who were opposed to, amongst other things, the hasidic practice they called *Rebbe-worship*. The misnagdim were mainly centred round Vilna, the capital of Lithuania, which was once part of the Polish commonwealth. The better-educated Litvaks, i.e., Lithuanian Jews, as personified by their spiritual leader and mentor, the eighteenth-century Gaon of Vilna, who preached that the true way to God is through intensive Torah study and scholarship, believed in learning for the sake of learning. A Gaon, in the Ashkenazi tradition, is a Talmudic genius; the title is rarely awarded, and is conferred only on a rabbi of exceptional learning. It was said that the Gaon of Vilna had mastered the Torah at the age of eight, and the hidden complexities of the Talmud by the time he was nine. The Hasidim, on the other hand, maintained that this was not the only way to God, as the impoverished Jewish masses in Poland had no means for all-day study. Unlike their Litvak opponents, the spirited Hasidim exalted in singing and dancing ecstatically, as if under a spell, to soulful Klezmer music played by fiddlers as an essential element in the worship of The Almighty. During these enraptured festivities, moderate imbibing of *schnapps* was, if not encouraged, certainly not frowned upon! Hence, the more animated Hasidim, who believed it was a *mitzvah* (divine command) to be constantly happy, earned the reputation of being joyful and fun-loving, and the traditionalist Misnagdim were thought of as scholarly but dour. The followers of these competing forms of Judaism were generally contemptuous of each other—it even went as far as the Vilna Gaon invoking a ban on the Polish Hasidim!

Apart from the animosity between Polish and Lithuanian Jewry, they were both also at odds with the Galitzianer, and of course vice versa. The last group hailed from the province of Galitzia, a part of the Austro-Hungarian Empire that ruled over a chunk of Poland. Both the Galitzianers and the Litvaks spoke Yiddish with a different accent from that of the Poles. Otherwise there was little outward distinction between them; there was only geography and of course the accent, which only became apparent when they opened their mouth. For instance, Polacks thought it funny that Litvaks could not pronounce the "sh" as in *shlemiel*—this came out as *slemiel*, and would have everyone in stitches. Nevertheless, the Litvak version of Yiddish is far more pleasant to the ear than the Polish rendering, in my opinion and that of many others.

These divisions were mainly societal, but they were enough to set the groups apart, and they rarely intermarried in those days. These communities are no more, but interestingly there still exists in the West until today a symbolic division among their Orthodox descendants, though this only manifests itself in the type of prayer-house their adherents belong to.

A Hasidic following was named after the place where its *rebbe* resided and from which he headed the community; for instance, there are Hasidic groups known as Belz, Gur, Kotzk, and so on. In our town there were several prayer and study-houses, each one called a *schtiebl,* literally a small room, with each *schtiebl* representing a different Hasidic sect. Every adherent would try to journey at least once a year to wherever their *rebbe* held court, and they would hardly leave his side over an entire weekend, starting with Friday afternoon. They would participate at the *rebbe's tisch* (table), over which he would preside, surrounded by his devoted disciples. This was especially at the last of the three festive Sabbath meals, when it was customary for the *rebbe* to deliver a *vort,* literally word, but in fact an in-depth Talmudic hair-splitting discourse that the adherents looked forward to the entire weekend. Such an experience was a most joyous occasion and a major event in the life of a Hasid. During the same weekend, the visitor would seek a blessing from his spiritual mentor, or advice on a matrimonial or family matter. Another possibility was to pass a *kvittle,* a missive, to the *Rebbe*, with a request for the Almighty to heal a sick relative, or asking that some other wish be fulfilled. Some of these Hasidic Masters were even said to possess mystic powers that could work miracles, and some had such a wide following that the places they held court at were well-known to the wider community because of all the disciples heading for it. This was so much the case that it's said Polish day labourers and peasants, when booking a fare, would ask for a ticket *do Rabina*—to the rabbi—without mentioning the name of the place he resided!

Every shtetl had to have its own Sabbath *klapper,* a sort of "town crier," for want of a better term. The *klapper's* duty was to hurry from door to door in the Jewish neighbourhood on Friday before sunset and *klap,* or tap, several times with a wooden mallet on the doors and shutters of Jewish shops to remind the shopkeepers of the imminent start of the Sabbath and summon them for evening prayers.

The *klapper* would rap harder on the shutters of shops whose keepers were prone to be lax with their time-keeping, urging them to conclude their business. The latter were tempted to take advantage of the last-minute trade prior to the onset of the Sabbath at sundown, when all manual work must cease, when trading and the handling of money is not permitted.

My father, Moshe-Aron, was referred to as *Reb* Moshke by his friends. The respectful title *Reb* was merited only by a learned man or a well-to-do householder. Father was an observant Jew, respected for his talmudic learning, wisdom, and modesty. As a young man, he had attended a yeshiva, a talmudic academy. Although not a Hasid himself, he was an admirer of the Gerer *Rebbe* of Góra Kalwaria, who headed a moderate branch of hasidism known as Gur. Father dressed in a modern manner and was clean-shaven, but as a traditional Jew he always kept his head covered outdoors, with a grey trilby during the week and a navy one reserved for the Sabbath. His political affiliation lay with the Mizrachi, religious-Zionist, movement. Unlike many people of the shtetl, my father was not ultra-, but rather modern-Orthodox. And our way of life was more rooted in Jewish traditions, imbued with a love of Zion, than focused on strict religious observance. Father embraced modernity, was a supporter of Haskalah, the Jewish enlightenment, and was a firm believer in Jewish ethics and values, combined with a worldly outlook.

My mother Gila, on the other hand, came from a traditional but not Orthodox background. She was mainly preoccupied with taking care of us children and running a substantial and welcoming kosher household. We were six siblings: my eldest brother was Moniek, then there was Izak, followed by my only sister Fela, Leizer, Abram, and finally me. Moniek and Leizer stood out as the most studious among us. Being the youngest in a large family, I was of course the centre of attraction and thoroughly spoiled. My registered Polish name was Rubin, with no middle name, and I was often called by the diminutive Rubinek. But my grandparents and older Yiddish-speaking relatives preferred to call me Rievele; this was after my paternal grandmother Rieva, after whom I was named. It was the custom to name children after their departed close relatives, to perpetuate their memory. And as I was the last to be born, I had to be named after my granny! As I got older I gained yet another affectionate name, ketzele (kitten), based on the family name, but this one I really disliked; I felt I merited a more grown-up name. Actually, pet names and nicknames were part of shtetl lore, and I shall talk about them later.

We kept the Jewish traditions and celebrated all the festivals, which were always joyous occasions in our home. Father observed the Sabbath customs and liked to don a festive satin robe on Friday evening in honour of the Sabbath. As it was too far to walk to the Synagogue, and observant Jews don't ride on the Sabbath, evening prayers were said at home. As Jews have done for centuries, on Sabbath eve Father welcomed in the figurative Shabbat bride with joy and the song "Come, My Love, to Meet the Bride." Before dinner, Mama lit candles in the silver candlesticks and said the blessing over them, and the family sat around the dinner-table set with best china and white linen, laden with food, while the delicious fragrance of traditional dishes filled the house. Next, Father recited *Kiddush,* the benediction, over a large silver goblet filled to the brim with sweet wine. After this came *Moitzi,* the breaking of two loaves of bread, symbolising the double helping of heavenly manna that the Israelites received for Shabbat in the wilderness. This came in the shape of plaited *challah* loaves, with round ones for festivals. Next, Father blessed his younger children with the priestly blessing. Laying his hands on my head, he recited "God make you like Ephraim and Menasse," the two mighty sons of the biblical Joseph, born to him in Egypt. Then he broke into the traditional Shabbat Eve hymns in his melodious voice, starting with "Welcome, greetings, O' ministering angels, angels of the Most High." Then, turning to Mama, he recited from the Proverbs: "A woman of valour, who can find? Her worth is far beyond pearls..." The sumptuous dinner, accompanied by traditional songs, was followed by the Grace after Meals. All this added to the magical aura of Shabbat in the home. The next morning we strolled in a leisurely way, as a family, to the synagogue for morning services, except for my mother and sister, who stayed behind to prepare the table for the festive lunch. In the evening, at the conclusion of Shabbat, it was Mama's turn to offer a blessing for the family for the forthcoming week. It was a touching little prayer in Yiddish, unlike most prayers, which are in Hebrew. It is recited by the mother of the household, and begins with *"Gott fun Avrum"*—God of Abraham, of Isaac and of Jacob, protect my family and guard the entire House of Israel in the coming week...

Family snapshot taken outside our home in the summer of 1937.
I was the youngest, aged six at the time.

My mother Gila, *née* Berman, was easy-going, but Father expected a measure of discipline from his sons, which we didn't really object to. Although devout himself, Father was not judgmental, and was tolerant of others. He didn't try to impose the burden of strict religious observance on us children, but his overriding desire was that we acquire a good religious grounding, and he strove to instil in us a positive Jewish identity. My older brothers were more interested in secular subjects, of which he also approved, but he never tired of saying that religious education would hold one in good stead. He maintained that it was important to be able to mix at every level of society, be it religious or secular, and he himself could interact with the high and low. He was fond of repeating the maxim, "Be a Jew in the home and a *Mentsch* (upright being) in the street." Father was blessed with a good baritone voice, and led the service in the synagogue on special occasions. He also read the weekly Torah portion from the *Bimah*, the raised podium in the synagogue auditorium. This requires a prodigious memory, as the Torah scroll is hand-written by a scribe, without vowels or cantillation notes. No pronunciation or grammatical mistakes are permitted, as this could alter the meaning of the Word of God; as the precept says, "Ye shall not add unto the word which I command you, neither shall ye diminish from it." Father was an articulate person who spoke Biblical

Hebrew fluently, and to prove a point with a learned friend he was fond of quoting scriptural verses in Hebrew or Aramaic from the sacred texts and commentaries. As he was a prominent member of the community, many came to seek his counsel. He was also a founding member of the Social Welfare Institution and Loan Fund for the needy of our town.

On the other hand, my mother's side of the family, the Bermans, though traditional in their ways, were not religiously observant. Their interest lay not in Torah study but in the chocolate and confectionery business in which they excelled. In fact, within the family, the Bermans as opposed to the Katzs had the amusing reputation of possessing powerful arms and strong, heat-resistant, hands, developed as a result of working with hot molten sugar for generations. They were accustomed to folding, kneading, and pummelling the stretchy mass, liberally sprinkled with edible talc to avoid any sticking, on steel tables as air bubbles burst with a loud pop. Their skill in the sugar business led to a rather unkind saying within the family: "The Bermans may have the brawn, but the Katzs possess the brains!"

Our German-sounding family name, Katz, predates the time when Jews were first given surnames in western-Europe in the sixteenth century and is not in fact of German origin despite its sound. The name had at some stage been Polonized by some naming official to the phonetic Polish spelling Kac, which sounds the same, as there is no "tz" letter combination in the Polish language. My pride swelled when Father explained that we were hereditary Hebrew priests by birth, belonging to the Kohanim, the priestly caste. Our name has its origin in the Temple of Solomon, no less. The name Katz is a Hebrew acronym for Kohen Tzedek, Righteous Priest, for those who officiated in the ancient temple of Jerusalem. This birthright is passed down from father to son ever since the destruction of the last temple by the Romans in 70 CE. All this made me feel rather important, having discovered that we descended from the brother of the biblical Moses, Aaron, who headed the tribe of Levi and was the first High Priest; a bloodline going back more than 3,500 years. The Kohanim were the nobility in ancient Israel. Father said that we would revert to that role with the coming of the Messiah when the temple is rebuilt.

My earliest distressing recollection is of being run over by a horse and cart as I darted across the street when I was about four years old. Fortunately, I escaped with just a broken leg. Apparently, I hobbled along with my plaster cast and when asked what I had there would re-ply, pointing at my leg, "*Watte fiessele*": a cotton wool leg! This amused my relatives no end, and the expression stuck. And thus I acquired yet another pet name; to all the doting uncles and aunts I was surrounded by, I was *watte fiessele*. But to my brothers I was simply *mazik,* a doting name for a mischievous child. I never liked these pet names, but only my lovely sister called me by my proper name.

Another of my abiding early memories is of being carried off into the woods by a *meshuggene,* a village simpleton, when I was about five years old. Fortunately, feeble-minded Mendel was placid and quite harmless. He dressed in a black caftan with peaked velvet cap, in the style of young Orthodox men. Mendel was not originally from our town; he apparently stemmed from a good background and was well-educated. People said that some tragic event in his life had in some way affected his mind. And so, one nice summer's morning, I disappeared with him from outside our home. Word spread and within minutes almost half the community went looking for me. Mendel and I reappeared in late afternoon, happily strolling down Sienkiewicz Street from the direc-tion of the woods, holding hands. I had had an exciting time gathering wild strawberries and blueberries in the forest, and didn't understand what all the fuss was about. When Mendel was admonished for taking me away, he replied innocently: "I saw this little boy with fair curly hair standing there and I thought he would enjoy coming *yagde* picking with me." He was never punished for it, since he and other characters like him were not only tolerated but formed part of the local scene. They hurt no one, and people would feed and help them. There was no crime within the community and there was no need to lock doors in the pre-dominantly Jewish neighbourhood. These unfortunate characters may have been at the bottom of the heap, but they were nevertheless part of shtetl life.

We lived in a somewhat isolated spot outside town, in a spacious home in idyllic rural surroundings next door to the family chocolate factory. I was free to wander and disappear for hours on end, together with my pet dog Dynguś, so long as I showed up at mealtime. I was really a country lad by environment, if not by background. We had no Jewish neighbours in our immediate vicinity—or any other neigh-bours, for that matter. I had no playmates and spent a lot of time on my own, but I was used to the solitude and my own company and because of it I suppose I grew into a solitary boy. The factory building and our adjoining home were built towards the end of the nineteenth century as *koszary,* or brick-built barracks for the czarist imperial army, mortgaged by the Pfeffer banking family, financed by the Jewish community in order to placate the czarist authorities. Our province had been under Russian domination, situated on the western edge of the Russian Pale of Settlement, within the boundaries of where Jews were allowed to settle. Apart from the factory complex, our home and the nearby school building, there was just open countryside. I loved exploring the area and have fond memories of roaming freely with my pet dog Dynguś at my side, leaping joyfully through the fields of corn, interspersed with red poppies and blue cornflowers, chasing butterflies, while Dynguś went after the field mice which seemed to entrance him. I enjoyed an exhilarating and adventurous boyhood in the country. That was my own secret playground; oh, how I wished it would remain like this forever. Apart from the nearby gently-swaying wheat fields, there were also potato fields with endless furrows running far into the distance. At harvest time, after the peasants had dug up the crop and departed, I would dig deeper for any leftovers and roast them in the banked-up ashes of a dying fire that I made with the wilted potato plants; there was no other kindling to be had in the fields. These, I thought, tasted more delicious than anything my mother prepared at home, in spite of her being an excellent cook. I did this all on my own; there were no friends to share in the fun and exciting adventures. Apart from Dynguś, only my brother Abram joined me occasionally, as most of the time he had his head buried in books, like our other brother Leizer. All the boys lived in nearby hamlets and anyway, their parents would not have let them play with the likes of me. There seemed no outward difference between us, but to them I was different—I was considered a "townie" and Jewish to boot.

These rural surroundings and green fields stretching as far as the eye can see imbued me with a love of the countryside, the wildlife, and gardening from an early age. I had my own patch against a sunny south-facing wall of our home, where I planted seedlings and grew flowers from seed. I liked cosmos and pansies in a variety of colours, as well as night-scented stock that filled the evening air with its deliciously overpowering fragrance outside my window. I grew it especially for my golden-haired sister Fela. Mathiola stock was her favourite, but mine was the sunflower, because of its rapid growth. It was exciting to discover just how wondrous nature is. I liked to watch things grow, and I ran out each morning to see by how much the sunflower had grown overnight. Every evening, after a hot day, I watered the plants with a watering can. I could observe their growth almost daily and this fascinated me; the sunflowers grew tall in the fertile black soil with large drooping seed-heads that ripened well in the short but hot Polish summer. It was these early beginnings that started me on the road to a lifelong passion for gardening. Gardening in the English sense was hardly a pastime in Poland; instead, people grew potatoes and cabbages out of necessity. Another one of my favourite hobbies was to climb the tall trees, like most boys at that time. There were majestic sycamore and chestnut trees surrounding our home and factory, and Dynguś would run circles around the base of the tree, wagging his tail, barking for me to climb down, or perhaps he wanted to come up and join me! Dynguś meant a lot to me—he was the only pal I had.

The original founder of the family business was my maternal *zeide,* grandpa, Leibish Berman. His forebears before him were also confectioners. He was a mild-mannered, loveable old gentleman who I adored and was close to. In spite of his advanced years, *zeide* Leibish was young at heart and had the reputation of being a harmless prankster, even in old age. As I got older, I frequently called on him on my way home from *cheder,* Hebrew school, in the town centre. To keep himself occupied after he had retired from manufacturing, grandpa Leibish ran a retail shop, selling confectionery rejects from the factory: misshapen chocolates, sweets, broken biscuits, wafers, and so on. Children would line up after school outside the shop eagerly holding up their *groszy,* keen to buy sweets. I can still picture my *zeide* trying to put the youngsters off by telling them that sweets were bad for their teeth, and he instead handed out the collectable picture cards. These cards of animals and acclaimed sportsmen were inserted into bars of chocolate and keenly collected by children. When I was a young boy, not yet able to read, my brothers helped me to memorise the various animals, and I would amuse my relatives by holding up a stack of these cards, calling out the correct name of each animal, reptile, or bird of prey. For instance, I could differentiate between a boa constrictor, a python, and an anaconda. As there were hundreds of these creatures, my parents typically thought they had a young genius in the making! This was hardly the case, but it was fairly apparent from an early age that I had a retentive memory and a keen eye for detail.

Our home adjoined the factory, where we produced not only a wide range of chocolates and sweets but also pre-packed biscuits, chocolate wafers, and in fact a large variety of confectionery, from the exotic Turkish delight and Greek halva down to sugar-coated *dragées,* sesame snaps, and the humble lollipop. There is hardly anything new today in the confectionery field that we didn't produce at that time; the only thing that has changed is the decorative packaging. It was a family-run business, and apart from my father, my two eldest brothers also worked in there, as did two uncles with all of their sons. No doubt my turn would have come one day; my ambition was to follow in my father's footsteps when I grew up. We employed a large workforce, and the goods were marketed under the brand name of "Amor" with the company trading under Berman Bros. & Partners. It was probably the third-largest chocolate and confectionery concern in Poland at that time, after Wedel and Plutos. We had a rail spur laid from the mainline to transport sacks of sugar, flour, barrels of cocoa-butter and chocolate mass, as well as other supplies, by the wagonload, and to facilitate distribution all over Poland. By the mid-1930s we had installed the most up-to-date German machinery, incorporating conveyor belt mass production methods. There were machines that could wrap sweets automatically in foil and coloured cellophane, spewing them out at incredible speed. Previously this had been done by hand, with rows of women sitting against long trestle tables heaped high with sweets, speedily wrapping the toffees, caramels, and fruit-filled sweets, dropping them into boxes resting in their lap. Some of these women were incredibly fast with nimble fingers. When full, the boxes would be weighed by the supervisor and the packers paid according to their output. Had it not been for the war, our business would undoubtedly have expanded into a concern of international repute.

One of my most amusing pre-war recollections is of my German cousin Leo Katz coming for summer visits from Halberstadt with his mother Manya. Leo's favourite sport was to throw sweets and chocolates by the fistful down from the factory loft window onto the street below and get a kick out of watching the barefoot urchins pounce on each other, grappling for them in the dirt. We could not communicate properly, as Leo spoke no Polish, so we dubbed him *Waffelman* in

German, after all the chocolate wafers he unloaded onto the ravenous street kids below. We who lived there didn't indulge in this pastime, as sweets were no novelty to us, but as Leo was a privileged and spoiled visitor from abroad, he was afforded the liberty of behaving in this precocious manner.

All my uncles and aunts on my mother's side were in the confectionery business, either in production or retail, all initially trained by grandfather Leibish. After the business had expanded and moved out of town, my grandpa retained a part of the original old factory in the city centre, at the bottom of Sienkiewicz Street. There were coal-fired ovens there for the baking of a variety of pre-packed biscuits, in particular the ever-popular *herbatniki*, tea biscuits. The large bake-ovens had to be kept going round the clock. And as the factory didn't operate on weekends, housewives who wouldn't cook on the Jewish Sabbath were welcome to bring their pots of *chullent,* the traditional bean and barley stew, on Friday evening for slow baking overnight. The dishes would be collected the next day on their way home from synagogue and served for lunch. It was the customary Shabbat meal, particularly during the cold winter months. Young girls dressed in their finery, with long glossy braids reeking of paraffin, could be seen hurrying home from our factory with their hotpots. Escorting the *chullent* was the responsibility and duty of the younger daughters of the households. The twin-handled pots were covered with brown art paper and tied with string at the top. For ease of identification, the family name was written on the paper. The more affluent housewife would include choice ingredients, resulting in a rich, fatty *chullent*. Apart from the compulsory butter beans, pearl-barley and potatoes, it would contain fine cuts of meat or such delicacies as stuffed *kishke* (intestine casing) or stuffed *helz'l* (chicken neck). But the poor could only afford a lean *chullent,* containing only the basic ingredients. It so happened that on occasion the oven temperature rose too high and the paper on top got singed, making the names illegible. People tried to memorize their pots, but they were all rather similar; white or black enamel. Consequently, it was hard to distinguish between such names as: Kamaszenmacher, Katzenellenbogen and Weinwurtzel. As a consequence, the poor man's modest Shabbat table was sometimes graced with the rich man's *chullent,* and vice-versa!

The familiar aroma of baked *chullent* wafted down the narrow alleyways at lunchtime on Saturday, combined with strains of Shabbat dinner melodies streaming from the windows of Jewish households. After the customary dessert of stewed apples or prunes, a boiling-hot *glezele thé* with a slice of lemon, sucked through a sugar lump, completed the festive meal. This was followed by a welcome afternoon nap by the head of the household, as little else was permissible for a God-fearing Jew on the Day of Rest; many things were considered to desecrate the sanctity of Shabbat, except to pray, take food, and procreate! Others would take a leisurely stroll in their best attire along the stylish Aleja, to see and be seen. When I went for such a walk, I was invariably rewarded on the way with an ice-cream sandwich, having progressed from a cone, from my favourite Italian ice-cream parlour. If the weather was not so kind, we would go to visit relatives instead; no invitation was necessary, as there was little formality in the warm atmosphere of the shtetl.

Ostrowiec was typical of many of the small towns where the Jewish population represented Judaism in all its diverse forms. Although most were devout and God-fearing, they were tolerant of their less observant neighbours. Generally there was harmony in the shtetl. However, in the thirties, some of the younger generation became more restless and politically motivated, and began to drift away from religion, particularly toward the secular branch of Zionism and the left-wing Bund. To the utter dismay of their elders, some rebellious young men would buy a *kiełbasa,* a pork sausage ring, on the fast day of Yom Kippur and eat it openly in the street, in a display of defiance against the Hasidim. This led to some confusion among the wider community. Poles were aware that pork is prohibited to Jews, but as a result of this display, some were intrigued enough to ask, "Tell me, Jew: what's the name of the Holy Day when you are allowed to eat pork?"

As a result of rising secularism, different political factions emerged within the community. The Zionists advocated the building of a Jewish national home in Palestine, the adoption of Modern Hebrew as the everyday language, and the repudiation of Yiddish, as the language of the Diaspora. The Socialist Bund (Workers' Alliance), opposed both the Zionist and the religious parties, agitating for a secular society in Poland. Unlike the Zionists, the assimilated Bundists, strangely enough, championed the Yiddish language and culture, but believed that only true socialism could solve the problem of anti-Semitism, social injustice, and other ills. They maintained that Jewish aspirations lay right there in Poland, prophesying that one day the Jewish and Polish masses would join hands and live in harmony as equals in a just society. Regrettably, few Gentiles shared their vision of a future Polish utopia.

The ultra-Orthodox also opposed emigration, but for a different reason: they urged their followers to await redemption in the *Galut* (Diaspora), staying until the Messiah would come, not just to Warsaw, but to distant Ostrowiec as well. As a result, most people remained where they were, in spite of all the poverty and widespread discrimination. However, some idealistic young pioneers chose to follow the Zionist vision of returning to their ancestral homeland to live in an egalitarian society, till the soil, and become farmers and manual workers, thus fulfilling a two-thousand-year-old dream of return to Zion and become a free nation in their own land. Others, driven away by poverty and hardship, preferred to seek their fulfilment in the *goldene medine 'Amerike'*—the land of opportunity, where the streets were paved with gold. The more affluent were naturally more inclined to stay put. Consequently, unlike many families, we had no relatives in the United States or in the Holy Land. However, there was the odd relative who went to seek adventure in a distant land. One capricious Berman cousin left home one day, ostensibly to buy a newspaper, and failed to return. Apparently, not considering his bride-to-be sufficiently pretty, he ran away to escape an arranged marriage with the girl, a second cousin, rather than face the music at home. Months later he sent word from some remote place in Latin America. Such family dramas were fairly common in those days. There was also Uncle Josef, whom I never knew; he was one of my father's younger brothers. My grandparents virtually disowned him because he brought shame on the family by becoming a staunch communist in his youth. Having rebelled against his traditional background, he left a comfortable home to become a manual labourer, a bricklayer, in Argentina. Henceforth, Uncle Josef was simply not talked about in our home. I only became aware of his existence as I got older. I was rather curious about him and felt sorry for him. I could never understand why Uncle Josef could not have become a bricklayer in Zawichost, where he lived, rather than in some strange faraway land, cut off from the family.

Traditionally, people were involved in trade and craft, but there were also rich Jewish mill owners and merchants who typically traded in timber, hides and cattle. Still, most people lived in grinding poverty and had to work hard to eke out a bare existence. Some were forced to rely on the generosity of others, as well as relatives from abroad, mostly the United States and Canada. Fortunately, there was a time-honoured tradition of mutual help within the community. Each better-off family had its circle of needy people whom it would take under its wing. The favourite pastime of my maternal grandma, Gitt'l Berman, was to look after her needy circle. On a Friday morning, *Bubbe* Gitt'l would load up a trolley with bags of sugar, cooking oil, nuts, raisins, and other products from the factory and make her way from one house to another as the housewives were preparing their modest Sabbath meals. She would first enquire what they were cooking, and then proceed to the kitchen to savour the dishes and advise them what was needed to improve the flavour, adding the required ingredients accordingly. Or she would simply forget a bag of sugar or flour on the table or on the doorstep, so that the recipient would be spared the embarrassment of a face-to-face hand-out. *Bubbe* Gitt'l died of cancer before the war, after a long illness. I can recall visiting her sickbed and eyeing the cut-glass bowl of oranges and grapes at her bedside. Imported fruit from far-off lands may have been taken for granted in the West, but it was scarce and expensive in the remote places of pre-war Poland. Such exotic fruit was only intended for the sick. Invariably, I ended up being rewarded for my visit with a fragrant orange wrapped in printed tissue paper, or a small bunch of grapes. Bananas I had never seen, let alone tasted, perhaps because they didn't travel well. I knew of the fruits, though, and associated them with the monkeys I had read about in comic books; I knew that Cheetah, Tarzan's chimpanzee, loved bananas!

Dr. Schieber was the family doctor, but many people could not afford to consult a qualified doctor so they called in Avrum Bajnerman, the *feltcher*, instead. The *feltcher* was a typical product of the shtetl that fulfilled an important need. As *feltchers* weren't qualified, their fees were considerably lower. Presumably, the word comes from the Yiddish *faltsch* (false), meaning sham doctor. Apart from attending to minor ailments, they also applied leeches, pulled teeth, but most commonly set suction cups, which was the recommended treatment for a fever or chest cough. This treatment was performed with a flaming taper wrapped in cotton wool that had been soaked in methylated spirit. The *feltcher* would dip the flaming taper into each cupping glass, creating a vacuum; he then placed the glasses swiftly on the patient's back in neat rows. I watched this done to relatives, and often a person's whole back—right down to the waist—was covered with small glass cups. In the case of a child, fewer and smaller cups were applied. The cups were thought to draw out the fever, and they left red rings which turned to purple bruises that took weeks to disappear. The strong smell of methyl spirit lingered on in the home for days, and was a sure indication of the presence of a sick person in the household.

Life was good to us in pre-war Poland; by local standards I had a very privileged upbringing, enjoying an exciting childhood in a close, loving, family environment with wonderful protective brothers and a delightful sister, who was one of the prettiest girls in town. Observing other, less fortunate, children, I really thought I was born under a lucky star. We were prosperous and lived in a spacious home with a maid and a laundry woman, which was essential in those days as linen had to be boiled, washed, and starched by hand. There was no central heating, although homes were well insulated with storm windows. Wood or coal-fired stoves had to be lit in every room in the early morning during the cold winter months. When the maid would have the day off, it was my father's duty to light the fires, as he always rose early to recite morning prayers. On really crisp mornings, he liked to warm up by first knocking back a small tumbler of neat 90-proof vodka before starting his day. In our home we had the usual modern amenities available at the time, like a hand-cranked gramophone player with a large trumpet-like speaker, a German-made Elektra radio, and a telephone, although there were few people to phone in a provincial town. There was no direct dialling, so for a bit of mischief, I would stand on a chair and reach for the instrument mounted on the wall. After I cranked the handle several times, a telephone operator would come on, reciting "*Halo centrala*," and I would replace the earpiece on the hook and run off! I found it puzzling how voices can be transmitted down a cable.

Life, though, was hard for most Jewish families in the bustling market towns of rural Poland. You could say that time passed by our small town, but that only added to its old-fashioned charm. Although certain twentieth-century inventions had so far eluded us, surprisingly some of the latest American fads did manage to reach us, like the yo-yo and chewing-gum. Coming from the family I did, I was rather tired of sweets and chocolates, but chewing gum was different. I considered it more grown-up and very American to chew gum, just like actors did in the movies. Most homes in the Jewish quarter had no running water, basic plumbing, or even electricity. There was no point in having a car, even if you could afford to buy one, as there was no petrol or service station in the town. There were, however, motor coaches for travel to nearby places, and the train for long-distance travel. The only method of transportation within the town was by *dorożka*, a horse-drawn carriage for passengers or a sleigh in winter; for conveying goods, the horse-and-cart was still in use. The *dorożka* had a fold-back hood for protection against the elements, and one of my more exciting jaunts, as I got older, was to hitchhike unnoticed, sitting back-to-front on the rear axle between the wheels. I had to be careful to ride unseen, as the coachman's whip, attached to a long flexible cane, could reach round the side and over the top to the back of the coach!

We had running water in our home, but water in the shtetl proper had to be carried in pails from the nearest well—and wells were not that plentiful. For that purpose, there was a *wasser treger*, water carrier, and another *treger* for the carrying of loads. Porters, together with tailors, cobblers, glaziers, carpenters, watchmakers, and surprisingly innkeepers, were almost all Jewish. The glaziers were a familiar sight, on account of people having their windows broken by stone-throwing Polish youths. The glaziers carried spare panes with them in wooden racks strapped to their backs, going from door to door. Each family had its regular water carrier, one of the wizened men who grew old prematurely, their shoulders rounded by the shape and weight of their wooden yokes. If you needed the services of a porter, they could be found standing on a certain corner of the Rynek, in their threadbare clothes, soliciting for business with their tools-in-trade; each one with a thick rope and grappling hook slung over his shoulder. These porters could carry heavy loads, like an entire wardrobe or a bedstead, on their backs. Bent low under the weight, they tottered on their feet with the rope tied round the load. They would spit on their palms, first into one hand, then into the other, before winding the rope around their massive fists as they attempted to lift the burden. These were powerful, broad-shouldered men, yet gentle with everyone, except when it came to defending the community against brawling Polish hooligans spoiling for a fight. Then they were always in the forefront, together with the butchers. When it came to a punch-up in the town centre, the Jews usually managed to beat off the others.

In keeping with the lively spirit of the shtetl and warmth within the community, everyone had to have a nickname; no one was immune. The nicknames could allude to their occupations, their humble origins, physical attributes or nervous habits, and so on. It was largely endearing and always meant in good fun. So we had Groinem *schnorrer* (beggar), who wheedled money out of others, and Zalman *hoiker* (hunchback), who may have been only slightly stooped, but it was enough to earn him the epithet. Then there was Gimpel *rotzer* (sniveller) and Froim *schmatazh* (rag merchant, i.e., tailor). There was even a man without any nickname, who was dubbed Moishe *blois* (simply Moishe), no doubt to differentiate him from another Moishe with a less favourable nickname. Luckily, our family had more benign names, which was rather a relief to me. My maternal grandfather Berman was Leibish *zuckermeister* (master confectioner), and my father's familiar name became Moshke *zuckermacher* (confectionery maker), as he was only a newcomer to the field, having come into this line of business through marriage to my mother.

Regrettably, I never had the privilege of knowing my paternal grandfather, who died before I was born. I was always fascinated by the amusing anecdotes connected with him and his capricious behaviour. My grandfather, Lazar Katz, earned the Yiddish nickname Leizer "*Daatch*," Lazar the German. Of tall stature and distinguished bearing, he was considered somewhat haughty by those around him. He apparently dressed elegantly in a well-cut suit with starched wing-collar and cravat, in the style of a German squire, which was out of character in a small town in rural Poland. From the mental picture I built up of him, I imagined him more of a rigid Prussian than a German squire. My grandfather Lazar lived with his wife Rieva in Zawichost, a picturesque village on the Vistula, not far from Ostrowiec. It was the site of an important historical battle in 1205 CE, between Lesser-Poland and Ruthenia, which ended in a Polish victory. Zawichost was also once an important Hassidic centre, and one of the historic places from where the cult spread far and wide. My father and his siblings were all born in Zawichost. A terrible tragedy occurred there one day, when his youngest brother Yisroel, a keen footballer and sportsman, in a show of bravado or perhaps for a wager, attempted to swim across the mighty Vistula River in full flood and drowned. He was only eighteen years old.

Grandfather Lazar owned an edible oil processing plant. There were presses there for the extraction of cooking oil from poppy seeds, sesame seeds, and other sources. Zawichost was strategically situated on the Vistula for that purpose, as grain and other commodities were transported by waterway. Although newspapers didn't always reach such remote places in those days, Grandpa Lazar nevertheless managed to keep abreast of current affairs and read newspapers out aloud to those gathered around him, anxious for news of the outside world. The authoritarian Polish regime of the day was not well disposed towards its Jewish minority, and there were threats to ban kosher butchering and to bring in other punitive measures which greatly worried the community. Thus, whenever a new decree was issued which the villagers were unsure of, they would hurry to Leizer *"Daatch,"* wanting to know simply: "Is it good for the Jews, or bad for the Jews?" Invariably, it was the latter. Grandpa Lazar was quite a character, pedantic and persnickety and yet a charming and dignified gentleman, or so I was led to believe. Among other fads, he abhorred the smell of onions and even more so garlic, which was often eaten in the shtetl. The story goes that he walked out of my parents' wedding reception in a huff when onions were served up with the salt-herring *hors d'oeuvre*. He was so peeved that he couldn't be persuaded to return to the reception hall until these were first removed from the tables! The antics attributed to grandfather Lazar were fondly recounted in our home, time and again, and eagerly listened to; they had become part of family lore. I dearly wish I had known my grandfather from Zawichost. Eventually, it dawned on me that I may have inherited some of my grandfather's fastidiousness, or so I was told by Mama, when she complained that I was too choosy!

My father came to live in Ostrowiec when he married my mother and thereafter entered the family confectionery business. My mother was a partner in the company with her two brothers, who had been handed the reins by my maternal grandfather. The Bermans were successful and highly skilled in the sugar business, and my father complemented this with his good business acumen. He undertook the responsibility for marketing and for constantly extending the product range. As part of his expansion programme, he introduced new lines of confectionery for different festive occasions. This included chocolate eggs and marzipan bunnies for Easter and novelties for Christmas tree decoration, like chocolate stars and baubles wrapped in colourful glittering foil. There were gingerbread men, chocolate-coated hearts, and beautifully piped and decorated Saint Nicholas, as Santa is called in Eastern Europe, as well as teddy bears and ponies and other animal shapes. The period leading up to Christmas was always hectic in the factory, and a most exciting time for me. I have fond memories of the festive season, with a huge outdoor Christmas tree beautifully lit up with fairy lights in front of the Amor factory building. It was a magical time of year, when there was snow on the ground and the thrill of tobogganing and skating on the frozen lake. Even the streets had hard-packed snow right through the winter, and so my toboggan and skates became my most prized possessions. I loved the snow; I went everywhere on my skates, which had straps fixed to them that they could be attached to any boots. And then there was the familiar winter scene of colourful sleighs, their runners carving into the pristine snow, drawn by trotting horses with tinkling bells hanging from their necks, their nodding heads exhaling clouds of vapour in the intense cold.

Occasionally, my parents took me on outings to other towns to visit family or attend a wedding or some other celebration. On these trips, I would be in my seventh heaven. If it was to Zawichost, my father's ancestral home, we would travel by a *dorozhka* carriage or, in winter, a horse-drawn sleigh, well tucked in, with me covered up to my eyes with sheepskins for protection from the severe cold, as the coachman snapped the reins. If we went farther afield, say to Kielce, where my favourite aunt, Hannah, lived, we would travel by train. I was at my happiest when we visited Kielce during the summer. Aunt Hannah was my father's only sister. Her husband, Josef Fajngold, owned a saw-mill and a wood-turning plant for the production of wooden heels for ladies' shoes, among other things. It was thrilling to go on those unforgettable visits and enjoy the company of my delightful elder cousins in beautiful, rural surroundings. They lived in an enchanting house set in an orchard, surrounded by many flowering trees in the spring and an abundance of cherries in early summer, and later plums, pears and apples.

At home my parents spoke both Yiddish and Polish to each other, while my brothers and sister stuck to Polish, but we understood Yiddish as well, by listening to our parents and their friends. Polish was more and more the first language of the younger generation. Some of the older shtetl-dwellers spoke only basic Polish, but on the other hand were well-versed in the Bible and in Jewish culture and traditions, and cherished learning. For many, Yiddish was their first language, but apart from Polish, they often understood Russian and German, on account of the frequency with which their home changed hands. Many also knew Hebrew, the language they prayed in daily. But the holy tongue was not for common, everyday, usage and this is where Yiddish came in. Yiddish is a mixture of German dialects dating back to the early Middle Ages; it also sometimes has a sprinkling of Slavic words, depending on where the speaker is from. Yiddish is written phonetically, in the Hebrew alphabet, from right to left. Hebrew words were added over the centuries to the Yiddish vernacular, mainly religious words, but also words of a caustic nature, added to outwit strangers, and making these words difficult for non-Jews to grasp. Yiddish-speaking people the world over could understand each other; it was the *lingua franca* of world Jewry. There were exceptions, of course, particularly Sephardic Jews in the Levant, where the language was not spoken. Yiddish came about when Jews fled the Rhineland to escape the fury of the Crusaders on their death-dealing journey across Europe to the Holy Land in the eleventh, twelfth, and thirteenth centuries. Many a Jewish community was put to the sword along the way. Religious persecution followed in the wake of the Crusades, and Jews were driven out of German lands, accused of spreading the plague, being bearers of disease, and poisoning wells. For those who escaped, there was only one safe direction they could go, and that was east, to Poland. They took their Judaeo-German language, *Judendeutsch*, with them as they went. But while High German remained rather humourless, Yiddish evolved into a folk tongue, full of wit and pathos, as well as laughter and tears like no other language; it was considered the language of the heart.

Migrating east in search of asylum, Jews found religious tolerance in Poland and the country acquired a reputation as a haven for Jews, who came to call it the "New Jerusalem." Jews were made welcome in the twelfth century by King Mieszko II, and protected thereafter by a succession of Polish kings and the local nobility. Jews had a long tradition of learning, employing private tutors, and so they were better educated at a time when few Poles were literate. It was this thirst for learning and knowledge that set them apart from their non-Jewish neighbours. Jews were also often skilled in the trades and experienced in commerce, with international connections. Ultimately they flourished in Poland, with the Jew often acting as the middleman for the magnates and ruling families. But over a period of time, they came to be resented by the peasantry and the common people for their success and for their association with the nobility. Jews administered the excise tax and were authorised to mint coinage. Some of the coins were even impressed with Hebrew inscriptions in praise of the ruling Polish monarch. Coins from the twelfth century survive, bearing the slogan in Hebrew "A Blessing upon Mieszko, King of Poland."

Records exist of Jews settling in Poland as early as the eleventh century. There is an acclaimed painting by the Polish master Jan Matejko depicting the arrival of Jews to Poland in 1096. There is even a mention of Jewish merchants from Spain reaching the country in the ninth century. Jews in Poland were not subjected to anti-Jewish measures instigated by the Church, as they were in Western Europe. There was religious tolerance at that time, and unlike other countries Poland didn't have enforced ghettoes. Furthermore, Jewish rights were enshrined by the Statute of Kalisz in 1264 by King Boleslaus the Pious. The Act guaranteed Jewish civil liberties and a measure of autonomy. This charter was in turn ratified by successive rulers, including fourteenth-century King Kazimir III. King Kazimir the Great, as he was known, showed much favour to the Jews by granting them additional privileges, resulting in him being labelled 'King of the Serfs and Jews' by the feudalists. Apart from enlisting Jewish talent to expand his economy and the royal treasury, the king's benevolence towards his Jewish burghers was attributed to his love for a beautiful Jewish girl, the enchanting Esterka. Legend has it that any male offspring from this union was to be brought up Christian, and daughters Jewish. Poland under King Kazimir was one vast, powerful country that stretched from the Baltic to the Black Sea, where Poles and Jews lived in harmony. As a boy, I was always fascinated by the funny names some Polish kings were known by. Apart from the usual descriptions, like the Great, the Just and the Pious, there were also the less flattering ones: Krzywousty (Wrymouth), the Elbow-High, the Curly, and so on. One of the greatest Polish monarchs was the Hungarian-born sixteenth-century Stefan Batory. He was the first monarch to decree against the accusation of ritual murder at a time when the blood libel was rife throughout Europe, including England, where the calumny first began in twelfth-century Norwich. There was even a Jewish king, Saul Wahl, who reigned for just one day when a successor could not be decided upon in time. But all this royal munificence gradually diminished due to meddling by the Catholic clergy. As the centuries passed, and the ghetto walls started to crumble in Germany and the West, and Jews obtained extensive rights thanks to the French Revolution and the Enlightenment, the situation for Jews in the East began to deteriorate. Poland had meanwhile fallen under the malevolent Imperial Russian domination.

My mother was an avid reader of Sholem-Aleichem, Peretz, Mende-le-the-Bookseller, and other leading Yiddish writers. As I mentioned, she was well versed in folklore and legends of the shtetl. Father was preoccupied with the family business and worked long hours, so it was mainly my mama who read me bedtime stories. Instead of fairytales, she related stories of ancient Jewish heroes and warriors. I listened, spellbound, as she recalled biblical stories of mighty Israelite warriors, from Joshuah, who conquered the Land of Canaan, to the victories of King David and the wisdom of King Solomon, who built the Temple of Jerusalem. She told me of the mighty Maccabees and the Hasmonean rulers, the leadership of King John Hyrkanus and Judas Maccabeus, of their valiant deeds with their small band of Maccabee warriors who defeated the Graeco-Syrians in 300 BCE, of the last Jewish revolt, led in 66 CE by Simon Bar-Kochba, who dared to rise up against the might of Rome, wresting Judea from the enemy, declaring independence. Emperor Hadrian, she told me, had to send additional legions from Rome to crush Bar-Kochba's last stand, resulting in the greatest calamity to befall the Jewish nation in ancient times, culminating with the Jews being scattered to the four corners of the earth. I could never get enough of these tales. There were also more recent protagonists, like the legendary Colonel Berek Joselewicz, hero of the Kosciuszko insurrection against the Russians in 1794. Joselewicz raised a Jewish cavalry, with young men flocking to his colours to fight for Polish independence. Unfortunately, their hero died on his horse, sword in hand, leading a charge. The failed insurrection led to Poland's dismemberment and partition in 1795 between Russia, Austria, and Prussia. Thereafter, Poland ceased to exist as an independent state and the name vanished from the map of Europe for more than a hundred and twenty years.

My mother liked to relate a little story, connected with a legendary Polish nobleman who converted to Judaism, as if it were true. He was known as the Righteous Proselyte of Vilna, the capital of Lithuania, which was part of the Polish commonwealth. According to legend, Count Walentyn Potocki, the son of a duke, was burnt at the stake in eighteenth-century Vilna for renouncing Catholicism and embracing

Judaism. At the eleventh hour, his father, the Duke Potocki, tried to avert his son's execution by imploring him to save his life and repudiate Judaism. It was all in vain; Walentyn Potocki chose to die a martyr's death. A Jew posing as a Christian apparently managed by bribery to secure some of Count Potocki's ashes and had them interred in the Vilna Jewish cemetery. Thereafter, the legend states, people began to tell the story of the "Righteous Proselyte," and a tree that grew to be old and venerable sprung up on his tomb, which became a place of pilgrimage for devout Jews.

Apart from learning about Polish history, I was also taught from an early age to take pride in the Jewish nation and its ancient history. My parents, particularly my mother, with whom I spent more time, strove to instil in me a love of our heritage and the yearning for Zion—anticipating the fulfilment of the age-old dream of return to our ancestral homeland. Because of our sins, we had been banished from our land. I was nurtured on stories of early Zionist heroes like the one-armed warrior Joseph Trumpeldor, who led the Jewish defence in Palestine against Arab bands after World War I. His dying words, pronounced as he lay mortally wounded, were often quoted: "It doesn't matter, it's good to die for one's country." This made me feel rather sad, but I also found it inspiring. I too wanted to go to Palestine and become a warrior when I grew up!

Looking at old picture postcards, I thought that the Promised Land was a place where old Jews in flowing robes with long white beards went to bewail the destruction of the Temple and to pine after Zion. Others went to live their days out in the Holy City, so that their remains would not have far to travel when the Messiah would come and God would gather up His people to lead them to the Promised Land. As I grew older, I took pride in reading about Jewish boxers and sportsmen like Zishe Breitbart, dubbed the modern-day Samson. Zishe was a Jewish champion, the strongman of Poland, who performed incredible feats of strength like being harnessed to and pulling an entire railcar.

There was a sad story from a bygone age that my mother liked to recount as an example of family devotion. It was a touching little tale, relating to the emotive custom of *Kever Avot*, the Jewish tradition of honouring the memory of one's parents by visiting their gravesides at least once a year, particularly on the anniversary of their passing, even if this entailed travelling far afield. In keeping with the timeless custom, one marks the visit by placing a small stone on the *matzeva, or* headstone. Often, in times gone by, families were ravaged by pogroms, poverty, and famine; there was a tale of two brothers who had survived such adversity but had become separated by war. Years went by, with each brother convinced the other was dead. Distances were great, and it was many years before one of them at last managed to embark on the journey of fulfilling his duty, only to find to his great astonishment that someone had placed a single stone on his parents' *matzeva*—a sure sign of life! Over the years the stones kept mounting up, and each brother became convinced that the other was alive, but alas, they never met up.

During my childhood, schooling was compulsory, but it hadn't always been so. Consequently some of the older generation weren't so fluent in Polish, with just enough to get by. And as they never attended state school, they stuck to Yiddish. As a result of widespread anti-Semitism and the discrimination they faced in all walks of life, they had no desire to integrate and learn the Polish language. This led to Jews closing in on themselves, creating a barrier between the two communities. Besides, many felt that Yiddish was a more expressive language, better suited to the manner of self-contained shtetl life. The ancient dialect also lent itself to self-mocking humour and subtlety, as well as song. Within the family, my brothers and sister considered themselves to be first and foremost Poles of the Jewish faith, with Polish as their mother tongue, but they also felt at ease with Yiddish, albeit with a more limited vocabulary. Unlike the more religious community members, we didn't keep our heads covered, and religious practices were reserved for the home—this is the way we were brought up. People could get by in the small towns without having to speak Polish, but problems arose if they had to deal with the police or other officials. From these problems, a strange genre of humour emerged: a mock language, a mixture of Polish and Yiddish, each phrase of which employed a play on words making it funny, and even rude. We imagined that this would so confound the officials that they would give up in despair. There were jokes about it, but I doubt if anyone would have dared address an official in this manner, out of fear of being clapped into the *Koza* (goat), as the local jail was called, or even worse, the notorious Pawiak prison, which thought struck fear into people's hearts. A disapproving mother could often be heard scolding her errant son by yelling at him that she could foresee the day when he would end up behind bars in the Pawiak, unless he would mend his ways.

With the defeat of Kaiser's Germany in the Great War and the dis-solution of the Austro-Hungarian Empire, and with Russia preoccupied with its revolution, Poland grasped the chance, with the help of the Great Powers to regain its independence in 1918, after earlier failed insurrections. With the rebirth of Poland and the end of the Czarist Empire, things began to look more promising for Jews in Poland. The country was led at this time by a popular revolutionary leader, Józef Piłsudski. And as he was fair to them, Jews hailed him as a friend and held him in special affection, with young Jews volunteering for his le-gions, which aimed to defend Polish independence. Following World War I, Piłsudski took power, after a military *putsch* in 1926, to become the benign autocratic ruler of the newly-independent country, ending more than a century of foreign occupation and partition. Earlier, he drove the Russians out of eastern Poland during the Polish-Soviet war of 1919-1921. In 1920 the Russians marched into our town, but were driven back by Polish forces. Polish soldiers then accused the Jews of siding with the Bolsheviks, which sparked a bloody pogrom. This was a mere excuse to ransack Jewish shops, and several people were killed.

As a young boy, I loved reading popular adventure stories glorifying the exploits of Marshal Piłsudski, my boyhood hero; they made me feel proud to be Polish. I loved to hear about how he led his legions against the Russian hordes in the primeval forests and wetlands of eastern Poland, about how his dashing leadership and the bravery of his cav-alry won through against terrible odds. In one daring manoeuvre he turned almost certain defeat into victory in 1920 by cutting off and surrounding a Bolshevik army at the gates of Warsaw, thus saving the besieged capital. This would come to be known in the annals of Polish history as "The Miracle on the Vistula." During my own childhood, the anniversary of this great victory was celebrated as a national holiday.

The liberal-minded Piłsudski, I learned in my youth, strove to im-prove the rights of all minorities, including the Jews. He opposed an-ti-Jewish measures and tried to contain the violence against them, but he didn't succeed in stemming the rising tide of anti-Semitism and na-tionalism of the thirties, fuelled by German Nazism. Marshal Piłsudski, with his distinctive handlebar moustache, was looked upon as a father figure and trusted leader, especially by the Jews. He once paid a visit to our town, and all the townspeople turned out in the Rynek to hail the great leader. His statue stands there to this day. The Jewish elders came forward to greet him on his entry to the town with specially baked bread and salt. According to Jewish custom, offering bread and salt is a sign of hospitality when welcoming a head of state or an important dignitary. It was said that the marshal had a predilection for Jewish cuisine: apparently he liked to be served stuffed carp or pike, "Jewish-style," on Friday evenings. When Piłsudski died in 1935, Jews wept. I was only four years old at the time, but I do recall my parents speaking of him in glowing terms, relating how Jewish people paid homage to the great man, lining the street and openly weeping when they heard of his passing. Later, my boyish enthusiasm and patriotism began to wane upon hearing my parents complain of anti-Jewish measures instituted by the hostile government that took over after Piłsudski. I realised more and more that we were looked upon as strangers who didn't belong in Poland and were being pushed to go to Palestine.

Jews would have good cause to mourn "Grandpa" Piłsudski, as he was known affectionately. After his death, a clique of army colonels led by Śmigły-Rydz governed Poland in the thirties. The administration became increasingly authoritarian, following a fascist course by aping Nazi Germany, at least as far as Jews and political opponents were concerned. A camp for political prisoners, known as Bereza Kartuska, was established; this facility put the fear of God into people. The chauvinistic regime grew more and more hostile towards its Jewish minority, and there were well-founded accusations of state-inspired anti-Semitism. After Jews had lived in Poland for almost a thousand years, the foreign-minister, Jósef Beck, formally declared in the Sejm (parliament) in 1937 that Poland barely had enough room for half a million Jews, so the three million Jewish inhabitants beyond that number would have to leave. Poland was, at that time, one of the least populated countries in Europe. At about the same time the administration came up with the Madagascar Plan, to expel the Jews to the French colony in Africa. They actually sent a mission there the following year to look into the feasibility of resettling Polish Jews there *en masse*.

The world depression of the 1930s was on, and the economic situation in the country steadily deteriorated, as did my family's fortunes. As if that wasn't bad enough, my father kept complaining bitterly about *podatki*, but I never understood the meaning of the word, except that these were tough times. I later discovered that *podatki* were in fact punitive tax demands, levied arbitrarily by the tax authorities against Jewish concerns. The rising tensions in Europe in the thirties resulted in more and more Jews being excluded from the public and economic life of the country. Not unlike in Nazi Germany, the ultra-nationalist Endecja party boycotted Jewish concerns. Endecja hooligans, modelling themselves on Nazi Brown-shirts, were posted outside Jewish shops to prevent Gentile shoppers from entering, resulting in ugly confrontations in the streets. The admittance of Jewish students to universities was further restricted, with those few who were accepted required to sit on the rear benches of the lecture halls. Some Jewish students protested by opting to stand during lectures, rather than sit on what came to be known as "ghetto benches." There was the story of a courageous Gentile girl who chose to stand in solidarity with her Jewish friend; this demonstration of loyalty was by no means unique. When Endecja thugs asked the Jewish student why she was standing up, she replied, "Because I am a Jew!" And when they asked her non-Jewish friend why she was standing, she answered, "Because I am a Pole!" She got her face slapped as a result. Families that could afford to do so sent their sons and daughters to study abroad, mostly to Paris and Vienna.

In September 1938, the month after I turned seven, I was enrolled in school for the first time. Primary schooling in Poland began at the age of seven, but I was already able to read fairly fluently by the time I started. By the time I turned ten, I had read and enjoyed the usual children's classics translated into Polish, stories like *Robinson Crusoe*, *Treasure Island*, *Uncle Tom's Cabin*, and so on. The hero I, like most boys at the time, most admired was Tarzan, and my preferred comic was Pat & Patachon, which was based on a French comic strip, I believe. But I didn't care too much for reading. Although fairly intelligent, I was not very studious; anyway, there were more interesting distractions for an outdoors-loving boy with an adventurous spirit. We lived next door to our factory, which was always a hive of activity, and as many of the employees were relatives, they pampered and fussed over me and let me stay and watch them work, so long as I was careful. I loved the constant hum of heavy machinery operated by huge electric motors that drove the long transmissions bolted to the ceilings, and the array of wheels and pulleys of varying size that propelled the heavy machinery via a maze of rotating vertical and diagonal drive-belts and pinions. All this produced a deafening hum of machinery that I found most exciting.

There were huge copper cauldrons full of boiling sugar, bubbling and splashing dangerously like volcanic geysers, as well as large rotating copper drums for the chocolate-coating of sweets. Never a dull moment was had. How I wished I could grow up quickly, so I could also work in the chocolate factory alongside my big brothers and cousins!

Primary School No.5, where I was enrolled, was co-educational and very near our home and factory. And as it was situated out of town, my brother Abramek and I were probably the only Jewish pupils at that school. I grew up believing that our God is an all-seeing God, and so during assembly I stood rigidly to attention, but I didn't cross myself during prayers out of an inner fear that the "Jewish God" would not approve and would strike me dead then and there. I also absented myself during religious instruction, which was given by a priest. This made me stand out, and as a result I was subjected to taunts and bullying. My nickname in class was "Kacyk," which I didn't really mind as it was not unlike my name, Kac. Anyway, I was called far worse names outside school. Although I had no friends amongst the boys in my class, the same was not true of the girls, I could sense that some of them sympathised with me and even liked me. Because of the way our society worked, we could not be friends openly, but I did get the odd furtive smile or wink. Following my first school year, I passed easily into the next class, with top marks in every subject except for conduct, where I got a poor mark. Not that I was unruly in any way; my trouble here was as a result of my classmates provoking me, shooting paper pellets and so on, and I had to stand up for myself—for which I invariably got the blame. Abramek, who was two years older, stood by my side outside school, and if we needed to summon extra help, our oldest brothers were never far away. Complaining to the headmaster was a waste of time. Fights broke out after school, and my mother had to nurse our cuts and bruises and apply cold compresses. The usual method of combat was stone-throwing and use of the *proca,* or catapult. I became a fairly good shot, and carried a supply of pebbles as ammunition on me, just in case. I was always on the lookout for a suitable fork-shaped stick that could be shaped into a good catapult. Oak or ash, being hard woods, were most suitable. One couldn't buy a catapult in a shop, it had to be made, and a good one was worth its weight in gold! I had a collection of them. The rubber came from bicycle inner tubes, and it had to be of the right elasticity and not too thin. The pouch holding the stone I cut out of the tongues of discarded shoes. The leather had to be just right, fairly thick yet supple, to give it strength, so it would take the strain when stretched. All this was terribly important; it was my preferred method of self defence. These after-school tussles taught me when to stand my ground, even if I got the worse of it, and when to beat a hasty retreat. I was agile and could run fast. Polish boys used to chase after me, calling names and hurling abuse, such as: *Parszywy Żydzie* (Scabby Jew), *Żydzie do Palestyny* (Jew to Palestine), and *Żydzie Beilisie* (Jew Beilis).

The last insult was a reference to an infamous blood libel trial that occurred during czarist times. A Jew named Beilis was put on trial on an invented charge of killing a Christian boy before Easter and draining his blood for use in Passover Matza. The protracted trial became a *cause célèbre*, and as a result of international pressure, mainly from America, the case was dropped. But in spite of Beilis's acquittal, the court ruled that Jewish ritual murder had taken place. After Beilis was set free, he fled to the United States for safety. The blood libel had existed since medieval times, when the Jews were also accused of poisoning wells and spreading the plague, and had over the years resulted in many such false accusations, which sparked pogroms throughout Europe against defenceless communities. Although ritual murder trials had been banned in modern-day Poland, the canard endured, hence the slur "Jew Beilis." Until I started school and was called a "Beilis", I was not aware of being any different from other Polish boys. I had to ask my father what they meant by "Beilis." I feel sure even now that the boys didn't know what they were saying; they had just heard the phrase and learned to repeat it.

Unfortunately, our town was not one of the more enlightened places where Gentiles lived in harmony with their Jewish neighbours. Still, we got by. There was a lot of backwardness in our rural province, but certain places were better than others, particularly the large towns. On occasion I had to run for cover or risk a beating on my way to Hebrew school, if a Christian funeral procession went by towards the cemetery near the Saski brewery. As the cortège passed on foot, bystanders would pause and, as a mark of respect, remove their caps and make the sign of the cross. Some mourners, however, chose to vent their anger by throwing stones at the windows of Jewish homes, or even assaulting passers-by, as they went. Hence a Catholic funeral was a signal to us to abandon the streets and secure the shutters. Danger was more likely during the sensitive period leading up to Easter Week, the time of the crucifixion, especially if the deceased was a young man—as if the Jews were to blame for his untimely death. As a seven-year-old, though mature for my age, I could never understand how anyone could condone such behaviour while bearing the coffin of their dear departed on their shoulders. Observing the scene from afar, I would think of the lifeless body in the casket that would never get to heaven with family and friends behaving the way they did. Ugly scenes like these made me aware of being disliked, but left me unable to understand why. This form of behaviour more than any other anti-Jewish manifestation had a strong effect on me, the image of which never left me. Such behaviour, at a funeral of all places, was alien to us—it was not the Jewish way and was totally different from Jewish funerals. Instead of taking it out on others, mourners expressed only sorrow and grief by sobbing, with close family members symbolically rending their clothes. And instead of retiring to the deceased's home to consume prodigious quantities of vodka, the bereaved in a Jewish house of mourning sit low to the ground in humility, surrounded by family and friends. Jews are obligated to comfort the mourner when paying their respect. It is customary to bring along some sustenance or to offer help in the kitchen, so that the family is spared such mundane chores while in mourning.

After school, which finished at lunchtime, there was *cheder*, Hebrew and religious-studies class, every weekday except Fridays. On Saturday summer afternoons the pupils would gather there to study Ethics of the Fathers, but I was exempt from the Saturday sessions, as I lived too far out of town and we were not supposed to ride on the Sabbath. On other days, if I was lucky I would hitch a ride by sneaking up behind a *dorożka*, sitting astride the axle between the rear wheels as the coachman cracked his whip, shouting *Vio! Vio!* Failing that, I would have to run all the way to the Jewish area of town. It was on the way there that I often got set upon by bullies, with no brothers to call on for help—for there was another *cheder* for older children. Once I reached the town centre, Jewish boys reigned supreme and no Polish boy would dare to start a fight because here they were outnumbered. Until then, however, I had to try and dodge them and avoid being ambushed. Sometimes they tried to cut me off, but I knew my way around the maze of crooked alleyways. These bullies were the bane of my youth, but I had to put up with it. I knew no better; this was how it always was.

Religious school started at the age of four, three years before we began state school. The school was in an adjoining room to the Hebrew tutor's private home. Black-bearded *Reb* Itche-Mayer Frojman was stern and strict, and the teaching method was by rote. Itche-Mayer sat at the head of the long table and the pupils sat on low benches either side of him, their heads barely reaching the top of the table. The tutor used an ivory pointer to indicate each letter or word, and the pupil beside him would repeat after him in Hebrew. After a few lines, the boy would go to the end of the bench and we would all move up one place in rotation. As we progressed, we repeated in unison after him passages from the Pentateuch in a sing-song chant, one verse at a time, translating into Yiddish as we went, while Itche-Mayer continually stroked his beard. From about the age of six, we were required to recite by heart the three lengthy passages of the Shema; the guiding principles of the Jewish faith; and other basic prayers. I was brought up from an early age to believe that there is an all-seeing God in Heaven and I never doubted his existence; it was a sin to allow such a thought to even enter your mind.

I distinctly recall the Akdomis, an intricate liturgical poem, being drummed into me. These rhyming early mediaeval verses in praise of the Creator are chanted at Pentecost, Shavuot. This Aramaic tongue-twister is difficult to pronounce, and we were expected to memorise lengthy passages from it though we never really understood it. Nevertheless, it was good for sharpening the brain; it was said that Jewish mental powers developed because of this form of study. If you weren't an attentive pupil you had your ears tweaked and cheeks pinched or, worse, you could be caned across the fingers. Perhaps it was due to our monotonous chanting that *Reb* Itche-Mayer would habitually nod off in the summer heat. But *Oy, va voi,* woe betide any boy distracted from his learning, as the tutor would open one eye, looking over his spectacles, to try and catch us out! We all feared his nasty temper, but at the same time we took it in good spirits, even the caning, when we would put on a brave face, trying to pretend it didn't hurt. Itche-Mayer had a *Belfer*, an assistant, who would occasionally stand in for him or help to keep order in the class. He also called on homes on Fridays to collect the teaching fees for the preceding week. Another duty of the *Belfer* was to take small children to *cheder*, carrying them piggy-back, which they looked forward to. Or he would hand out sweets to encourage the children's attendance. Itche-Mayer had a sideline, selling "tuck," sticky little caramelised bars of poppy or sesame seed, at playtime and after class at half a *grosz* per piece. Needless to say, I was not a very good customer, as I had all the sweets I wanted at home and was in fact rather sick of them. I was popular in *cheder*; all the boys were rather envious of me and tried to cosy up to me because of our chocolate factory!

Dynguś, my bright-eyed and alert pet dog, was always at my side and went everywhere with me. He was not allowed to enter the school, but he waited patiently for me to come out. We had not bought him; he just turned up at our doorstep one day with no collar on and took to me instantly—and the sentiment was mutual. He was like a smaller version of a cross-Border Collie with black and white patches, and just as intelligent. Dynguś, the name my brothers came up with, was I presume, after the Australian Dingo, or perhaps the pagan folk carnival of Śmigós-Dyngus, when young Poles chase after village maidens to chuck buckets of water at them. Anyway, I liked the name and loved the dog. I must have had him for about two years, until just before the war began, when he disappeared the way he came—a portent perhaps of bad things to come. I suspected that he had fallen afoul of a mean dog catcher; they were in the habit of catching any dog, not just strays. After the loss of my pet, I was devastated for a long time and just couldn't get over it. Dynguś was a loyal pal and I missed him a lot. It would never be the same without him. I had no friends where I lived: Polish boys would not have me for a friend, and Jewish boys lived too far away, in the town centre, and never dared venture out to visit me. I had no school friends either, as I spent my time trying to avoid the other students or fight them off after school. I only had the company of my brothers, and as I had no young cousins either, I spent a lot of time in adult company. My big cousins used to take me to football matches that often ended in a free-for-all, and we would have to run for our lives before the end of the match. This didn't stop my cousins from going to football, but I had to give it up when my father forbade it. From an early age, I had an irresistible sense of adventure, so I wasn't scared, but I never questioned my father, whom I looked up to. Looking back, I suppose I was a mischievous lad outdoors, but obedient at home, and I never had to be punished.

Any description of the Jewish shtetl would be incomplete without a mention of the familiar village fools. As I've said, we had our share of these eccentric characters—they were part of shtetl life. For example, there was simple-minded Ely, known as "Ely the Ladder" or "Ely the *Golem.*" Soft-hearted Ely worked in our factory as a handyman; he often demonstrated his concern for all living creatures. For instance, whenever the cat got on the factory roof, Ely the *Golem* (which was used to describe a slow-witted person in Yiddish) would immediately abandon his workbench, dash outside, and prop a ladder up against the wall so that it could climb down safely. Then there was *"Eliyahu Hanavi,"* "Elijah the Prophet," who would drape himself in flowing white robes from head to toe and race through the streets towards the Jewish cemetery. As he went, he implored everyone along the way not to tarry and to repent, to prepare for the coming of the Messiah.

The cemetery was in the centre of town, and one could not miss it. As reverence for the dead was an important tradition, people would visit, as I mentioned, on the anniversary of a parent's passing and often during the Hebrew month of Elul, before the Days of Awe, when it is customary to pray for eternal rest for the dead and to beg them to intercede with God on behalf of the living. There was a certain mystery associated with the graveyard, and shtetl folk were steeped in superstition. I thought that ghosts and evil spirits lurked there in the night, and I would shrink away from the vicinity after dusk even if accompanied by an adult. Though I was scared of "Elijah," I was also curious and mystified by him. I was sure he was a ghost! Draped in a white robe, he hardly showed his face. "Elijah" enacted his prank on festivals; as people made their way to synagogue, he would go in the opposite direction towards the cemetery, and would never be seen emerging from it.

I believed, as a child, that in the middle of the night the ancient *matzevot* moved aside to let ghosts emerge from their dank graves. The restless souls would go roaming, and to pass anywhere near the cemetery at that time, I felt, was risky indeed. It was said that in the pitch-black of night, the dead converged on the ancient synagogue to pray—as ghosts, they didn't need a key to enter! And should any living soul appear, they would quickly scuttle back into their dark graves, and the gravestones moved back into place so that no living soul would ever set eyes on them. During the day though, my friends and I considered the graveyard quite harmless. In fact, it was exciting to scale the cemetery wall with my *cheder* pals, to go scrumping for fruit, which grew in profusion in the overgrown ancient cemetery. Apart from bushes laden with berries, there were trees with branches weighed down with apples, plums, damsons, small juicy pears, and so on, depending on the time of year. I left the cut-glass bowl of fruit in our home untouched, finding these fresh fruits more appetizing. As the roots of these ancient trees must have reached deep down into the graves, other people said that the fruit from the graveyard was taboo. Perhaps that's why my friends and I found it more tempting—the thrill of the forbidden fruit! We suspected some of the fruit to be bedevilled and even contaminated, so we played a game of "risk," daring each other to take the first bite. The tombstones bore the equivalent of the Hebrew letters, T-N-Z-B-H. These abbreviated initials stood for the Hebrew, "May his soul be bound up in the bond of eternal life." We boys didn't know this, and we took it to stand for a Yiddish acronym, interpreting it as: Toyte-Nemen-Ziegel-Bauen-Heizer: Dead-Take-Bricks-Build-Houses. It is hardly surprising that my nightmares at this time were all connected with the graveyard, demons, and ghosts! Another place I dreaded was the forbidding Catholic Church of Archangel Michael, which occupied the highest point in town, with its tall spire dominating the skyline. It was a large church, the only one in Ostrowiec, and when the bells pealed they could be heard all over town. As there was no way of avoiding the church to get to the other side of town without taking a long detour, I would race past it as quickly as I could, as did all the Jewish boys. It wasn't until after the war that I plucked up the courage to go inside the dark and forbidding church, just to satisfy my curiosity and overcome my youthful superstition.

Among the other quirky characters in our town I have a vivid recollection of were the "Three Gogges," three inseparable, almost identical sisters who were totally deranged. They were in their thirties, perhaps; tall, lean, and quite good looking in a wildcat sort of way. The three sisters roamed the streets together barefoot, scantily dressed in rags, with long, unkempt, matted black hair and piercing Gypsy-like eyes. I'm sure people passed on their discarded clothing and shoes to them, but they must have preferred to dress in the way they did. The Gogges would curse at any male passer-by and hurl abuse at him as they went. As boys can be rather cruel, we followed them in the street and taunted them, as we did with all the feeble-minded *meshugenes*, but the Gogges were incredibly strong and could be quite dangerous. They were capable of throwing large rocks at their tormentors, so we learned to keep our distance. The three Gogges lived in a cave-like dwelling, formerly a smithy, against a hillside on the edge of the meadow, and if we couldn't see them out on the streets, we would go looking for them and try to entice them to come out. When they did emerge, we would scatter in all directions, screaming in panic. We truly believed they were witches, and would call after them, "*Baba Jaga, Baba Jaga*," referring to a folklore ogress who stole young children and carried them off into the remote forest, before cooking them in a pot for dinner.

My cousin Avram Berman was a keen amateur photographer, and his particular interest lay in taking pictures of the more unfortunate shtetl characters. Avram also travelled to other places in an effort to seek out interesting subjects to record for posterity. He had a professional wide-lens Leica camera, and built up an extensive photographic library which would have been priceless today.

The staple diet of the poor, apart from the usual cabbage and potatoes, was salt herring. This would be prepared at home with a little oil and vinegar according to taste, with a chopped onion on top, and it was delicious when eaten with black bread. The salt herrings were sold loose, out of a wooden barrel, as was sauerkraut, borscht, gherkins pickled in brine and dill, and so on. One could reach deep into the brine with one's hand and pull out the choicest pieces. "Big Ethel" ran a provisions shop well stocked with these barrels. To find a good herring, the discerning shopper would sniff under the gills, and if any regular dared suggest the herrings weren't fresh, temperamental Ethel would admonish the customer and hurl back at him indignantly, "Oi there, Moishe-Yukel, I tell you the herrings are fresh, they don't smell, I smell!"

However, fresh food was purchased weekly on market-day from peasant farmers who brought their produce to us from nearby farms and hamlets. The Rynek would spring to life in early morning, teeming with people, both Jew and Gentile. At the same time, the peasants would buy manufactured goods from the Jewish shopkeepers in town, which they could get "on tick," and so everyone came away happy. Market-day was Thursday; this made it convenient for the Jewish housewife to stock up for the Sabbath. The peasants arrived at the crack of dawn in anticipation of a good day's trading. They came on a multitude of carts, often drawn by scraggly old horses, with the carts doubling up as makeshift stalls. The poor nags had to stand most of the day, harnessed to the shafts of the wagons, munching from nosebags suspended from their necks, with their heads nodding and tails swishing from side to side to drive away persistent flies. Apart from the usual dairy products, the farmers also brought fruit and vegetables. There was butter, eggs, and heart-shaped white cheeses wrapped in muslin. Freshly-churned butter was kept cool wrapped in cabbage leaves, an original substitute for greaseproof paper. Cheese and butter could be tasted prior to purchase by scooping up a *soupçon* on the thumbnail to make sure it had not turned rancid. There were also aromatic dried mushrooms strung in garlands, with freshly-gathered ones in late summer. There was seasonal fruit; my favourite was wild strawberries and blueberries, picked in the forest, in early summer; they were delicious when eaten with *smietana,* sour-cream, and sprinkled with sugar.

But most important, the peasants brought lots of clucking hens to market. Without them, there could be no chicken soup for the Sabbath table. These were sold live, and choosing a good one was quite a performance. The shopper would first inspect several hens from different carts before making her choice. The discerning housewife would look for a plump bird which would add flavour to a good chicken soup. There was no demand for scrawny old chickens, except perhaps by the very poor at the end of the day's trading. After the shopper pointed to a certain bird in the cage, the farmer would grab the struggling, squawking, hen and cross its wings, to stop the poor thing from beating its wings and taking off, before handing it to the customer for consideration. She would first size up the chicken by lifting it up and down several times to ascertain its weight. Then she would tuck the struggling fowl under her arm, with its head and neck facing backwards, and poke its bottom to try to locate any eggs. Egg yolks were an added delicacy to a tasty, golden-coloured chicken soup. If satisfied so far, she would turn the bird upside-down and blow vigorously onto the poor creature's bottom, parting the feathers to see if the skin was yellow and plump. After the customary haggling was over, the deal was clinched. It only remained for someone to hurry with the chicken to the Jewish slaughterer—and this was the duty of the elder daughter in the family. After a brisk day's trading the peasants departed one by one, each aiming for his preferred tavern, where the vodka and beer flowed freely. Their horses left behind prodigious quantities of manure, mixed with swirling rivulets of liquid discharge which covered the entire cobbled square. It only remained for an army of sweepers to clean up the huge mess!

A bustling market day in Ostrowiec, as I remember it from my youth. This image is printed in Andrzej Lada and Aleksander Salij, *Ostrowiec-Swietokrzyski* (Ostrowiec: Comex, 1991).

I have a vivid recollection of the circus that used to come to town once a year and perform in the Rynek, the main hub of town. It was the annual event to look forward to. It was spring, with the severe winter weather behind us, and so it was already a most exciting time of year for me, as it was for all the boys and girls in our town. We followed the clowns who walked through the streets on stilts, like giants, to advertise that the circus had arrived. It was at the circus that I saw a black African and a Chinaman for the first time. Previously, I had only read about such exotic people in children's books.

One night, one of the lions escaped from the circus and ran into the house belonging to one of my uncles, Velv'l (Wolf) Berman. Wolf had the reputation of enjoying a drink or two on a Saturday night with his Gentile boozing pals, who accepted him as their equal, and returning home in the early hours of the morning. Wolf was a giant of a man, who liked to demonstrate his prowess by performing feats of strength in the *piwiarnia*, the local tavern. He was known, for example, to do press-ups with a keg of beer above his head. He was also known to drink a small barrel of local Saski brew in one night for a wager, or more likely for bravado. He also laid claim to mastery in beer-swilling contests, by sinking the equivalent of a yard of ale in record time. It was no mean feat for a Jew to outdo Poles, who were renowned drinkers. However, people said that the general population was inclined towards violence and wife-beating when drunk, but not so our Wolf. He was a mild-mannered, gentle person and despite his reputation not a habitual drinker. When sober, he insisted he only drank once a week, on Saturday nights, and only socially, or so he claimed.

The day the lion escaped from the circus, it being a Saturday night, Wolf was as usual in the ale-house with his red-nosed Gentile buddies, soaking up the beer. Meanwhile, the lion entered one of the rooms in his house off the Rynek through an open window. The beast then plunked himself down, right up against the bedroom door where Wolf's wife Sheyndla was sound asleep. The story goes that the lion kept grunting and groaning at her door. As a result, Sheyndla woke up, got out of bed, and tried to push the door open, but couldn't. Thinking that her massive husband was flat-out against the door, sleeping off the drink, she shouted at him angrily: "Velv'l, *bist du shoyn weiter shikker?*"— "Wolf, don't tell me you're jolly well sloshed again!" No matter how many times this tale was repeated at our dinner table, it never failed to amuse us, and we children nearly fell off our chairs trying to imitate the lion's roar.

Sometime in early July 1939 my first school year ended, and there was the long summer holiday to look forward to. But that went by all too quickly, and when the last days of that glorious summer began to wane I could hardly wait for school to start, in spite of all the bullying and taunts I had been subjected to. Sadly, however, events took a different turn and my school never even opened its doors. At dawn on the very day that school was due to begin, massed German armoured divisions surged across the Polish border without any formal declaration of war. As a result, I never went back to school, and my education, which had barely begun, was at an end. The happy times were over; it was to be my last summer of bliss with my loving parents and siblings around me. I always look back to that wonderful summer with nostalgia and fond memories. How I wished with all my heart that time would stand still, but sadly the halcyon days were over, and with them went my secure and carefree childhood.

CHAPTER 1

War! War! Is Their Cry

It was summer of 1939, and the clouds of war were gathering. After all his previous territorial claims, a ranting Adolf Hitler now turned his attention to Poland, demanding that the Free City of Danzig and the Pomeranian Corridor, which gave Poland access to the sea, be ceded to the German Reich. I had just turned eight, and didn't really understand the political implications involved. I heard grown-ups speak of war, and like all boys I thought war and shooting rather exciting. But I soon realised the gravity of the situation from the way my father and brothers stayed glued to our German-made Elektra radio in a way I never saw them do before. The Polish national radio would begin its main newscast at noon with the *Hejnał,* the haunting bugle-call from the Kraków Tower, which I always liked to listen to. This harked back to medieval times, when hordes of Tartar horsemen from the East raided the city. The bugle-call from an archer's slit would be interrupted in mid-note, signifying that the Polish trumpeter was hit by a Tartar arrow. This was followed by stirring martial music and slogans glorifying the national leader: "Our beloved and brave commander, Marshal Śmigły-Rydz, stands with us, no one would dare intrude on our homeland!" We were taught these adulatory songs at school, in praise of the national leader. Another absurd slogan vowed: *Nie oddamy guzika od palta,* we will not yield a single button from our overcoat. In view of this rather silly bluster, a quip soon made the rounds: "No, we will give up the whole coat instead!" The puffed-up military leaders punched above their weight, with little to back up their delusion of power. After all the German annexations and broken promises, they still looked upon Hitler's threats as idle bluff. People were critical of the regime; some said that the mobilization order went out too late, failing to suitably prepare the nation for war. The government tried to reassure the public that all those Panzer columns on parade in Berlin were only mock-ups, made from cardboard. The over-confident Polish leadership, dominated by inept army colonels, totally underestimated or deliberately played-down the German might that was about to be unleashed against the defenceless people of Poland.

On 1 September 1939, the British Prime Minister, Neville Chamberlain, under an earlier commitment made to Poland, delivered an ultimatum to Adolf Hitler at his chancellery in Berlin to the effect that unless Germany agreed to withdraw its forces from Poland within 48 hours, a state of war would exist between the two countries. And when that expired with no response from *Herr* Hitler, Britain found itself at war with Nazi Germany. Within a matter of hours, France followed suit, and World War II had begun.

The morning of 1 September was fine and sunny; at least in my part of the country there wasn't a cloud in the sky. It was the day my new school year was due to begin, I could see the schoolhouse from my home; it never even opened its doors. At dawn that day, Hitler unleashed the Luftwaffe and his massed divisions across the Polish border. My family stayed glued to the wireless set as the Polish state radio kept repeating warnings of approaching enemy aircraft formations: *"Uwaga, uwaga, nadchodzi"*: "Attention, attention, approaching..." This was followed by coded military messages transmitted over the air-waves. The small Polish Air Force was no match for the Luftwaffe, having mainly obsolescent biplanes to pit against the most powerful air force in Europe. Almost immediately we heard the drone of German aircraft overhead and the distant sound of heavy explosions, apparently aimed at Polish army formations somewhere in the vicinity. I was tremendously excited when for the first time I saw a huge German bomber plane close up, as it passed low overhead above our building, its black cross clearly visible. It happened so quickly that it never occurred to me to take cover. The swastika and the Teutonic Black Cross would in time come to haunt us. However, there was no actual fighting in our area, and that lone aircraft was all we saw of the war. We were aware nonetheless that the Germans were advancing rapidly, and were deep into Poland, and all we could do was wait with trepidation for the invaders to reach our town. Not in our wildest dreams could we have imagined what far-reaching consequences this would have for us, and how it would shatter our lives.

After the German Blitzkrieg, or lightning war, began, it took their forces no more than a week to reach our area. The Panzer columns needed no more than another three weeks to roll deep into Poland, with little to stop them until the Russian lines. The Red Army had meanwhile marched into Poland from the east, with the German and Russian armies meeting at Brest-Litovsk on the River Bug, effectively splitting the country in two. This was formalized under a secret pact made between Nazi Germany and Soviet Russia during the signing of their Treaty of Non-Aggression, stabbing Poland in the back. The astonished Poles didn't know what had hit them, and hardly resisted the Russians, as they were not at war with them. The dauntless but badly-led Polish army, like its air force, was armed with antiquated equipment and had hardly any tanks. Some people believe that the dashing Polish cavalry remarkably tried to wage an obsolete form of warfare on horseback, wielding lances and swords and hopelessly charging armoured Blitzkrieg formations. The Polish army was forced to fall back to avoid encirclement, and then tried to regroup in front of Warsaw to defend their capital. The Luftwaffe pounded the city mercilessly, and Poland had no choice but to capitulate, which it did on 27 September after its leaders, including the military commander-in-chief, escaped to Rumania together with some of the remaining military forces.

We stood utterly bewildered outside our home and watched with disbelief as the first German units arrived. The grim-faced soldiers on BMW motorcycles wore green rubberised trench coats and had goggles on their helmets and machine guns mounted on their side-cars. They were covered in dust and grime, and looked tired as a result of their lightning advance through Poland in a matter of days. These stern-looking reconnaissance riders totally ignored us as we stood outside our front door. A little while later, two open-top staff-cars arrived and seemed to reconnoitre the area, but they too soon rode off. These were followed later in the day by hordes of Wehrmarcht soldiers wearing grey-green uniforms and polished knee-high boots. They came riding bicycles, with their rifles slung across their shoulders. In contrast to the earlier ones on motorbikes, these smiling and chatty soldiers astride this innocuous form of transport didn't appear at all menacing. We soon realised that they weren't frontline troops, but a supply and engineering detachment made up of older reserve soldiers. Field kitchens also arrived, pulled by sturdy draught-horses. The Germans' favourite dish seemed to be a thick, highly-seasoned Hungarian goulash that I didn't like the smell of as they sat on the grass, eating it greedily out of mess-tins. In retrospect, it would have been hard to imagine that the compatriots of these benign-looking soldiers would one day be capable of such brutality. The conquerors had the motto *Gott mit Uns*, God is for us, stamped on their belt buckles, around a swastika in the centre. They had every reason to believe that God was marching with the Wehrmacht. *"Heute Deutchland, Morgen die Gantzer Welt"*: "Today, Germany belongs to us, tomorrow the entire world," they sang as they went. Everything seemed to be going their way, sweeping all before it, all to the glory of Hitler *und Vaterland*.

This initial reconnaissance unit must have been relying on old maps or out-of-date intelligence, and expected to find a Polish army detachment based here—hence their interest in our locality. However, any Polish troops in our area would have earlier retreated north-eastwards in the face of the German onslaught from the west.

The Wehrmacht soldiers completely ignored us as we watched them proceed to set up camp on the land adjoining the factory and our home. There was a large barrack-square there, suitable for their parades and goose-step drilling. Actually, our factory building as well as the nearby schoolhouse were originally built as *Kasernen,* permanent brick army barracks, and were used for that purpose during the First World War. A garrison of the Czar's Imperial Russian army had been stationed there at the time. One had to be very careful when digging up the soil; cannon shells and other munitions were often unearthed, left over from the Great War.

Right from the start, Father endeavoured to foster friendly relations with our Wehrmacht neighbours, who were at first punctilious in their behaviour towards us, treating my parents with the utmost respect. Father did his best to ingratiate himself to the portly and affable *Herr Feldwebel* (sergeant-major), who seemed to harbour no prejudice against Jews and was appreciative of the token gifts he was presented with. Father said we need not have worried; things might not turn out too badly after all. Those old enough, like him, remembered that German and Austrian soldiers were well-disposed towards Jews during the First World War. In fact, Jews at that time in the part of Poland under Czarist-Russian rule, including ours, where Jews had been oppressed, welcomed German troops in as liberators, but with the rise of Hitler all that changed. My father and older brothers were well aware of the ill-treatment of Jews in Germany. They knew about the Nuremberg Racial Laws, and Kristallnacht, the Night of Broken Glass, when synagogues throughout Germany were set alight and Jewish shops and property damaged or destroyed, with thousands of Jews sent off to concentration camps. We had also received worrying reports from my father's younger brother, Paul, who lived in Nazi Germany and was married to a German citizen, describing the anti-Jewish measures enacted there. The obese Göring quipped: "I would not want to be a Jew in Germany today!" Furthermore, he ordered Jews whose names were not distinctively Jewish to add "Israel" or "Sarah" on to them. This, we realised, was to mark them out as Jews, and if they introduce similar measures here, "we can live with that," Father said. However, soon after that we heard that Uncle Paul had his business confiscated, and was desperately trying to get out of the country. Early on in the war, we received a Red Cross postcard from him, informing us that he had reached the port of Hull in England with his wife and young son Leo. This was the same Leo who in happier times we had dubbed *Waffelman* when he visited us with his mother, spending his summer holiday with us in Ostrowiec.

Years later we learned how fortunate my uncle and his family were to get out of Nazi Germany when they did. They reached safe shores at the brink of war thanks to a chance acquaintanceship Uncle Paul made on a ship, which would serve to save his life and those of his wife and child. In the mid-thirties, after the Nazis introduced the infamous Nuremberg Racial Laws, Uncle Paul sailed for Palestine with a view to settling there with his family. This was easy enough at the time; the Nazis were only too happy to see the Jews go, leaving their assets behind, providing they had a visa for another country. However, Uncle Paul was concerned by the undeveloped conditions prevailing in Palestine at the time, and decided they would remain in Germany. On the return voyage he had the good fortune to befriend an English couple, by the name of Vinograd, from Hull. A few years later, as the situation for Jews in Germany became untenable, the Vinograds sent my uncle the necessary papers that would enable him and his family to escape to England as the war was about to begin. An admirable gesture indeed, resulting from a chance meeting on a boat, which saved their lives.

After the Germans marched in, it didn't take long for the whole Nazi apparatus of oppression to be put into effect. It began with the Jews being deprived of basic rights throughout Poland. This was followed soon after by a campaign of intimidation and brutality, with the Gestapo and SS claiming their first victims by randomly shooting several religious men in the street, under the pretext that they were Communists. How could a God-fearing Hasidic Jew ever be a Communist non-believer? The Germans lost no time in doing away with "undesirable" people who

appeared odd to them; this included the mentally deficient, street beg-
gars, and cripples, who were the first to disappear from sight. Life for
my family, however, didn't change significantly in those early days, since
we lived out of town, away from the congested Jewish area where the
first sporadic humiliations and excesses took place. But as time went on,
Father would come home from the town centre with ever more depress-
ing news of harsh measures implemented against the community, of
people arrested for no apparent reason, and of random confiscation of
chattels and property. Jewish businessmen, including my father, meanwhile had their bank accounts frozen, leaving them penniless; luckily,
my father had made some provision beforehand. In his wisdom, he had
converted much of our family's assets into more portable forms, like
pre-Revolution Russian gold coins, called "piglets," and diamonds. Both
of these were conveniently small and could be hidden easily or sewn into
clothing. Later on, as our situation deteriorated, a "piggy" or diamond
would be exchanged for cash with the Polish racketeers who grew rich
on the backs of hapless Jews. Polish General-Government money was all
right for certain staples, like bread and potatoes, but otherwise pretty
worthless. Diamonds, gold coins, and American dollars were the currency *par excellence* for obtaining vital things like forged documents and
buying your way out of tricky situations, and my father's foresight was
instrumental to us as the war progressed.

Towards the end of 1939, Jewish refugees started to converge on our
town, having been evicted from Konin in western Poland, a town lying
halfway between Poznań and Łódź. This area was annexed and incorporated into the Reich, or Greater Germany, to make way for its God-given
right to *Lebensraum*—living space for the Master Race. All the Jews from
this area were driven out of their homes at short notice and pushed over
the border into central Poland, now designated General-Government,
the official name for occupied Poland, with Dr. Hans Frank as its Nazi
overlord.

The train carrying these unfortunate refugees halted at Ostrowiec
railway station, having been shunted from town to town, dropping off
people along the way to seek a shelter for themselves. Father went to
the station and "adopted" three of these homeless families. One family
was named Judkiewicz, and the man of the house was a tailor; another
was the Cohen family, who were egg merchants; and there was a third,
whose name I can no longer recall, though I do know the head of the

family was a pharmacist. In all, about one thousand refugees were simply dumped in our town, for the Jewish community to shelter. We took these unfortunates into our home and shared with them what was now our cramped accommodation and our soon-to-be-depleted stock of food. These deportees had lost everything; they came as they stood, with few belongings. Some wondered if this was an indication of what was in store for us too. "But all they lost were their material possessions," Father said, "and if things get no worse than that, we will endure." Father, the inveterate optimist, kept repeating that, and things like it, no doubt intending to allay our anxiety, especially Mother's, and keep our spirits up. A common expression at the time that people kept repeating went: *"Es wird alles vorbei gehen"*—it will all come to pass. Few would have imagined that worse would follow.

Soon enough, the arrogant Master Race began to throw their weight about, starting with plundering Jewish shops and businesses, brazenly helping themselves to goods without paying. More affable officers used less crude methods by demanding credit they had no intention of making good, or simply handed over old German currency that was no longer in circulation. This dated back to the era of hyper-inflation in Germany, and one could do nothing about it. Although sugar, the essential raw material without which our business could not function, was in short supply, Father nevertheless endeavoured to keep on friendly terms with our Wehrmacht neighbours by being over-generous with the factory produce, thereby hoping to gain their goodwill. He believed that in the ever-worsening situation developing around us, this could help to make our position more secure, living as we did cheek-by-jowl with the German military.

At about this time, some young Jewish men from our town and elsewhere began to flee eastwards, in the direction of the Soviet-occupied former Polish territory; mostly to the Lwów area. The Red Army had marched into Poland from the east two weeks after the Germans had invaded from the west, as permitted by the secret agreement to divide Poland, which had been added to the shameful non-aggression pact between Nazi Germany and the USSR that gave Hitler the green light to invade Poland. Consequently, the country was carved-up between Germany and Russia on a vertical line along the River Bug, well to the east of Warsaw, with the Nazis taking the lion's share. The Soviets kept the former Polish-Russian frontier open during this early period, and didn't try to stop refugees from fleeing to their lines. Like other young men from our town, my two eldest brothers, Moniek and Izak, had their knapsacks packed, ready to head for the Russian lines in eastern Poland. Father thought Moniek and Izak could be at risk by staying behind, as they were of military age, and he urged them to head for the Russian lines without delay. He thought that the rest of us would be safe where we were. But at the last moment my two brothers went against our father's wishes and stayed behind to help look after the family. They were, after all, adults, and Father never imposed his will, he only offered advice. My parents were not so young; Father was in his late forties and my mother about three years younger. Had my two brothers gone away, the next oldest was Leizer, who was only thirteen at the time. The selfless decision made by my two brothers would ultimately cost them their lives, but would help to save ours, as I'll later discuss.

As it happens, even had they taken our father's advice, there is no way of knowing what would have happened to them. Later on, when Germany invaded the former Polish eastern territories and Russia in June 1941, those Jews who had fled to the Russian lines were trapped by the rapid German advance through Poland and into the Ukraine. Those who managed to flee deeper into Russia, ahead of the advancing Germans, survived. Those who stayed behind in the Russian-occupied eastern zone of Poland would perish, almost to a man, at the hands of either the Germans or the collaborating Ukrainians. Had my brothers made the journey, we would have constantly agonised over their fate.

CHAPTER 2

The Nightmare Begins

The first heavy blow for my family came at the end of 1939, barely three months after the German invasion. The Gestapo, secret police, lost no time in paying us a visit to inform my father and uncles that under the Aryanization Programme of Jewish Concerns, they would now install a *Treuhaender*, a custodian, to take charge of our family business. And as our factory was by far the largest Jewish concern in Ostrowiec, two *Treuhaender* were in fact appointed. This in effect meant that our business was being confiscated, with immediate effect, and we would from now on have to work for the benefit of the Third Reich. These administrators were *Volksdeutsche*, ethnic Germans, as opposed to *Reichsdeutsche,* Germans born inside Germany. They were from the city of Poznań, which had its name Germanized to Posen. They spoke both Polish and German, as they had been under Polish rule between the wars and could now choose to declare their loyalty to the German Reich. These fifth-columnists were now rewarded by being installed in Jewish concerns, in recognition of their pro-Nazi activities prior to the German invasion of Poland.

Our new German bosses treated us well at first; as they knew little about the confectionery industry they needed to rely on our expertise to carry on with the day-to-day business, but all rights and decision-making were taken away from us. It was rather like a master-and-servant relationship. My father and uncles had to simply come to terms with the new situation, that they were subordinate to the Germans, their new masters. The oft-repeated German slogan at this time was: *Wir Bauen eine Neue Europa*: We are Building a New Order in Europe. From then on, my father, brothers, uncles and cousins became ordinary workers in their own business and were made to toil for their German masters for little financial reward. In time that, too, was stopped. I suppose we were fortunate to be allowed to stay on in our home, which adjoined the factory, but this too was not to last.

Early in 1940 the reign of terror began in earnest, with new restrictions and prohibitions levelled against Jews almost daily. The occupation authorities lost no time in ordering all Jews in General-Government Poland over the age of ten to wear a white armband on their upper right sleeves, imprinted with a blue Star of David. The size of the star had to be no less than 10cm wide. In the part of Poland annexed to Germany, Jews had to have a yellow star patch that bore the word *Jude* stitched to their outer garments. The decree made it clear that non-compliance would result in severe punishment. Vendors soon appeared on street corners offering the armbands for sale, ahead of the date we had to begin wearing them. The armbands were made of white cloth, but one could also buy more permanent ones, made of rigid white celluloid, so that the Blue Star would be clearly visible from afar, as decreed. The cloth armbands had a tendency to roll up, we discovered, thus partly obscuring the star, which was strictly against regulations. We were now a marked people, no longer free to move about at will, and if you tried to pass for a Gentile Pole, you took your life into your hands. From then on, every Jew carried his identity on his sleeve, back, or front, depending on the part of Poland in which he or she lived. Apart from ease of identification, the wearer of the Jewish Star became a target for derision. Actually, this singularly distressing decree was not original: the Nazis adopted it. It harked back to the Middle-Ages, when Jews in Christian Europe were demonized, and forced to wear the yellow "Badge of Shame." In certain countries, the required uniform was, rather than a badge, a tall conical hat, indicative of the devil's horns, so that the public could easily identify and stigmatise the Jew as the offspring of the devil or Satan. In certain countries, notably France, Jews were made to wear a yellow patch in the shape of a circle, called a *rouleau*. Yellow signified treachery, greed and insanity.

In time even harsher measures were to follow. All education was stopped and schools were closed to Jewish children. Jews were not allowed to travel on trains or go to parks; all places of entertainment were closed to them. In fact, we were forbidden to do anything of a pleasurable nature, under threat of severe punishment. We were now effectively trapped in our small town, unable to travel. Radios, bicycles, and cameras were the first to be confiscated. A night-time curfew was also put into force, depending on the daylight hours. Street posters listed all the things forbidden to a Jew:

1. A Jew is not allowed to own or ride a bicycle.
2. A Jew is forbidden to go to the cinema or theatre.
3. A Jew is forbidden to travel by train or other public conveyance.
4. A Jew is not allowed in the park.

The list continued from there.

A Jew was not even allowed to keep a dog. Although I missed my pal Dynguś, I was glad I no longer had him. For a start what would I have fed him on? He would never have understood why I had to be so cruel to him as to let him starve. And had I still had him, I could not have made myself give him up to those beasts. Cameras were confiscated, and radios had to be surrendered to the authorities. Thereafter, listening to foreign broadcasts carried the death penalty. As a result, we were now cut off from any news of the outside world, and had to rely on rumours. Food rationing for certain commodities was introduced for the general population, but there was no provision in place of rationing for Jews. We were not entitled to any food rations; we simply had to fend for ourselves, existing on little more than bread. In time, that too became scarce.

At about this time there emerged a tiny ripple of hope in the form of the Madagascar Plan. Actually, the Poles were the first to come up with the scheme back in the thirties, when they proposed expelling Polish Jews to the French colony of Madagascar, off the African coast. They ran out of time when Hitler turned on Poland in 1939, but in 1940 the Nazis considered resurrecting the Polish plan, to expel all the Jews under their control to the tropical French island in the Indian Ocean and turning it into a Jewish reservation under German jurisdiction. This no doubt would also have appealed to the Poles, not that they had any say in it now, as it offered the prospect of emptying the country of its Jews. But we Jews never took it seriously, though in the light of what was happening to us under the Nazis, even this solution seemed preferable. In the end nothing came of it. Hitler soon dropped the scheme as too difficult to implement for logistical reasons. He no doubt feared that the British Royal Navy would sink any German shipping on the high seas. It certainly wasn't the cost in human cargo that deterred the Führer; his concern must have been for the German tonnage! So the Nazis decided on the Final Solution instead, hoping to solve once and for all what Hitler termed *"Der Judenfrage"*: the Jewish Question. As a result of the aborted Madagascar Plan, a satirical pre-war song was revived and did the rounds in the ghettoes. It was about a mythical Jewish-African slave republic. The lyrics were in Polish, with added subtle Yiddish/Jewish humour. I can no longer recall it word for word, but it went something like this:

Oy, Madagascar (Refrain)

I'm a wild savage,
a true cannibal they say.
So I'm off to Africa,
I have a colony there, you know.[1]
Oy, Madagascar...
Dusky, sweltering and steamy,
a land that's half-wild.
I will buy me an elephant
and a wild horse.
I shall have a proper colony
or nothing at all.

Coconuts and bamboo trees,
the tribes there are savage.
So I may find it better,
because where there's culture,
there's conflict and strife.

Oy, Madagascar...

I'll make a pass at a native girl,
I have my ways you know.
With her it will be black on white,
because that's just what I like.

Such a dark-skinned mummy
and a white-skinned daddy,
will beget chequered babies
and it will all come right.

---

1 The lyrics carry on about opening a kosher diner there, as well as a *mikve* (ritual bathhouse).

My father liked to tease my uncle Josef Fajngold, who lived in Kielce and was married to Father's only sister, my favourite aunt Hanna, that he strongly resembled Adolf Hitler; in fact others thought so too. He had similar dark features, the straight nose, and the "Charlie Chaplin" moustache with glossy plastered-down hair that was fashionable at the time. Of course, he didn't grow the mustache to mimic the German dictator; he wore it long before Hitler became known as the chancellor of Germany. Early on in the war, we heard from Uncle Josef that he was forced to shave off the moustache that he was so attached to after he was threatened by a Nazi in the street. He was lucky to get off with just a warning; he could have been shot on the spot for impersonating the Führer! Something similar happened in Ostrowiec to a friend of my father's, who was stopped by a German in the street and asked for his surname. He replied, Hipler, Sir! The German thought the man was making fun of his beloved Führer. Mr. Hipler, too, got away with it this time, apart from a good whack on his shoulder with the Nazi officer's swagger-stick. But while moustaches can be shaved off, the man was helpless to do anything about his name. To be saddled with an unfortunate name like that was terrible: his fate would in the future depend on the whim of whatever Nazi he was confronted by.

By now there were frequent so called *łapanki,* street raids. Army trucks would suddenly screech to a halt, and German soldiers would jump off them and force young Jews into the trucks with their rifle butts. These prisoners were pressed into compulsory work gangs for a specific project, and when the task was complete they were usually released, sometimes after only a day or two. Before long, though, Jews were grabbed off the streets, ostensibly for work, but never to be heard from again. Others still were snatched for permanent slave labour to nearby Starachowice or Skarżysko-Kamienna, the latter to become known as one of the most notorious slave labour camps: prisoners who worked in one of the factories there turned yellow from the picric acid they were exposed to in the production of explosives. Then there were arbitrary arrests for no apparent reason except to use the victims as a means of extortion. Families had to pay hefty ransoms to have their relatives released, or else their dear ones would never be seen again.

The streets became unsafe for Jews. People chose to stay indoors whenever possible. Individuals were picked on at random in the street and subjected to intimidation and painful humiliation, especially rabbis and old men with beards. It became a popular pastime for soldiers and gendarmes armed with scissors and clippers to hack off beards and *payot* (side-curls) in the street. My maternal grandfather, Leibish Berman, to whom I was very close, had a long white beard resembling that of a biblical patriarch, which I liked to stroke. It was not that he was particularly religious; it had more to do with the tradition for wise old men to wear beards in those days. One day, he was accosted by some German thugs on the street; they ridiculed him at first, then proceeded to cut his beard off, but only on one side of his face. My grandpa considered this the ultimate insult to his dignity. When he reached home he wouldn't cut the rest of it off, as most men would have done. My grandpa was a proud and dignified old gentleman, and he decided to defy the Nazis in this token way. He was from then on reluctant to go outdoors, but if he had to, he would wrap a scarf round his chin and face as if he had an earache, thus hiding what was left of his beard.

Jews were not allowed to share pavements with an *Übbermensch,* a German master-man. If you saw one approach, it was prudent to step into the gutter and doff your cap, or else have your face slapped by some enraged Nazi thug and perhaps be pushed into the gutter. If a German thrust his right arm out in a Hitler salute, on no account was a Jew permitted to respond in a like manner. It wasn't that anyone would have wished to, but if someone did raise his arm reflexively or to please the German, it could prove fatal. The privilege of a Hitler salute was reserved for the *Herrenvolk,* master race. It was actually forbidden for a Jew to acknowledge a German in public, save by stepping into the gutter and humbly averting his eyes.

Elderly religious men were held up to ridicule and made to carry out the most demeaning of tasks, like scrubbing pavements and even going through the motions of licking them clean on all fours. For a bit of amusement, German policemen and soldiers forced bearded old men to sing and perform comical dances in a circle, mimicking a Hassidic dance, subjecting them to painful indignities to the accompaniment of cruel derision and laughter. Rabbis had their faces slapped and their hats knocked off their heads. They were made to put on prayer shawls and *teffilin*—the cube-shaped black leather boxes containing scriptural passages inscribed on parchment that religious men strap to their left arm and forehead first thing in the morning, as a constant reminder of God's laws—in the middle of the street for the entertainment of their tormentors. As the German supermen stood by mocking and jeering, others took snapshots as souvenirs for the folks back home or for Nazi propaganda purposes, as an example of the superiority of their *Kultur*— such superiority was demonstrated by the harassment and humiliation of elderly men!

CHAPTER 3

The Large Ghetto

The next devastating blow filled everyone with worry and dismay. This came in the early spring of 1941, when the German authorities issued an edict requiring all Jews living in the outlying small towns and villages around Ostrowiec to abandon their homes and move into the predominantly Jewish area in the city centre, which was also the poorest and most squalid part of town, where a "ghetto" was to be established. This would come to be known as the Large Ghetto. It was also referred to as the Open Ghetto, as it was left open at first, without any wall or fence. At this time, one could come and go as one pleased. However, no one was allowed to stay overnight outside the ghetto boundary. Every Jew had to return by evening, before the start of the curfew. At the same time, any non-Jewish family who happened to be living inside the designated ghetto area had to move out by the specified date and go into dwellings vacated by Jews elsewhere in town. As a result, the Jewish population of Ostrowiec swelled from ten thousand to sixteen thousand almost overnight, with people from the neighbouring small towns and villages, as well as refugees evicted from distant towns like Konin, some even as far away as Vienna, pouring into the ghetto.

As we lived outside of the designated Jewish area, we were to be forcibly evicted from our home by the appointed date unless we decided to vacate voluntarily beforehand. We would also be locked out of our business, which would from then on be out of bounds to us—something Father found particularly hard to accept. "What exactly is a ghetto?," I kept asking people. I knew this was serious, but no one would explain; they had no time for me, they were too busy with all the preparations in the factory and at home. I had never heard of a ghetto before. Then I thought I'd ask my two eldest brothers, who, I decided, should know, but they didn't say much either. They were the strong, silent type. I suppose they were not sure themselves what it entailed, and they just got on with the packing. When I asked Father, he said, "You may like it there, Rubinek—it's a place where a lot of people live close to one another. It may not be too bad there after all; you'll have lots of friends of your age to play with." But I was not convinced; I didn't like the sound of "ghetto." All I was sure of was that I didn't want to leave my play area, where I had my secret dens. I just couldn't take it in, nor understand why all this was happening to me, one thing after another. Everything I held dear and loved was being taken away, bit by bit. First my dog went missing; then I had to give up my bicycle and the radio. I had liked to tune into to distant, crackling stations, speaking strange languages. And now we were to be forced out of our comfortable home. I would have to give up my lovely room and everything in it, as well as the freedom to roam and play in the area I was so fond of. "I don't want to be hemmed into a ghetto!," I kept crying, seeing it—quite accurately—as a place where I would no longer have the freedom to roam in the fields and woods where I grew up and that I loved so much. I kept protesting and could not be consoled. I sobbed and sobbed, but to no avail. It was like a bad dream— a nightmare from which I could not wake. "I don't want to leave home," I kept repeating, as mama was crying. "If we have to go, we will go!," Father said, putting his foot down. We listened to him; he always made the decisions. He was better informed than my mother. He must have known the Nazis meant harm, but he played it down to soften the blow. There was no choice; we simply had to gather up our essential things, load them onto a couple of pushcarts, and head for the poorest part of town, where the ghetto was to be established. Although it was early spring, Father strongly advised that we put on as much winter clothing as possible, just in case. He must have had a premonition that we were in it for the long haul.

Hundreds of bewildered families did the same, all converging in family groups upon the same densely populated area, with the strong supporting the weak. They came from all different directions, some with handcarts and wheelbarrows and even old prams, but most carrying bulging old suitcases tied with string, or just supporting bundles made of sheets tied together on their backs. It was a sad and pitiful sight. Some of our fine furniture had earlier been blatantly commandeered by German officers—everything was up for grabs, to them. They came and picked what they wanted, and my parents could say nothing, let alone complain—for complaining could draw severe punishment. The rest of it we had to abandon to be pilfered by local people after our departure. We were allowed to take with us only personal effects: cooking pots were a must, as were the bare essentials. Luckily, this included our goose down quilts, which were essential to keep us from freezing in the severe Polish winter. We had already been deprived of our freedom; now we were also thrown out of our home, with our business confiscated and our livelihood and possessions all taken away or left behind. Father, above all, as the breadwinner and head of the family, was utterly devastated; his whole world and everything he had striven and worked for had come to nothing.

The objective of the ghetto was to do away with small communities in rural areas, to isolate Jews from their non-Jewish neighbours, and to concentrate them in holding centres near railway lines, as the first stage in facilitating their eventual evacuation. Once the Jews were trapped inside the congested ghettoes, the German plan was to slowly starve and weaken them so they could more easily be coerced into what the Germans called *Aussiedlung* (relocation). The goal was to sap us of our strength and the will to resist.

Living conditions in the ghetto were very cramped. We were allotted accommodation by the Jewish Order Police with a family named Zylberberg, at 13 Iłrzecka Street. Our family of eight and my cousin Franka, who had lived with us since the war had begun, were crammed into one room, which was hitherto the Zylberbergs' family salon; they had to make do with less space. Some of the refugees from Konin who had been lodging with us since they had been thrown out of their own homes were also allocated rooms in the same house. Sheets and blankets were strung across the room between the bunk-beds to provide a modicum of privacy. Once settled inside the ghetto there was just one thing that I liked about it, as my father had predicted; the place was teeming with boys and girls of my age. Suddenly I found myself surrounded by many friends I could play with, as I never had before. We played the usual children's games: hide-and-seek, tag, cowboys and Indians—but we never played chasing or shooting "Jerries," for no one would have wanted to be a "Jerry" and besides, we were too afraid of them. It was easy to pretend you were a Red Indian by attaching a feather to your cap, but how does one dress up like a German—by putting on a swastika armband? That would have been too much, and too dangerous.

About seven months later, in December 1941, the hitherto open ghetto was walled in and sealed off from the outside world. From now on, we were forbidden to go beyond the designated ghetto boundaries.

The *Bekanntmachung* made it clear that any Jew found venturing outside the ghetto wall would be shot on sight. In spite of the extremely cramped conditions inside the ghetto, our room was kept spotlessly clean. My cousin Franka, who was from Kielce and was a talented milliner by profession, had a fetish for cleanliness. She could be irritating at times, but her work pleased Mother. The family tried to make the best of the situation, and we even managed to earn some money clandestinely. My father and brothers managed to produce boiled sweets, secretly, in a small way, in our cramped abode. This was sold to one of our former Polish traders outside the ghetto. The necessary colourings and essences we took with us from the factory. The sweets needed to be smuggled out of the ghetto and brought to the Gentile contact on the "other side," as we called it, and as I was too young and not up to the task, Abram, who was two years older, was entrusted with the job. This was a dangerous practice, for any form of enterprise was strictly forbidden. And as the melting of sugar combined with flavourings gives off a strong, sweet-smelling odour, the job had to be done hastily during the night. All the equipment was scrubbed clean after each production batch and hidden away, to cover all traces.

Our Berman relatives from Łódż, who also now found themselves inside our ghetto, were equally enterprising: they found a way of producing laundering soap. I liked to watch them boil up the carbolic mixture, made from low-quality ingredients, each an ersatz version of what they might use in better times, that had been smuggled into the ghetto; the mixture was then poured into wooden moulds in which the soap would be allowed to cool and set into bars. How they managed to obtain the necessary ingredients, I still don't know. It's amazing how enterprising and resourceful people can become, even in such difficult circumstances, if the need is great enough. Soap was a precious commodity, as hygiene became a big problem due to overcrowding.

As time went on, the situation in the ghetto grew progressively worse. An acute shortage of food developed. This applied to the general Polish population as well, of course, but for Jews it was far worse. At this time it was still fairly easy, although hazardous, to slip out of the ghetto to the "other side." We could remove our Jewish stars and try to join a line for bread in the Polish sector. This was not a guarantee that you'd receive any; as soon as someone with Jewish features joined the queue, bickering and jostling would commence, with murmurings down the line: "Jews eating Polish bread!" If a Polish policeman appeared in the distance, it was best to scarper! Often the Poles themselves would chase away any Jew from the bread line or even strike out at him.

Our family was not too badly affected at first, as my father had managed to bring plenty of money to the ghetto, where he kept it carefully hidden. This enabled us to buy extra food, smuggled into the ghetto, at exorbitant prices of course. Contact with Poles outside the ghetto for this illicit trade was still possible at this time, although it was risky. Contact was also made with Poles at the workplaces where Jews laboured alongside Christian Poles in local industrial plants. While they worked together, Jews were not given wages and had to manage on fewer calories. Despite these conditions, this situation was better than that of some other ghettoes, particularly in large cities, where Jews were not taken to outside workplaces, and remained cut off from the local population. We knew this and other facts from escapees from other ghettoes, like the Warsaw ghetto, where contact with the "Aryan side" to obtain food was forbidden, and the rule was strictly enforced. This, coupled with the sheer size of the population in overcrowded conditions, led to starvation, and epidemics took hold, with young children dying in the streets, begging for bread.

Our ghetto was bad enough, though. As a result of the overcrowding and squalor, sanitary conditions deteriorated, making disease inevitable. Consequently, the first of several typhus epidemics broke out not long after the ghetto was sealed off. Although there were Jewish doctors present, including some distinguished ones who had been expelled from major cities such as Vienna, there were few drugs to prescribe. The rampant epidemic lasted several weeks and took a terrible toll; almost ten percent of the ghetto population died as a result of the outbreak. While the epidemic was raging, we were quarantined and confined to our homes; this led to even more privation and hunger. We were only allowed out during designated short periods, in a frantic search for food.

As I suffered a lot with inflamed tonsils and frequent sore throats, my parents decided that I should have my tonsils removed while it was still possible. The doctor in the ghetto who performed the operation had no anaesthetic, nor any painkillers to prescribe. I screamed in agony as he ripped my tonsils out with what looked like long scissors and tongs. Reclining in what seemed to be a dentist's chair, I watched as the blood gushed out of my mouth into a metal receptacle suspended around my neck. Afterward, the doctor wryly remarked that ice-cream would be good for slowing down the bleeding. The doctor knew, of course, that there was no ice-cream in the ghetto, nor any other delights. I had almost forgotten what it tasted like—it was a distant memory.

It must have been early June 1941 when we were alerted to the din of large Panzer columns moving along the Kunowska road that ran through town just beyond the ghetto, heading in an easterly direction. The rumbling of motorised vehicles could be heard from inside the ghetto. At the time we didn't understand the significance behind this large military movement. It transpired that the Germans were massing troops for an all-out attack against Soviet Russia that Hitler had code-named "Operation Barbarossa," thus breaking the Nazi-Soviet 10-year non-aggression pact that the Führer had ratified less than two years earlier, and which he had clearly never intended to keep. The rumbles we heard turned out to be part of Army Group South, which moved through our town heading for Przemyśl in southeastern Poland, in a direct line for Lvov and Kiev in the Ukraine. It was part of Hitler's dream of conquest for *Lebensraum* in the East. He called it *Drang nach Osten,* Drive to the East; this was his long-planned war of annihilation against the Soviet-Union. About the operation, Hitler had boasted, "The world shall hold its breath this day!"

As an inquisitive nine-year-old, I was fascinated by soldiers and military hardware, particularly the mighty Wehrmacht. Tempted to see what this was all about, I removed my Star of David armband and slipped out of the ghetto, which was not too difficult at this time, nor exceptionally dangerous, I felt. As a young boy I would hardly attract attention. I was three months short of my tenth birthday, when wearing the Jewish-star became compulsory. But I wanted to wear it sooner; I was rather proud of it and also wanted to appear older than I really was. I stood there for hours on end, out of sight of the Germans, not far from the reviewing stand where high-ranking officers took the salute as the mighty German military juggernaut rolled past. This went on intermittently for several days and nights. The confident German soldiers sang lustily as they went: *"Wenn Die Soldaten Gehen Marschieren. . ."*—"When soldiers come marching through town, all the maidens open their windows and doors. . ." The soldiers were sitting in rows, ramrod erect with rifles held between their knees, atop large half-track troop carriers with artillery pieces in tow. Some of the soldiers wore field-green rubberised trench-coats with goggles on their helmets; this made them appear particularly daunting. To a small boy like me, they looked fearless, like giant supermen.

At about this time, the Germans also introduced a popular army marching song frequently sung by the goose-stepping soldiers, *"Wir Fahren Gegen Engelland"*—"We move against England." We didn't know they had planned an invasion of England, and considered the song rather amusing, for they never sang about their other adversaries. No doubt it was the intrepid Churchill and the defiant British that most needled the Führer! Having lost the Battle of Britain, Hitler now turned his attention east, by unleashing his massed divisions on 22 June 1941 against Soviet Russia, in a titanic struggle. Soon after, the triumphant Nazis trumpeted with glee their lightning and unstoppable advance deep into Russia. Victory posters went up, proclaiming boldly, *"Deutschland Siegt Auf Alle Fronten!"*—"Germany is Victorious on all Fronts!" Large 'V' signs appeared on the streets to impress the general population, with the Nazi propaganda machine proclaiming that the 'V' symbol stood for German victory over "Jewish" Bolshevism. The general population was exhorted to greater effort under the banner of the "New Order in Europe."

Even before we were consigned to the ghetto, the Germans had appointed a Judenrat, a Council for Jewish Affairs. We called it *Komitet*, or Committee, at first, but later we referred to it by the German name, Judenrat. It was housed in the former Jewish High School building. The Committee comprised mainly professionals, along with some of the leading members of the community. A Jewish militia, armed with wooden clubs, was also formed, and they were nominally under the control of the Judenrat though all of their orders came from the Germans. The young men who joined the Ghetto Police did so with the aim of helping to protect their families, and for the privileges that came with it. The task of the Judenrat was to administer ghetto affairs and provide manpower for the German war effort, issue work permits, and so forth. The German authorities also used the Judenrat as a means of transmitting their orders to the Jewish community. The Judenrat was made up, in the main, of well-intentioned men of integrity who were duped into believing that by obeying German directives they would be serving the interests of the wider community and helping protect their own families. Later on, when their services were no longer required, their privileged status would not help to save them. In the end, all Jews were equal in German eyes.

My father was one of those invited to join the Judenrat, but he declined, wisely as it turned out. However, he had several good friends in their ranks, and these connections proved useful in helping him to obtain the all-important *Arbeitskarte* (work permit) for himself and my two elder brothers, which he trusted would protect them from the impending evacuation. There were not enough of these to go round. They were generally only issued to fit men under the age of thirty-five, preferably those with work skills, and a small number of women. The Judenrat had to make the difficult decisions of whom they should issue these vital permits to, as they would become a matter of life and death. As my father was, of course, over thirty-five, it took a great deal of effort, money, and connections to arrange for his permit.

As time went on, the German authorities required ever-increasing collective contributions from the ghetto community, under the pretext that this would help protect them and stave off deportation. The pay-offs were exacted in cash, valuables, expensive furs, and jewellery, and whatever else we still had. Another method of extortion was to arrest a prominent member of the community or well-to-do person on a trumped up charge for some small infringement, and then demand a hefty sum from the family, via the Judenrat, in return for his release. All the time the Germans kept raising the stakes and tightening the screws. Father came home almost daily with devastating news of friends and acquaintances who had been killed or arrested, or had simply disappeared without a trace. No one could know where the next blow would fall, or who would be taken away next. The Nazis targeted individuals whom they considered *Prominente*. Would Father be next? They had taken away less prominent members of the community, so there was no telling. We lived in constant anxiety.

Father had always been defiantly optimistic, but by the latter part of 1941 he became more and more suspicious of Nazi intentions, and could see through their deceptions. He started to predict the disaster that could engulf us, and began to lay plans to save his family. Father possessed an analytical mind; he was convinced there was a gradual plan unfolding that could lead to the destruction of all the Jews. He decided we should start by making plans for a suitable hiding place locally, for when the need arose, and further laid plans for my sister Fela to head for the so-called "Aryan side" of Warsaw, posing as a Gentile. She was to find accommodation and suitable employment that would help to act as a cover. At the same time, she would try and prepare a safe-house for Mother and for me on the "other side," that is, outside the Warsaw ghetto, for when the need would arise. It was essential for Fela to make the move right away, to give her time to blend into the general Polish population so she would not arouse suspicion later on. I had what was called at the time a reasonably "good appearance," but my sister went well beyond that and looked to be the typical "Aryan" type. She could readily pass for an ethnic Pole with her light blonde hair, blue eyes, and Slavic high cheekbones. She also had a good command of Polish, without the trace of Yiddish that some Jews, especially those coming from smaller towns, spoke with. My mother, too, had the right looks, although her accent was perhaps not as good. To allow for that, Father came up with a clever idea: at least for the duration of the journey to Warsaw, or whenever she got into a tight spot, she was to pretend she was unable to speak, and wear a discreet tag pinned to her lapel, saying she was deaf and dumb.

Father managed to procure through Polish contacts the necessary forged documents for the three of us: a *Kennkarte,* or an Aryan identity card, each for Fela and Mother and a birth certificate for me. All this would not have been possible without money, lots of money. The identity cards were not entirely foolproof, as they bore fake issuing stamps and the official's signature was also forged, but the actual blank cards were genuine enough, and of course the fingerprints were theirs. Presumably these blank cards had been stolen from the authorities by Polish clerks, with the photographs and fingerprints added afterwards. These documents would be sufficient for a random check in the street, but would not stand up to a detailed examination by the Gestapo. At my age, no identity card was required, only a birth certificate, and as this bears no photograph I was able to have the genuine article, issued in a different province. This had once belonged to a Christian boy in the name of Stefan Teodor Wojs (pronounced Voice). Stefan had died of an illness, or at least this was what we were told, and I would simply take on his identity. For all we knew, Stefan could have still been alive! The trade in documents became big business for certain enterprising, well-connected Poles. The real Stefan was a year younger than me, which was just as well; being under-nourished since our arrival in the ghetto I was small for my age. Polish birth certificates specified the person's religion, and in the case of a Jew it stated *Wyznanie Mojżeszowe* (Mosaic persuasion), but my new birth certificate included the all-important *Rzymsko-Katolickie* (Roman-Catholic) religion. All forms of identity in Poland indicated the bearer's religion, which marked out people of the Jewish faith. This fact greatly assisted the Nazis in identifying them, even though they may not have had Jewish-sounding names.

Early in 1942, my sister, who would henceforth be known by the Polish name of Walerja Matera, or Wala for short, escaped from the ghetto and set off by train for the "Aryan" section of Warsaw. She was just eighteen years old. In the meantime, I was to remain where I was. Unlike Fela, I had slightly identifiable Jewish features, but what was worse, as a circumcised boy I would have endangered her prematurely. It was therefore decided that we would wait until it became absolutely necessary before making the move. Warsaw was decided on because one could more easily blend into the general population of a large city. It would have been too risky to do so locally, where people were inclined to know one another. Provincial people are also more likely to make it their business to pry into their neighbours' affairs. Newcomers to rural neigh-bourhoods would immediately arouse suspicion and be at the mercy of blackmailers and informers. At this time, a 5-kilogram bag of sugar or flour was the German reward for reporting a Jew who was outside the ghetto. Posters went up to that effect, and certain roguish people were tempted to cash in. As a result, some of them set about selling their Jewish neighbours for a bag of sugar or flour. Non-assimilated Jews tended to speak Polish with a Yiddish inflection; others may have had certain Jewish mannerisms that Poles could easily detect—unlike the Germans, who couldn't always tell a Jew from a Christian Pole. They had to rely on Polish collaborators to identify and track the Jews down. Any Jew caught outside the ghetto wall was immediately "liquidated," the common Nazi term for being shot on the spot.

Poles are a very patriotic people, and they resented the German oc-cupation. To their credit, unlike certain other countries they did not collaborate with the occupiers, except in the case of the Jews. Here, however, they were guilty of complicity and even betrayal, or at best total indifference to the fates of their former neighbours. Doing away with the Jews offered unscrupulous people the opportunity for material gain; as a result many enriched themselves at the expense of the Jews. If you wanted to slip out of the ghetto, it was not too difficult at this time, but you would be at the mercy of a largely hostile population on the lookout for Jews, anxious to strip them of their possessions and collect the reward. As far as my research shows, Poland became by far the worst country for a Jew to find himself in in all of occupied Europe, and I have never seen convincing evidence to the contrary. There were always honourable exceptions, of course, but these brave individuals were extremely hard to find. Granted, one cannot reasonably expect people to put their lives on the line for relative strangers, but one would have expected them to at least look the other way.

After the earlier sporadic shootings, the first large-scale killings in Ostrowiec took place in April 1942, when a so-called SS-*Straffkommando,* punishment unit, descended on the town. People were shot at random, and others were sent off to unknown destinations, never to be heard from again. A few weeks later, postcards arrived to inform their relatives that their loved ones had died of pneumonia in some remote place or at Oświęcim. At that time, we didn't understand the significance of this place, except that it was a small Polish town in the south-west, near Kraków. It would later become infamous by its German name, Auschwitz.

Prior to the impending "resettlement" operation, the Germans employed deception tactics to calm the community, spreading information via the Judenrat that we were to be evacuated in family units and relocated further to the "East," to parts of the Soviet Union the local population had fled to ahead of the German advance. There, we were told, the Germans would set up essential industries for us, with good working conditions, and we would be living in family camps. Life would probably not be easy and we would have to work hard, but it was more important that we would be safe there and the killings would stop. Many fell for this deception—not that they had any choice, but they wanted to believe it, refusing to dwell on the unthinkable. Having witnessed the cruelty and random shootings in our own town, others could scarcely believe the Nazis would come up with such a humane solution as to resettle all of us in the east. Yet, one never likes to accept one's imminent demise, and "as long as there is life, there's hope," people said. Tragically, as we now know, it turned out to be an illusion, but then, how could anyone possibly have foreseen the terrible fate that awaited them?

To add to the confusion and anxiety, some bewildering reports began to filter through. A few escapees reached our ghetto from Radom and Lublin, larger towns to the north and east, where "resettlement" operations had taken place a few weeks earlier. These people came to warn us, and many of us were shocked by their accounts of the ghastly atrocities committed by the Germans and their accomplices against those who didn't present themselves willingly for evacuation, and those who tried to hide. Others dismissed the atrocity stories brought back by the eyewitnesses as untrue or at best exaggerated, or just isolated incidents that could never happen to us here. "Surely such monstrous crimes cannot possibly be perpetrated on such a scale by a civilised and cultured nation like the Germans," was typical of the reactions to the atrocity stories brought back by those who got away. It was impossible for most people to imagine that the Germans would come up with such a diabolical plan as to eliminate all the Jews of Europe—surely not women and children? It sounded too preposterous. Few could envision the fate we were hearing about awaiting us as well. Many were deeply devout, with an unshakable belief in God on High, who would, they insisted, protect them from harm. Rabbis advised their flocks to put their trust in the Almighty, the God of justice and compassion. With nowhere to run and no weapons or other means of defence, there was no choice but to submit to the will of God, "who would surely not abandon His People in their hour of need."

In the final days, before the anticipated repatriation to the East, the entire community was in turmoil and a state of shock. Some of the people began to suspect that there could be some sinister reason behind the impending "resettlement operation" after all. The young and fit tried frantically to obtain a place in what was called in Polish a *Placówka,* a workplace outside the ghetto. Many believed that a job in essential industry offered the only hope of avoiding the evacuation trains. Our protection and security, the Judenrat advised, lay in hard work and in complying with the German demands. This seemed disingenuous, since so far we had obeyed their orders and submitted to their whims, and yet the killings had certainly not stopped. Some time earlier, the Judenrat had come up with the idea of trying to protect at least some of the children by putting them to work, to make them appear productive in the eyes of the Germans and thus improve their security. There were a few different tasks we could do, and Father arranged with his Judenrat friends that I would be one of those chosen, together with about twenty-five other boys and a few girls, for one of them. We were to clean old bricks at the brickyard; chopping old mortar off of them with a special steel tool. It was not unlike an ordinary hammer at one end, with a chisel-head at the other. Some of the bricks we worked with were hardened blue-bricks that were difficult to clean because of the way the mortar had bonded with them. These blue-bricks were used for lining the furnace walls at the local steelworks, where many ghetto inmates were employed as slave labourers. As we worked, sparks would fly from the hammer and the hardened bricks, and needless to say we had no goggles to protect our eyes. Some children ended up with splinters in their eyes and other injuries, like smashed fingers and torn-off fingernails, until we got the hang of the work. To try and impress the Germans, we were made to march through the ghetto streets singing Polish school songs, like "A Daisy Grew in the Meadow." We formed up in a line in twos, led by a Jewish policeman out in front. Holding our tools-in-trade on our shoulders like toy rifles, we marched to our workplace, singing aloud as we went, returning home later in the same way. Other children were allocated different tasks.

In the last days before zero-hour; crowds of anxious people besieged the Judenrat building, fretting over what was to become of them, all desperately pleading for work permits which at least offered a chance of life. But there weren't enough of these to go round: the Germans had set a strict allocation. For the old, the young and the infirm, there seemed no hope. Some families, including ours, were storing any provisions they could lay their hands on. At the same time, families were feverishly preparing hiding places. Some of these hideouts were ingeniously clever, concealed behind false walls, in lofts, and in cellars. My family was among those putting the finishing touches to our hiding-place below ground. Those who had business connections with Poles appealed to them for help, as well as to their Gentile friends and neighbours. Others tried to seek out peasant-farmers willing to hide them for money on their land, where it was somewhat easier and safer to hide than it was in town. If they were discovered, the farmers could always claim the Jews had hidden on their land without their knowledge. Parents desperately tried to place their babies and small children with Christian couples willing to take them in. It was easier to do this for girls than for boys; some Christian orders were prepared to save souls for Christianity, but preferred girls to boys for obvious reasons. Some desperate mothers simply "abandoned" their babies on convent steps during the night, and in the morning the mother superior would be faced with the terrible dilemma, having to decide, in the case of a girl, whether the baby was Jewish or simply a foundling.

On that grim last weekend before the resettlement operation was due to begin, the air in the ghetto was heavy with foreboding. In their despair, many turned to God, remaining in prayer houses, sitting low to the ground and reciting Psalms and dirges from the Book of Lamentations by the Prophet Jeremiah, which is read on *Tisha b'Av*, the ninth day of the Hebrew month of Av; the saddest day in the Jewish calendar. On that day, the First and Second Temples in Jerusalem were destroyed, by the Babylonians and the Romans respectively. On the same date, the Spanish Inquisition and other terrible tragedies deliberately imposed on the hapless Jewish nation throughout its blood-soaked history began. The Nazis also liked to indulge in this perverse form of symbolism. The mood in our ghetto that weekend was sombre indeed; it seemed that no one slept in their beds that Friday and Saturday night, but we all stayed up to pray for heavenly intervention to avert the evil decree planned for the Sunday. During the day, many remained in the *Ohel,* the vault erected above the grave of the revered *Ostrovtzer Rebbe*. As was the custom, they prostrated themselves at his graveside, praying and sobbing for the protection of their families. Some left prayer-notes at the *Rebbe's* graveside for their entreaties to be fulfilled. Others, in their grief, wept at the graves of their deceased kin, appealing to souls departed. The devout believed that the righteous stood at God's right hand, and have the power to intercede on behalf of the living. But alas, all those desperate pleas, drowned in tears, would not suffice to protect the supplicants from the terrible fate that was about to engulf them.

CHAPTER 4

In the Hen-House

The *Aktion* was carried out by an Einsatzgruppe, a roving Special Task Force, comprising German SS officers, including Latvian and Lithuanian volunteers. The Einsatzkommandos openly wore armbands with the initials JVB (*Juden Vernichtungs Bataillon*)—Jew Extermination Squad. These special units arrived on the first of several cattle trains in which their victims were to be transported to the East. SS-Obersturmführer Schild was drafted in to direct the entire operation. He had earlier overseen the Aktion in the nearby town of Radom.

Our disaster struck on a bleak Sunday morning, 11 October 1942. Before dawn on that day, the entire ghetto was encircled by the German gendarmerie, assisted by the Polish civil police from our town. The blaring steelworks siren that could be heard all over town sounded at 7 a.m. This was the signal for all Jews to head forthwith to the assembly point in the Rynek market square in readiness for their evacuation "to the East." The instructions had earlier been proclaimed on street posters, in German and Polish. We were ordered to take with us personal luggage of no more than 15kg each, but were strongly advised to take our money and all valuables with us. Failure to report for resettlement, or disobeying orders, carried the death penalty. All young men and women in possession of work permits were instructed to assemble elsewhere, outside the *Arbeitsamt,* labour office, on Florian Square, where they were kept under guard for the duration of what came to be known as the *Aktzia,* from the German word *Aktion,* operation. Most of these young people were never to see their families again.

My grandfather Leibish declined a place in the shelter our family prepared and offered it instead to younger relatives. He was eighty-one years old, and in a last act of disobedience to the Nazis, he decided not to report to the assembly point as ordered. Instead, he was seen on that fateful Sunday morning defiantly walking up the incline towards the Jewish cemetery, wrapped in his *tallit,* which was heavily adorned with silver braid. I can still picture him vividly, wearing his tallit and bowed in prayer. Under his prayer-shawl he wore a *kittel,* a white linen robe. The *kittel,* a symbol of spiritual purity, was the traditional wedding gift from a young bride to her groom, and he wears it for the first time under the wedding canopy. Then, when the time comes, the corpse is dressed in it for burial. My grandfather was making his way to the grave of Grandma Gittel, who had died before the war, and there he sat beside her grave, deep in prayer, suitably attired and ready to meet his Maker. It was the sad lot of my eldest brother Moniek to find him there shot dead, lying face down across the grave of his beloved wife.

On that ill-fated Sunday morning, *Reb* Yankele Hertzog, the much-loved synagogue beadle, was seen walking briskly towards the assembly point, cradling a Torah scroll tightly to his chest. The new life we had been promised in the East would have been unthinkable without the Torah. A Gendarme observing this "strange scene" delivered a hard blow to the beadle's head with the butt of his rifle, and *Reb Yankele* slumped to the ground senseless, but still zealously embracing the sacred scroll in his arms so it would not, heaven forbid, touch the ground. It is a grave transgression to allow a holy Torah to fall to the ground: when this happens the entire community is required to fast every day for forty days as penitence.

From the assembly point in the market square, we learned later, the unfortunate mass was herded towards a siding near the railway station. On the way, stragglers were set upon with whips and rifle butts, and the Germans unleashed their ferocious dogs on them. People were shot for slacking or simply for stepping out of line. There was total mayhem and carnage on the streets as children were shot in front of their parents, and parents in front of their children. After reaching the station area, the assembled victims were kept at the railway sidings without food or water for many hours before they were finally forced into the tightly packed freight cars—a hundred and twenty people to each wagon. The cars were then shut tightly and transported to an unknown destination. At the same time, the infirm, the bedridden, and patients at the Jewish hospital who could not be moved were shot, brutally murdered as they lay in their beds.

During the *Aktzia* a particularly distressing tragedy occurred involving one of my cousins, who was hiding somewhere in town. As Dinah Berman with her newborn baby was cowering in a dugout below the ground, loud German screaming could be heard coming from above. At that critical moment, her baby began to cry. The other people in the bunker, terrified the baby's cries would betray their hiding place, frantically implored her to do something to pacify the baby. Dinah placed a pillow gently on its head, intending to muffle its cries, and tragically smothered her own infant. The hide-out was detected anyhow; only one person survived, by feigning death, to tell the story.

Many such heart-rending stories circulated following those harrowing days. Panic-stricken women and mothers, crazed with grief, were seen roaming the streets, some wailing, others in a daze as if out of their minds, desperately searching for their dead babies and lost children. Others still were chased through the streets and shot at by the frenzied soldiers while hopelessly trying to save themselves, attempting to force their way into other people's hideouts. This exposed everyone to even greater risk, as it could easily resulted in the hiding places being discovered and their occupants killed. The Latvian and Lithuanian auxiliaries attached to the *Einsatzgruppe* were the most savage assailants, infinitely worse than the Germans. Witnesses said that these sadists delighted in tearing away infants clinging to their mothers' protective bosoms, then swinging the babies by the legs to smash their heads against the nearest wall, within sight of the insanely distraught, screaming mothers.

My immediate family was able to avoid the *Aktzia* at this point, though we could hear and imagine what was happening in our hiding place. Some time prior, we had thought up an ingenious hiding-place in the form of an underground shelter dug beneath a small hen-house. The owner of the house in the ghetto where we were assigned a room also owned a timber yard on the Iłrzecka Street, across the road from us. The Zylberbergs, who were no longer trading, were a well-respected Orthodox couple with a grown son and two daughters. They had earlier kept hens inside the timber yard, to augment their meagre diet with eggs. By now there were no chickens left—they were eaten when hunger took hold in the ghetto—but fortunately the hen-house remained intact. My family came up with the idea of building a concealed bunker below the hen-house, using it as camouflage, in partnership with the Zylberberg family. Father suggested that we offer them some space in the hiding place in exchange for the use of their timber yard, and they readily agreed. Apart from my two eldest brothers, their son Hershel also assisted in the project. The work consisted mostly of digging and carrying away the excavated soil bit by bit. This had to be done in strict secrecy, and it took weeks before the anticipated *Aktzia* to complete it. To begin with, the complete wood and chicken-wire structure was moved aside, as were the boards it stood on, without disturbing the layers of caked-on chicken faeces mixed with feathers. It was important to preserve this as camouflage for the top of the bunker, when it would be complete. Then a large rectangular ditch was dug where the coop was standing. The pit had to be big enough to accommodate about a dozen people in sitting positions. The excavated soil had to be hauled away in sacks during the night and scattered elsewhere, leaving no trace of fresh soil within the timber yard—that could have given away the whole thing. A thick metal pipe for ventilation was positioned in one corner of the pit, which ran vertically from the *bunkier* upwards, beyond the roof of the shed that the hen-house stood in. This pipe had to be boxed in above ground with old timber to mask it. When the work was complete, the entire hen-house was replaced on top of the excavated hole where it had previously stood, leaving no clue of a possible hiding place below it. As the hen-house only measured about 2 x 2 metres, the adults had some difficulty squeezing through the small door of the cage. Once we were inside, we could move a couple of the floorboards aside, and step down a short ladder into the bunker itself. Inside it we placed two low benches for sitting back-to-back. We also took down some provisions and buckets of drinking water, as well as a large drum for sanitation.

Late in the night the day before the *Aktzia* was due to begin, five of my immediate family members went down into the bunker, with my two eldest brothers remaining outside. Fela by then had been safely out of the way in the "Aryan" part of Warsaw. We took care to proceed cautiously, so as not to be seen entering the timber yard. Any sign of movement there could have betrayed the hide-out. We then squeezed, one by one, through the small opening into our *Bunkier*, which was hardly more than a large pit below ground, albeit a skilfully camouflaged one. Together with us were Aunt Temma from Łódź with her husband Meir and their son Heniek and daughter Helcia, as well as members of the Zylberberg family.[2] About twelve people in all were crammed into the small shelter. Once we were settled below ground, Moniek and Izak

---

2   Of the Zylberberg family with whom we shared the hen-house bunker, only Hershel survived. He lives in Melbourne, Australia, where we met up in 2006. Hershel carries on the family tradition in the lumber business.

closed the small door to the hen-house and hung a small padlock on it, without actually locking it. From the outside it looked like an innocent, empty coop, complete with a good layer of fowl droppings, mixed with feathers for good measure. No one could have suspected what was below it. My brothers then locked the timber yard gate from the outside. The yard was hemmed in by brick-built houses on three sides, with a high wooden fence and gate in the front, facing the street. All we could do now was hope and pray that our hiding place would stand the test and that my brothers would be able to come back to release us when it was safe to do so.

Conditions in the bunker were very cramped indeed, and it soon became unbearably hot down below, although it was cold outside. The air soon turned foul and stifling; the stench was unbearable. We were short of air, and took it in turns to sit next to the pipe opening. It wasn't possible to light a candle, for lack of oxygen. We sat in the dark in total silence, craning our necks to listen for any sound from above.

Early the next morning, to our utter horror, we began to hear loud German shrieking coming from the street, almost above our heads. This confirmed our worst fears that the operation had begun. Loud shouts of *Halt! Halt!* were followed by shots and yet more shots, on and off all day. There was utter turmoil on the street above us. It sounded as if people were running to and fro, screaming hysterically, just beyond the timber yard, with intermittent shooting throughout the day. We sat huddled together, numb with fear; every shot reverberated through the bunker and made us shudder. We were in a terrible state, not daring to utter a word. We kept still, thinking that the Germans might have dogs to sniff out people below ground. Time stood still down below, and every hour seemed like a day. The only visible difference between night and day were the faint shafts of light coming through the chinks between the boards above our heads, the boards our eyes were constantly focused on.

After three long days and nights, the sound of shooting gradually subsided at last and began to sound more distant as the action moved away from our vicinity. This was followed by an eerie silence. We realised the *Aktzia* was at an end, but what next—where would we go from here? We had no idea what awaited us on the outside, and how many people were left in the ghetto. Our bunker, just inside the timber yard, was right next to a busy road, so why was there no movement of people and no sound of life four days after it all began? Why had Moniek and Izak not come to release us as planned? We feared that perhaps everyone had been taken away, including my brothers. What would become of us? It didn't bear thinking about. Where were all those with work permits, why were they not returning to the ghetto at night after the day shift? We were in agonies, thinking that perhaps everyone without exception had been evacuated and we would be left all alone to rot inside the bunker. Although we could have gotten out without any outside help, where would we go? Father, as usual, tried to calm our fears by saying we could safely rely on Moniek and Izak to come back for us when they considered it safe to do so. To add to our woes, we started to run short of drinking water, as we had not foreseen the intense heat that would build up below ground with a dozen people in such a restricted space. Fortunately, Abram wriggled out of the bunker by carefully removing a couple of planks and the padlock without disturbing the whole chicken-wire structure. Luckily, he located a tub of stagnant rainwater inside the timber yard, collected by the Zylbergergs for growing tomatoes and cucumbers. This was sufficient to improve the situation for a couple of days, and perhaps before then we would get some rain.

After we had endured the hell-hole for about a week, one early morning we thought we heard some movement from above. We craned our necks and held our breaths to listen carefully. Suddenly the silence was shattered by shrill German voices. We went deathly quiet as our blood ran cold—the Germans were upon us! They started by furiously smashing down the hen-house, cursing and kicking the boards aside with their hobnailed boots. Earth and debris was falling on top of us, and then we came face-to-face with enraged Germans looking down on us from above, grinning widely, pleased with their find. We were petrified as they pointed their rifle muzzles down at us. This was it—it was all over! We were sure they were about to finish us off then and there, shooting down into the pit, and there we would be conveniently buried below ground. Cowering, overcome with fear, we all embraced and waited for the shots to ring out. But surprisingly they didn't shoot, and instead ordered us to come up. They kept yelling, in their usual high-pitched, arrogant fashion: *"Alle Raus, verfluchte Juden, Raus!"* (All out, you damn Jews, out!) Stunned, we had no choice but clamber up the ladder, one by one, tottering on our feet, dazzled by the intense light. I could hardly keep my eyes open—after being in the dark for so long, they took time to adjust. In the intense light the Nazis' grey-green uniforms looked a different colour. They kept on yelling: *"Los, Los! Schnell! Haende hoch!"* (Move, move quickly. Get your hands up!) The Germans were always in a hurry.

Once out of the bunker with our hands raised, we were reluctant to move, not knowing what they were going to do to us. The Nazis prodded us with their rifles to make us move quicker out of the shed and into the timber yard. Then, to our utter horror, they started to put us up against a brick wall, with our backs facing them, to be shot. I felt blood rushing to my head—this was it, my life was over! I stood wedged between my parents, holding onto them tightly. Mama was weeping uncontrollably as the Germans levelled their rifles at our backs. I flinched every time I heard the bolt-action as each soldier in turn cocked his rifle, waiting for the order to fire. As our last moments ticked away, the crying changed to quiet sobbing. We tried to steady each other as we said our last good-byes, now more composed and resigned to die, but I just couldn't be calmed. Looking up at my father, I cried, "Daddy, I don't want to die!" Father never begged for mercy. Instead I heard him whisper a prayer; it must have been the confession of *Vidui*, the prayer of the dying. Then he raised his voice and lifted his eyes up to the heavens, invoking the hallowed words of the *Shema:*

"Hear, O Israel, the Lord our God, The Lord is One!"

The affirmation of God's existence, recited by every believing Jew who is able to utter it before breathing his last, was also the first Hebrew prayer I was taught as a young boy, and recited upon waking in the morning. To try to calm me down, Father said we were about to part from this world, but I must not worry or cry; it would not be for long. He promised we would all be together again in the next world. I believed and trusted my father, but I was still scared. I had been raised to believe that life is eternal and that man's body returns to earth and reverts to dust, but the spirit lives on and returns to God, who gave it. From a young age, I was taught that every being has a *neshomeh,* an inner soul that departs from the body and ascends to heaven the moment one expires, and that the dead will revive with the coming of the Messiah when God will gather up His people and lead them to the Promised Land. As I stood there awaiting death, I just couldn't grasp that this was really happening to me. Why was my short life at an end? What I dreaded most was the moment the bullet would pierce my body and I would fall to the ground motionless. What was it like to die? How much would it hurt? Not daring to look up, I kept my eyes tightly closed, bracing myself for the fatal shot that would end my brief years.

The executioners seemed to be taking their time now. As the agonizing seconds and minutes went by and no shots rang out, I opened my eyes slowly to see what they were waiting for. Were they deliberately trying to draw out the anguish? We stood there trembling from fear and cold while they contemplated our fate. After some minutes of silence and whispering to each other, they began to yell at us. They were furious, threatening us with "*umlegen*," to do us in, for daring to disobey orders. The Nazis in their warped cynicism expected us to be willing victims, to accept our fate graciously. They were appalled that we should have disobeyed orders and hidden. Disobedience was something unthinkable in German eyes, and for that alone we deserved to die. The Nazis were obsessed with order and obedience. And the irony of it all, of course, lay in one very simple question: would we have earned the right to live had we obeyed their orders? In the end, I don't know what made them decide not to pull the trigger, but we were spared once more, at least for the time being.

They chased us out of the timber yard, shoving and prodding us along the way, past streets and buildings now emptied of people. There was an overwhelming stench of death in the air. As we neared the cemetery, we began to panic again, thinking that they were taking us to the usual place of execution against the cemetery wall. But before we reached it, we drew level with the lemonade factory, into which the Germans pushed us with their rifles. To our great relief we found ourselves with other people who had likewise been rounded up. Trapped inside our bunker we had known nothing of what was happening on the outside, though we did hear shooting and terrible screams. On our way to the factory we had also seen the empty streets and derelict houses we passed. It was from the other people in the factory that we heard for the first time the harrowing details and the full extent of the cruelties inflicted during the *Aktion*. We could hardly believe our luck when we heard of how others had been gunned down as they were hauled out of their hiding places. How were we spared? Father said, "The Guardian of Israel is watching over us. He must have heard our pleas." Father often invoked God. He was a believing person, and I never doubted him.

We were fortunate not to have been discovered by the roving *Einsatzgruppe*, which had already departed for the next ghetto marked for obliteration. The Latvian and Lithuanian killers would not have spared us. Fortunately, we were detected by a German search unit equipped with a listening device, whose task it was to flush out people who had evaded the roundup and to put them into a holding centre until a further transport to the "East" could be organised. When we emerged from the bunker, I noticed that one of the Germans carried a device resembling a mine detector, with the help of which they managed to locate us. This apparatus consisted of a long handle with a disc at the bottom, and the operator who carried it had earphones on his head. As we hardly spoke, we could only assume that this device was so sensitive that it could detect breathing and perhaps even body heat. This search-and-destroy operation was carried out with the usual German thoroughness, and the search unit was assisted by two local Polish policemen who went by the names of Kaczmarek and Bombel, who operated as a pair. These two villains had specialised in tracking down Jews; knowing the "beat" well, they had guided the Germans to the most likely hiding places. These methodical house-to-house searches lasted for about a week, by the end of which time most of the Jewish community was no more, including practically all of my extended family, who must have numbered more than sixty people.

Our temporary prison was in the basement of the lemonade factory. The windows were fitted with iron bars, with German guards posted outside. We right away started to look for a means of escape, fearing the Germans would kill us sooner or later. At one point, panic broke out in the basement when someone shouted a warning that the guards were threatening to lob hand grenades in through the iron grilles. At first escape seemed impossible, but then we found we could bend the iron bars a little. After dark I made my escape by squeezing through the bars. As I was very skinny, I was able to get through with little difficulty: once the head is through, the rest follows easily. The family inside managed to bend two of the iron bars sufficiently to enable my brother Abram to squeeze through as well. We took cover in a vacant derelict house nearby, from which we were able to observe the lemonade factory doors. Shivering in the dark and cold, we kept an anxious eye on the basement where my parents and Leizer, as well as the other relatives who were with us in the bunker, were being held. There wasn't a scrap of food to be found in the empty house we were sheltering in, but luckily there was water. All we could do was wait and see what the Germans decided to do with the people in the factory basement. We were very hungry, so Abram slipped out after dark into the nearby empty houses to see what he could find. After groping in the dark for some time, all he came back with was two small onions; the ghetto had been stripped bare by the starving population, and finding any food at all was most unlikely. To our great relief, though, the next day the detainees held in the lemonade factory were released into what now came to be called the Small Ghetto, as a result of the perimeter wall having been moved inward considerably.

It was the Germans' not finding enough people to make a transport to the "East" worthwhile that saved us. As far as the Nazis were concerned, this was only a temporary reprieve anyway, until the next time, by which point they hoped to round up more victims. Later that evening I was happily reunited with most of my family, with only Fela missing. My brothers told us then that the reason they hadn't come to lead us out of the bunker was because they were aware that the Germans were still mopping-up in the town, searching for people in hiding.

During the *Aktzia*, eleven thousand ghetto inhabitants were transported to their deaths, but their destination and fate was still unknown to us. A further fifteen hundred who were found hiding, resisting, or trying to escape were shot in the town by the *Einsatzgruppe* during the operation. These victims were buried in three mass graves, five hundred of them in each one, on the edge of the Jewish cemetery. This left about three thousand people, comprising those the Germans considered productive labour and some so-called illegals—unproductive children like me that the Germans were not aware of. Those with work permits had to be over fifteen and under thirty-five; as a result, the elderly and practically all of the children had been taken away. It was only because of the local heavy industry that the Nazis had decided to maintain a ghetto; otherwise the entire community would have been transported out and destroyed without a trace, as were so many other communities. Were it not for that, those of us who had managed to evade capture would not have had a ghetto to go back to and hide in.

Most of the friends I had played with in the ghetto I never saw again. As far as the Nazis were concerned, there were no children left, but some had still managed to evade the round-up by going into hiding. After the initial shock of the *Aktzia,* the situation began to slowly settle down, and the people who had successfully hidden emerged from their hiding places and started to slowly filter back into the ghetto. As a result of the population increase, sanitary conditions deteriorated inside the Small Ghetto and another epidemic broke out. My brother Abram and my eighteen-year-old cousin, Helcia Berman, contracted typhus, which is highly contagious. Helcia, who had survived by hiding with us in our bunker, sadly succumbed to the disease, but Abram, being more robust, fortunately managed to pull through.

Towards the end of 1942, the German authorities came up with what they claimed was a humane solution for us all. As they explained it, it sounded quite promising. They made it known that an order had been issued by Dr. Hans Frank, "The Hangman of Poland," to establish official *Judenstadter*, literally, "Jew-towns." The concept of the *Judenstadt* was to be an autonomous Free Ghetto along the lines of Theresienstadt, in Czechoslovakia, near Prague—the "showpiece ghetto" we had heard about, for the *prominente*, or privileged. The Germans spread glowing reports about the new *Judenstadt*. People were assured that the "unproductive" and mothers with children would be safe there and treated humanely, as in Theresienstadt. Our allocated location was to be in the medieval fortress-town of Sandomierz, overlooking the River Vistula. Anyone who wished could now register for transfer to the *Judenstadt*. No one was coerced to apply; relocating was for once voluntary. The Germans assured everyone that the worst was behind us, and that the "bad times" were over. They declared a sort of amnesty for any "illegal," who could now safely come out into the open and not be punished for having gone into hiding. They stopped shooting people out of hand, to create the illusion of leniency, and to make the *Judenstadt* idea more convincing. It sounded quite reassuring. We would even be allowed to take all our belongings with us! To further mislead the people, there were just two minor requirements to be accepted: you had to arrange for your own transport to Sandomierz, and you had to pay a sum of money for the privilege of joining the safe haven. The sum demanded was not set too high, so as to give the needy the same opportunity as the better-off to qualify for this promising sanctuary. Regulations were relaxed, and the travel ban between towns was lifted for a period of time, to enable everyone to travel in safety to their designated *Judenstadt*. The easing of all these restrictions made the proposition sound all the more above board.

Several days of activity and excitement followed. People were preoccupied with feverishly preparing for the journey ahead. They made plans to hire Polish coachmen, dorozhkies, and carts. Some even forfeited their life-preserving work permits to travel in family units together with their hitherto "illegal" relatives. Others emerged from their hiding places in the countryside to return to the ghetto, prior to setting off on their journey to the *Judenstadt*. Similarly. unsuspecting people from other places also made their way toward this promised "safe haven." My father, however, was not easily taken in by Nazi promises. It sounded too good to be true to him, and he warned relatives and friends, trying to dissuade them from falling into a possible trap.

I had only one surviving aunt by this time, Temma Berman, my mother's sister, who had evaded the earlier round-up by sheltering in our bunker. She could not be dissuaded from falling for this cynical ploy together with her husband and young son. Sadly, my aunt was by now broken in body and spirit, having lost her beautiful fair-haired young daughter Helcia to typhus; she hoped to find solace in the *Judenstadt*. People were by now so depleted that any offer of life was too tempting to resist. People in such a state of mind didn't plan ahead, and only thought of surviving the next few weeks. They would eagerly seize on any lifeline, especially as there had been encouraging reports circulating, of families who received postcards from earlier deportees, confirming that they were alive and well. These postcards later turned out to be a cruel hoax, and were written under duress before the writers were killed.

One grey and dismal December morning, with fresh snow on the ground, I watched from a safe distance and almost envied the people going on what looked to me like an outing, happily exchanging farewells with those staying behind. Having loaded up their belongings, they mounted their dorozhkies and carts, and the ghetto gates swung open to let the convoy through as they headed out to an unknown fate. At the head of the long column of about one thousand people, sitting aloft on a horse-drawn carriage, was their patron and protector, Rabbi Yehezkel Halsztok, son of the legendary Ostrowtzer *Rebbe,* of blessed memory. The exodus moved off amid an air of excitement, mixed with trepidation. A few hours later, as soon as the convoy reached its destination, the Germans lost no time in singling out the rabbi. The Nazis dragged him off the coach and threw him to the ground, mocking and ridiculing him in front of his community before shooting him dead. The people soon realised it was all a cruel sham; they had been lured into a death-trap. It was too late now, though: the iron gates were locked shut behind them and their fate sealed.

My sister had by now been living under an assumed identity in the Aryan section of Warsaw for some time. And as an "Aryan," she was able to move about the country, though rail travel was always risky for a covert Jew as trains were carefully watched. Father, of course, had suspected a Nazi deception all along, and he sent word to her in Warsaw via our Polish contact to proceed to the town of Sandomierz without delay to investigate the *Judenstadt* there and try to locate our relatives, from whom we had received no word since their departure. Fela didn't hesitate for a moment, and she immediately set out for Sandomierz at great risk to herself, in the hope of making contact with our aunt and uncle there and guiding them back to our ghetto. When she reached Sandomierz, she found that as an "Aryan" it wasn't possible for her to enter the *Judenstadt* ghetto. She did, however, manage to observe through chinks in the wall the dreadful state of the people within. To her dismay, as Father had suspected all along, this was no "model ghetto." The conditions there seemed worse than in Ostrowiec—it was a cruel Nazi deception.

Fela closely observed the plight of the people within from different points on the perimeter wall. Incredibly, she was sure she caught a glimpse of Aunt Temma in the distance for a few brief moments, as a sad, hunched-over, bereft figure, wandering about aimlessly as if in a daze. But it was impossible to get inside to make contact with her—she was too far away. Fela waited for some time, hoping she would somehow reappear. My sister despaired at not being able to rescue her aunt—she was so near her, and yet unable to help.

CHAPTER 5

Gone to Pitchipoï

After the *Aktion* was over, the perimeter wall of the ghetto was moved and reduced, to cover a smaller area, as it now had fewer people to accommodate. But over a period of time numbers started to swell again, with evacuees brought in from other places. As a result, living conditions steadily deteriorated. Surprisingly, there were still some children, such as myself, who had evaded capture left prowling around the ghetto, but as far as the Germans were concerned we no longer existed. Also "nonexistent" were some of the old, the infirm, and mothers with children, all of whom the Nazis considered unproductive and called *um-legal*, illegal. As an illegal, I had to stay out of sight from then on and, and to remain ever watchful while moving about the ghetto. Those with work permits received food rations, although they were barely sufficient to live on, but children received nothing. Our situation had become particularly desperate; we had to fend for ourselves. Of the few children still around, some were left without parents and soon became further malnourished, which started to affect their growth, as mine had been affected already. We referred to our absent friends as having "gone to Pitchipoï" an imaginary far-off place, in ghetto jargon. My mother also used to speak of a distant place she called Pitchipoï, which could be either utopia or hell, when recounting Yiddish tales of a bygone age. Although there were ominous rumours, we just couldn't grasp in our young minds that they could be true, that anything so terrible could have befallen our missing relatives and friends. The way things were here, we wondered if they weren't better off in the distant land of Pitchipoï. We also had a simple card-game we called Pitchipoï, which we played sitting cross-legged on the ground in some concealed corner of the ghetto where we were hidden from view.

Inside what now became the "Small Ghetto," all supplies and services were cut off, to make our lives even more unbearable. There was no fuel for heating, so we had to tear up floorboards. Electricity was cut off, so all we had for lighting was a crudely-made lamp that burned carbide, a wartime substitute for paraffin that was rather temperamental and kept going out, giving off a foul odor like rotten eggs. The water supply was cut off as well, with only one central water-pump to serve the entire ghetto. We had to pump the water out and then carry it home in pails and cooking pots.

At about this time my eldest brother Moniek was suddenly taken ill with some unknown complaint. During the *Aktzia,* Moniek was part of a work gang made to lug dead bodies to a mass grave, and thus had to witness the shootings and the merciless German and Lithuanian savagery. It was while collecting the dead that Moniek came across the body of our grandfather. All this affected him acutely, and he returned after his ordeal totally exhausted and broken in body and spirit. Soon afterwards he contracted some blood disorder, as far as we could tell, and died within days. Although there were doctors in the ghetto, including some very good ones from Vienna, a thorough diagnosis was not possible and would have been futile in any case, as there were no drugs to be prescribed. Moniek was a wonderful brother to have. He stood out as an exceptionally talented young man who we all looked up to as a role model. His death affected us deeply; we were utterly devastated. He was a tall, handsome young man of twenty-two and a brilliant student, and was one of only a few Jewish boys to have been admitted to the Lyceum, prior to university, despite the *Numerus Clausus,* which restricted the entry of Jewish students to high school and university. However, since war intervened, he never made it to university. We were a close-knit family, and until now we had all managed to survive as a complete family—in fact, we were the only large family in the ghetto to have done so. Until now, we had found a way out of every predicament, but with Moniek's death we realised just how vulnerable we really were. Hitherto, no doubt due to my youthful sense of invincibility, I had believed that no harm would ever come to my family. I still had no concept of death, at least not where my family was concerned, in spite of death being all around me. We stood at his bedside, utterly helpless, as he was burning up with fever. And then he whispered softly for Mother to moisten his mouth, which she did with a cotton wool taper soaked in water, and as she was brushing his mouth gently, he stopped breathing. Mother let out an agonising scream as Moniek slipped away. Moniek's death came as a terrible shock to me: he was the eldest, and my parents' crowning glory, and everyone's favourite. He was completely selfless; he put everyone before himself. Seeing our parents so distraught and heartbroken affected the rest of us profoundly. Things would never be the same again without Moniek; he was the first to die, and we never got over it, it left an aching void within the family. He was deeply missed.

My eldest brother Moniek who died in the ghetto.

A new exploit, *wyskoki,* Polish for "leap out" sprung up in the ghetto. This entailed going on forays into the uninhabited former Jewish section to look for spoils. *Wyskoki* was a daring fear, and only undertaken by bold young men, including my brother Izak. They would sneak like thieves in the night outside of the ghetto to their former homes, or to the homes of absent relatives, to look for hidden treasure. We considered these nocturnal expeditions fair game. Poles were free to plunder Jewish homes, stripping them bare, but they didn't know where to dig for valuables. It was only fair that we should benefit from what the Poles called "Jewish booty" rather than them, or the Germans. Those who didn't have the stomach for doing the work themselves would tip off others to the location of hidden family treasures, and share the haul with them. Polish policemen, fully aware of the *wyskoki* enterprise, made it their job to try and catch red-handed any Jew who dared venture out of the ghetto on these clandestine missions. My father, of course, didn't approve of Izak risking his life in this way, but he had by now lost some of his former authority and confidence, and would no longer impose his will. In any case, we all lived on borrowed time. Izak was a brave and tough fellow, who I believed could fight his way out of any tight spot. I was immensely proud of him, and considered myself very fortunate to have such hardy brothers, particularly in these dire circumstances. Of course he played it down, calling it "just five minutes of deadly fear," meaning it's only the first few minutes that count, when you first made the crossing.

The Gestapo and SS headquarters was in the former high school building on top of Sienkiewicz Street, on the edge of town, and at this time, the SS and Schupo (German urban police) carried out almost daily shootings inside the ghetto. We knew some of the officers by name: some of the worst perpetrators stationed in our town were Langer, Hollweg, Wagner, Holzer, Ostmann, and Willand. In addition, there were two particularly cruel Austrians who went by the names Peter and Brunner, and who mostly operated as a pair. They derived equal pleasure from inflicting pain. One name was rarely mentioned without the other, and whenever "Peter and Brunner" showed up inside the ghetto, word spread rapidly and people scurried away quickly. This deadly pair often delighted in inflicting suffering just for the joy of it. The two swaggered about the ghetto in their smart breeches and polished knee-high boots, carrying whips and leading vicious, snarling dogs they relished setting loose on their victims. This deadly twosome hardly ever left us without first finding and liquidating a victim or two. They either shot them on the spot or forced them to walk with their hands behind their heads to the execution wall near the cemetery, or the nearest rubbish dump, leaving their bodies there like refuse. Dustbins in rural Poland were usually large box-like wooden structures with a tilt-up lid, and were overrun with vermin.

Gestapo-officer Brunner had a ferocious Alsatian dog he called Churchill who he liked to set on his prey with the command: "*Churchill, nehm den Jud*" (get the Yid) or "*Mensch, nehm den Hund*" (man, get the dog). The killer-dog would react to his command and sink his teeth into the victim's flesh. His partner in crime, the SS man Peter, sported a mouthful of gleaming gold teeth made by the accomplished Jewish dentist Ludwik Wacholder, who had also lived in the ghetto. Peter had been so pleased with his dentures that out of gratitude he had promised the dentist personal protection, which he repaid a few weeks later by nonchalantly shooting Wacholder dead with his own Luger. Perhaps he developed a toothache, or felt he no longer needed the services of a dentist.

At this time, we were still unsure what fate befell our relatives and all those thousands transported out during the *Aktzia,* as well as those lured into the *Judenstädt,* the so-called safe haven. People were of course very concerned for the well-being of their absent relatives. There were many rumours, but people tried to delude themselves by refusing to think of the unthinkable. It would have been beyond the grasp of most people to imagine that anything as diabolical as the truth could have befallen their loved ones. However, events started to unfold when a very courageous young woman, Miriam Gutholtz, who had earlier gone to the *Judenstädt* with her family voluntarily, returned one day alone, with the shattering news that shook everyone to the core and caused dismay in the beleaguered ghetto. She recounted how in early January 1943, her family, together with people from Ostrowiec and hundreds of others, was herded into cattle cars at Sandomierz and sent on an unknown journey. Before the train reached its destination, some young men who suspected the worst managed to tear up a couple of planks in the wagon, and Miriam with her boyfriend leaped out of the speeding train into the snow and were met with a barrage of machine-gun fire from the escorting guards in the end carriage. She lay motionless in the snow in the extreme cold for some time, waiting for nightfall. After dark Miriam crawled up to her boyfriend, only to find to her horror that he didn't stir—he had not been as lucky as she—he was dead.

In spite of suffering from frostbite, Miriam managed with difficulty to drag herself to a nearby farmhouse, and luckily the compassionate farmer offered to help her. The spot turned out to be almost at the gates of Treblinka, which the farmer confirmed was a death-camp. The kindly Polish farmer contacted Marian Hamera, a Gentile well-wisher Miriam knew in Ostrowiec. Mr. Hamera worked for the German authorities as a master locksmith, and had a permit that enabled him to travel freely about the country. Without hesitation, Marian Hamera came to Miriam's aid, smuggling her back into the ghetto, and as she suffered from frostbite he had to almost carry her. Miriam Gutholtz brought with her the devastating news which confirmed our worst fears: the *Judenstädt* "safe haven" was a cruel lie and a callous Nazi trap. Worse still, she told us that the packed evacuation trains that entered Treblinka emerged empty soon after. The so called "resettlement" was a deception on a massive scale, and all our loved ones transported to the "East" had in fact been gassed, burned, and transformed into ashes within hours of their arrival.

Miriam described the nightmarish journey and the cries of anguish she heard in the tightly-packed wagons without sanitation. People were gasping for air and water; the wailing was uncontrollable. Some suffocated. Others went out of their minds or died of thirst along the way. The dead remained standing, supported by the living, as there was no room for them to fall. During stops along the way, village boys lining the track at junctions started an enterprise, selling bottles of water. People offered their valuables for a little water. Some young scoundrels first took the money, and then cruelly emptied the bottles onto the ground. The outstretched hands of the dying were desperately reaching out as the train slowly pulled away from them.

Miriam's miraculous escape and return to the ghetto had a devastating effect on everyone; our worst fears were now confirmed, and any earlier illusions quickly evaporated. Panic gripped everyone, sending shock waves through the entire ghetto. A desperate cry went up: "Brothers, save yourselves at all cost!"

Suffering from frostbite, Miriam had to have her toes amputated before gangrene set in. The surgeon had no anaesthetic to administer. Our parents had been good friends, and I vividly recall accompanying my parents to visit Miriam's sick bed. Many people went to see her, many coming to show their admiration for a true heroine and symbol of courage and endurance.[3]

The Germans delighted in inventing cruel deceptions to ensnare their victims, by first raising their hopes only to dash them later—their cynicism knew no bounds. One day they made it known that they needed skilled workers for an important project in another town that would ensure the workers' safety. Many Jews took them at their word

---

3   When I went back to Ostrowiec in 1992, I looked up Marian Hamera, who assisted Miriam Gutholtz to make it back to the ghetto from the gates of Treblinka. Though old and frail, he recounted the sequence of events for me. He has since died. Miriam Gutholtz survived Auschwitz and went to live in Israel. Having lost her toes to frostbite after her leap from the death-train, the brave lady walks with difficulty on toeless feet.

and came forward, as vital work offered a chance of life. Some of these volunteers didn't even have the required skills but hoped to bluff their way in and thereby save themselves. However, they were destined for what the Germans euphemistically called *Sonderbehandlung*, special treatment. When the Germans were satisfied with the response, the volunteers were assembled, then transported to their "work destination," which turned out to be Pirlei, at nearby Radom. There they were all asphyxiated in a specially adapted mobile gassing-van, which had its diesel exhaust-pipe redirected into the vehicle. Earlier, a larger group of one hundred and fifty victims was similarly lured away under some pretext, and ended up in a place, perhaps Bełżec, where they were similarly gassed to death with the diesel-engine exhaust pipe from a truck connected to a specially adapted gas-chamber. These were part of the early gassing experiments with carbon monoxide. "Special treatment," we soon realised, was cynical Nazi camouflage-language for just plain murder. In time, people learned not to volunteer for anything, however enticing; word got round that only a *freier,* a sucker, would volunteer. We despaired at what foul trick our tormentors would come up with next.

In spite of all the misery, there were some diversions in the ghetto which helped to keep up morale. Willy, an evacuee from Vienna, set up a *Lokal,* or nightspot, he named *Badewanne* (bath-tub) in a dingy ghetto cellar. I'm not sure what was on offer in the way of entertainment, apart from home-brewed hooch—the *Badewanne-Lokal* was off-limits to a scamp like me. However, out of curiosity I liked to loiter around outside in the evenings, and picked up the *Badewanne*-club signature tune. It had a catchy little melody that I still recall, though I know only a few of the lyrics. As Willy spoke no Polish or Yiddish, he sang it in his native German:

> *In die Badewanne bin ich Kapitän....*

> In the *Badewanne* I am blissful
> In the *Badewanne* I feel so comfy
> So I must find me *ein Mistress*
> And during love-play, I'm so cosy

> *In die Badewanne bin ich Kapitän....*

The rest of the lyrics, I suspect, were rather risqué. Though I was a streetwise ghetto vagrant by then, I still knew nothing about such things as mistresses, let alone love in a bathtub!

There were two main work places for the ghetto inhabitants which at least offered some security for their workers. By far the largest was the Ostrowiec steelworks, with its name Germanized to Hermann Goering Hochoefen-und-Eisenwerke. The other was the former Głowacki brick factory, now renamed Jaeger Works. There was also the construction firm of Bauer *und* Losch, as well as the smaller Austrian-owned Ellin plant at Bodzechów, near Ostrowiec, which produced electrical parts, also employing slave labour from our ghetto. Other people were assigned work on temporary projects, such as road building, snow clearing, and the like.

My brother Leizer, who was four years older than me, was allocated work at the brickyard on the narrow-gauge railway, repairing and maintaining the track, running between the brickyard and the steelworks. Since he was an intelligent and capable lad, the Polish locomotive driver Radzik singled him out and arranged for him to become his assistant and engine stoker, which was considered a "cushy" and worthwhile job. In time, Mr. Radzik also got to know my father and was sympathetic to our plight, helping out with food and in other ways. Ultimately his wife would become the contact between my parents and my sister in Warsaw, travelling there periodically to deliver messages and money from my father. At about this time rumours started to circulate that the Germans were about to carry out another *Aktzia* inside the ghetto. Leizer told Mr. Radzik all about me and how I had to hide in the ghetto, and asked if he would consider giving me shelter in his home at least until after the impending round-up operation was over. Mr. Radzik thought it over and eventually agreed to take me in, but it was understood it would only be for the duration of the *Aktzia*.

On the prearranged day, in the pitch of night, I found a way out of the ghetto by squeezing through a scooped-out opening below the wall that I had earlier sussed out and prepared. Then I proceeded to make my way to the Radzik home. Escape from the ghetto was becoming more and more hazardous. Moving about the town after curfew was in itself dangerous, but at least there were no hooligans about at night to claim their reward for informing on a Jew. I had to proceed with utmost care, as anyone ignoring the curfew could be shot on sight. Luckily, it was a dark, moonless night. First I had to pass through the town centre, once predominantly Jewish but now deserted and desolate, inhabited by stray cats. Instead of taking the most direct way, I followed the perimeter of the market square and past the forbidding Catholic Church of St. Michael, with its tall steeple, which I always viewed with trepidation—all the more so on this dark and grim night. I carried on down the hill, along the whole length of Third May Avenue, past the bridge on the Kamienna River, to the edge of town. Keeping close to the walls, I made my way one block at a time, pausing now and then to listen carefully before proceeding further.

When I finally reached the right locality, I got confused and had trouble identifying the Radzik home. I hadn't been there before, and the whole area was in pitch-darkness—as it was not a built up neighbourhood, it had no street lights. To my dismay, there were several wooden bungalows there, all of a similar type, and I didn't know what to do next. I was in a terrible dilemma: lost and confused, I could hardly chance on just any door and thereby expose the Radziks to unnecessary danger from suspicious neighbours. At first I thought of giving up and returning to the ghetto, but that would be admitting defeat, and I might never get another chance. In the end, I decided on a house where I saw a dimly-lit lantern flickering in the window. I hesitated at first, then after tapping on the door gently, tried the handle, praying I had the right house. I barely had time to glance over my shoulder to see if anyone was watching when Mrs. Radzik edged the door open and peeked through the crack. She looked alarmed at the sight of a frightened and pitiful Jewish boy at her door. To my utter dismay she whispered quietly, yet firmly, through the gap, "You must leave now, please go away!" My heart sunk and blood rushed to my head. This seemed like a death sentence to me. She was anxious for me to go quickly, but I stood my ground without budging, looking imploringly towards her husband standing in the background. Mr. Radzik then stepped forward, grabbed me by the hand, and pulled me inside, shutting the door behind him. A heated argument followed between husband and wife. Mr. Radzik was willing to take the risk for a few days, but his wife was too afraid. I cannot say she was indifferent to my fate; her reaction was understandable; she was primarily concerned for the safety of her young son, an only child. In the end it was the wife who prevailed, and I had to leave and head back to the ghetto. This was a terrible blow to me. I felt cast aside, convinced that nothing could save me now. I had nowhere to run and nowhere to hide.[4]

The way back to the ghetto was even more hazardous. I thought I caught a glimpse of the shadows of a pair of patrolling Germans, silhouetted against a wall. It was just beginning to grow light, and without the cover of darkness I was an easy target. I dashed from doorway to doorway, keeping in the shadows of the buildings. The picture I recall shows a scene of utter desolation in the former Jewish area. The homes had been ransacked and the furniture smashed. Doors stood open and windows slammed in the wind in the abandoned homes. Household goods, articles of clothing, odd shoes, broken chairs, pots and pans lay strewn about the courtyards, as if they'd been first picked up and then discarded by pilferers for more tempting booty. Bed linen and torn curtains were hanging out of wide-open windows, fluttering in the breeze. Feathers from ripped bedding lay scattered on the ground, blown about by the wind. These had presumably been slashed open in search of hidden valuables. Holy books and torn parchment scrolls lay desecrated and unfurled on stairways. There was no sign of life except for the startled cats that scattered before me in different directions. The stray cats had multiplied, and had made the former Jewish neighbourhood their habitat. I knew some of the homes here; they belonged to uncles and aunts who were no more. This poignant and desolate scene will stay with me until the end.

Once I was back inside the ghetto a sense of hopelessness set in. Our gloom deepened by the hour. The situation was now desperate; we realised that we could no longer count on any help from the non-Jewish contacts and acquaintances my father had earlier had. We could rely only on ourselves, and we needed more time to prepare the hiding place that my father and brothers were planning for the members of the family who were most at risk, before the next *Aktzia* would begin. We believed it to be imminent.

At about this time my dashing and handsome cousin, Meier Berman, together with other young men from the ghetto, made contact with representatives from a Polish resistance group, supposedly operating in the

---

4   During my 1992 Ostrowiec trip, I enquired about the Radzik family, who went on to help my family on many occasions. But alas, the couple had died some years before. There had also been the son who I had seen on that grim night in their home, but tragically he too had died, in an accident at the steelworks where he was employed. This was a grave disappointment to me: I got there too late. I wanted so much to meet up with him and convey my appreciation for his parents' kindness.

area. After several secret meetings and negotiations, the deal was settled. The young Jews involved were required to pay a hefty sum towards
the purchase of their firearms and for the privilege of joining the Polish
partisan unit. On the given day, 9 February 1943, they were guided, in
two separate groups of seven men, to an underground bunker in a forest near a place called Bukowie, not far from Ostrowiec. Having first
handed over their money, ostensibly in exchange for guns, they were
treacherously killed in the most gruesome manner—torn apart with
hand grenades that were tossed through an opening into the bunker.
This, while waiting to be issued with arms and further orders for their
first operational assignment. After a few minutes, when all went quiet,
the killers entered the bunker to finish off anyone who moved. Meier
was killed outright, but incredibly two young men, Shloime Zweigman
and another named Nasielski, survived by feigning death. Nasielski got
away, but was never heard from again. Zweigman, although injured in
the massacre, managed to make it back to the ghetto to tell the story.
This was the subject of a trial after the war.[5]

They had had the bad luck of falling into the hands of some criminals
belonging to an *Armia Krajowa* (Home Army) unit from nearby Kunów,
instead of the *Armia Ludowa,* (People's Army). Those belonging to the
latter were in the main socialists and left-wing sympathisers, who were
more likely to accept Jews into their ranks. Unfortunately, the latter
were never a significant force in our area. They were more active in the
remote forests in the east, where they could more easily be supplied
by the Russians. This was not the only such shocking incident in our
town—another group had also been deceitfully murdered in a similar
manner by an armed Polish gang. These heinous acts put an end, at
least for the time being, to any further attempts by young men from the
ghetto to seek contact with partisan groups in the area. Their ardour to
fight back was blunted; they were convinced by recent events that Poles
just could not be trusted.

Some time earlier, my courageous brother Izak had somehow managed to make a crude replica of what he called a *parabellum* handgun in

---

5   Some of the Polish AK men who had a hand in the murder of Jewish partisans were put on trial
after the war. Two were sentenced to death, though their sentences were soon after commuted
to short prison terms. One of the killers was later pardoned. The trial was a travesty of justice.
Shloime Zweigman survived the war and went back to Poland to give evidence. He made his home
in the United States.

the tool room at the steelworks. How he managed to do it, I don't really know, as Jewish labourers had no access to the tool room. I held the gun in my hand: it looked real enough, but it could not have fired a bullet. Nevertheless, he planned to hold up a German with it and take his gun away. He imagined that with his own weapon and having demonstrated his daring, he was more likely to be accepted by the partisans. Naturally, Father opposed this reckless scheme, which could have led to terrible repercussions, with vengeance wrought not only on the family but on the entire ghetto. Izak had put aside his rash plan for another time, but after these loathsome murders he gave up the idea altogether. We were doomed anyway, but many felt that had we received help and support from our Polish compatriots we could have at least made the Germans pay a heavy price.

My cousin Meier Berman, killed by Polish AK gunmen.

Below is an example of Nazi duplicity: it is in the form of ghetto currency, bearing the Star of David on the one side and a seven-branched candelabrum, the ancient Jewish symbol of state, on the reverse. All of this was designed to give the impression of autonomy and normality, not unlike the *Judenstadt,* Jew-town, ruse. The Two-Mark promissory note was issued by the Jewish Elders of Litzmannstadt Ghetto, the largest ghetto after Warsaw. We had always known Litzmannstadt as Łódż, but the Nazi's had changed it to this German name. All other currencies were confiscated and declared illegal. This replacement ghetto-money was a sham, and pretty worthless. The Nazis resorted to all manner of cynical tricks to mislead the Jewish population and lull them into a false sense of security.

CHAPTER 6

Like a Ghetto Rat

The second *Aktzia* was now imminent. We didn't know exactly when, but we knew it was on its way. After Moniek's death, the burden of responsibility for safeguarding the more vulnerable members of the family fell to my now-eldest brother, Izak. The next one down, Leizer, was only fifteen at the time. Izak, who willingly undertook the most daring tasks to protect us, was just twenty years old. Father, who possessed such good judgment, was always there with sound advice, but he was now about forty-eight years old and physically incapable of undertaking the daring exploits of my brothers. He had been considerably weakened by his exhausting work at the Ellin plant in Bodzechów, where prisoners were treated harshly. Because of his age and deteriorating physical condition, he could not obtain work at any of the plants in Ostrowiec, where work conditions were somewhat better. Had he not faked his age to appear younger, he would not have qualified for any work at all—and that would have been a sure sentence of death. Although we had long since been cut off from our source of income, Father still found the means when palms needed to be greased or strings pulled, or when it became necessary to buy "*protekteje*" (connections and favours), an expression frequently used in the ghetto. Father had incredible foresight, and was able to predict future setbacks and how best to prepare to meet them. He now strove to at least save the younger members of the family and Mother; he didn't include himself in any of the plans, and never took his own life into consideration.

Our saving grace was that as a family we were totally committed to each other—this was our secret weapon against the Nazis! Father and my elder brothers, and to a certain degree all of us, were endowed with the resilience and tenacity so essential to remaining alive. Observing the people around me, I considered myself very fortunate and proud to be part of a family such as mine. And yet again, another ingenious idea for a hiding place was hatched. There was a single-storey house which our company, "Amor," had leased before the war from its non-Jewish owner, as a confectionery retail outlet. This small house, with its shop in front, now stood vacant and boarded up. But what was so interesting about the place from our point of view was its unique location: it bordered on the ghetto wall at the far end of the Jewish cemetery, right on the ghetto boundary. The house, as well as the cemetery wall, actually formed part of the ghetto perimeter wall, and its windows conveniently bricked up. The front entrance was through the shop, which faced the street and the Polish side, at a point where the Browarna and Polna roads converge. The rear entrance faced the ghetto, and this was also boarded up. We took a calculated risk, banking on the Germans' one-track mind and hoping that they would not search this house, standing as it did in a sort of no-man's-land on the edge of the ghetto. Izak had taken a couple exploratory trips there during the night, to try and find a way into the place. He made an impression of the padlock with some suitable soft material; from it he managed to forge a skeleton key at the steelworks.

Properties owned by Poles in proximity to the ghetto bore a rectangular plaque with a large letter "P" on it, in blue. These were affixed to the outside of the building to indicate it was a Polish establishment. Our intended safe house, although Polish-owned, did not, for some reason, carry this sign, perhaps because the house formed part of the ghetto wall and was bricked-up and unoccupied. It was crucial for us to obtain such a sign, which would define the property as being outside the ghetto and thereby less likely to be searched. Presumably these signs were allocated by the authorities, but Izak had to think of another way of obtaining one. One night he scaled the ghetto wall and went on to secretly remove one such sign from a Polish house somewhere in town. This was no mean feat, as these plaques were mounted high up at the fronts of the buildings. He then affixed the sign to the rear wall of what was to become our safe house, so that the "P" sign would be clearly visible from inside the ghetto, from which direction the Germans would be operating. We hoped that they would be diverted by the sign. I'm still amazed at the creativity and fortitude that went into our everyday lives and all the effort spent in order to survive—surely that too was a form of resistance.

The 9th of January, 1943, was bitterly cold. There was hard-packed snow and ice on the ground, and one could somehow sense the foreboding in the air. This time the Germans dropped all pretences, making no attempt to hoodwink the people. By now, few of their intended victims had any illusions about them, and could no longer be taken in by the Nazis' diabolical deceptions—we all knew what was in store for us. This time, only three of us—Mother, Abram and I—made our way to our safe house, accompanied by Izak. To avoid detection, we slipped out of the ghetto in the middle of the night, walking cautiously without uttering a word. We cut through the Jewish cemetery to the other side, which marked the ghetto limit. There was a full moon that night, with hard-packed snow on the ground and a severe frost that crunched underfoot with every step that we took. The extreme cold almost took our breath away as we picked our way silently in between the headstones, towards our destination.

The place that housed our former factory-shop was completely empty, apart from a convenient heap of straw and cardboard litter in the middle of the shop floor. It was bitterly cold and pitch-dark inside. With the windows bricked up, we had to feel our way inside in total darkness. We buried ourselves in the straw and under the cardboard, which provided some insulation from the cold, as well as additional precaution against discovery, should the Germans force their way inside. The straw made us feel itchy, but it helped to keep us warm. Izak then locked the front door with the heavy padlock and hurried back to the ghetto, leaving the three of us inside. Although Mother and Abram were attached to work-posts, we didn't consider this sufficient to protect them from the impending round-up and selection. Mother was not so young anymore and Abram was barely fourteen, but being tall for his age he got by so far; one had to be fifteen to qualify for labour. We hoped that Father's and the others' work posts were safe and would help protect them from harm, as our lives, too, depended on them coming back to release us. We were locked in with no means of escape, as all the openings were bricked up. Perhaps Izak had made some contingency plan which we were not aware of. The mere thought of my brothers failing to come back to release us was unthinkable.

As anticipated, early the next morning we began to hear the crackle of rifle shots, which confirmed our fears that the hunt for Jews was on. The shots coming from the outside were punctuated by screaming and desperate cries for help. Our fear was unimaginable; we were terrified of the lock being shot off or the door smashed in, of being discovered at any moment. The waiting was tortuous; every hour seemed like a day. And when the turmoil in the ghetto started to die down the following day, we despaired: Would there still be a ghetto to go back to, and what would become of us? With no means of escape, we were haunted by the thought of being doomed inside the bricked-up house without food, water, or light.

This time, however, the operation inside the ghetto lasted no more than a couple of days and then all was quiet again. I nearly jumped out of my skin when on the third night we heard the key turn in the lock. We began to breathe again when we realised it was Izak, who had come to take us back to the ghetto. On reflection, apart from us, the Polish owner of the property had also had a lucky escape. Although he was unaware of us hiding in his premises, had we been discovered the Nazis would have gone looking for him and he could have suffered the same fate as us, despite his uninvolvement. However, this was not the time for such thoughtfulness. I feel sure my father and brothers never considered the moral issues involved—only the will to live was uppermost in their mind.

The immediate danger was over for now, insofar as the *Einsatzgruppe* had left town. I clearly recall the full moon and starlit sky that night. It was piercingly cold; the deep frost glistened and reflected off the moonlight as we made our way back through the cemetery, seeing along the way the terrible aftermath of the bloodshed that had occurred here only a day or two before. The dead lay where they fell, in between the headstones. I have a clear picture in my mind of a lifeless young mother shielding her dead baby in her arms, swathed in a cloth tied to her shoulder. It was a calm night, and total silence reigned. During a sharp frost one hears every footstep, and the slightest movement. The lofty ancient trees in the cemetery didn't stir in the frosty calm—tall silent witnesses to the carnage that had been perpetrated here only the day before. Stiff corpses were lying in all manner of grotesque postures in the snow, with their frozen limbs pointing in different directions. Almost tripping over the bodies between the headstones, we recognised some of the faces in the moonlight, with their eyes frozen open. The snow was stained by a pool of blood around the head of each victim. Most had been despatched with a single bullet to the nape of the neck. The Nazis allocated one bullet per Jew, according to a method they cynically called *Gnadenschuss;* a quick, merciful death. The terrified victims had tried to hide wherever they could; many sought refuge in the graveyard, where they were hunted down like animals. Their bodies were left where they fell, and could not be buried while the ground was frozen solid. They were later cast into a mass grave on the edge of the cemetery.

It transpired that nearly everyone, including members of the Judenrat, who no longer enjoyed immunity, were forced into the cattle-trucks and transported to their deaths. The only people to be spared were those attached to the Steelworks and the Jaeger plant, and some of the Jewish *Ordnung* Police. At the same time, all of the workers at Bodzechów, including my father, were slated for transportation. But miraculously, overseer Kierbel had him taken out from among those selected to die. Pointing at my father, he insisted to the German in charge, *"Ich brauche den Jude"* (I need that Jew), claiming he had special skills for essential war-work. Kierbel later brought my father back to the ghetto, and Bodzechów was liquidated thereafter. During this *Aktzia,* over a thousand people were transported to Treblinka death camp, and about three hundred shot inside the ghetto, many of them in the cemetery. This time, few of those in hiding escaped detection. There now remained only one thousand workers, of whom eight hundred were assigned to the Steelworks and the rest to the Jaeger plant.

Having survived the second *Aktzia*, we were again comparatively safe, but for how long? We emerged from hiding into what was left of the even smaller ghetto, and when we realised that only about half the inmates remained, we wondered how long the Germans would keep it open to accommodate just one thousand slave labourers. Where would we go and what would become of us, when they decided to do away with the ghetto altogether? We had no prospect of finding a permanent hiding place outside the wall. People talked of running to the woods, but there were no extensive forests in our area. The nearest was the Swiętokrzyska-Wilderness, some 80kms from Ostrowiec, but one could not survive there for long without help from local people, especially in winter. It turned out that these woods were in any case dominated by nationalistic groups hostile to Jews. In our rural province, the relationship between Christians and Jews was particularly strained. There was a lot of ignorance and backwardness in our area; the population comprised mainly the lower working-class and illiterate peasant farmers, all staunch Catholics steeped in superstition with deep-rooted prejudices. As a consequence, the help extended to Jews by Poles in our area was minimal.

As an under-age boy in the ghetto, I had ceased to exist and had to remain permanently out of sight of the Germans—children had no right to live. Until now, my family had done most of the thinking for me. So far we had managed to survive, with all those who remained sharing the same fate. When we had food, we shared what we had, and when one went hungry, we all did. I would now have to think more and more for myself, and to rely on my own initiative and wits, as most of the time my family members were not around to help. In time I located several good hiding places in the lofts of abandoned and derelict buildings. It was now February 1943. There was no heating fuel, the cold was intense, and I suffered a lot from itchy chilblains. It was easier to try and keep warm in lofts, which were often full of discarded clothing, books and memorabilia; the things that people store away in such places. To relieve the boredom I rummaged through these and found albums with old snapshots in sepia of people long gone, posing stiffly in their best attire with serious unsmiling faces. The houses were built close together, forming a kind of warren, and I found a way of getting from one house to another and from loft to loft through a network of holes in the walls, like a ghetto rat, without having to set foot in the street. I had peep-holes at strategic points through which I could observe the nearby streets to keep a sharp lookout for any lurking danger. The buildings were deserted, and even the houses that were lived in were empty during the day, with the occupants at their work places. So I always looked forward to the evenings, when I would be together with my family, and the ghetto would again feel more secure. I was not the only child hiding like this—there were a few other boys here and there, and one day I met Pesia Balter, the only girl I knew getting by the way I did. She was about three years younger than me, and I was glad to have the company, while she was happy to have the reassurance of an older child's presence. The brave little girl tried hard to hide her discomfiture, and I remember clearly that whenever she heard the sound of hobnailed boots approaching whatever hideout we were using, she'd wet her panties. Later, we lost touch, going our separate ways. Like me, she had older brothers to guide her.

Some 57 years later, I met up with my ghetto pal quite by chance in Los Angeles. I recognized her in a group, went up to her, and asked "Do you know who I am?" "Why, should I?," she replied. I said that the little girl I knew long ago didn't have blonde hair, so she parted it, revealing dark roots! We fell into each others arms. When we shared the tales of our experiences, she was curious to know if I had been aware of her embarrassment at the time. I replied that I was too scared myself to have noticed, as indeed I was.[6]

My main area of operation was a narrow passage, leading to a long cobbled yard with dwellings on either side. The way in was through double gates from the Iłrzecka Street at one end, and at the other it led to the Jewish cemetery. It was through this alleyway that the ruthless killers Peter and Brunner used to pass, forcing their victims to walk ahead of them to the place of execution at the cemetery wall. This same route also led to their headquarters outside the ghetto at the top of Sienkiewicz Street, in what was previously the secondary school No.1 that my brothers had attended. The doomed victims were made to walk with their hands up, followed by Peter with his Alsatian dog a few paces behind, pointing his Luger pistol at the victim's back. I would clench my fists as I observed these scenes, sometimes close up, through peepholes.

I can vividly recall how these men looked; their wicked faces stand before my eyes. SS-officer Peter was in his forties, fair-haired, tall and slim with a pock-marked complexion and deep-set evil eyes. People said he, like his companion, spoke German with a Viennese accent. He wore breeches and riding boots, and carried a hunting whip which he repeatedly lashed against the side of his well-polished boot as he went. Peter sported that mouthful of gleaming gold teeth that the Jewish dental-surgeon Ludwig Wacholder had made for him before Peter had killed him. His henchman, Brunner, was also Viennese and in his forties. He was stocky, with receding brown hair and a rounded, more jovial face, but just as sadistic as his companion. This macabre ritual of escorting their victims to their executions took place in late morning, as if they had to kill a Jew or two before returning to their quarters for lunch, which was prepared for them by a Jewish cook and her attractive daughter, who were kept there as slaves—they clearly detested Jews, but must have had a penchant for Jewish cuisine. After a wearisome morning's

---

6   In 2002, completely by chance, I was reunited with Pesia Balter, the brave young girl in the ghetto loft. Having changed her name to Paula Lebovics, she was working as a volunteer for the Spielberg Holocaust Foundation in Los Angeles. On seeing her there during a visit, I recognised her instantly after 57 years. All the staff gathered around in disbelief, including the director of the centre—there wasn't a dry eye in the place. Spirited little Paula had ended up in Auschwitz, and had survived.

Jew-hunt, followed by a tasty lunch, they no doubt relaxed with a good cigar and fine Cognac in hand, listening to Beethoven or Wagner.

I closely observed the anguish of the condemned, walking to their execution with dignity. Resigned to die, they bore on their faces the ashen imprint of a death mask. As I watched the little group go by, I found it hard to believe that within minutes this man would no longer be breathing life. Though death was all around me, I still could not quite understand what it meant to die, and it was difficult for me to believe how a person could be alive one minute, and dead the next.

There were now almost daily executions, with the Germans picking their victims on the smallest of pretexts. Perhaps the person didn't stand to attention rigidly enough, or maybe he didn't doff his cap in time, implying disrespect or defiance. On the other hand, some Germans considered a Jew raising his cap to them a reprehensible sign of familiarity. They were so unpredictable that one could never know how to react and how to placate them. Sometimes they would pick their prey for no reason at all, and just shoot them out of capriciousness; at other times they may have simply taken a dislike to a particular person. After a few killings, they would notify the Judenrat to collect the bodies of executed "Communists" or "attempted escapees." Some of these victims were hiding, like me, and shot during searches. My greatest fear was of a systematic sweep by a search-party. I tried to cheer myself up by the thought that here I had the advantage. I had good hideouts from which I could see them approach and watch their every move.

Most victims went meekly to their deaths without resisting. People had been instilled with so much fear that they were afraid of mass reprisals, particularly against their families. Any individual act of resistance would have been folly; if a German had been killed inside the ghetto, they would have exacted the most savage retribution on us all and perhaps razed the entire place to the ground.

There was now utter despair among the "illegals" like me; we realised just how hopeless our situation had become. At this time, the Polish word on most people's lips was *likwidacja*; the threatened liquidation of the ghetto. One never knew exactly when the blow would fall, but we knew it was only a matter of time before I and the others would be left with no place to hide. Within the family, only Mother and I would have any chance of joining Fela in Warsaw. But my sister was by now in great danger herself; we learned that she'd had some narrow escapes.

Unfortunately the other members of the family would have no choice but to remain where they were, at the mercy of the Germans. We now reached a new low, which we had never seen before.

Chance meeting with Pesia, now Paula, in Los Angeles.
A camera was on hand to capture the moment.

CHAPTER 7

The Brickyard

During March 1943, word got round that the ghetto was about to be liquidated, and that an *Arbeitslager,* or labour camp, was under construction near the steelworks just beyond the town, to house the ghetto inmates. We knew this from the carpenters and workmen from our ghetto who were put to work there, preparing the ground and erecting wooden barracks. As a result, abject fear broke out; everyone realised that our time was running out, and once we were incarcerated inside the camp, behind electric wire, it would be final and we would never get out alive. This caused particular dismay among those in hiding like me, referred to as *umlegal*, or illegals. As an 11-year-old, I was too young to present myself for labour duty; worse still, I would lose my shelter within the ghetto walls, which had until now offered good scope for hiding on familiar ground, and where I could remain with my family. The ghetto lofts, nooks, and crannies were my last hope of refuge, and time was running out.

The only solution was to try to find a hiding place outside the confines of the ghetto, but that would be impossible without help from local people. Father had a number of Polish business contacts from before the war, but no one was prepared to take the risk of harbouring a boy—a girl, perhaps, but not a boy. The last remaining option was for Mother and me to join Fela in Warsaw, as we had planned all along. Mother could have passed for a Gentile—she had the necessary papers prepared—but when it came time to leave she refused to be parted from Father. As far as I was concerned, it was decided that I would definitely join my sister in Warsaw, but it would have to wait until the last possible moment, so as not to endanger her prematurely. As a boy, I would be a liability and a danger to her; Jewish males carried with them their inescapable identity and besides, Fela had by now her own difficulties to cope with in the "Aryan" section of Warsaw. As for the other members of my family, there was no other choice but to remain in the ghetto and await transfer to the camp. There were now strong rumours that the time set for the liquidation of the ghetto and the transfer to the *Arbeitslager* or *Lager*, as we came to call it, was to be April 1943. In view of this new development, and not knowing what was in store for us, people made frantic efforts to find alternative hiding places outside the ghetto walls. At about this time, two of my cousins, Moshe and Yossel Berman, decided to abandon the ghetto in spite of having what were considered secure work places. They had made contact with two Polish farmers from the nearby village of Denków who teamed up together, and were prepared to hide them on their land for money. Putting their trust in these two peasant farmers would turn out to be an error of judgment.

By now there was a shortage of manpower due to the depleting ranks caused by the frequent killings and epidemics, so the Germans announced that anyone could safely come forward to be registered for work. Some boys of fourteen could qualify, if they were tall and looked fit enough, like my brother Abram, but I was not yet twelve. This sudden generosity to issue work permits to all who came forward was yet another deceitful Nazi trick to lure them out of hiding and into the net. Of course, people no longer trusted the Germans, but as many lived in such dire straits outside the ghetto, in constant fear of being denounced, they could no longer take the strain and decided to return, considering it the lesser risk. Others still, who had run out of pay-off money to Polish blackmailers, were left with no choice but to return to the ghetto.

As the ghetto was about to be liquidated, my sister's fiancé, Shauli Rappaport, to whom she had become betrothed prior to her departure for Warsaw, pledging to marry when the war was over, escaped from the ghetto to join his brother in some hiding place. As he was making his way across town, being of Jewish appearance, he was set upon by Polish hooligans who robbed and beat him, then dragged him to the Gestapo, from whose clutches he never emerged. The "Aryan" streets were not safe for Jews, not so much because of the Germans but because of the Poles. The Nazis were inclined to trust their own infallibility, and were gullible enough to believe that Jews were only to be found inside ghettoes and camps, but Poles knew better.

The only possible place where I could try to hide, it was decided, was at the Głowacki brick factory that the Germans had renamed Jaeger Works. The complex covered a large area that offered good scope for hiding, with vast grounds and a number of old factory buildings and warehouses with extensive bushes and shrubbery nearby. I would have to be on my own from now on, and learn to fend for myself. But as two of my brothers were assigned work at the plant, it would hopefully be possible for me to have contact with them. So the brickyard it was; there was no other choice except to head for Warsaw to join my sister, but it was still too early for that, as it could cause problems for her. Knowing what awaited me all on my own, I tried to delay my escape to the brickyard for as long as possible, but it was imperative not to leave it too late and thus run the risk of being trapped in the ghetto while the liquidation was in progress.

At the end of March, a day or two before the expected closure of the ghetto, I had to make my escape before the transfer to the *Lager* was due to begin. It had to be done in daytime, as the brick factory area was uncharted territory for me. I knew of the opening below the ghetto wall that I had made use of before, when I had last escaped, but it had since been filled in. I inspected the spot beforehand, and to my relief all I had to do was to scrape away some of the soil, so I could wriggle under the fence. I put my head through first, glancing right and left to see if the coast was clear before emerging on the other side. I quickly straightened up, looking around again to make sure I hadn't been seen. Then I dusted myself down quickly and hurried on my way. I carried with me two small blankets, or rather one blanket cut in two, as well as some rations: pieces of stale bread, *sucharki* (dried rusks), and a small jar of home-made plum marmalade; food we had managed to save up over a period of time. As it was still daylight, I had to avoid attracting attention while cutting across town, as we were only too aware that people from the ghetto were easily picked out by their scraggly appearances.

I had never been inside the brick factory before, and didn't know my way around, though I had a general idea of the area from my brothers' description and the rough sketch they'd made for me. I managed to find a way in by carefully scaling the barbed-wire fence and scurried towards the marshy swamps adjoining the factory compound, hiding in the dense bushes and reeds growing around the ponds, as planned. I tried to settle down as best I could until such time as my brothers would appear with the camp workmen. I always liked the wide outdoors and the green fields, but I didn't think I would like it now, under these conditions. As luck would have it, my escape was followed by a whole day and night of torrential icy rain. Sheltering in the bushes, I got soaked to the bone as I lay there curled up in the wet blankets, shivering from cold, lashed by wind and rain. I built up a den, using layer upon layer of branches and reeds, and as the water level rose higher I had to abandon the sodden lair and move to a more raised patch of ground. I was in a sorry state, trying to shelter as best I could from the driving rain beating down diagonally, without letup. By late evening, utterly exhausted and distressed, I cried myself into a fitful sleep, and in the morning it was still raining. I found that my stash of bread and biscuits had turned to mush, but it still helped to assuage the discomfort of my empty stomach. I ate some of it before it would all disintegrate and be washed away. I ate more than I should have—it was meant to last, and I didn't know where the next crust of bread would come from.

I had spent the first night under open skies, and now I was in a miserable state. How was I going to survive for any length of time living like this, all on my own? I would be forced to give up before long. I lay there in wait, brooding over my plight and anxiously watching for my brothers' arrival with the work party. As no labourers from the camp were brought in that morning, I realised that there had to be a reason behind it; the "operation" in the ghetto must have begun. When no one appeared the next day either, I began to fear for my family, imagining that they had all been taken away and I would be left all on my own to perish in the marshes. However, the next morning, to my considerable relief, I peered out of the bushes to see the column of labourers appear in the distance. I could observe them from afar, but must not be seen approaching them. Out of sheer joy I wished I could run and greet them. By the early evening the workmen were assembled, counted, and then escorted back to the camp; it was not possible to make contact, but I was able to rest assured that they'd be back. By midday the following day I caught a glimpse of my brother making his way cautiously towards the tangle of thickets where we had arranged to meet. Leizer got something out of his pocket, which I soon gobbled up, but what was more important, he brought with him the marvellous news that the family was safe. He and Abram were still assigned to the brickyard, with Father and Izak to the steelworks, for now. Mother was allocated work inside the camp kitchens, a work-post that would turn out to be advantageous; it would enable her to conceal scraps of food for the family.

My brother described the transfer of the prisoners from the ghetto to the newly-erected camp. He said that on the first of April, all the ghetto inmates were first assembled, counted down, then marched in the torrential rain I had experienced as well towards the new *Lager*. The heavens opened, and the rain lasted the whole day and night. People said that the heavens were weeping for the Ostrowiec community. After several centuries of Jewish presence in the town, this was to be the end. The new camp was situated a few kilometres from town, not far from the steelworks, on the Częstocice meadow, near the sugar refinery. After the ghetto was emptied, its walls would be torn down, and Ostrowiec became *Judenrein,* cleansed of Jews, as the Germans called it. The liquidation of the ghetto was carried out by German SS, assisted by Ukrainian auxiliaries who thereafter policed the camp and escorted the inmates to and from their work places. The *Lager* came under the direct authority of the SS, and was run by the *Werkschutz*, factory security personnel and the Ukrainians. The latter were drafted in specifically as concentration camp guards. The Germans didn't take kindly to their uncivilised Ukrainian underlings, who were recruited by the Nazis as hired killers. The job offered worthwhile fringe benefits: apart from the uniform, there was plentiful Vodka and cigarettes, but what was even more enticing was the prospect for theft and plunder. Prior to the opening of the labour camp, there were no Ukrainians stationed locally. Previously, they had only come as part of the death-dealing *Einsatzgruppen,* together with the Lithuanians and Latvians, and would depart after the *Aktion* was over. The Ukrainians, conspicuous by their black uniforms, brown leather collars, and black forage caps, were more trigger-happy than most German guards, but on the other hand were responsive to bribes if there were no German officers about. Unlike the Nazis, for the Ukrainians this was not a matter of ideology but simply a job. The illiterate and uncouth Ukrainians had the power of life and death over the inmates, but in the presence of their German masters they were careful to obey orders.

Apart from making bricks for building and hardened fire-bricks for lining the steelwork furnaces, Jaeger was turned into a plant supplying various items for the Nazi war effort, like sledges for the Eastern front. Although the brickyard area offered good scope for hiding, I hated staying near the ponds there. Apart from the discomfort, the area was teeming with water-rats. These were almost the size of cats, with glossy greyish-brown fur. The coypu-like rodents were not scared of people, as they had no predators, and would usually ignore me, but if I tried to chase them off, some scurried away and others stood their ground. I carried a robust stick with me at all times.

A partial view of the swamps I shared with frogs and water rats. This was taken in early April when the trees were still bare of leaves, the same time of year I first began to prowl the area.

There was one particularly large alpha-rat that I got to know. He was rather pudgy and slow-moving, and compared to the others he could not be frightened away easily. If you tried to chase him off, he would raise himself up on his hind legs and bare his incisors as if to hiss at you.

There was also a multitude of frogs, of varying size and colour. The place was teeming with them, some very tiny, no bigger than a thumb-nail, others as large as bullfrogs, constantly leaping and diving into the water with a plop, creating rings that spread through the pond—the only thing that disturbed the evening calm. The water-rats liked to be active in the early evening, swimming silently and effortlessly, leaving ripples in their wake throughout the pond. Sleeping restlessly with my hand on the stick next to me, I was all too wary of the wildlife around me, and could never truly relax. The willow thickets were still bare of leaves but were just about to come into bud, so I prayed for spring to arrive early—that would help to alleviate my plight and provide me with better foliage cover.

April in Poland is far too cold to sleep rough, and I would get frozen through in the nights. By daybreak my joints were stiff with cold, and took time to loosen up. Apart from several layers of clothes and my two small blankets, I had no real protection against the weather, and when it rained I got drenched right through. It was imperative that I find shelter under cover, at least for the night. The Jaeger plant offered good scope for hiding inside the many buildings, some almost derelict, but I was too afraid to make use of them. I didn't know my way around. Nonetheless, I began to cautiously explore the whole complex by just following my instincts. I knew that there were Polish night watchmen, who could have tipped off the Germans to look out for me. Although I could easily have slipped into one of the buildings before it was locked for the night, I had to avoid being trapped inside and discovered there the next morning. The first thing I had to make sure of was, is there another exit or escape route, just in case? The brick-drying kilns were invitingly warm and cosy, but they only had one opening and no means of escape, so I kept away from them.

My first agreeable hiding place under cover was in a large wooden shed which I noticed no one went into, so I decided to shelter there one evening from the biting wind. The large barn was padlocked, but I found a loose plank and managed to ease my way in by sliding an overlapping board to the side and then back into place, not to leave any trace. Once inside, I felt my way around in the dark. I burrowed into the stacked-up bales of straw and fell into an instant deep sleep. During the night, I thought I heard a garbled voice, which startled me. But feeling snug and warm, I went back to sleep quickly. By dawn, I slowly woke up, thinking that something had stirred close by. Holding my breath, I stayed motionless, listening out carefully. Perhaps it was some little animal I had heard in the night, I reasoned, and so I tried to go back to sleep again. When asleep, you while away the time and forget all your troubles and even hunger. But minutes later my sleep was again interrupted, and I realised by the repeated rustling of the straw that this was no animal: animals are lithe, so this had to be another human presence in the barn! To my considerable surprise, our two heads emerged from the straw almost simultaneously. We had been trying to sniff each other out until we came face to face! I was astonished to find there was another boy hiding in the barn. It turned out to be a boy called Marek, who must have had a nightmare and talked in his sleep—that was what I'd heard in the night. I knew him vaguely, as I had come across him some time ago in the ghetto. Apparently, Marek had also heard me sneak into the barn the previous evening and decided to keep still and wait until morning, and he too fell asleep. Marek and I became instant friends. We made a deal to operate as partners from then on, come what may; we even decided to share our small stash of food. Now that there were two of us, I felt more secure, and the company helped to relieve the monotony. I hoped this would be the beginning of a lasting friendship and a long stay together. Marek was a sturdy lad, more experienced at living rough than I was, and I started to learn from him. I imagined him to be Robinson Crusoe, and I was his Man Friday, from the fascinating book I had read at home, before the war. Being a couple of years older than me, Marek took charge, and I was happy to follow him. He was familiar with the area, having prowled there for some time. Things started to look more promising. I now had a roof over my head, and although the sharp straw got into my clothes and made me itch, I was well protected from the penetrating wind and rain. This was heaven compared with sleeping out in the open. The only remaining problem would be finding food.

In this image, I am exploring the brickyard with my family, pointing out the different places I hid in during the war.

As fate would have it, this relative comfort was not to last. The Germans must have been aware of Jews hiding in the area, and they carried out searches from time to time. At dawn one morning, before the labourers were brought in, we were woken by shrill German voices and choking smoke. The Germans must have known fugitives were likely to shelter in the barn and had set it ablaze. They must have used a jerry-can of gasoline, because the place flared up quickly and began to burn furiously. To our horror, peeping through a knothole, we spotted two green-uniformed *Schupos*. I don't know why they didn't simply shoot off the padlock and come into the barn to get us, or shouted a warning to us to come out. Perhaps they wanted to burn us out and see how Jews frizzle alive! Or possibly the *Schupos* were wary of armed Jews frequenting the area, trying to make contact with relatives from the camp. With no time to lose, we made for the loose plank and crashed out and bolted away, running for our lives like we had never run before. Luckily, the policemen were at the opposite end of the barn, and partly obscured by the dense smoke, so we had a head start. But as soon as they spotted us, they gave chase, yelling: *"Halt! Halt!"* firing their revolvers at the same time, aiming to kill. Marek and I instinctively split and ran in different directions. As bullets whizzed past my ears, I kept zigzagging, making it difficult to take aim. While running, I kept crying out for my mother: *"Mamusia! Mamusia!"* My only thought was of how to reach the next objective I was aiming for without being hit. I kept my eyes firmly fixed on the spot I was hoping to reach. "Oh God, please help me to get to the next bend"—that's all I thought of. Fortunately, of the two *Schupos,* the one that came after me was not so young and rather obese. Amazingly, you finds extra strength when in mortal danger, strength you never thought you had. I kept on running long after the bullets were out of range and no longer echoed about my ears. I just ran and ran, until I could run no more. I dropped to the ground breathless, panting rapidly. Reeling from my narrow escape, I cowered in the undergrowth, crying out for my *mamusia*. I had never needed her more than now. After I recovered, the first thing I started to think of was food, and the only food we had was left in the barn. All I had to eat was dandelion leaves, which were just starting to push through the ground. I also munched the roots I dug up with my *Hitlerjugend* dagger. They tasted rather bitter, but I realised they could not be toxic as I knew that rabbits liked them. I was too scared to go back to the brickyard, and I kept away from the area for the rest of that day.

After dusk, I had no choice but to go back to the brickyard and ponds and the company of my furry friends the water-rats and croaking frogs. I could not have been tempted back into the comfort of the barn, even if I had wanted to, for it had been reduced to a heap of smouldering ashes, together with any food we had. And to add to my woes, I had also lost my blankets, which were irreplaceable. But worst of all, I never met up with Marek again after our deadly escapade. I wanted to believe that my pal had also gotten away. He was a full head taller than me, and with his long legs he could run very fast. While running, I saw fleetingly, as I glanced sideways, that the distance between Marek and the pursuing *Schupo* was ever widening. Over the next few days I forlornly combed the area in search of my friend, desperately hoping to find him, but he had vanished without a trace. I longed for Marek's company; it helped to relieve the loneliness. Being older and bigger than I, Marek was a source of strength, and I felt more secure with him around. Staying on the run is much more difficult when you are on your own. Besides the worry of being on one's own, the solitude can play tricks on you and drive you crazy. I even started to talk to myself, but this, I discovered, actually helped give me courage. My friend never came back, and I never saw him again—he was gone. Marek had no family; they had all "gone to Pitchipoï" and he was the only one to escape. I hoped that his luck hadn't run out along the way. I wanted to believe that he came to no harm and found shelter somewhere. Though I was well accustomed to danger, this was the first time I had actually been shot at. I was in danger all the time, and had survived with narrow escapes before, but being a live target was an altogether much more frightening experience.

Another acceptable and warm place to shelter in for the night was the locomotive repair-shop, where the narrow-gauge locomotive was kept locked up overnight. My brother Leizer, though only about sixteen, was intelligent and gifted. As Mr. Radzik's assistant and stoker, Leizer asked him if he would mind his young brother slipping unseen into the locomotive shed for the odd cold evening, to be locked in for the night. It was, of course, in Mr. Radzik's home that I had tried to take shelter when I had escaped from the ghetto. Being a kindly man, he agreed. But we decided to give it up after a while; we couldn't carry on taking advantage, as this could put his job and life at risk. As it was, he helped out with food and in other ways. Whenever Mr. Radzik was around the loco-shed, and if it was safe for me to approach him, he would share his lunchtime sandwiches with me. It usually consisted of thick slices of black bread and a small chunk of *kiełbasa,* wrapped in a white cloth; this occasional bit of protein helped to keep me going. I'm sure his wife would have thought of sending a little extra for me too. Anyway, winter meanwhile subsided, the days were lengthening, and spring was in the air. I was thrilled to see the first flight of storks, which were a common sight in these parts in summer. For me it heralded the arrival of spring, which I had thought would never come.

As time went on, I got to know the area better, as well as the various installations. I sussed out more comfortable sleeping quarters inside old factory buildings. It was important to keep changing lairs, in case I was seen entering a particular building. The warmest places were the brick-drying kilns; when left to cool off, they retained the heat for some days, but since as I mentioned there was only one opening to each kiln, with no means of escape, I would only shelter there for the odd chilly night, and I only went in late at night. Ever watchful, I stalked the area warily. Over a period of time I developed an animal-like instinct, with my eyes and ears alert to every sound. Eventually, I got to know the entire complex and grounds really well—the movement of German guards, the Polish night watchmen, shift times, and so on. During the day, apart from the Ukrainian guards who escorted the labourers to and from the camp and also guarded them at their work-posts, there were also now and then, the *Schupos* to watch out for, as I had earlier discovered to my cost in the barn. Apart from them, there were also the yellow-uniformed Gendarmes, or rural police, who earned the Polish nickname *kanarek*, canary. The Jaeger plant came under the control of the "canaries" stationed nearby, on *Aleja*, 3rd May Avenue, near the Kamienna Bridge. The elusive canaries scared the living daylights out of me; they were in the habit of appearing out of nowhere.

As time went on, the weather improved and spring was in the air. The days kept getting longer, bringing with them welcome relief and the pleasure of soaking up warm sunshine. Aquatic wildflowers soon sprang into life, and the warmer weather also brought out the phosphorescent fireflies, dancing, weaving, and skimming the surface of the water in the twilight, and the crickets also began to chirp. Unfortunately, the warmer evenings also brought with them the unwelcome mosquitoes. Buds unfurled into leaves, and the shrubbery started to sprout and soon burst into blossom. And, as an added bonus, all of this plant life helped to provided me with lush camouflage. In May, the air became heavily scented with lilac, and in early summer with the deliciously fragrant sweet jasmine, followed by acacia. To assuage my hunger, I gorged myself on the white acacia blossoms which grew there in profusion. The fragrant pea-like white blossoms hanging in racemes are edible and sweet-tasting. I don't know if they were of much nutritional value; though they helped to fill my stomach, they didn't really satisfy my hunger. I also realised that the blossom gave me the "runs," so I had to go easy on the stuff.

One night I lay hidden inside a large warehouse used for storing timber, which was kept locked for the night. I was up in the loft, just below the eaves, resting on a stack of timber boards and trying to settle down, curled up with my knees drawn. From there, I was able to observe the outside through a small window. I was dozing restlessly, waiting for dawn to break, mindful of any sign of danger. Somehow, I had a gut feeling that perhaps I should not have chosen this place on this particular night.

These brick-drying kilns provided the best protection from the icy winds.

By dawn I was up and ready, anxiously waiting for the doors to be opened so I could slip away. While peering out of the window I noticed to my utter horror that several "canaries" were waiting outside the entrance to the building, no doubt ready to begin a search as soon as the doors were opened. I was scared out of my wits, but I was ahead of them: I had an escape route prepared. Experience had taught me never to shelter in a building that only had one entrance with no means of escape, so I had first made sure that there was another way out. I had noticed that there was a small hatch, high up below the eaves, at the gable end of the building. From there I managed to lower myself onto the roof of the adjoining structure, slipping quietly away out of sight of the "canaries." I was lucky that time. It had been a mistake to take shelter there; I must be more careful, I reminded myself, or they will hunt me down one day. . . .

My hiding and running at the Jaeger brickyard had developed into a deadly cat-and-mouse game. I had become like a hunted animal skulking the area, wary of the Germans who must have known I was there, as I had been spotted more than once. I feared it was only a matter of time before they would catch up with me. My parents, on hearing about my deadly encounters, were of course proud of their youngest, as they referred to me, surviving the way I did, but at the same time they worried for me. It was decided that perhaps it would be better if I were hidden inside the *Lager*, if a way could be thought out of getting me inside the camp. They must have come up with some idea. We could not be sure if it would prove any safer, but at least I would be together with my family in the camp and certainly more comfortable than sleeping outside. Apart from the constant fear of being caught during the day when the risk was greatest, it was the spring's chilly nights that had troubled me the most. But this had since improved, so there was no immediate need for me to make the move. Though I was alone, the nights were much safer, so I counted down the minutes until evening would arrive and I could relax more. Every day, before dusk set in, the daily routine of deciding on the warmest and safest place to stay overnight would begin. It made sense to keep rotating lairs.

Hiding at Jaeger had its compensations, compared with being in the *Lager*, especially after the weather turned warm and the days were long; I was out in the open, as opposed to being shut in behind barbed wire. We were now in late spring or early summer, and I had by then settled down reasonably well to the day-to-day routine, all the time learning new hiding skills, moving about stealthily and trying to sense danger— part of the art of survival. My brothers brought me food they scraped together from their camp rations, but a lot of the time I went hungry. I often thought about the delicious food I had shoved to the side at the family table; I had been such a picky eater at home. Now I could think of nothing tastier than a freshly-baked country loaf to satiate the hunger gnawing at my stomach.

As time went on, hunger forced me to start taking greater risks by venturing out of the confines of the brickyard into the nearby streets, to join a line for bread outside a baker's shop. I tried not to attract undue attention, but that wasn't easy. I must have looked strange, like a boy from the wild, with my long matted hair. Boys of my age had their hair closely cropped for hygienic reasons; it was a school requirement. I hoped that no one would suspect I was Jewish while I waited in line for bread. When people began to get a bit chatty, I tried to avoid conversation by just shaking my head or making jumbled sounds. This exposure to the street was to provide me with a good initial experience in trying to pass for a simple country lad. I didn't venture out very often or very far, in case I attracted undue attention. People would have realised I didn't belong to the neighbourhood. I also looked rather strange, like a boy from the wild. I didn't want to provoke any of the muttering down the line of "Jews eating Polish bread!" that I had heard about. My brothers brought me the money, and they in turn smuggled portions of bread back into the camp for the family, to augment their rations. I was pleased to be able to help them for a change, but they were not happy that I was taking additional risks.

I always kept a small *Hitlerjugend* dagger on me, inside a leather sheath, which my brother Izak had given me back in the ghetto, on me. It didn't worry me unduly that it had a swastika on the porcelain hilt; I never really gave it much thought. Being on my own; the dagger helped me to feel more secure, having the means to defend myself if necessary. It was also useful for dividing food, opening cans, and as a general tool. I kept it attached to the side of my leg, held in place by the buckle and strap of my tattered plus-four trousers. To help relieve the boredom and take my mind off my hunger, I tried to keep busy by carving small objects with the knife. I made flutes and whistles out of bamboo and pliable willow branches, and as a result my woodcraft improved. I set bird traps with the aid of bricks. I used a long piece of string tied to a peg, propped up against a tile, and when a bird hopped in I pulled on the string and the tile dropped and closed the opening, trapping the bird inside. For bait I used worms and chafers that I placed inside the trap. I always released the sparrows, warblers and other birds. I would have been tempted to eat the larger quarry had it been possible to make a fire. Mallards also frequented the ponds, which would not have been too difficult to trap or bring down with a stone, which would have made a tasty meal indeed. At twilight, starlings moved swiftly in clusters, trying to bed down for the night in the high grass. Large flocks of crows filled the late afternoon sky, crowing excitedly as they went. These in turn were followed at dusk by the dark and sinister-looking bats, weaving in and out, beating their wings. I was scared of bats; it was said that they could fly into your hair and get entangled, and as my hair was rather long, I kept my hands on my head until darkness fell, and the bats would settle down for the night, inside sheds or hanging by their legs from tall trees. To try and relieve the never-ending monotony, I listened to birdsong and the chirping of crickets and observed the wildlife around me, but most important, I had to remain on the lookout and never take my mind off any sign of approaching danger. The only thing I had to look forward to was meeting up with one of my brothers. On most days I would make my way to one of two pre-arranged spots hoping to meet up with one of them; it was mostly Izak who came, as he worked at this time loading bricks onto boxcars. If no one turned up, I would come back the next day and the day after. I had no wristwatch; nor did any of the prisoners. On a clear day, I could more or less tell the time of day by the sun's position against a certain chimney stack. We always tried to make our rendez-vous at about the middle of the day, but this would depend on whether it was possible for my brother to slip away from the work gang unseen.

As I gained more confidence, I started to explore the banks of the nearby Kamienna (river) and the surrounding area to look for something I could pick from an allotment or greenhouse. I never strayed too far out; it was safer to stick to familiar ground should I run into any trouble, and I always returned to the brickyard before evening. While scouting the area, apart from looking for food I also searched for a comfortable den I could hole-up in, as it was prudent to keep changing lairs, but I never found anywhere safe enough outside of the brickyard. The whole Jaeger complex was surrounded by either a brick wall or barbed wire fencing, except for the area adjoining the swamps, which was left open, probably because it wasn't considered necessary to fence this area in. I mapped out a path between the soggy swamp and the dense shrubbery, with the use of branches and stepping-stones to avoid getting wet.

During all those difficult months at Jaeger, I survived mainly on coarse-grained bread, thinly spread with *powidła*, a tasteless plum marmalade that seemed to contain more beetroot than fruit. I never had a cooked meal or anything hot to drink throughout that entire period; the un-boiled water never did me any harm. Although there was plenty of kindling about, it was not safe to make a fire, as this would have attracted attention. Again and again I remembered with chagrin how I had been such a choosy eater at home. Now I hankered after my mother's cooking. She was such a marvellous cook. However, by early summer I was able to ease my hunger with vegetables, and later with berries and fruit I picked furtively from nearby allotments and orchards. This diet resulted in the most uncomfortable bellyache! Another problem was my hair; by this time it had grown long, but I could not risk going to a barber's shop in town. My long hair and down-at-the-heels appearance was attracting attention, and I had to stop venturing out to the bread shop altogether, as I could have been picked on by urchins as a "boy-tramp." Looking at my reflection in the pond, I recognized that I resembled some creature from the wild, with my shabby clothes and weather-beaten face, my skin deeply tanned by the sun. To try to keep clean, I washed in the pond as best I could. Not having any soap, I must have really smelled. I also never had a change of clothes during that entire period. I would rinse my underpants and vest in the pond and put them out to dry on the sedge grass. Looking back, these deprivations were the least of my worries. My most pressing concern was to keep ahead of the German "canaries" and live through each day. The discomfort didn't bother me as much as the tension and fear.

One of the cruellest Germans frequenting Jaeger was a *Schupo* known to the prisoners as Willand. One early morning, soon after the work party arrived from the camp, he ordered the prisoners to form up in the square, just inside the main gate. He made it known that he intended to make an example "as a deterrent to any troublemaker." Willand then randomly pointed to several men from the line and ordered each one to step forward a few paces. He then nonchalantly shot each one in the head at point-blank range. Any who moved after that he coolly finished off as they lay on the ground, just to make sure. I clearly heard the commotion and the shots as they rang out. I realised that something was amiss, knowing that the prisoners were assembled in the yard. I managed to sneak a look, and saw the victims lying on the ground with the killer standing over them, gun in hand. I kept my distance, staying well out of harm's way. Incredibly, one man named Akierman, though injured, survived the execution by feigning death—I saw him, later, at the brickyard. I had known him to stay overnight at Jaeger. It was said that he had contact with partisans and kept a weapon hidden at the brickyard. I had tried to keep clear of him, as these activities alerted the Germans to the presence of armed Jews; this also spelled danger to me. I had a keen sense of self-preservation and tried not to invite additional risk. The few armed Jews hiding in the vicinity were not welcomed by Polish partisan units in the woods, so they had no choice but to operate independently, in small groups. Often brothers would team up together; for instance, in our area there were the Sztajn, Pancer, Koppel and Kempinski brothers, but out of that group only one Kempinski was to survive the war.

I lost all track of time. It meant little to me, except for the never-ending boredom. Apart from day and night, I knew time by season: warm or cold. But one date is deeply etched in my memory. It was the day after Polish Constitution Day, May 3, when one of my most frightening and traumatic encounters took place. As this is a significant day in the Polish calendar, it merely helped me to recall the exact date, but it's the events of the following day that I will never forget. On that day, 4th May 1943, my brother Izak managed to slip away from his work gang and came to see me at the pre-arranged spot. It was a warm and sunny afternoon, and we sat on the ground exchanging news about the family at the camp. He also brought me some very welcome scraps of food that Mother had spirited away from the camp kitchens. She risked her life doing this for me. Being all alone in this wilderness, I often thought of *mamusia*, and yearned to be with her and embrace her. I missed her a lot, not having seen her or my father for so long.

As Izak and I were enjoying the last rays of afternoon sunshine filtering through the foliage and and he was about to start back to rejoin the work party, shots rang out and seemed to get closer and closer. Peering out of the bushes, we saw a man in the distance running in our direction pursued by Ukrainian guards who paused now and then, took aim, and fired their rifles. Then the man half-turned and fired back with his handgun, emitting little puffs of smoke. We realised it had to be one of the Pancer brothers, who were known Jewish partisans. He and his pursuers were getting dangerously close to us, so we also started to run, in case they stumbled across us. Bullets whistled past, and to our dismay we found ourselves running ahead of the fugitive and his pursuers, all running in the same direction. We were out in front, followed by the desperate Pancer, with the Ukrainians closing in on him, shouting in their own language: "*Stoj!*" "*Stoj!*" but we kept on running. Izak and I changed direction to get away from them and avoid the river that lay ahead. Two of the Ukrainians came after us, while the others went after the partisan. Luckily, we were now in tall grass and scrub, ducking and weaving, thus making it difficult to take aim. I had the presence of mind to sling aside my *Hitlerjugend* dagger but we could not avoid running towards a concrete wall that lay in our path, topped with rows of barbed wire. As I tried to clamber over it, I gashed my leg on the rusty barbs and fell backwards to the ground, shouting to Izak, "Run! Run!," but he stayed with me. In no time at all the two Ukrainians were upon us, with their rifles pointing at our heads, as we lay panting on the ground. I found it hard to believe that this was happening to me again; here I was, staring death in the face. How did we end up in this mess? It was all because of a wrong split-second decision; it was a mistake to have started to run. It's difficult to fully describe how it feels to be so close to death. Lying face down on the ground, I tensed my body, shrinking from the impact of the fatal shot about to ring out. It sent my heart racing and temples throbbing, and I felt like vomiting. Only a person who has faced such a situation can know how it feels. But as some seconds went by and no shots rang out, I thought that perhaps there was a glimmer of hope; every moment of life is so precious. Shouting in broken German, the frenzied Ukrainians ordered us to get up, prodding us out of the scrub towards a clearing. Soon after, the other Ukrainians appeared, dragging with them the doomed Pancer, who had also been captured. They kept beating him mercilessly with their rifle butts and kicked him repeatedly as he lay on the ground, bleeding profusely from the head. The brave man never cried out once. Izak also received a few rifle blows to his body, but they left me alone. The Ukrainians then ordered us to kneel on the ground, thinking they were about to finish us off by shooting us in the back. Cringing from fear, I felt like throwing up as I braced myself for the shot to find its mark. Just then a guardian angel in the guise of a Jewish policeman appeared out of nowhere. Realising what was afoot, he ran up to the Ukrainians imploring them not to shoot, as we were not connected with the gunman. Syngier the policeman, who had been a close friend of my eldest brother Moniek who had died in the ghetto, explained that we were part of a special work-gang from the *Lager*, and assured them that we would be severely punished for "loafing at work." By some miracle the Ukrainians relented, having been promised a pay-off by Syngier that my father was to make good. As a result, we were spared. Pancer, however, was escorted away and later put to death by hanging on the camp square. This was the prescribed form of execution for armed resistance; otherwise a Jew simply deserved a bullet in the head.

The primitive Ukrainian auxiliaries were not averse to a bribe, if there were no Germans present. The reason we were not killed on the spot was because that method of killing was against German orders when dealing with a "bandit," as the Nazis called partisans, who would first have to undergo interrogation by the Gestapo to extract any information before being publicly hanged in the camp as a warning to others. The Ukrainians later handed Pancer over to their German masters and left us in the charge of the policeman, who afterwards let me go. He escorted Izak back to the *Lager*, as the prisoners had already departed for the camp. Before he let me go, Syngier gave me a stern warning to leave the area: "Boy, you must find somewhere else to hide, if you stay here they will surely catch you," he said, and he would not be able to save me again. After my close brush with death, we realised that my time at Jaeger was coming to an end. My luck could run out any day now, and there would be no reprieve next time.

The leg I had lacerated on the rusty barbed wire started to give me trouble and slowed me down considerably. It was festering, and I had no antiseptic ointment. I bound my leg up with rags and, having learned that it had disinfectant qualities, applied urine to the wound—which made it sting sharply. It took some time to heal up. I carry a long scar on my left shin as a memento to this day. Meanwhile, my next hiding place was being prepared for me inside the *Lager,* but for the time being I had to remain where I was for some weeks, until the preparations were complete and a way was found to get me inside the camp. To stay alive, one had to be one jump ahead of the Germans and never wait for the inevitable.

In 1947 a case was filed against the Jewish policeman by the Historical Commission in Poland for misdeeds committed against a fellow prisoner. In his defence, Syngier claimed that he had saved the lives of two Jewish brothers. He managed to trace me to London, hoping I would repay the debt I owed him by providing testimony in his favour, for saving me and my brother from a firing squad. I don't know exactly what he was accused of, but he did save my life and in spite of his alleged wrongdoings, I felt duty-bound to help him. I prepared the necessary deposition, which I had legalized at the Polish Consulate in London. Incidentally, my sworn affidavit (facing page) was witnessed and authenticated by the Polish Vice-Consul, Mgr. Pawel Lewkowicz.

Apparently my evidence resulted in the case against Syngier being dropped. He was then free to leave for Canada, where I understand he was shunned by the Ostrowiec survivor community in Toronto.

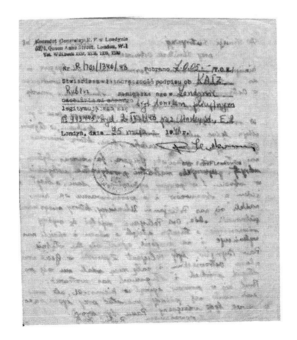

Copy of the testimony I submitted in favour of Syngier.
I wrote it in Polish, it is dated 23 May 1948, two years after I reached England.

CHAPTER 8

A Shallow Grave

By late summer 1943, my family had come up with yet another inventive idea for a hiding place for me. This time it was within the *Arbeitslager,* the labour camp, right inside the barracks. It was important that I make the move before the autumn weather set in, as I could not have gone on much longer living the way I did. I could not have endured a winter at the brickyard. My life there had also become a constant battle for survival, and my luck seemed to be running out. It was time to move on. We didn't know if the camp would be any safer, but in any case there was no other alternative. I would at least be together with my family and better protected from the elements.

But first I would need to get inside the *Lager.* The only way, we decided, was by joining up with the inmates on their way back to the camp in the evening before they reached the camp gates. But before that, I needed to familiarise myself with the route the prisoners took, a distance of some five to six kilometres, by following them at a distance and finding the best place to sneak into the column of prisoners. I did this over several days, exploring the route carefully, in my own time. The spot chosen as the most suitable was fairly near the camp gates. We felt there would be less chance of being picked out by the escorting guards if I would only be marching with the prisoners for a short distance.

On the pre-arranged day, I left the brickyard in good time, well ahead of the prisoners, and made my way to an area dotted with mounds of slag-metal waste from the steelworks along the path the inmates would be taking on their way back to the camp. I then hid behind a slag-heap and waited for the columns to appear. It was early evening when I first saw the shuffling inmates coming into view from two different directions, one from the brickyard, which I was to join up with, and the other from the direction of the steelworks, a little farther away. As the middle of the column drew level with me, I jumped forward deftly, merging with the marching ranks. My brothers, Izak and Leizer, knew the exact spot and were on the lookout for me, keeping to the outside of the column so they could shield me from the eyes of the escorting guards. Flanked by my two brothers, I linked arms with them to support myself and make myself appear taller. As we marched along, I had some difficulty keeping in step with the others, and was pushed forward by the men from behind, as they were not allowed to slacken off, but I soon got the hang of it by lengthening my stride, and letting me brothers help me along.

As we approached the *Lager,* the camp gates were swung open by two guards, one at each gate. The person I understood to be the camp commandant, Zwierzyna, was standing with his cohorts and guard dogs next to the sentry-post as the five-abreast column filed past. A Jewish policeman kept yelling out *"Mützen ab, Augen links"* (caps off, eyes left). I managed to slip through without any trouble. Once past the gates, the prisoners quickly dispersed, each towards his respective barracks, and my brothers took me to theirs. The column from the steelworks soon followed, with my father and Abram among the new arrivals. I immediately began familiarising myself with the camp routine. The first lesson I learned was that we were no longer ghetto inmates; we were now *Häftlinge,* prisoners. I must have been the only young *Häftling* who had willingly imprisoned himself! Soon after, the hungry prisoners started to form up with their mess tins for the evening soup ration they waited for all day. Inside our barracks that evening, I was happy to be reunited with my father and later with my mother, for the first time since the ghetto was liquidated more than five months earlier. I was overjoyed to be with them again; it was comforting and reassuring merely to be in their presence. I was shocked, though, to see how bad Father looked, how different from how he'd been when I had last seen him. Mother could not remain with me long that evening, as "free-time" was soon over and she had to return to the women's barracks before lights-out, when the curfew would begin.

That evening I learned why Father looked so gaunt. He had been assigned to hard labour in the WVHA section, unloading wagons of scrap iron and iron ore with a shovel; a shovelful of ore is unbelievably heavy. This had a terrible effect on him. My father was now in his late forties, and had hitherto been strong and energetic, but the punishing work at the steelworks had taken its toll. These vital iron ore supplies kept coming from neutral Sweden throughout the war, and fed the blast furnaces of Nazi-occupied Europe, greatly assisting their war effort. Sometimes the ore arrived in freight cars with Russian markings, which we observed on the sidings near the camp. We were very curious about anything Russian. These long wagons, made of solid steel, were enormous compared to the smaller German or Polish wooden boxcar variety. Father said he was convinced that Germany would never win the war: "The Russian steel output must be so immense that they can afford to build freight cars out of precious steel instead of cheap timber," he'd say. "Can you imagine how many tanks and heavy guns they must be turning out? Everything about Russia is so vast, it just cannot be conquered; eternal Russia will be Hitler's graveyard." Poor Father tried to take heart from whatever he could—he dearly desired to survive long enough to see Nazi Germany crushed.

A partial view of the vast Ostrowiec Steelworks.

It was not, as you may have guessed, enough to just steal into the camp; I now had to somehow hide from the Germans. Again, my ever-resourceful family had an ingenious idea for a hiding place. It was in the form of a dugout below the bottom-tier bunk that my father and brothers slept on. Below the boards of the bottom row of bunks there was a void about 25cm in height. This space was hidden from view by the boards that supported the bunks. To start with, two of the boards had been prised up and the nails removed. Enough of the soil that formed the ground under the space was scooped away and shoved to the sides to accommodate me, in a prone position on my back. However, the space was too shallow for me to turn over, or to lie on my side. The two loose boards were then replaced on top of me, and covered over with the prisoners' straw-filled mattresses.

My brothers and father had no tools with which to prepare the dug-out; no tools whatsoever were allowed in the camp. However, Izak had managed to conceal on his body a piece of metal from the steelworks, with the aid of which he had scraped away at the compacted hard soil during the night, using his bare hands.

At long last I was now able to have my hair cut. Izak borrowed a pair of clippers from the camp barber and cropped it short—oh, what sweet relief! Soon after I got into the *Lager*, Izak was assigned the same punitive work as my father, shovelling heavy iron ore. This was considered the hardest task of all. Doing twelve-hour shifts, one could not survive such punishing work for long on camp rations. What's more, Izak helped Father out with his workload whenever possible. My father was born in 1893, and was by then almost fifty years old. It pained us to see him return to the barracks at night utterly drained and exhausted. I will never forget how the whites of his eyes stood out; his face and hands were covered in red iron ore dust—he was but a shadow of his former, robust, self. Mother, as I mentioned, was working in the camp kitchens, which at least had its compensations. And Abram's job was to crawl inside the furnaces after they had cooled off, and to use a special tool and hammer to chop out any fire-bricks lining the furnace walls that had been damaged and needed to be replaced. He was just fourteen years old.

The *Lager* was situated near the Częstocice sugar-beet refinery, not far from the steelworks. The camp consisted of a number of long wooden barracks, with no windows aside from narrow raised skylights running the lengths of the roofs. The barracks stood in straight rows, all facing the *Appellplatz* (assembly ground). The camp perimeter was built in a square and enclosed by three rows of electrified barbed-wire fencing, with four watchtowers, one in each corner. Ukrainian sentries manned these day and night with mounted machine-guns trained on the camp fence and the barracks, to spy on the prisoners, and revolving searchlights illuminated the fence during the hours of darkness.

There was no escape; the only way in or out was through the camp gate. Two sentry boxes, painted with the customary red and white diagonal stripes, stood on either side of the camp entrance gate. The guardhouse and barrack block housing the German SS and Ukrainian guards was situated just outside the camp fence, near the entrance gate. Thus, the guards had a clear view of the entire camp and the barrack doors, which all faced the assembly ground.

Inside each of the barracks there were three-tiered wooden bunks (plank beds) running the length of the barracks on both sides like shelves, with a gangway down the middle. Narrow rectangular bags the width of the bunks, made out of coarse sacking and filled with straw, served as mattresses. The straw came through the loose weave and was irritating and itchy. There was no change of clothes: the clothing you stood in was worn day and night, and no underwear was issued. You had what you came in, and this was disinfected from time to time. A small, wood-burning cast-iron stove stood in the middle of each barracks, with the stove-pipe running through to the roof. Every prisoner was issued with one blanket. This was insufficient to keep warm, so on cold nights our family would huddle closely together for warmth.

There were separate quarters for women, who were few in number. The Germans didn't consider women capable of hard labour, and they had enough men. After the day shift, men and women could mingle before and after "soup time" until lights-out and the start of the curfew, which varied according to the daylight hours. After curfew, it was advisable to stay in one's barracks or risk being shot at from the watchtower if caught in the beam approaching the electrified fence. If a prisoner had dysentery, as we often did, it was prudent to stay well clear of the fence when making a dash for the latrines.

There was only one latrine and washroom hut that had to serve the entire camp. There were two doors: women entered at one end and men at the other. A low timber partition provided a modicum of privacy. The open latrine had a crossbar running the length of the shed, serving as a thigh support, above a rectangular pit. The only time I could make use of the latrines was after dark, before the curfew. My legs didn't reach to the floor, so I had to watch my balance—the pit was quite deep! The stench from the open cesspit was overpowering, and from time to time, our captors formed a *Scheisskommando* ("shit detachment") from amongst the prisoners to reduce the level of excrement to stop it from overflowing. The reduction was done by passing buckets, hand-to-hand, to another freshly-dug pit. Needless to say, this was considered one of the most abhorrent tasks—and was all part of the systematic plan to break down our morale and degrade the inmates. The Germans referred to us as *Untermenschen* (sub-humans), who deserved no pity and who could be killed with impunity and without remorse. One didn't become a sub-human overnight, of course. It was a gradual process. Inevitably, this treatment led to a degree of breakdown in morals among some of the young men and women, who felt they didn't have long to live and so lived for the moment.

German guards were fearful of the infectious diseases which took hold in the camp from time to time, so they tried to keep their distance. They rarely ventured inside the barracks and never came at night, so there was no need for me to hide inside my "coffin," as I thought of it. When they entered the barracks in daytime, it was to mete out punishment or to carry out the occasional barrack inspection. The ever-present danger was when the labour security officers Goldsitz and Rhade, accompanied by Ukrainian guards, came onto the camp square for *Zahlappell*, roll-call, in the early hours. One could never be sure they would not enter the barracks in search of some missing prisoner who failed to report for roll-call, so I always remained hidden flat on my back in my dugout. I was able to emerge by myself and to hide again by myself, which is the only thing that saved me. I would only come out after the guards had left the camp with the prisoners, when the blowing of whistles and the barking of orders and dogs had ceased. I remained inside the barracks, keeping close to my bunk, never venturing out during daylight. If danger lurked, I was able to quickly slide sideways, on my back, into the dugout, and to replace the boards on top of me. It was on one occasion, as I was lying down below, flat on my back, with the boards almost touching my face, that I realized that it was like lying inside a wooden coffin in a dank grave. I felt breathless down below, so I had to come up for air as soon as it was safe to do so. To this day I have a phobia about lying on my back; it brings back traumatic memories, and I'm unable to sleep that way.

Now and then there were the barrack inspections, when each prisoner had to stand rigidly to attention in front of his bunk. As the German officers entered the barracks, a cold shiver would run down my spine as the barracks' senior brought the prisoners to attention with the command: "*Achtung! Mützen ab*" (Attention, caps off). These were terrifying moments for me; I could hear every sound down below in my "coffin" as the SS guards passed within a few feet of me. A sudden cough or sneeze could have spelled disaster for me and my family. Father told me to hold my nose, which would stop me from sneezing. I also kept my eyes closed, so I could hear better. I held my breath while the inspection-party walked past the line of prisoners, and only relaxed when I heard them move away from my bunk. A little while later, the order *Weitermachen* was heard, as they left the barracks and the inmates eased off and dispersed. Everyone in the barracks knew of my presence there. I was, of course, a source of danger to them, if discovered, but nonetheless they liked me and considered me their mascot. It was tacitly understood that should I be reported, my big brothers would not hesitate to exact their revenge. We were pretty sure, though, that it would never come to that. Most of the men knew each other and their families intimately from way back, and a close bond existed between them. It may have been different in the larger concentration camps, where strangers of different nationalities were lumped together and some contemptible person may have been tempted to "rat" on his fellow in the hope of saving his skin or earning an extra crust. Extreme hunger can do terrible things to people.

Roll-call was at five-thirty in the morning, after reveille at five. At six a.m., two separate columns of workmen set out from the camp, going in opposite directions towards their respective work places. The day shift lasted until just before nightfall, seven days a week, with the occasional Sunday off. The daily food ration consisted of 180 grams of coarse black bread that tasted as if it contained sawdust and two ladles of a watery soup, usually made from cabbage or turnip and the odd potato floating around, with little protein. As in other camps, a favourite talking point was of a thick soup where the spoon would stand up on its end. In the morning the prisoners received a ladle-full of black *ersatz* coffee, apparently made from sugar beets, and a hunk of sticky, and sometimes mouldy, bread. If the bread was too mouldy, it was best soaked in water, and after the mould floated to the surface you could squeeze it out. I was not entitled to any rations; I couldn't even be seen approaching the vat on the *Appellplatz* where the slop was doled out. My family shared their rations with me, which meant less for them. Each prisoner was responsible for carrying his *menaszka* (mess tin) with him, and a spoon if he had one. If he had no spoon, he would have to slurp his food. To each, the tin was his most prized possession. Some people only had a tin can for a mess tin, with a piece of wire attached for a handle. If lost, the tins were difficult to replace, and "no mess tin—no soup" was the camp rule. Hence they were kept about the prisoner's person, usually tied to the waist with string. The same applied to any spare piece of clothing a prisoner may have had, as there was nowhere safe to keep it. Leather shoes were unobtainable, and when their shoes wore through, the prisoners were issued with wooden clogs instead. We called them *Hollenderki,* Dutch maidens.

The inmates in our *Lager* wore a motley variety of worn out, shabby clothing. You only had what you arrived in, and when that fell apart, prisoners were issued with *pasiaki,* a blue-grey striped pyjama-like outfit of shirt and pants. In the early days, some prisoners were brought in from other camps wearing these curious stripes, which were hitherto unknown to us. The Star of David armband that was worn in the ghetto was discarded in the camp, for here we were all caged in, and there was no need for the Germans to set us apart from the rest of the population. There were no prisoner markings either, as there were no political prisoners in our camp, only Jews. There weren't any names, nor even numbers like in Auschwitz; prisoners were simply addressed with a stabbing finger movement and a piercing shriek: "*Du Jude!*"

One day a grisly discovery was made when a sack tied with string was found lying against the camp fence. Inside it were found two severed heads that turned out to be those of my cousins, Moshe and Yossel Berman. In better times, it had been Moshe who would take me to football matches in support of the local team, KSZO. The two brothers, as I recounted earlier, had escaped from the ghetto before its liquidation to be hidden by peasant farmers in the nearby village of Denków. After the two peasants, who were in it together, had presumably laid their hands on their money and my cousins were no longer of any use to them, they butchered them in the most gruesome manner. Their severed heads were thrown against the camp fence in a macabre display of hatred and contempt for their erstwhile Jewish neighbours, and their decapitated bodies were dumped elsewhere. When the headless bodies were later brought into the camp for burial, it was found that their wounds were consistent with having been run through with pitchforks, several times. They must have made the fatal mistake of keeping all their money with them—or perhaps the peasants discovered where they had hidden it.

From time to time, the camp guards would carry out searches to try and extract any valuables they could from the wretched inmates to stuff their own pockets. One day they declared that they had good reason to believe there were American dollars hidden in the camp which had to be handed over immediately, promising that no harm would come to those who complied. Of course, no one believed them, and no dollars were forthcoming. The guards then carried out a thorough body search. All they found was a few dollars on two brothers, sewn into their clothing. As a result, they were taken out onto the *Appellplatz*, where the other prisoners were to witness their execution. One brother shouted out a desperate last plea, imploring the executioners to shoot him first. "I don't want to see my brother die!," he pleaded. Surprisingly, the Germans obliged and granted him this last wish.

One prisoner in particular, a Jewish policeman named Puczyc, who was not a local, was to be avoided. He was unpredictable and could turn violent; no doubt believing that this would curry favour with his superiors and help save his own skin. One day, he appeared from behind our barracks and came across my mother boiling up some potato peelings in a mess tin standing on bricks over some flaming twigs. She had smuggled the peelings from the camp kitchens for her children. When Puczyc realised what she was up to, he kicked it over with his polished knee-high boot. A local man would not have done this to her: our family was well-respected before the war. Father had done much for the good of the community and the needy of our town. Even in this nether world, some people sought his counsel and came to listen to a *Dvar Torah,* words of wisdom, which he liked to quote from the Hebrew Scriptures.

As there was no rabbi left alive, it fell upon Father to conduct clandestine services on the High Holy Days in our barracks. There were no prayer-books, but my father knew them by heart. As worship was forbidden, the prayer meetings had to be short, so he only focused on the salient prayers. I sat on my bunk and listened; a hushed silence filled the barracks as Father offered prayers in his melodious soft voice, the strains of which carried much feeling. I can still hear the poignancy of *Odom Yesodo Meofor;* "Man's origin is dust and to dust he returns and gets his bread at the peril of his life." Another passage that stands out in my mind said, "In Thy hand is the soul of every living creature; the soul is Thine, and the body is Thy work, O Lord of the Universe, have pity on Thy creation." The atmosphere in the barracks was heavy with emotion. In view of our plight, these solemn words took on an especially deep significance. I remembered these poignant words, and as I got older understood their meaning with greater clarity. I realised just how meaningful they were, and how appropriate to the situation. Not everyone joined in the prayers, of course. Many abandoned God, just as He had abandoned them. From the depths of despair they had cried out for help, but they had not been answered—God remained silent, and the world looked on and said nothing.

Although there was nothing to laugh about, a sort of bleak humour emerged in the *Lager*—we were Jews, after all! Earlier, in the ghetto, we had been too shocked to make light of the events that had befallen us, and there were more important things to think of at a time when everyone was preoccupied with avoiding deportation trains and bullets to the head. But as time went on, we became more accustomed to our situation and could afford to raise a laugh at our predicament. Once we were incarcerated in the *Lager,* caged in like animals, it was final—what were we to do? "What was, was, and is no more," as one sardonic ditty went at the time. The opening words to another ditty, steeped in irony, presumably alluding to an old flame in the good old days, went like this: "Where were you when the money was there? Now you're here when the money's all gone!" In the camp there was time to think, and a cheerless humour emerged, helping people to cope with the grim reality and to preserve their sanity.

A *Lager* jargon also developed. It was made up of sardonic, self-mocking plays on words, and was a form of escape from reality. The expressions were full of pathos about our plight and precarious existence, about the daily routine, and about the food—or rather the lack of it. People joked bitterly: "Here every day is like Yom Kippur (the Day of Repentance, the central fast day of the Jewish calendar); we all dress up as if it's Purim (a holiday partially marked by the wearing of costumes), and we live in a *Succah* (wooden hut, such as the one used on Sukkot, the holiday of Tabernacles)," as if camp life could compare with the joyous festivals of the past. Nicknames were invented and given to various guards and cruel tormentors. Hitler became *Hittlemacher*, cap-maker, in Yiddish, and so on. This jargon spread from ghetto to ghetto and camp to camp by word of mouth. The usual phrase to encourage someone on the brink of giving up the will to live was *"Gibt nisht up die bonne"*—don't surrender the ration coupons. Satirical songs and poems were written. All of this helped to ease the inmates' hardship and raise their morale, which the Nazis were determined to break—it was a form of spiritual resistance.

Prisoners eagerly exchanged scanty bits of information about the course of the war gleaned from Polish workmen at the steelworks, some of whom may have had access to clandestine radio reports from London or the Underground. When we heard by way of rumour that the Wehrmacht had suffered a significant defeat at Stalingrad some months before, we could scarcely believe it. This marked the tide of war changing, but we didn't know it at the time; now we were aware of the full extent of the Russian victory. This piece of sensational news lifted our spirits and raised our hopes. Prior to the battle of Stalingrad, many of us had believed that the Germans would win the war and that our chances of survival were slim.

Any information about the progress of the war was hard to come by. The Ukrainian guards had orders not to talk to prisoners and, regardless, would never admit to German reversals. To the contrary, they liked to taunt us, saying *"Russki kaputt!"*. The suggestion that Soviet Russia was done for, was very disheartening for us, as we looked to it for our salvation. In our part of the world, the only direction from which any rescue could come was the East—the Western Allies were a distant prospect.

By this time the prisoner population started to swell, with inmates being brought in from other prison camps like nearby Skarżysko-Kamienna, and some from as far away as Warsaw. It was from them that we first heard about the epic Warsaw Ghetto Revolt, when the ghetto inmates rose up against their Nazi oppressors, and about the indescribable destruction and enormity of crimes committed elsewhere. They also brought with them songs of defiance and bravery, along with more nostalgic and plaintive songs. One indignant song said, *"Tzu bin ich fun ein schtein geboir'n...?"* Was I born of a stone and did a mother not hold me in her arms? Another poignant one was *"Es Brent"* ("Our Village Burns"). This became a rallying cry; it carried a message of resistance couched in the lyrics: *"Evil winds full of anger rage and ravage and yet you stand there looking on with folded arms. Should our shtetl with us together, go up in ash 'n fire, and when the slaughter's over, leave just charred and empty walls. . . . Brothers! Grab the buckets, douse the fire with your very blood, show what you're made of! Brothers don't just stand there looking on with folded arms, as our poor little shtetl burns. . . .*

One piece I liked, *Matyushka Russiya,* came a little later. It was a wistful song, full of yearning for Mother Russia, which symbolised freedom from the Nazis. I have not heard it sung since those dark days. Sung in Yiddish, these are but a few of the lyrics, as I remember them:

> *Matyushka Russiya,* Oh, how deeply I pine for you. (Chorus)
>
> I yearn for the Russian *lieder* (melodies),
> for the heartfelt brothers and sisters.
> I yearn for the Russian *mentsch* (being)
> that is resolute and sturdy.
> I yearn for the Russian soul,
> who is as free as the wind.
> Suddenly, a raging tempest on the earth is unleashed.
> Wild beasts run amok,
> people hunted down and trampled on.
> War, War is their cry!
>
> *Matyushka Russiya,* Oh, how deeply I pine for you. . . .

At that time, we all had immense solidarity with Soviet Russia. All our hopes rested on the valiant Red Army who bore the brunt of the war, and only they, we believed, would come to our rescue. Only "Mother Russia" evoked any hope as far as we in Poland were concerned. Inmates complained bitterly, "Surely, the outside world must know what is happening and what the Nazis are doing to us!" The inmates felt abandoned by a callous and uncaring world that remained silent, for their silence encouraged the Nazis. People naively thought that the cynical American and British leaders would have much to answer for, when the war finally came to an end, for being indifferent to the fate of those doomed to destruction.

As a result of the arrival of newcomers from other prison camps, the regime in our *Lager* progressively worsened; conditions and sanitation deteriorated further. Hungry and frail bodies attract disease, and a typhus epidemic broke out yet again, with many dying as a result. I was plagued with body lice, which were impossible to get rid of. As lice spread disease, particularly typhus, the prisoners were sent to periodic showers and for de-lousing sessions, where they were dusted down with a lice powder which I, as an illegal inhabitant of the camp, could not take advantage of. I was infested with the blood-sucking parasites, and they tormented me, particularly at night when I was trying to sleep. They were in my hair, although it was closely cropped, and in my clothes, particularly in the seams. Somehow the lice, especially the nits, got into the most hidden crevices. I would sit for hours on my bunk, carefully going over each piece of clothing, searching for the plump little beasts, crushing them between my thumbnails. They got so fat from feasting on my blood that when I squashed them they burst with a click, revealing traces of human blood. The itchiness almost drove me crazy. I couldn't stop myself from scratching until I lacerated my skin. The pain seemed preferable and easier to endure than the constant itching. Strangely enough, at the brickyard I had never suffered from lice, although my hair had been long. I suppose there was no one to catch it from, and I had tried to keep clean by washing in the lake.

Then there were the elusive jumping fleas that were difficult to catch. These mainly inhabited the barrack floor and liked to go for your ankles and legs. And there were of course the nasty-smelling bedbugs that one had to contend with. These were easier to locate, as they were dark brown in colour. When crushed they emitted an unpleasant and peculiar sweet odour. Bedbugs, compared to lice and fleas, are large, and they are mainly active at night. They can give a nasty bite that leave a little red bump for several days. As it was not possible for me to go with the inmates to the showers and de-lousing sessions, I had to make do with rubbing myself down with a wet rag inside the barracks. Due to lack of nutrition and poor hygiene, I suffered a lot from festering sores and painful boils. The long days spent in the *Lager* were extremely boring with nothing for me to do, apart from searching for the noxious little parasites. I only had the evenings to look forward to, when the family returned to the barracks after the daily work shift.

Now and then the barracks were fumigated. This was an anxious time for me, as the equipment was operated by German sanitary personnel, in white overalls, and due to the harmful fumes, I could not remain inside my dugout below the bunk. Even outside the barracks the chemical fumes had a choking effect on the inmates. Fumigation was performed in the evening after soup time, while the prisoners sat outside on the ground. I was shielded by my family until we were ordered back into the barracks. The camp grounds were covered with black shingle from the steelworks smelter; there wasn't a shrub or even a blade of grass to be seen. Neither trees nor any other greenery grew in the *Lager*. There were no birds or birdsong, and no butterflies. Even mice and rats kept away from the camp; they would hardly find a crumb. Only flies were not deterred.

By late autumn 1943, the situation in the camp was worsening by the day; there were now more frequent shootings and acts of unspeakable cruelty. As I was afraid of being discovered, I went back to the brickyard for a short period, and as before, I sneaked back into the camp with the prisoners when we thought that things had calmed down somewhat. One day, the two partisan brothers Sztajn were captured. I knew them, as I used to come across them during my time in the vicinity of the brickyard. I'm not sure exactly where and how they were caught, but the two brave men were brought into the *Lager* and hanged on the *Appellplatz*, having first been subjected to torture; they were apparently in a terrible state. The entire camp was forced to stand and watch as the stools were kicked from under them. The bodies were left swinging on the gallows for hours as the inmates were made to stand and watch. The prisoners stood in stony silence, full of admiration for two brave men who had possessed the courage and an opportunity to fight back.

At around this time, one morning following the *Appel* (roll-call) the prisoners were made to stand for hours on the assembly ground. As they waited, Moishe Gutholtz, an orderly from the *Krankenstübe* (sick bay), cracked and could take it no longer. He turned on his tormentors, railing at them: "You vile murderers, what do you want from us?" Then the burly Gutholtz threw himself at *Werkschutzführer* Rhade, grabbing him by the throat from behind with one arm while with the other he removed the Luger from its holster and thrust it in his ribs. Moishe pulled the trigger, but the gun jammed, so he briefly let go of the German's neck to pull the lever back so he could fire. During that moment, Rhade recovered and started to grapple with Gutholtz, and they both fell to the ground. The Ukrainian guards rushed up but could not take proper aim at Gutholtz, as he and Rhade were rolling in the dirt in each other's grasps. The guards, unable to take aim, beat the courageous man senseless with rifle blows to his head and body. When he finally let go of Rhade they shot him, but he still held on to the gun in his tightly clenched fist, though he appeared to be dead. Incredibly, after Gutholtz's body was carried away by his fellow inmates to be buried, he whispered to the burial party: "Brothers, cover me lightly." An alert German caught on to the situation and ran up. Reaching for his Luger, he put it against Gutholtz's temple and pulled the trigger. The Germans and Ukrainians then went wild, striking out in all directions, firing at random into the line of prisoners, killing several and injuring others. Some inmates tried to rush the guards, while others tried to calm them and hold them back. They had no chance; there was no escape and no-where to run to, except into the arms of hostile Poles. Resistance was simply suicide, but by holding back, they had a chance, however slim, of surviving to tell the world of the horrors they had endured. Only survival was paramount; nothing else mattered.[7]

Towards the end of 1943, in order to cover the losses incurred, hundreds of prisoners from other prison camps were brought into our *Lager*. They came from such places as Piotrków, Radom, and Płaszów, near Kraków—over five hundred prisoners came from the latter. These were referred to as *Krakowiaks*, after the folk dancers of that province. As a result of the squalor and poor sanitation, yet another epidemic broke out. Thankfully, I was not infected and in my entire time there never got seriously ill, apart from colds and of course diarrhoea, which was so common as to be not worth mentioning. I must have built up immunity to typhus, which is highly contagious. Had I fallen ill, there would have been no chance of treatment. I took heart from the saying that Father liked to repeat: "What doesn't kill you makes you stronger."

One day, Polish steelworkers tipped off the Germans that several Jews were hiding at the steelworks. They guided them to where they were sheltering, and indeed six young men were discovered. The Germans in turn left it to their Ukrainian lackeys to mete out the appropriate punishment for attempting to hide. The savages cast them alive, one by one, into the roaring furnace at the foundry. One of the victims was my mother's cousin, by the name of Fiksenbaum. After this hor-

---

7   The site where the Ostrowiec slave labour camp stood has since been turned into cultivation allotments where the locals grow their cabbages, without so much as a plaque to record what took place there. Nor is there any record of the former Jewish community.

rific incident, it was time to put into effect my long-planned escape to Warsaw. We could not risk leaving it any longer. I didn't want to be separated from my family, but my parents urged me to go, before time ran out.

CHAPTER 9

Deadly Encounter

In preparation for my long-planned escape to Warsaw, my family and I tried to envision all possible scenarios, with a strategy prepared for any eventuality. To begin with, I had to familiarise myself with all the details contained in my false birth certificate: name, place of birth and parish, names of "parents," maiden name of my "mother," and so on. But most important, we had to think of a way around the crucial problem of my circumcision, which would be the first thing that would be checked in the event of any suspicion. There were random checks in the streets by Germans, and any male with Jewish features would be unceremoniously asked to drop his pants behind the nearest courtyard gate. Unless medical necessity made it imperative, circumcision among Catholic Poles was not practiced; in fact they considered it repugnant, as the mark of a Jew. This assisted the Nazis in identifying any Jewish male trying to pass for a Gentile.

Thus, in the weeks prior to my setting out on the momentous journey to Warsaw, we had to overcome the problem of my circumcision. Again my family came up with a brilliant and yet simple idea with which to deceive the Nazis. My sister in Warsaw managed to acquire some special glue which she sent to Ostrowiec via Mrs. Radzik. I think it may have been some dental adhesive. I decided to call it my *"cudny klej"* (magic glue). I right away started to experiment with the substance by carefully applying the required amount to the tip of my penis, then drawing the skin over the glans as far as I could, then pressing the skin together to form a point and holding it firmly together until the glue set, thus making it appear as if I had not been circumcised. However, there were certain snags involved. First of all, it was painful while it lasted. What was worse, the deception would not withstand a medical check, or even close scrutiny by experienced eyes. It would be sufficient only for a cursory check in the street. Furthermore, the glue would not hold for long, only several hours. If I passed water, it would not last even this long, for urination would cause the glue to gradually lose adhesion. And, most crucially, none of this would be any good unless I had prior notice to perform the procedure, as and when required. I doubt if this ploy would have worked with an adult, but in my case it did, though it was extremely uncomfortable while the glue held. At first I didn't think I would be able to bear it for any length of time. The degree of comfort, I later discovered, depended on the skill of application, which came with practice.

One wintry December morning in 1943 after reveille, on my planned day of escape, I bid a sad farewell to my brothers inside the barracks, having parted with my mother the previous evening. I had been reluctant to leave her. She was very tearful, but after a while she let go of me, saying, "Go, go, my son, and live." The parting this time was very difficult, and I was praying with all my heart that the embrace would not be the last. Leizer and Abram formed up for the brickyard, and I set out together with my father and Izak to join the column of workmen lining up for the steelworks, which was in the same direction as the railway station, where I had to go. Fortunately, it was a misty and dismal morning, and the weather would help to hide me from the escorting guards. I shivered in the penetrating cold as I positioned myself in the middle of the column between my father and brother. Like before, as I was too short to masquerade as an adult, I had to make myself appear taller by holding on to them as we shuffled past the camp gates, where the guards fleetingly scrutinised the marching column as it went past. *Kommandant* Zwierzyna was there as usual, with his henchmen at his side, and their baying German shepherd dogs straining at the leash.

After we had been marching for about twenty minutes, we approached the Częstocice Sugar Refinery, and it was time to say my final farewell to Father and Izak. I shall never forget my father's last words to me as we parted; he blessed me, whispering in Hebrew: "May the Lord protect you…" Before letting go of me he said in Yiddish: "*Rievele, gib achting oif dir, und fergess nischt*"—Take good care, and never forget. Father's final words to me, *Never Forget*, have always rung in my ears. What exactly did he mean by them? Did he mean don't forget your parents, your faith, or who you are? He must have had a premonition that we were parting for good. He knew that if I survived I would never forget my parents or my faith; so what he was really alluding to, I am convinced, was: "*Never forget* what was done to us!" Father knew we were doomed, and what haunted him most was the thought that the Nazis would cover up their heinous crime and there would be no one left to tell what had happened. I, at least, had a chance of surviving.

As we drew level with the refinery building entrance, I broke away from the marching ranks and quickly dashed into the courtyard, taking cover behind the double gates, trusting that I had not been spotted by the escorting soldiers. Crouching behind the gates, shaking like a leaf, I listened to the sound of the prisoners' wooden clogs clunking on the cobblestones as it slowly receded. Once the clatter was almost inaudible, I slowly emerged from behind the gate into the middle of the deserted road, and with a faint wave of the arm I wished my family one last farewell. As this was out of town, there was no one about, so I stood there for a while with tears streaming down my face and watched until the rear of the column slowly disappeared into the hazy distance. I feared for the fate of my family; who could know when I would see them again?

Before moving on, I wiped away the tears, trying to regain my composure. As I stood there all alone, a feeling of loneliness came over me and all sort of doubts entered my mind. I was convinced that I was ill-prepared for the task ahead of me, to act the part of a Christian boy with all that this entailed. I had been hiding, in one way or another, for so long that I got scared of people in the street. The simple knowledge that I would act frightened brought on new fears, and I worried that my attempt to escape would end in disaster. I knew that I had to shake off the image of the frightened boy who belonged in the ghetto and start to think more like the real Stefan Wojs. If I saw a German approach me now, I must not waver or duck out of sight as I had in the past, but look him straight in the eye. One false move could give me away, and if I tried to run it would be fatal. As a young boy, if you were caught in the ghetto, some relatively humane German might let you off to live another day, but on the "Aryan" side, you would never be given another chance; the Germans never liked to be outfoxed.

Prior to my escape, although I didn't want to leave the reassuring protection of my family, I had yearned to be free, beyond the barbed-wire, but when it came to it I lost my nerve. As I stood there all alone in the deserted street, separated from my parents and brothers, a feeling of hopelessness came over me. Hitherto, I had known where they were and was sure in the knowledge that I would see them again soon. Family meant security, but now it was different: who could know when I would see them again? For many months past, I had faced the kind of danger and hardship I had learned to cope with, and I knew how to get by in familiar surroundings. Hiding, I was adept at, and when it came to running I was light on my feet. I had a certain confidence in my hiding and running skills, but that was no longer the right thing to do. This time it was different; it was a challenge, although long in the planning, I was not prepared for and which would require different skills and a different kind of courage, I was not sure I had. In the past I had to avoid people; they could never be trusted, be they German or Polish, they spelt danger and harm. Previously I had moved in the shadows, but now, should I come face to face with a German, I must not waver, and if challenged I would have to bluff it out, as there was no chance of escape.

All this raced through my mind and sent my heart throbbing as I wondered how I would cope with it all. I was reluctant to proceed, and stood as if frozen to the ground. I knew the "Aryan" streets were rife with danger for a boy like me, and I wanted to turn back. I should have stayed with my family in the camp where I belonged, and shared their fate, come what may. I despaired that I would be recognised on the street and wouldn't get far. How can one disguise such fear? All sorts of dire things went through my mind. I imagined that my middle name Teodor sounded Jewish and would give me away. I knew I looked like a boy from the ghetto, skinny and pale with sallow cheeks and protruding eyes as a result of months of malnutrition. Big eyes were considered a Jewish trait by Poles, who often spoke of "sad Jewish eyes," so I tried to keep them partly closed. I started to practice the "squinty-look" while still in the *Lager*, by getting into the habit of lowering my eyelids to make my eyes appear narrower. On the "Aryan" side your appearance became an obsession; your very life depended on it. Your looks could either betray you or save your life. I had to get a tight grip on myself, as time was ticking away and I had a crucial appointment to keep. To turn back now would be to admit defeat and dash any hope of survival. I had to make a determined effort to regain my composure. I tried to imagine that I was not Jewish, and further tried to avoid even "thinking Jewish." But that was not easy, considering where I had just come from. To give me confidence, I tried to focus on the more positive things I had in my favour, that would help me along. I kept repeating over and over again to myself, as I went, that I didn't look Jewish with my fair complexion and my blue eyes, which were not that big, that I possessed my Christian birth certificate, and most important, that I had my magic glue—with all of these advantages, I would surely get by.

Having steadied myself, I wiped away my tears and pulled my cloth cap down to shade my face. At last I began to inch forward in the direction of the railway station. On the way there, as I passed some steelworker's cottages, I was astounded to see that life was going on as normal. Here was this peaceful scene in front of my eyes that I could scarcely believe was real, as if there was no war on, and nothing had changed. Here people lived normal lives, and old men still tended their vegetable patches, as they had in the past. Boisterous children played noisily outside their homes; boys played on swings and girls skipped rope or hop-scotched on pavements. I had forgotten a normal world existed beyond the *Lager*. It seemed as if I had been locked away behind barbed-wire for as long as I can remember. I paused for a while out of sheer curiosity, hidden behind the bushes, just to observe the scene. I looked at the tranquil setting with envy. As a boy from the camp, I was too afraid and even ashamed to show my face. My world, though only two or three kilometres away, might just as well have been on a different planet from the one where these happy children played. I could have carried on watching them for much longer, but to keep to my schedule, I had to get moving and stop day-dreaming. Why, oh why, I wondered, did I have to be born Jewish?

I had a rendezvous arranged with my sister at the nearby railway station. Fela now went by the Polish name of Walerja Matera or Wala, as she liked to be called, for short. She had come from Warsaw together with her non-Jewish friend Bronia, short for Bronisława, who was to lead me to the place where I was to be sheltered. It was advisable for the two friends to keep apart by travelling separately, in case Wala was found out. My sister did, however, come along in a different coach, in case I didn't show up for some reason and she would have to get in touch with Mr. Radzik, our mutual contact. There was no other way for the family to keep in touch with my sister in Warsaw, and there was no other way for her to contact us. Bronia was a young Gentile woman whom Wala had befriended in Warsaw. She had undertaken to lead me to my destination, but not to let me travel at her side, and if I ran into any trouble along the way, it was tacitly understood that I would be on my own. Bronia's main task was to purchase my train ticket. It would have appeared rather suspicious for an 11-year-old boy (as I was, according to my false birth certificate) to be buying his own, and the presence of an adult also avoided the risk of having to talk and answer awkward questions. Rail travel was always hazardous, as stations were closely watched by the Gestapo, who often stood in the booking-hall, and the German Bahnschutz, the railway-police, accompanied every train. It was, however, a risk we had to take, as there was no other way of travelling long distances. While I was still on my own, as the station came into view in the distance, I made for some bushes to do all that was necessary to transform into an uncircumcised boy. I hadn't had anything to drink that day so I would not have to pass water, as this would have caused the glue to slowly dissolve. The later this procedure was performed, the better, because of its limited effectiveness. I could never be sure I would get a chance to do another application just when it became vital. I then slipped the tube of glue into a concealed pocket inside the lining of my peaked cap, which was the same as all Polish boys wore at the time. Satisfied that nothing was overlooked, I hurried to my rendezvous.

I no longer recall what the identifying signal was, but Bronia needed no clue to pick out a lone, hollow-eyed boy walking hesitantly towards the station. Bronia approached me and handed me a small "decoy" package to carry, wrapped in brown paper tied with string. This contained a slab of *słonina*, Polish-style solid bacon fat. Poles were very fond of this, but due to food shortages it was scarce during the war. I stood next to Bronia as she purchased my rail ticket. The purchase went off without any hitch and we left the waiting room, as it was safer not to stay in people's sight. After Bronia had slipped me the ticket, I kept my distance from her while waiting for the Warsaw train to arrive. I could hardly believe it when I first set eyes on my sister, whom I had not seen for so long. She was hovering around, keeping a protective lookout. We had not seen each other for almost two years, yet we didn't dare to greet each other, apart from a furtive nod, in case we were being watched. We could not be seen together, as I could have implicated her. We looked like brother and sister, but we had different surnames. When Jews were moving about in the "Aryan side" there was a basic rule to be observed: if one is stopped, the other walks on.

The Warsaw train was late in coming, and after a long time I saw the semaphore rise as the locomotive slowly drew into the station. Bronia and I boarded the same carriage, but at opposite ends, while "Wala" entered a different carriage, all according to plan. The train was packed to capacity, including standing passengers and German soldiers. Some compartments displayed the Reich's Eagle with extended wings, clutching a swastika in its talons, and this denoted that the carriage was reserved for German personnel. I waited for the train to move for what seemed like an eternity, while the German railway police went through each compartment checking documents and questioning passengers, and, if necessary, inspecting baggage. They were no doubt on the lookout for people with Jewish features, resistance men, and other "undesirables." Some of the German soldiers on the train appeared to be walking-wounded from the Russian Front. By now we knew that the Wehrmacht was getting the worse of it in the East. The compartments were all full, and I could not find a seat, so I was forced to stand in the corridor. This was the worst possible place, as I was directly in the path of the railway police and passengers walking up and down the train.

After a wait that seemed endless, the guard at last blew the whistle, the engine sounded a couple of blasts, as the train shuddered and jolted back and forth several times before pulling away. I breathed a sigh of relief as the steam engine gradually built up speed and began its journey to Warsaw. The familiar Polish rustic scene of endless pine forests rushed past, with the trees weighed down with fresh snow. Inevitably, my thoughts turned to the family I had just left behind, and to all the relatives taken away from this station, along this very track, in sealed cattle wagons, supposedly hurtling to the East, but in fact heading North, on their last journey. Like them, I had started on my way, but I had at least a chance of life, when I could so easily have been on the death-train to Treblinka were it not for the strategy of my devoted family and my dedicated sister, which had changed my destiny. To have stayed where I was, whether in the camp or at the brickyard, spelled nothing but doom—only Warsaw held out any hope of survival.

After we had been travelling for about an hour, I became aware of hostile glances in my direction from a tall, repulsive-looking man in civilian clothes with deep-set eyes. I felt his fixed stare from afar and guessed that he was Gestapo, from his tell-tale dark grey leather coat and brown felt hat. As far as secret police go, the Gestapo were not very subtle in their appearance. I suppose the intention was to intimidate and engender fear. When he crooked his forefinger at me, motioning me to him, I pretended not to see him. His gesture sent a cold shiver down my spine but I made no move, as if frozen to the ground. The Gestapo-man then took a few steps forward and I flinched as he barked *"Jude!"* at me. The startled passengers quickly moved aside to make room along the corridor. I thought, this is it, my number is up! My heart must have skipped a beat or two as I tried to make out that I had no idea what he was on about. He pushed me towards the end of the carriage, away from the inquisitive passengers, and pulled my cap off, thrusting it into my chest, as I recoiled backwards. I forgot that I should have removed my cap out of respect for a German. He then grabbed me by my shoulder with his paw-like hand and shook me to and fro several times, pointing at my package, wanting to know what was inside it. Pressing my fingers to my lips, I began to make a mumbling sound as if I couldn't speak. It was all part of the plan: should I at any time be challenged, I would pretend to be a mute. Without having to speak, I was less likely to incriminate myself. The brute then grabbed the parcel of *słonina* and ripped it open, shouting, "*Polnische Schweine, Verboten!*" Without being asked, I held up my birth certificate in my shaking hand. But he just pushed my hand aside dismissively, brazenly grasped my trousers with both his hands, and pulled them down with one firm tug! I instinctively covered my crotch with my hands as if out of embarrassment, and at the same time forced out a couple of sobs, hoping to arouse pity. The German took a good look, and after realising he had made a mistake, sheepishly stalked out of the carriage, having embarassed himself in front of the gawping passengers. I heaved a sigh of relief: the disguise had worked and stood the test! But it was a close call. Wala was in the next carriage, thankfully unaware of my encounter, but it must have been acutely distressing for Bronia, who was in the same carriage as me and must have seen it all. Soon after the ordeal was over, Bronia brushed past me along the corridor to give me a furtive wink and a warm nod of approval.[8]

There was a purpose, however implausible, to the slab of *słonina* that I carried with me. As pork is abhorrent to Jews, we hoped that by carrying it, it would add credence to my being "truly Polish," we thought, perhaps naïvely. For the same reason, Jews masquerading as Gentiles often chose to adopt distinctively Polish surnames, opting for names with the word "swine" forming part of the surname, like Świniarski

---

8   I asked my sister why Bronia should have wanted to help me, since she didn't seek any financial reward. The apparent reason for Bronia's sincerity was that, being of rather plain appearance, she had always found it difficult to socialise. Only Jewish friends were kind to her. We learned after the war that Bronia was herself taken prisoner during the 1944 Warsaw uprising, in which she took part. She was sent as forced labour to Germany, and, tragically, died in an Allied air raid.

(swine-keeper), as if no Jew could ever countenance such a name. There was rationing for most commodities, and trafficking in black-market goods from the country into the cities was strictly prohibited. Pigs and farm animals were meant to feed the Wehrmacht. However, providing there wasn't much involved, a German policeman would usually turn a blind eye to a young boy, especially a mute. A small amount of contraband *słonina* could also have helped to account for any nervousness on my part. I am still amazed at just how much thought and planning went into it all, leaving nothing to chance.

The journey onwards, in stops and starts, seemed to last forever, but in fact we had only been travelling for about three hours when the train stopped at yet another station. There were German soldiers lined up on the platform, armed with rifles. Some boarded the train and started to order young men and women off it, lining them up on the platform. It turned out to be a *łapanka,* a round-up, of able-bodied people to be sent to Germany as civilian labour. Realising what was afoot, Wala had the presence of mind to join several old peasant women, who wore typical floral country-style kerchiefs on their heads, huddling in a corner. Wala also put a headscarf on, to try to hide her face and her youth. But her eyes must have given her away, and she was ordered off the train, unlike the grey-haired old *babushkas* with their wrinkled, weather-beaten faces. Fortunately, Bronia, being petite and not of robust appearance, was not taken. Peering out of the train, I was beside myself, seeing my sister on the platform in an anguished state, pleading with the officer-in-charge to let her go. As the train pulled away, I saw my sister slowly disappear in the distance. I was overcome with anguish at the thought of being separated from her for good and all our carefully laid plans coming to nothing, but I tried not to show it, in case the Gestapo man reappeared. Wala was about to be taken to Germany for compulsory work, which would be a terrible blow to me. I would be forced to return to the camp, or worse still the brickyard, where it would be hard to survive in winter for any length of time.

For a young woman with the "right looks" like my sister, being caught in a round-up as an "Aryan" would normally be considered a stroke of good luck and a virtual guarantee of survival: it provided a meal ticket and a roof over one's head in Germany, and paradoxically, Germany was a safer place for Jews than Poland. Some young Jewish women in fact tried to get themselves snatched off the streets in this way. Unlike Poles, ordinary German civilians didn't have an obsession about Jews in their midst and were not as a rule on the lookout for them, and having the official status of *Ostarbeiter* (a worker from the East) afforded a certain measure of legitimacy. Ordinary Poles and other nationals, as opposed to political prisoners, were put to work in Germany as conscripted labour, to replace German manpower called up for war service. In the case of women this usually meant working in light industry or on a farm, and on the whole being treated reasonably well. Ironically, the only danger in towns and factories was from Allied bombing.

However, in the case of my sister, she had to at all costs avoid being taken to Germany, as this spelled disaster for me. When the train finally reached Warsaw, my final destination; Bronia broke the devastating news to me that I had nowhere to go. Perhaps she could have found out where the woman I was to be taken to lived, but without Wala and the regular payments I could not have remained there for long, and perhaps would not even have been taken in. At a loss as to what to do with me, Bronia decided to take me to see a mutual Jewish friend, Lola Blajberg, who lived in Wawer, outside Warsaw. Lola was employed as a maid by a well-to-do Polish family—under an assumed identity, of course. Lola knew me from home; she was one of three young women from Ostrowiec, including my cousin Franka, who were all passing for non-Jews, with false papers, in the Warsaw area.[9] It was prudent for the three close friends not to live together, but they kept in touch, helping each other out in any way they could, by sharing contacts and information, and even helping each other financially. Lola was a brunette, with striking good looks in a classic Jewish sort of way, so she always wore dark glasses to hide her large brown eyes and to attenuate her prominent nose. Lola became quite distressed at the sight of me at her door as Bronia broke the news to her. Poor Lola—what could she do with a Jewish boy on her hands when her own situation was, to say the least, chancy? My prospects looked pretty grim, and I faced the nightmare of having to return to where I had just come from. In the end it was decided to wait a couple of days, to see if by some miracle Wala returned. Lola meanwhile hid me in a spare room in her mistress's house and covered me over in

---

9   My cousin Franka Fajngold was snatched off the street in 1944 and taken to Germany as an "Aryan" for compulsory work. She was liberated there by the Americans the following year. After the war she made her home in New York, married Dov Sachter, and had a son, Joe. She has since passed away.

a bed with heavy feather-filled bedding, without the knowledge of the owners, who were conveniently absent at the time. Lola took a huge risk doing what she did; she was a true friend. Her kindness could have cost her her priceless job, or even more. And even if it was just a job, it was a job she could not have replaced easily, and one that also meant a roof over her head.

Although the bed in which I hid was the largest, most comfortable, and cleanest bed I had been in since the war had begun, I just couldn't sleep. My pillow was wet from weeping as I tried to cry myself to sleep, praying with all my heart for my sister to find some miraculous way of coming back for me.[10]

Meanwhile, Wala was taken with the other detainees from the train to an assembly point where they underwent medical checks to determine who was fit enough for compulsory work in Germany. This was carried out under the supervision of Red Cross observers, to ensure fair treatment. My sister had to somehow get out of the Germans' clutches for my sake. She wept all through the night, knowing that her eyes tended to become red and puffy when she cried. She had a bit of a cold anyway, so she deliberately coughed a lot through the night, trying to aggravate her throat and lungs. By morning, during the medical check-up, she pleaded with the German doctor in a hoarse voice in front of the Red Cross officials. She explained that she had to look after her chronically sick widowed mother, who would surely die without her care and attention, and there would be no one left to look after her young brother. The German doctors may have taken this into account when they declared Walerja Matera had failed the medical examination—my sister was not fit enough to serve the *Vaterland*!

Early the next day, as I was lying motionless under the weighty bedding, the door creaked open and Lola put her head through to give me the thrilling news that my sister was waiting for me outside the house. I could hardly believe it—it was a miracle! I quickly threw off the bedding and dashed outside. My sister and I fell into each other's arms, for I was now able to embrace her for the first time since she had escaped from the ghetto almost two years earlier. We were both elated. I would

---

10   Lola Blajberg also survived the war and married an old friend of hers from Ostrowiec, Shlomo Politanski. She became a nurse sister and lived in Hadera, Israel. Lola was childless and has also since passed away.

now be able to proceed to the safe-house my sister had arranged for me. As I looked pale and thin, like a boy from the ghetto, the young ladies decided to put a kitchen stool over my head to hide my face. I thus skipped along the streets behind Wala and Lola, all the way from Wawer to Anin, keeping the *taboretka* balanced on my head, until we reached the place where I was to be hidden in the confines of a small room, with a wardrobe for a hiding place.

CHAPTER 10

My Guardian Angel

I had lost all sense of time when I was at the brickyard or in the *Lager*. There was no way of keeping track of hours or days; there were no diaries or clocks and every day was like the next. We more or less judged the time of day by our wretched routine—especially "soup-time," as everything else revolved round that. I am only able to recall events by the season, by whether it was summer or winter. I know that it was the middle of winter when I set out, as I put on all the clothes I had in order to keep warm. It was bitterly cold when I reached my destination after my nightmare train journey.

The Warsaw Ghetto no longer existed when I arrived in the city. It had been razed to the ground in the spring, during the Warsaw Ghetto Uprising that began on 19 April 1943, after a smaller, initial revolt in January. The cynical Nazis deliberately timed their final assault on the ghetto to coincide with the eve of Passover, the festival that symbolises freedom from slavery. The Nazis were sticklers for perverse symbolism. The next day was Hitler's birthday, and the obliteration of the ghetto was intended as a special gift from Himmler to his Führer. By that point, the desperate defenders were few in number and poorly armed, yet they managed to hold off the German onslaught for some time. In fact, it took more than four weeks for the Nazis to put down the uprising, using overwhelming firepower until the entire ghetto was reduced to rubble, together with the people who resolved to die fighting rather than on their knees. My sister had witnessed the conflagration from outside the ghetto wall. She told me that she couldn't stop herself from going almost daily to shed a tear and pay homage to those brave men and women.

One day in particular stood out in her memory. It was Easter Sunday. The uprising had been going on for days; it was spring, and the sun was shining as the ghetto was dying, engulfed in fire and smoke. There was a festive air about the "Aryan" streets as the devout people of Warsaw emerged from their churches dressed in their finery, cheerfully exchanging the customary Easter greeting "Christ is Risen." Girls in traditional dress paraded up and down the fashionable boulevards as they always did at Easter; it was no different than any other year. The girls showed off their colourful outfits, with intricately embroidered aprons over their velvety skirts. Each girl had a floral chaplet resting on her plaited flaxen hair, with a posy of spring flowers in one hand and in the other a small wicker basket full of colourfully painted Easter eggs. After confession, and free of all sin, the worshippers strolled leisurely in the bright sunshine, under a blue sky. Then they all converged on the ghetto, eager to see the *auto-da-fé*: the spectacle of Jews burnt alive. "Christ is Risen!"—but the Jews burn to a cinder! Glory Be!

My sister described the carnival-like atmosphere on the streets, all of the merry-making that took place to the accompaniment of raucous music emanating from a nearby spring fair where people were having fun. The merry-go-round kept turning, as it always did at Easter. Meanwhile, animated spectators stood gawping from a safe distance as the Germans pounded the ghetto with artillery shells and set it ablaze with flame-throwers, block by block. Jewish mothers, crazed with grief and shielding infants in their arms, were seen leaping from tenement buildings to certain death. The entire ghetto was like an inferno; raging flames swallowed everything in their path. Fiery sparks and ashes rose to the heavens, and grey particles whirled and danced in the air; some soared skywards into infinity, others glided gently down to settle on the pavements outside the ghetto wall—the only way to freedom. The victims' bodies may have burned, but their spirits were not consumed nor defeated, my sister firmly believed, as she stood back behind the German cordon, trying her utmost to hide her emotions and the tears welling up in her eyes. Wala felt as if something within her was dying at the same time as the ghetto died. She was desperately hoping for a word of sympathy or a gesture of support for those consumed by German flame-throwers, but none was heard. She had to be careful not to betray her own identity, and she waited in vain for one brave soul to cry out: "Stop! Shame on you! Those dying inside those walls are fellow citizens and human beings like us!" But all she could see was glee on the Poles' faces, and all she could hear ringing in her ears was the phrase "The bugs are burning in the ghetto," repeated down the line of spectators.

By the time I reached Warsaw, there were—in theory—no Jews left. The entire area of the former ghetto had been reduced to rubble, and the debris cleared and sifted for valuables by slave labourers before the area was ploughed under to make way for the proposed Adolf Hitler Park. My sister had arranged shelter for me in Anin with an elderly Christian lady; *Pani,* or Madame, Gozdzialska, who lived with her chronically-ill niece Wanda, whom she took care of. Anin was near Praga, a working-class district of Warsaw on the right bank of the Vistula. In contrast to Praga, Anin was a prosperous, leafy place, where some of the more affluent had their summer retreats. *Pani* Gozdzialska's modest abode hardly fitted that description, though it was situated in a delightfully green area, dotted with silver birch and pine trees. *Pani* was a spinster of around seventy years of age, with silver-grey hair tied in a bun at the back. She always wore a faint smile on her gentle, deeply-lined face, which reflected the hard life she had coped with. She was a small, frail-looking figure who nevertheless possessed immense vitality for her age. Claiming descent from a Russo-Polish noble family, she spoke Russian fluently, though the language was taboo. It was fairly obvious that she had known better days. *Pani* was well-educated and expressed herself in an effusive manner, waving her hands about in the air like an ageing, dignified, stage actress who had come down in the world. In private, she was fond of mixing in with her Polish the odd wise Russian folk-expression—she had many of them.

Her background was no doubt a legacy from Czarist Russia, which had occupied a large chunk of Poland prior to the First World War, after which the country regained its independence, ending over a hundred and twenty years of partition and foreign rule, when there was no Poland on the map. *Pani* often talked about the "Russian soul," full of praise for the country's talented people: their culture, their musical tradition, and their flair for song and dance. Oh, how she longed for them to come and drive the hated "Swabians," as she called the Germans, out of Poland. At times I wondered if she was talking about the same people that had so oppressed the Jews under the Czars, and who were responsible for all the terrible pogroms that my father remembered from his youth and often spoke about. Looking back, I don't think *Pani* was politically minded: she praised "Mother Russia" but was not pro-Soviet; she was a devout Catholic. She longed for Poland to be free again, and only Russia, she believed, possessed the might to defeat Nazi Germany.

Pani Gozdzialska was an incredibly brave lady and I came to love her dearly; she put her life at risk for me. Since she was poor, the money offered may have been a consideration, but it wasn't her main motivation. First and foremost, she did it out of human decency and Christian consciousness. She was a person sensitive to the suffering of others, and regarded it as her moral duty to help those in distress. *Pani* had fallen on hard times, and the money for my keep must have been a help to her. She lived in a small rented flat in a building housing four families, with us occupying one of the two first-floor flats. *Pani* had never had much contact with her neighbours, and now had even less, because of my presence there. The entire flat consisted of a small living room and a tiny bedroom with a sloping ceiling. Although filled with clutter, the place was always well-scrubbed. The bathroom and toilet were outside the flat, on the landing, which presented a problem for me, and I rarely made use of it, as I had to avoid the neighbours. I had to make do with a bowl of water and a chamber-pot. In one corner of the living room there was a tiled stove for cooking, which provided the only heat for the flat. In another corner stood a treadle sewing machine; *Pani* had been taking in alteration work from a Jewish tailor in Praga, but this work had dried up when the Jews were confined to the Warsaw Ghetto. The lady of the house slept in the living room on a sofa-bed, and I shared the other room with her incapacitated niece Wanda, sleeping on the floor, curled up in a corner with a blanket.

Wanda was about thirty-five years of age, but looked older. Sadly, she was deformed and suffered from epilepsy; she also had lung trouble and coughed a lot. She was short and square, with a hunched back, and her large head and goitre neck sat on wide shoulders. Looking back, I see that Wanda was quite intelligent but rather misguided. She was moody and didn't speak well of Jews, which was nothing unusual. She believed the old canard that Jews use the blood of Christian children for matza served at the Passover Seder meal, which I said was just too silly for words. "Well, If they no longer do, they certainly used to," she would say. I was taught from childhood that the blood of any animal is absolutely forbidden to Jews, although other religions permitted it. What got me worried was when she said that "because Jews rejected Jesus Christ, the Lord rejected the Jews, damning them to eternal purgatory, and so they will never get to heaven." I hoped this didn't apply to me, "As I quite like baby Jesus," I told her. Wanda was obsessed with religion, and hardly ever talked about anything else. Her sentiments must have stemmed from her strong Catholic convictions, which, as preached from the pulpit, fostered animosity to Jews. She would never admit to Jesus having been a Jew. "Even if he was," she said, "the same cannot be true of the Virgin Mary!" Wanda was embittered and kept brooding over her disability, which was understandable. She was practically bedridden, and spent a lot of time drowsing. When awake, she sat up on her iron-framed bed, reclining against feather pillows set beneath a large gilded cross on the wall above her head, whispering the rosaries. Or she would mutter under her breath, carping about me, which added to my misery and loneliness. *Pani* never admonished her niece for her bad behaviour, no doubt making allowances for her condition. Besides, she never knew the full extent of it and I never let on; I considered myself more than fortunate to be there at all.

In one corner of the room stood a small table covered with an embroidered white cloth that Wanda used as a communion table to kneel against when in prayer. On it stood a gilt crucifix surrounded by devotional statuettes and a small vase of faded artificial flowers. The walls were adorned with images of saints and of the Virgin Mother and Child. An icon of the Black Madonna wearing a gold crown took centre stage. The Madonna of Częstochowa was revered as the Queen of Poland. But the most dramatic to me was an effigy of Christ on the Cross, with blood dripping down his face from beneath a crown of thorns, which I could hardly take my eyes off of when I caught sight of it. This, together with a benevolent-looking Jesus holding forth in the palm of his hand an exposed bright red heart made me feel uneasy and guilty for being a Jew. I viewed the cross with suspicion and fear, aware that Jews associated it with endless persecution over the centuries. If we were expecting a visit from the doctor for Wanda, I would sit as quite as a dormouse, hunched up behind a wardrobe that was placed across a corner of the room, hardly daring to breathe. Or if there was the risk of a police search, I would sit with my knees drawn up inside the wardrobe. Because of the neighbours down below, I spoke in whispers at all times and didn't move about the flat unnecessarily. I wore no shoes and walked on tiptoe, mainly confined to the bedroom, as the living room was near the landing and the neighbours.

Spring had meanwhile arrived, and sometimes at night I could stand on a stool in front of a raised window that was safe for me to look out of to breathe the fresh evening air. The air was heavily scented with lilac, and in early summer with the sweet jasmine that grew in profusion in this leafy area. I longed to go outside, but could never venture out to enjoy the freedom. This, for me, was the hardest part of being locked away like this, for I longed to go outdoors. There was little food in the house, but compared to where I had come from, I had little to complain about. There was bread–though never enough for a ravenous growing boy, and occasionally, *Pani* would bring home a few grammes of costly salami or *słonina*, which would go to the bedridden Wanda first, since animal fat was considered good for lubricating the lungs and relieving a tubercular cough. Dinner usually consisted of one dish, either a thick soup or a stew known as *bigos*, a traditional Polish dish of sauerkraut with bits of meat, usually rabbit, and pieces of sausage for special occasions. These had to last for two or three days, with little in the way of protein to go into the pot. Wanda ate very little, and *Pani* even less, but I made up for them.

Pani Gozdzialska was an active person, always busy doing things. Apart from going to church, she sometimes disappeared for days on end, and I never discovered for what reason. I suspect that she may have been helping Jews somewhere, perhaps by bringing them food, but she would never talk about it. I was not happy at being left alone with the petulant Wanda, as she resented my being there, and I was always anxious for *Pani* to return. Although I felt sorry for Wanda, I avoided speaking with her unnecessarily, as our conversations invariably ended in a squabble or her cutting me off. I tried to keep to myself, just living with my thoughts, brooding over my confinement. I daydreamed about the family I had left behind in the camp, concerned for their wellbeing. I only had Sundays to look forward to, when my sister would come to visit.

I was bored to tears, and spent the long days reading anything I could lay my hands on. Hence, my literacy and general knowledge improved. My entire education had amounted to just one year at school before the war and some private tuition and violin lessons early on in the ghetto, but at least I could read fluently. Most of the books available at the Gozdzialska home were of a religious nature. It was, of course, important to familiarise myself with the Catechism for children, in case I was ever questioned on aspects of the Catholic religion and made to recite prayers. I rehearsed the basic prayers with *Pani,* learning the *Pacierz* (Our Father), which every child recites, by heart, hands clasped, kneeling down beside the bed, before climbing in. I received a lot of help and advice on church worship from her. It was also important to learn about Polish feasts and customs. There were many of them, mostly of a religious nature but also of pagan origin, as well as folk traditions. I now had the opportunity to cultivate the Warsaw dialect with the two ladies of the house; my more rural accent was somewhat different from the Warsaw lilt. What's more, I had become used to chatting in Yiddish in the ghetto, as it was all around me then, and as a result my "Jewishness" had become more apparent. Now I tried to guard against any Jewish mannerisms. For instance, *Pani* explained that talking with one's hands was considered a Jewish trait by Poles. One slip of the tongue or wrong nuance would be enough to give me away if I had to come out into the open and act the part of a Catholic boy. I could never be sure I would sit out the war where I was.

In the apartment I found a big stack of back copies, spanning several years, of a periodical from before the war. They contained stories of a religious nature and reports on major events from around the world, as well as articles of general interest. It was like a Catholic *Readers' Digest*, combined with *National Geographic*, and partly illustrated. I read these avidly from cover to cover, gleaning information about far-off places I could only dream of. A world where boys like me had fun running free with their friends, went to school, kicked a football, breathed fresh air, and enjoyed the freedom I had been deprived of. I had never been very studious; I just loved the outdoors and adventure. Now I had no choice. There was nothing for me to do but read, and the more I read the more I hungered for knowledge. Learning things, like that America was named in honour of the navigator and explorer Amerigo Vespucci, although he was not the one to discover the continent, was fascinating for me. I was eager to learn about the world events and upheavals of the thirties. Apart from the rise of Hitler, there was the civil war in Spain, the aerial devastation of Guernica, the brutal Italian attack on Abyssinia, the Sino-Japanese conflict, and more. The publication ended, to my disappointment, with the outbreak of the war. Some of the events I read about I had heard my father talk about at home, but they had never meant much to me—I was too young and happy-go-lucky. Now, however, I tried to absorb all I could. I was particularly fascinated by Great Britain and its Empire. Looking at a world atlas, I would see this little island marked in red, and virtually two-fifths of the rest of the world's land was shaded in the same color. I just couldn't understand how such a small country, much smaller than Poland, could rule over a vast part of the planet containing a quarter of the world's population! I also remembered that some of the nicer things in our home bore the inscription "Made in England," when I hadn't really known what it meant. I read about England's frequent floods, and imagined the island to be always under water. The more I read, the more curious I became about the island nation. Hitherto, I'd had little knowledge of England, other than what I had read in children's adventure stories, and those were invariably connected with the sea. I had never even set eyes on the sea-shore!

To augment the household income, *Pani* located some regular work for me to do at her house. It entailed filling filter-cigarettes with tobacco. This was done with a simple device designed to inject the tobacco into the long filters, called *gilzy*. Long filters were fashionable at the time. There was a knack to filling these blanks so as not to damage the fine cigarette paper, and in getting the density just right, not too soft or too firm: the former would affect the shape of the cigarette, and the latter would use up too much tobacco, an expensive commodity in wartime. I was allocated a certain quantity of tobacco to fill a given amount of blank filters, and learned to do the job properly, but after a while this work dried up as things became scarce.

I was always concerned that if push came to shove and she was confronted by some bullying German, the unpredictable Wanda would give me away. Had *Pani* been taken away, as she surely would have if a Jew was found hiding in her home, Wanda would have been lost without her, with no one left to take care of her, but simple logic doesn't always apply when one is in such a state of mind. On my part, I tried hard to be helpful and endear myself to Wanda, but she wouldn't have it and snapped back at me. During her epileptic bouts, which were fairly frequent, if *Pani* was out I did all I could to help her. I tried to limit her uncontrollable convulsions, to keep her from falling out of bed and hurting herself, or from swallowing her tongue. I watched *Pani*, and she told me what to do in the event of her absence. After every fit, as Wanda calmed down and slowly came to, she would look at me askance with her eyes half-closed, and would shrink away from me as if I carried the plague. I would never own up to helping her. I could have been of more help yet, when she was conscious, but she preferred to struggle on without me when she had a choice. And so the long, dreary days and weeks passed, with me sharing a room with an unfortunate sick person who harboured a grudge against me that I could never understand. The faith I was born into seemed to trouble her more than the ongoing risk of my presence in the household.

My sister, meanwhile, lived and worked in Warsaw doing odd jobs, usually domestic, or working as a waitress in a café. Whenever danger threatened, she would move on and try her luck at something different, in another part of town. On one occasion, Wala went to visit a girlfriend who was, like her, living with false papers. Her friend resided in a suburb of Warsaw she was not very familiar with. It was prudent to always remain inconspicuous—by avoiding ostentatious clothes, for instance. Not to draw attention to oneself was rather difficult in the case of my sister, who possessed such striking good looks. She tended to attract admiring glances.

As Wala emerged from the station she got somewhat disorientated, and a Polish policeman noticed her and ran up to her, saying, "You look lost," and asked if he could be of any help. One had to avoid Polish policemen at all costs. Called *granatowe*, or "Navy-Blues", on account of their navy-blue uniforms, they tended to be on the lookout for undercover Jews, anxious to strip them of their possessions, as they believed that people on the run were inclined to carry their valuables on them. The policeman saluted her smartly in the soldierly manner, by putting his index and middle fingers to the cellulose peak of his cap. The Polish two-finger salute symbolises Honour and Fatherland, but his intentions were neither honourable nor in the cause of his mother-country.

Wala courteously declined any help, insisting she knew perfectly well where she was going. Nevertheless, the "navy-blue" latched on to her and walked beside her, and whenever she turned the corner or changed direction he did the same, claiming he was going the same way. After walking for some distance with her, he carried on pestering her; asking impertinent and personal questions. Then, out of the blue, he accused her of being Jewish and went on to blatantly demand *schmaltz* (Yiddish for chicken-fat, and Warsaw slang for "'Jewish" pay-off money). "Me, a Jew? That's hilarious!" she laughed it off. After she persistently refused him any money, he retorted, "All right, then, have it your way, young lady. In that case, you will have to accompany me to the station, where we have ways of establishing who you really are, and you will live to regret it!"

My sister had no choice but to call his bluff and agree, saying, "In that case I will report to your superiors that you tout for bribes!" These were words no Jew would have been expected to dare utter to a policeman. As they carried on walking towards the police station, he sidled up to her and asked sheepishly what she had inside her package. It instinctively occurred to her that perhaps she might be able to seize on his interest in the package to shake him off. The more inquisitive he became, the more tightly she held on to it. After more badgering, she offered to give him some money out of her purse, just to be rid of him, but said, "On no account can I part with the package," clutching it ever closer to her chest. His sheer greed whetted his appetite all the more, and he swallowed the bait.

In the end, she made it appear as if she wavered, then at last she agreed to hand it over to him, but only on condition that he let her go, to which he readily agreed. They were by then in clear view of the precinct, where policemen were milling around outside. So as not to arouse the suspicions of his colleagues, he suggested that they say goodbye amicably, like old friends, in front of the police station. When it was time to part company, Wala handed him the package and he thanked her profusely, with every reason to be well pleased with the outcome. As he took leave of her, the "Navy-Blue" dipped his head, kissed her hand, and clicked his heels in the best courtly manner. My sister promptly fled the area and returned home, without even visiting her friend.

The policeman no doubt rushed back to the privacy of the station, eager to check out his haul, only to find that apart from a small gift for her friend, the *sac de toilette* contained nothing more than a nightgown, a hairbrush, and other cosmetic items—the sort of things a young lady needs for spending a weekend with a friend!

My sister (right) with Lola Blajberg on a wartime Warsaw street. Wala seems to be carrying a little packet similar to what got her off the hook!

As a covert Jew moving about "Aryan" Warsaw, one lived on the edge of a precipice, in constant fear of betrayal and at the mercy of Polish extortionists and informers. Called *szmalcownicy,* from the Polish word *szmalec* for grease, these scoundrels stalked their prey on the streets of the capital, sometimes operating in gangs of two or more, hunting down people of Jewish appearance to blackmail them or even turn them in. These dregs of humanity referred to their Jewish quarry as "cats." I've never understood the connection—perhaps it was just underworld slang. Wala thought that she had on occasion been tailed by these *shmaltzovniks,* but she somehow managed to shake them off by disappearing into a crowd or jumping onto the running board of a tram car. Or they simply gave up their pursuit, perhaps unsure if they had made a mistake.

Every day brought with it new threats and dangers. One took a terrible risk by venturing outdoors, dreading the tap on the shoulder, and when one reached the relative safety of the home, if one had a home to go to, there was the constant worry of having been followed, or the ever-present fear of denunciation by a neighbour, followed by a knock at the door—the stress was relentless.

One day, during the spring of 1943, Wala sensed danger, and found herself once more in a dicey situation, having to quickly look for another place to stay. She had a useful Polish contact who, knowing she was Jewish, had helped her out in the past. This time she recommended her to a distant relative who was looking for a housekeeper. The place turned out to be in the vicinity of Małkinia and the death-camp of Treblinka, a fair distance from Warsaw. Wala was fully aware of the notoriety of this place, but as it was no longer operational after the October 1943 revolt in which prisoners had destroyed one crematorium and many had escaped, and she needed a job and a place to stay. Her new employers turned out to be a bicycle repair-shop proprietor, his wife, and their young daughter. The wife was a schoolmistress, and an exceptionally nice person. Her elderly mother also lived with them, and the man of the house strongly disliked her. He turned out to be an unscrupulous egomaniac, always full of himself. Wala took an instant dislike to him, calling him "Alpha"—the ultimate scoundrel. I never discovered his real name, as my sister only referred to him by that epithet.

As soon as Wala arrived, she realised why Alpha needed her. Up in the loft of an adjoining annexe, he was sheltering a wealthy Jewish couple from Warsaw with a young son. As he was getting handsomely paid for this, he could afford to hire someone to look after them. Wala was to prepare their food daily and take it up to the loft, remove their waste regularly, and generally take care of their needs. The first time Wala went up to the loft and came face-to-face with the frightened, anguished family, she was shocked and taken aback, just as they were, but this soon changed into the feeling of mutual affinity that arose when one Jew met another in such dire circumstances. While they were a charming enough family, it occurred to my sister that by staying in this position she was endangering her own life even more, and so she planned to leave. Jews in hiding were often blackmailed or even betrayed by jittery neighbours, afraid of collective punishment. Alpha was too unstable and too risky a character to trust, and she was afraid of staying there. He would cope without her, if he had to. It was Wala's opinion that the cad only looked to the financial reward, and was unprepared for the danger and inconvenience that comes with sheltering Jews. It would have been wise to leave, Wala knew, but as she grew fond of the hapless family, she decided to stay on for a while to help out. Whenever she went up to the loft, she would sit for some time with the despondent couple and try as best she could to cheer them up. She reassured them that their confinement would soon come to an end, as the tide of war had turned decisively against the Germans. The couple had been wealthy and accustomed to the good life of pre-war Warsaw, and it was difficult for them to cope with the hardship of their cramped and miserable confinement. Alpha's elderly mother-in-law did the shopping for them, and as she was not endowed with too much sense, she spent money freely on delicacies from under the counter which were scarce and expensive. The old lady kept going back to the same shops, buying quantities of food, and carelessly spending sums of money difficult to justify for a small household in wartime. This was bound, sooner or later, to arouse the suspicion of the shopkeepers and inquisitive neighbours.

One day, the bicycle shop proprietor sent his apprentice home to Wala. The boy came riding a bicycle from the repair shop and brought with him a picnic basket with food for his wife and little girl, who were spending a few days away in the country. The boy came with instructions from his boss for Wala to take the food to his wife, and as it was a fair distance to cover both ways by bicycle in a day, Alpha suggested that she spend the night in the country with his wife. She did so, and the next morning made an early start, eager to return home, concerned for the Jewish family in her care whom she had left behind the day before. On reaching home, she was horrified to discover that the Jewish couple with their son, as well as the mother-in-law, had all been killed. Their bodies were slumped over the rubbish dump in the back yard, where they had been shot dead by the Gestapo.

Alpha lost no time in blaming his mother-in-law for the tragedy, on the grounds that she had invited suspicion on the household with her indiscreet spending. He claimed that she must have been informed on by a local shopkeeper. After this revolting crime, Wala immediately ran away, suspecting that Alpha was behind the heinous deed. It was fatal for Jews to keep a lot of money with them: it was sheer greed that had led to the crime. Wala discovered from the woman who had recommended her that it was indeed Alpha who had betrayed them to the Gestapo, accusing the old lady of sheltering the Jewish family in the loft without his knowledge. It seemed fairly obvious that Alpha planned the blood bath for that very day by sending Wala away to stay with his wife and child, who were conveniently absent. Had Wala been there when the Gestapo arrived, he could not have claimed he had no knowledge of Jews in his household or hidden in the outhouse, and he had nothing to gain by having Wala killed as well, which she would have been had she been in the house when the Gestapo arrived. The grasping Alpha had it all planned: he had thought up a way of cheating the Jewish couple out of their money and doing away with the ongoing risk of harbouring them. Simultaneously, it gave him a chance to disposing of the old lady he detested. He realised Wala would not be a burden to him—he could tell her to leave whenever he wished, as she had been hired for the sole purpose of looking after the Jewish family. After they were gone, her services would no longer be required. Had he intended to carry on sheltering the family and been content not to steal all their money, he could have prevented the old lady from inviting suspicion, but he saw an opportunity in her indiscreet behaviour to arrange that no suspicion should fall on him. By pointing an accusing finger at others, he allayed any suspicion his wife may have had of him being implicated in her mother's death.

Once she was back in Warsaw, where she found another job, Wala came to see me in Anin from time to time, usually on a Sunday morning, her day off, when she paid the dear *Pani* for my keep. Occasionally she brought me a special treat, a *millefeuille,* my favourite pastry, from a noted Warsaw patisserie. *Pani* Gozdzialska was almost destitute, and the money Wala gave her helped to pay the rent and to arrange for Wanda's medical treatment and drugs, which were very expensive in wartime. At the same time, my sister filled me in on her latest escapades and the daily hazards of moving about the streets of Warsaw. Occasionally she brought news of the family, by way of Mrs. Radzik from Ostrowiec, who made the journey specifically to bring messages and money from Father.

Mrs. Radzik did her best to reassure my sister that they were safe and well, although we knew how much they must be suffering in the camp. Her husband, the locomotive driver, continued to have contact with my father and brothers at their workplaces, and he carried on helping all he could. In the early days Wala used to come to Ostrowiec and steal into the ghetto to visit the family. This became too dangerous by the middle of 1942, and thus it was Mrs. Radzik who travelled to Warsaw instead. While it must be recalled that it was Mrs. Radzik who had turned me away from her door, she did help in other ways with great courage if the task involved didn't put her family at risk, and was kind enough to act as a courier.

During my time in Anin, my sister survived a number of hair-raising experiences. At one point she was employed by a patisserie-shop owner, a *Volksdeutsche,* and his attractive Polish wife. Wala worked in their home, at the rear of the shop, as a live-in maid. After a while, she somehow sensed that her German employer began to suspect her, but as he was very much under the thumb of his assertive wife, he didn't dare to interfere in the domestic affairs. The lady of the house appreciated having a good, hard-working maid in exchange for just board and lodging, with no questions asked. However, the wife may have likewise begun to suspect her, maybe because she had to act evasively at times. But with the maid posessing the "right looks" as well as the necessary identity papers, and with her husband being German, she probably felt she was not taking much of a risk.

One day, Wala answered the doorbell at the back of the shop when the lady of the house was out. As she slowly opened the door to see who it was, a man wedged his foot in the gap, and other people appeared out of nowhere, forcing their way in. Wala was horrified: she had been specifically instructed not to open the door to anyone, and had thought she was only opening it wide enough to see who was there. As it turned out, the proprietor of the shop had apparently received telephone threats from people who wished to punish him for his German ancestry, and these intruders were here to make good on the threats. There were three young men and a woman, brandishing revolvers and threatening to shoot. Then they dragged her *Volksdeutsche* employer in from the shop. Realising the seriousness of the situation, my sister pleaded with the intruders that she was only the maid and not a German, but it made no difference, and they were both tied up. The gunmen declared themselves to be AK resistance fighters who had come to "settle the score with the *Krauts,*" but said the captives' lives might be spared if they handed over all their money and valuables. Wala was afraid the intruders would shoot them anyway, even if they got what they wanted, believing that she too was a German collaborator.

Wala was in a terrible dilemma, and thought of divulging her Jewish identity and offering to join their group. But then, what if they were just common criminals, pretending to be the resistance? There were enough of those bandits about. Or, if they really were Home Army members, most were anti-Jewish and would probably refuse to take her with them. Consequently, she would have blown her cover to her employer, shown ingratitude, and confirmed his suspicion that she was Jewish. As a consequence, she would be arrested, or at best forced to leave his household. On the other hand, if she kept quiet, the Gestapo would come to interrogate her and detect her false ID card. Her *Volksdeutsche* employer would probably claim that Wala was part of the plot, as she had let them into the house, though she was warned not to. It was inevitable that she would have to pay with her life, either for being in league with the gunmen or as a Jew.

While all these scenarios raced through her mind, my sister realised she was in a no-win situation and decided to hold back and say nothing. The gunmen, having taken the cash from the till and ransacked the house for valuables, leaving Wala and her employer on the floor, gagged and with their hands tied behind their backs. When they were completely done, they ran out, as they had come in, through the rear door. The girl robber, as an after-thought, turned back and snatched Wala's shoulder bag, which had been hanging in the entrance hall. Inside the bag, apart from her money, Wala had her vitally important *Kennkarte*. This spelled disaster for her; the Gestapo might never believe her identity card was taken, assume that she had no papers at all, and automatically suspect her of being Jewish.

My sister was in a desperate situation from which she couldn't possibly extricate herself. Lying tied-up on the floor as she was, she was hopelessly trapped! Later that afternoon, her employer's wife returned, untied them both, and immediately called the Polish police. Wala thought now would be the time to make a run for it, before the police arrived, but she realised she wouldn't get far without identity papers. Had she still had her fake *Kennkarte*, she would certainly have done so. There was no alternative now but to stay put and face the consequences. Following the Polish "Navy-Blue" police, the sinister Gestapo also arrived and began to question Wala, to ascertain if there had been any collusion between her and the gunmen. Fortunately, the *Volks-*

deutsche's wife came strongly to my sister's defence, stating that she had inspected her papers before she was hired, and they were in order. This helped satisfy the Gestapo, at least for the time being. However, she was ordered to report to the *Kommandantur* the next morning for further questioning and to make a full statement. Again she thought of making a run for it before morning, which seemed the obvious thing to do: "run while you can" was the golden wartime rule. Again she chose not to: although she dreaded having to face the Gestapo again, she knew that there was no other way of getting a replacement ID card, without which she was lost.

The next morning Wala made a full statement to the Gestapo and tried to be helpful and impress them with her precise description of the event, knowing that they would cross-check it with that of the proprietor. She cursed the bandits for stealing everything she had: "I'm just a simple housemaid and I'm not in the least worried about my documents, but the thieving swine stole my money, all my hard-earned cash!" she complained bitterly. The Gestapo officer in charge believed her and didn't give her a hard time. To her utter amazement, he told her she would be issued with a replacement *Kennkarte*, subject to further enquiries. She gave them the exact same fabricated details contained in her false document, hoping they would have no way of checking it out; she couldn't think of anything different. Meanwhile, the Gestapo provided her with a temporary certificate to tide her over until her replacement *Kennkarte* is issued. She was asked to provide passport photographs and to report to the registration office where her fingerprints were taken. Soon after, she collected the genuine article to replace her stolen fake! What seemed like a rotten bit of luck that could have led to disaster turned out to be a true blessing in disguise.

Meanwhile in Anin, one early morning in the spring of 1944 a Gestapo car with a loudspeaker mounted on the roof criss-crossed the streets of Anin, which is built on the grid system. It declared a curfew with immediate effect, ordering everyone to stay off the streets and to remain indoors. The announcement went something like this:

> ACHTUNG! ACHTUNG! (Then in Polish) *"Everyone must stay indoors until further notice. Anyone disobeying orders will be severely punished. BANDITS and CRIMINALS are hiding in your area. A*

*house-to-house search is about to be carried out. Anyone found shel-
tering or assisting these criminals will be shot."*

In Nazi jargon, "Bandits" and "Criminals" were Resistance fighters
and Jews, respectively. The announcement sent a cold shiver down my
spine; they were about to start a sweep for Jews in hiding! I had to act
quickly. The wardrobe would be useless; it would never stand up to a
search. If I ran outside during the curfew, I was bound to be caught and
shot. The curfew was in force, and there was nothing to do but remain
indoors and openly try to brazen it out. All I could do was disguise my
circumcision, as I had before, and await my fate. There had been raids
from time to time, but on a smaller scale. This was to be a widespread,
systematic, manhunt, which I learned was a result of the assassination
of the German police chief Franz Kutschera by the Resistance in neighbouring Praga, where the AK Underground was particularly active.

When it dawned on her what was happening, Wanda, who never addressed me by my name, went into hysterics, shouting: "You must leave
now, before you get us all killed!" *Pani*, on the other hand, went pale in
the face but remained composed, as if resigned to her fate; she never
feared for her own safety. Ignoring Wanda, who was beside herself, she
said calmly, "Stefciu," as she called me when she wanted to emphasise
something, "You must do as you see fit to save yourself." She did not say
whether I should try to run or stay, and I knew she would never turn me
away. She gave me a blessing, raising her hand to make the sign of the
cross above my forehead.

I was afraid that when the intimidating Germans appeared, Wanda
would not be able to contain herself. It would have been far better to
avoid a face-to-face encounter with Wanda present, but it was too late
now, and it would be too risky to make a dash for it—the streets were
swarming with Germans. Peering out of the window, I could see soldiers
in steel helmets, with weapons in their hands as if ready for action. An
officer was yelling out commands as small groups of soldiers fanned out
in different directions. Having taken the necessary precaution I had not
needed to resort to for some time, ever since my encounter with the
Gestapo-man on the Ostrowiec to Warsaw train, all I could do was pray
to God that no Gestapo or SS men would come into our home. I considered ordinary Wehrmacht soldiers less menacing, and not so used to
tracking down Jews.

As they burst into our building, I heard the shrill German voices I was so familiar with; they took me back to the ghetto. The terrifying sound of hobnailed jackboots stomping on the wooden stairs grew louder and louder; I knew they were coming for me! My heart was pounding rapidly as we waited for the knock at the door, and the suspense was unbearable. I nearly jumped out of my skin as the door burst open and three steel-helmeted Germans burst in: two tall *Waffen*-SS officers, almost touching the ceiling, and a *Feldpolizei*, a field-policeman, distinctive by the chest-plate in the shape of a small shield that was suspended from a chain around his neck. They began by searching the flat, rummaging through the drawers and cupboards for anything incriminating. Then the arrogant military policeman who seemed to be in command shouted *"Ausweis Karten!"* which he proceeded to scrutinise carefully. He must have become suspicious when he noticed that my surname was different from the other two, and it didn't seem I was related to them. My chest tightened with fear and sent my temples throbbing as he looked at me sternly. Then pointing at me, he barked at the old lady *"Ist er Jud?"* Wanda crossed herself frantically and kept repeating, *"O rany Boskie!"* (Christ's wounds).

Pani turned deathly pale. Ignoring the word *"Jud"* (Yid), she tried to explain in a faltering voice that I was an orphaned relative. "Dear God" she pleaded, "have pity on an old woman, burdened with a cripple and an orphan!" But her words fell on deaf ears; the German didn't seem to understand a word of Polish. The two *Waffen*-SS men just watched and didn't interfere—apart from searching the flat they left matters up to the military policeman. Suddenly, turning to me, he started to gesticulate by moving his hand up and down, yelling: *"Herunter, Herunter!"* I ignored him at first, pretending not to understand, but he kept pointing at my pants with his hand moving up and down. I began to sob as I bashfully lowered my trousers and immediately pulled them up again, as if acutely embarrassed. Just then, Wanda started to hiss and splutter, making the sounds which preceded a convulsive attack. The astonished soldiers took their eyes off me. Wanda began to writhe spasmodically as the Germans looked at each other in amazement, shrugged their shoulders, and burst out laughing. Then the officer with the chest-plate swore aloud: *"Donnerwetter!"* he said, and turned to face the door and storm out, with the others following on behind. I heaved a sigh of relief as *Pani* fell to her knees in thankfulness. "Praise Be *Jezu Christus!*" she uttered, crossing herself several times in rapid succession.

When Wanda finally came to after her fit, she could hardly remember a thing, and perhaps it was just as well. I had one more lucky escape and it was all thanks to Wanda; her seizure had saved me and consequently all of us. It distracted the Germans from further questioning and caused them to lose interest and give up abruptly. It must have been Wanda's acute fear that brought on her epileptic attack at that crucial moment. To me, her seizure was nothing short of a miracle; I was convinced that my guardian angel was still watching over me and had come, once more, to my rescue.

CHAPTER 11

An "Angel" in Nazi Uniform

At about this time, Wala was working as a waitress at the "Adria," a fashionable Warsaw café patronized by German officers. Though this would appear a foolhardy thing to do, it was in a way safer to be right under their very noses; that is, if you had the "right looks" and the nerve. Working in such a place helped to deflect any suspicion by Poles, as if no Jew would have dared to be so brazen. I marvelled at my sister's audacity and courage—she had nerves of steel! Wala found a suitable room nearby, and as she now had a genuine *Kennkarte* and a job to match, with such excellent cover; she felt that her fortune had at last changed for the better.

However, within forty-eight hours of moving addresses, everyone was required to report with their identity papers to the building superintendent. He had to make sure that newcomers to the block were included on the list of tenants, and would then register them with the authorities. This assisted the Gestapo in keeping track of people. Wala wanted to keep her name off the register to avoid attracting attention, for she was afraid that her frequent changes of address might invite suspicion—she wanted to lie low for as long as possible, and hoped that the superintendant would turn a blind eye. By showing a reluctance to comply, she hoped to give himt the impression that there was some genuine reason for not wishing to register, perhaps connected with the underground, which was by this time very active in Warsaw. No one messed with the Polish Underground! However, she was unable to avoid his glare, and he kept reminding her whenever she went in or out of the building of the need to report with her identity papers. Wala still tried to delay it for as long as possible. My poor sister had no choice but to pin her hopes on this superintendant, and people in his position were notorious for informing on Jews.

One particular evening Wala felt uneasy. She didn't like the insidious look on the superintendant's face when she entered the building, and somehow had a premonition that something was going to go wrong that night. She didn't undress, and lay restless, fully clothed, on her bed, as if she was ready to run, although there was no chance of escaping. Later that night came the knock at the door she had been dreading. "Open up! It's the police!" The superintendant, it seemed, had denounced her. The informer stood at the courtyard gate with a sly look on his face as he watched her being led away by two Polish policemen, one on either side of her. At first she was taken to the police *komisariat* on Jagiellonskiego, where she stood up well to the interrogation. As hard as they tried, the police were unable to break her and prove she was Jewish. Out of frustration, the treacherous and corrupt "Navy-Blue" police turned her over to the German Secret Police, better known as Gestapo.

The Aleja Szucha (Szuch Avenue) Gestapo Headquarters was infamous. It was widely believed that no one taken to this torture facility under suspicion of being Jewish during this period ever emerged alive. I learned about my sister's arrest soon after it happened, told by my cousin Franka, who came to Anin right away with the devastating news. Everyone knew that Aleja Szucha was the end of the line, for Jew and Pole alike. I was beside myself, and all we could do was turn to the Guardian of Israel and ask Him to protect my poor sister. We prayed for some miracle. *Pani* Gozdzialska also joined in, and offered prayers to Jesus Christ for Wala's safe return. The next day, when my sister hadn't showed up, we became more convinced with every passing hour that we would never see her again. My devoted sister, who had given me the only chance I had of surviving by plucking me from the labour camp and the brickyard wilderness, was gone. My cousin and I were totally grief-stricken. We wept uncontrollably in each other's arms, and in my grieving heart I bid her a final farewell, though I still found it hard to believe that I would never see my wonderful sister again. Although my cousin Franka had long since discarded all Jewish practices, we lit a candle in her memory and sat in mourning, low to the ground, in keeping with Jewish custom.

Aleja Szucha was known as the most notorious Gestapo interrogation centre in all of Poland. The forbidding edifice had previously housed a Polish Government Ministry. This infamous facility was to be later mentioned at the Nuremberg Trials as an example of utmost Nazi brutality, where Polish political prisoners, suspected members of the Resistance, and Jews were subjected to brutal interrogation and torture. The suspects were arbitrarily sentenced in batches by a summary court and hastily executed in the prison yard, within earshot of the other prisoners awaiting interrogation. For the most part, Jews were not brought to Aleja Szucha at this time, as they were not entitled to the privilege of any court hearing, however summary. Jews were marked out for instant death without any form of legal process. The only "Jews" brought to Aleja Szucha were like my sister, mostly females, held under suspicion of being Jewish or of resistance activity. The fate of any suspect Jewish male denounced or caught on the "Aryan side" was unceremoniously determined on the spot—men and boys were simply made to unbutton their trousers behind the nearest courtyard gate, and if they were found to be circumcised they were shot out of hand. At this time, suspect Jews were not as a rule taken to Aleja Szucha for interrogation, unless there was some reason for doubt.

My sister was cast into a dimly-lit basement together with other suspects, mainly women with only a few men, all under suspicion of being Jewish. Most bore signs of having been beaten and tortured. My sister feared that these could be her last hours and that she might never live to see another day. The majority of her fellow prisoners appeared to be Jewish. Polish political prisoners were kept apart from Jewish suspects. They were held on the upper floors in so-called "tramway cells," which had two rows of wooden benches with a central gangway, resembling a street tram. The very first thing Wala did on reaching the Gestapo prison was flush her eternity ring down the lavatory. It was a gift from Father and the last valuable item left to her, as she had sold everything else of value as and when she ran short of money. During the expected interrogation, she intended to pass for a simple country girl, thereby giving herself time to answer questions and keep them down to a minimum. To have shown any form of sophistication, either in speech or by the wearing of jewellery, could have given her away.

Most of the suspects were in a sorry state, having been deprived of food and drink and being taken out in turn for interrogation and torture. Some desperate prisoners in the dungeon spoke quite openly, having resigned themselves to death. Wala never revealed her identity or confided in any of them, and wisely tried to distance herself from them. She suspected that the Gestapo had planted an informer in their midst to spy on their prisoners. She felt that most of the prisoners were doomed anyway, and her life, too, hung on a thread, but in her genuine identity card she at least had one trump up her sleeve. One male prisoner of Jewish appearance protested his innocence loudly, perhaps for the benefit of any spy present, and repeatedly informed the others that he was not Jewish, but had been circumcised for health reasons when an infection made it imperative. He even held up a certificate from a hospital to prove it. Wala had a feeling that he was nevertheless a Jew, though, and after he was taken upstairs for his first interrogation he was never returned to the cell. Another male prisoner declared defiantly that he had poison concealed on his body, and he would never let the Nazi tyrants get him first. Some were returned to the cell after a while; others were in no state to walk and had to be carried back. The prison cells echoed with the cries of the tormented as they were led directly from the torture chamber into the yard for execution. Shots resonated through the cells, further unnerving the distraught prisoners.

Early the next morning, it was my sister's turn to be questioned. Fortunately, her interrogation was not inside a torture chamber but in a room sparsely furnished with a desk and chairs. As usual for such places, a picture of Hitler hung on the wall. Wala was interrogated by a Gestapo *Obersturmführer* (Lieutenant) in full uniform. He first scrutinised her documents, which he must have earlier found in order or she would not have gotten this far. As the German spoke no Polish, he questioned her through an obnoxious German-speaking Polish interpreter, no doubt a *Volksdeutsch*, who lost no time in charging Wala with being Jewish. His Polish was faultless, rather better than his German, Wala thought. The interpreter seemed determined to condemn her out of hand, relying, no doubt, on the informer's evidence. But the Gestapo *Oberst* immediately overruled him, insisting that they take their time and go through the procedures laid down by Nazi theories on racial purity. They began by studying the shape of her skull, taking note of the size of her nose and ears, looking for any Jewish traits. She was next made to walk up and down the room, as they observed her every step. According to Nazi racial pseudo-science, it was possible to identify a Jew by his or her gait! Although Wala was as Aryan-looking as any Pole, the interpreter was adamant that she was Jewish. The Gestapo officer was not so convinced, and he again had to restrain the interpreter and cut him down to size. It became fairly apparent that the German didn't care much for the manner of the Pole. Nevertheless, the interpreter kept persevering, trying his utmost to catch her out and prove the German wrong. Trying a different approach, he would suddenly break into German from the Polish, hoping for a slip of the tongue, as many Jews spoke some German, but he could not make any headway. No matter how intimidating or threatening he became, he was careful not to lay a hand on her, no doubt wary of the German officer, who stuck to the rules. The *Volksdeutsch* tried all sorts of different tactics to entrap her. He would fire questions at her in quick succession, or scream loudly, "What's your name?," hoping she would drop her guard. But she kept her cool, calmly repeating "Walerja Matera" over and over.

My sister Fela with her fiancé, Beniek Majerczak, soon after the war.

Next, the *Oberst* himself stepped in and made it a point to ask Wala why she had refused to register and had broken the law. And if she was innocent, as she claimed to be, why should anyone have wanted to report her to the police? Keeping her composure, she replied that it was purely out of malice on the part of the superintendant, and for no other reason. She told them that he had kept pestering her, and that she had found him lewd and repulsive and had to repeatedly reject his advances. This was the only reason why she wanted to avoid the man upon entering and leaving the building; there was no other reason. "*Herr Oberst*," she pleaded, "As you can see, my papers are in order. I have nothing to hide; I'm just an ordinary country girl and I didn't realise I was doing anything wrong!"

This explanation seemed perfectly feasible to the Gestapo officer, who was by now more than convinced of her innocence, and he told the interpreter to make sure he noted this down in the report he was writing; translating Wala's words into German as he went along. The Gestapo officer, now fully satisfied that Wala was not Jewish, lost all further interest in the case. Not wanting to waste any more of his time, he became restless and started to pace the room, or stood by the window, hands on his hips, looking outside as the interpreter stubbornly kept on with the grilling. But the interpreter never managed to break her. By lunchtime, he broke off for a while and produced some sandwiches, which he began to enjoy while sitting on a corner of the lieutenant's desk. The German immediately admonished him for his bad manners, and ordered him to go and find something for the suspect to eat, the poor suspect who had been falsely accused and who had not received any food since she had been brought in.

By this time the *Oberst* had had enough, he finally ended the interview once and for all, ordering Wala's immediate release. What's more, the interpreter was made to grudgingly escort my sister out of this terrible place and bring her all the way to the main gate; cursing blindly along the way. As Wala was about to be rid of him for good, he called after her one last time: "You were dead lucky this time, *cholerna Żydówa*"—you choleric Jewess!

Before Wala could finally breathe a sigh of relief, she had to get past the barrier and clear the sentry-boxes at the top of the street. The whole of Szuch Avenue was closed off to traffic and pedestrians. She strode off briskly, not daring to look back, afraid she would be called back and still unsure whether she was really out of danger. My sister had literally emerged from the jaws of death.

It is commonly believed that no one taken to Aleja Szucha at this period in time, under suspicion of being Jewish, emerged alive, save for my incredible sister, who managed to pull it off. She could only put it down to divine intervention, believing that the Gestapo *Oberst* had to be a messenger of Jewish descent, disguised in Nazi uniform, sent down from Heaven to rescue her.

What really saved my sister was not only her good "Aryan" looks, her tenacity, and her courage in adversity, but her authentic *Kennkarte*, which the Germans themselves had furnished her with only a few months before. Presumably that is why she was never subjected to torture, unlike the other prisoners. She would never have come out of Aleja Szucha with her original forged document, which would immediately have condemned her. I was inclined to think that the Gestapo officer was no angel; under the circumstances he could not have reached any other decision. He had to let her go. So the real miracle had occurred a few months before, when the armed resistance raiders took the bag containing the false identity card. After her ordeal, Wala made straight for the Vistula and sat there by the river-bank to collect her thoughts after her terrible experience and decide where to go from there, with no abode, no job, and little money. As she sat, a thief sneaked up from behind and grabbed her handbag, which was lying next to her on the grass. To her utter dismay, her priceless "Aryan" *Kennkarte*, which had just saved her life, was gone! She would have no choice but to turn to the German authorities for a replacement. But this would have to wait; she dreaded the thought of having to confront them again. For now, she had someone who would guarantee her "Aryan" status—a colonel of the Gestapo, no less!

Later that afternoon, when Wala turned up in Anin, I thought she had come back from the dead. It was truly beyond belief and nothing short of a miracle—my joy was indescribable.

The former Aleja Szucha Gestapo Headquarters in Warsaw.

An interrogation room at Aleja Szucha Gestapo Headquarters, now the Museum of Martyrdom. A portrait of Adolf Hitler hangs on the wall with torture instruments resting on the table and chair.

CHAPTER 12

Jewish Pilgrim at the Black Madonna

It was 6 June 1944—or perhaps I heard the news a day or two later, as notable events about the war often reached us some time later. I was always eager for *Pani* to come home with any news of the outside, but this time she brought the most dramatic news ever, coming straight from central Warsaw. Generally a placid person, *Pani* was in a high state of elation as she recounted the thrilling news that British and American forces had crossed the *Kanal la Manche*—for the English Channel is referred to in Poland by its French name—and landed on the French coast. Normandy was not mentioned by name at this time, only *Kanal la Manche*. I quickly fetched the atlas, and from it we naturally deduced that the Allies must have taken the shortest route and landed on the French coast somewhere near Calais. But the actual progress of the invasion force was not known to us, as we had no access to BBC broadcasts from London and were unable to follow the course of the fighting.

We'd had no idea the Allies were about to invade; we had only looked east, to Russia. Occasionally, Pani would bring home a secret bulletin, circulated by the Underground, but aside from those we had to rely on rumours, and one could never be sure where they originated from; only those from secret sources were considered reliable. Mostly they came from German "street barkers," or loudspeaker radios which spouted Nazi propaganda on the streets of Warsaw, giving out news that one had to take with a pinch of salt.

A Nazi party newspaper translated into Polish and circulated in the capital—I'm no longer sure, but it may have been called *Nowy Kurier Warszawski*—admitted that the landings had taken place. But the paper insisted that the Atlantic Wall was holding fast and that *Festung Europa* was impregnable, confidently predicting that the Allied invasion force would be thrown back into the sea. *Pani* brought home a copy of the issue, which she would not have done normally; good Poles didn't like to be seen buying German newspapers. However, this time she was tempted to get a copy out of sheer curiosity, in view of the dramatic news, and we were hungry for information. I listened intently as *Pani* tried to read between the lines, attempting to detect the propaganda lies put out by the Nazis. With the invasion of Europe finally on, and the Germans in full retreat, *Pani* got more talkative and described the various armies involved on the Allied side. She told us of the great resources and might of America, spoke in glowing terms of the Royal Navy, who "ruled the waves," and described the fighting spirit of the British "Tommy," whom she held in high esteem—well, almost as high as the soldiers of the Red Army!

This momentous news filled us with great hope. Surely the war could not go on much longer now, with the opening of the "Second Front" in Europe and the Allies firmly established on the mainland. What was more, a few weeks later, on 20 July, *Pani* reached home with yet another piece of sensational news: an attempt had been made on Hitler's life, and he might even be dead, despite of the strenuous denials of the "street barker."

As a result of all the dramatic news from the war fronts, I felt confident enough to slip out of the house in the evening once or twice, before the start of the curfew, to enjoy the welcome fresh air and to fill my lungs and stretch my legs, after having been confined indoors for six months. At first, my legs felt as stiff and foreign as yet-unused wings must feel to a fledgling. I kept trying to sprint away to see if I still remembered how to run and if I was as quick on my feet as I had once been.

In view of the continuous good news, *Pani* suggested that as a form of thanksgiving we would all go on an outing. And what better place to go than to the monastery shrine of the Holy Mother of Częstochowa? We would go there on pilgrimage to pray for early deliverance from the Nazis, and at the same time offer prayers for a cure for Wanda. This shrine is the foremost place of pilgrimage in Poland, dating back to the fourteenth century. It houses the Icon of the Black Madonna and Child. *Pani* suggested that it would be safe enough for me to come along as well, to which idea I readily agreed. I looked forward to coming out into the open after being shut away for so long. To mark the event, *Pani* wanted to make me look presentable to fit the occasion, so she gave me one of her "pudding-basin" haircuts, which was desperately needed, before we set out together—me, *Pani*, and Wanda in her wheelchair—on the thrilling journey.

We travelled by train to Częstochowa, a town some distance to the west of Warsaw, on a glorious summer's day below a beautiful azure-blue sky. It had rained during the previous night, and the air was clear, fresh and fragrant, heavily scented with the odor of Mock Orange, which people in Poland refer to as Jasmine. Anin was so beautiful and verdant; I had never seen it properly before. When I first got to Anin it was winter. How lovely the world looked that morning! I relished the liberty of moving about freely, listening to the birds chirping away noisily. It was wonderful to bask in the warm spring sunshine that I had been starved of for so long. It gave me an elated feeling in my head, as if I was floating on air. After being cooped up for so long, I wanted to remain outdoors in the fresh air and sunshine, just walking on and on, hoping the day would never end. Pushing Wanda' wheelchair, I skipped along as happy as a lark—now and then Wanda had to tell me to slow down!

By the time we reached the vicinity of Jasna Góra, a host of pilgrims was already there. They had been arriving since early morning, counting their Rosary beads along the way. In their exultation, the faithful kept repeating, "Our Father" and, "Glory Be" while eagerly pressing up the incline along the tree-lined avenue that led to the shrine. In their devotion, some penitents even walked on their knees for the last stretch, continuously intoning "Ave Maria," the prayer to the Virgin Mary, as they went. A pilgrimage to Our Lady of Częstochowa, who had the reputation of bestowing miracle cures, was of great spiritual significance at this turbulent time. The Madonna had been revered as the Queen and the Protector of Poland from foreign invaders throughout the country's troubled history. When we finally got near the image above the altar, I was rather surprised to find that the image was not very large, and that the sorrowful-looking Madonna was not really black but rather coffee-coloured, having darkened with age.

Religious passions were running high; the crowd was seething with patriotic zeal. Religion in Poland goes hand-in-hand with nationalism. This was not a very comfortable setting for a lone Jewish boy pretending to be something he was not—I felt like an unwelcome and not entirely sincere intruder, making the sign of the cross and going through all the motions. As the procession emerged from the church, holding aloft gold crucifixes, I was kneeling on one leg with the throng and felt the pungent whiff of the waving censer. Inside the Church during Mass, the Priest intoned the *"Kyrie Eleison, Christe Eleison"* as the worshippers responded, "In the name of the Father, the Son and the Holy Ghost,

Amen." Something within me stopped me from going forward to the altar with *Pani* and Wanda to receive the Host in the form of a wafer, representing the body and blood of Christ. Although she never mentioned it, I somehow felt that *Pani* may have wanted me to go forward with her, but she could sense I was hesitating. In any case, it is a sin to take communion if one is not baptised, and she must have been aware of this. It was an ironic situation for a Jewish boy to find himself in, and I also got carried away in the religious fervour and prayed, not to an icon or effigy, but to the same Father in Heaven, in the only way I knew—the way I was taught as a boy at Hebrew school. I prayed for the protection of my family wherever they might be. I could never imagine that they were not well, or that any harm would ever come to them.

It wasn't comfortable to be a Jewish boy during these inquisitorial times. It would have been so much better to just give up being Jewish, but it isn't something one can do easily. Though I could try to deny my faith, I could never escape my destiny, because those around me would never let me. They would always keep reminding me, "A Jew will always be a Jew." Thus, I felt, I might as well remain what I was born into. I was compelled to deny my identity to stay alive, and at times I even regretted being Jewish, but deep down I could never forget who I was, and where I came from, whether it was here at Jasna Góra or when it later became prudent for me to be seen going to church on holy days.

Before we started back home, *Pani* offered to give us each a little souvenir to mark the occasion. Wanda chose some amulet or another to adorn her room, and I picked a picture postcard of the Black Madonna and Child as a keepsake.

Within days of our trip, as if all our prayers had been answered, the booming of heavy guns became clearly audible in Anin. This had to be the beginning of what I had waited and prayed so long for! We knew that the Allies had landed on the mainland of Europe, but we had no idea that the Russians were advancing rapidly through Poland. At night, one could see gun flashes in the eastern sky and a red glow on the horizon— a sure indication that the front line was drawing close to Warsaw, heralding our imminent liberation. I was too excited to go to bed that night, and stood on a chair by the window for a long time, with the lights out, gazing into the night sky and the gun-flashes in the distance. This had to be long-range Russian artillery, I thought. I was too excited to go to sleep. This must be it—the Red Army was on its way! The next day *Pani* and I went out on the streets and watched with glee as the Germans were feverishly preparing to pull out. They were loading up their trucks with fine furniture and desks—taking all their ill-gotten gains, no doubt confiscated from private homes, back with them to the *Vaterland*. I was so thrilled, I felt like leaping in the air for joy. The nightmare was at last coming to an end. I could hardly wait to see what the next day would bring.

CHAPTER 13

The Warsaw Inferno

Tuesday morning, 1 August 1944, as I remember, was warm and rather humid, with hazy sunshine. The thunder of heavy guns could be heard in Anin, and it came closer with every hour; surely this was a clear indication of an early end to my ordeal. After years of struggle and going in daily fear for my life, I was about to be freed. I could hardly believe it; I was so excited that my head kept spinning around. It also occurred to me that it was ten days before my thirteenth birthday, a significant event in the life of a Jewish boy. The occasion, known as a Bar Mitzvah, marks the day a Jewish boy undertakes the obligation to keep all 613 precepts, between Man and God and Man and Man, like an adult. The best birthday present I could possibly have would be to celebrate my Bar Mitzvah in freedom.

Early that morning, my sister arrived unexpectedly in Anin in an exuberant mood. Tuesday was not a day she normally came to visit, but on this day she couldn't get there quickly enough, she was so excited to tell me that the Germans were in full retreat from Warsaw, and liberation could be only a matter of hours away. "Stefciu," she said, "we have cheated the Nazis and survived—this calls for a real celebration!" And as there was no need for me to hide anymore, she said, we would set out for central Warsaw together to explore the big city and await the entry of the triumphant Red Army, to experience there the never-to-be-forgotten moment of our liberation. I got ready in no time at all, and we bade a brief farewell to *Pani* and Wanda, planning to be back later in the day. What's more, Wanda raised a smile and even warmed up to me; perhaps her not-so-friendly attitude had been due to nothing more than acute fear. We promised *Pani* that I would be back with her that evening, or the next day at the latest. We were sure that when we returned it would be as free people, at liberty to come and go as we pleased.

It was very exhilarating to be out and about in the open. We boarded the bright-red painted *"Kolejka"* suburban electric train from Anin-

Wawer to central Warsaw. It was all very exciting. I looked forward to exploring the capital, which I had only seen briefly before, with my sister. We crossed the broad Vistula via a lattice bridge that connected Praga with the main part of Warsaw. On the way, we could see German military vehicles in headlong retreat across the Vistula bridges, all going the same way, from east to west. When we reached the city centre, there were far fewer Germans in evidence, with only the odd military vehicle speeding past, fleeing in dread of the avenging Russians. It was a marvellous sight. I had often wondered if this day would ever come, and what it would be like to see the hitherto invincible Wehrmacht turning tail. While mingling with the crowd, I remained as always on my guard. Wala tried to impress upon me that I could relax.

"Stefciu," she said, "there's nothing more to fear, and no need to shy away from people! The Germans are on their way out, and the shmaltzovnik Jew-hunters are now out of business. They can't touch us anymore!"

I could only answer, "I know, but it will take some time for me to get used to it." For almost three years now, I'd had to avoid people, making myself as invisible as possible by keeping out of sight. Wala was far more confident than I, and had a nice demeanour about her; she was good at mixing with people, especially now that the Nazis were as good as gone.

Wala knew Warsaw well, and she showed me the sights. We explored the capital together with carefree abandon, jumping on and off the running-boards of street trams out of sheer excitement at being alive and free. I felt like a slave who had just been unchained. I had never been to downtown Warsaw before—it was beautiful. I was bewildered by the busy, crowded streets, the tram cars, the impressive buildings, the majestic palaces and old castles, and the historic Old Town area. It felt as if it was all a dream. Soon after lunch, though, we noticed that some feverish activity had begun; young men and women were scurrying about the streets purposefully, as if running messages. Later that afternoon, the streets began to clear and grew almost deserted, as if everyone was responding to a signal. A deceptive calm descended on the city and even the big Russian guns seemed to have fallen silent—it was the lull before the storm.

Surely, there had to be something in the air. There must be some reason for all this frantic activity, we assumed. These people must know

something that we don't. We decided that perhaps we should also abandon the streets and try to take cover. Somehow, it never occurred to
us to return to Anin. Wala suggested that we look up a friend of hers
who happened to be living nearby and avail ourselves of his hospitality, and at the same time try to find out what was afoot. To my utter
surprise the "friend" turned out to be a Polish police officer, the very
sort of person I always tried to keep clear of! Confronted by a "Navy-
Blue" in the open door, my first instinct was to turn tail and run. Wala,
unlike the scared, untrusting animal that I was, took these things in her
stride. They were perfectly normal to her, and so she had failed to warn
me. Bolesław Piatkowski had been introduced to her as a sympathetic
friend by our cousin Franka Fajngold, who went by the grand name of
Apollonia Szybowska; she had the colourful personality to match the
name. "Apollonia" had by now been seized as an "Aryan" on a Warsaw
street and sent for forced labour in Germany. Rather surprised to find
us at his door at this hour, Bolesław, or Bolek as he liked to be called,
nonetheless greeted us warmly and didn't hesitate to invite us into his
apartment on *Ulica* Wolska, in the Wola district of Warsaw. We were
also delighted to be introduced to his charming wife and their teenage
son. Bolek Piatkowski was a liberal-minded person, and as an avowed
anti-Nazi, he was favourably disposed to Jews. As a rule, Polish policemen by their very nature were reactionary and hostile to Jews, so it was
rare indeed to find the likes of police officer Piatkowski in the ranks
of the "Navy-Blues." For a policeman he was atypical; he was both a
passionate Polish patriot and a good socialist. We had a nice feeling
about him, and suspected him of belonging to the Armia Ludowa, the
clandestine left-wing People's Army.

Wala asked Bolek if there was anything afoot out in the street. "Yes,
there certainly is," he replied. "We are expecting a call to arms at any
moment that will trigger an armed uprising all over the capital!" Apparently, this was not a very well kept secret, but Wala had had no inkling
of it, and nor had *Pani* Gozdzialska in Anin. Soon after, Bolek went and
changed into his civvies, and Madame Piatkowka invited us to join the
family for afternoon tea in the *salon*. I thoroughly enjoyed the delicious
home-made shortcake biscuits and the traditional Polish *babka* cake,
which I hadn't had in a long time. Sitting around the table, we tried our
best to relax by making small talk, but it was difficult to hide the state
of suspense we were in, and the conversation inevitably turned to the

subject of the explosion that was about to erupt. At exactly five in the afternoon our conversation was cut short by sudden bursts of small-arms fire, and we turned deathly silent, just looking at each other. Soon after, Officer Piatkowski stood up to his full height. He was tall and imposing, and on leaving the table he said in a grave voice that he was sure the insurgency had started. "This is it! It's begun," he said. He went into another room and produced a hitherto banned Polish national flag, which had been hidden since the war began, and unfurled it from the balcony railing.

In no time at all other people, up and down the street, did the same, and put out their red and white flags, hanging them from flagpoles and out of windows. What a marvellous and stirring sight it was! We were going to teach those darned Jerries a lesson they would never forget! Bolek fetched his service rifle and slipped a white-and-red armband over the left sleeve of his civilian jacket, saying he had orders to report to his unit. Bolesław Piatkowski then bade his wife and us a hasty farewell, confidently expecting to be back before long. As he reached the door, he turned back and said to my sister, "Walusia,"—that is what he called her—"it would not be safe for you to try and get back to Anin now. You and Stefek are welcome to remain in our home until the danger is over." And as a parting gesture, with his voice full of emotion, he said: "You have nothing more to fear as Jews. Warsaw will soon be free and things are about to change. There will emerge a new Poland, a better and just Poland for all!" We were very touched by what he said, and tears came to our eyes, especially those of Wala, who is easily moved. We realised that he must be an officer in the resistance and therefore must know what he is talking about. Bolek then turned towards the door and promptly left the apartment, taking his teenage son with him. That night a welcome shower fell on the city after a warm and sultry afternoon. During the evening the firing died down somewhat, and we had a reasonably quiet night. However, we were far too excited to get much sleep.

Now that the uprising had started, we were sure that by morning the Russians would have crossed the Vistula to relieve the capital and be welcomed with open arms by the entire population. But when morning came, there was no sign of the Russians. The shooting became more intense, echoing all around us, from the nearby streets. Later on, heavier arms also came into play and loud explosions could be heard from near and far, but we didn't know how things were progressing. Were we winning? Over the next couple of days, the surrounding streets resonated with the ever-increasing sound of gunfire. To our dismay, Warsaw was now fully caught up in the uprising and we, trapped in Wola, turned out to be in the thick of it. That district was to experience some of the initial and most bitter fighting of the entire uprising. And still, days later, there was no sign of the Russians. Our dream of imminent liberation began to fade rapidly.

One of the reasons we had decided to travel to central Warsaw was that in the event of any heavy fighting between the Russians and Germans it was considered safer to be in the big city. We knew that liberation was imminent, but had heard nothing about a possible uprising. We also wanted so much to experience first-hand the triumphal entry of the Red Army into the capital. There was no going back now to the safety of the Gozdzialska home, and it began to look as if we would have cause to regret our hasty decision on that auspicious morning. Unknown to us at the time, on the very day we left Anin an advance column of Russian tanks, racing from the north-east, reached the outskirts of Praga, right next door to Anin. Had we stayed there, we would have come close to gaining our freedom that day. This Russian forward column was either ordered to pull back or forced to retreat by the German forces, but had we stayed, we would have at least been on the right side of the Vistula and that much closer to the Russian lines, with no wide-flowing river to separate us.

The Armia Krajowa, the national Home Army. had timed their uprising to start as the Red Army's General Konstantin Rokossovsky, who was of Polish origin, was at the gates of the capital and the liberation of the city was a foregone conclusion. By then there were few Germans left in evidence and it took the insurgents little time to take control of a large part of the city at great cost, apart from some pockets of stubborn German resistance. The intention of the Armia Krajowa (AK) was to beat the Russians to the punch and wrest the capital from the Germans. They intended to score a military as well as political victory by taking control of the capital and asserting their independence in the name of the Polish Government-in-Exile in London. It was they who orchestrated the uprising and who gave the order for the uprising to begin without consulting Moscow, thereby irking Stalin. The AK was under the direction of the London Poles, who were strongly opposed to

Soviet Russia, which made matters worse.

The AK was politically on the right, and apart from being implacable enemies of the Russians, many of its members were also anti-Semitic. It is well documented that the AK leadership ridiculed the Jews' fighting ability and didn't want them in their ranks. When Jewish fighting units appealed to them for arms during the Warsaw Ghetto uprising, they considered arming them a waste of good weapons, although arms were in fact purchased from Polish sources. General Tadeusz "Bor" Komorowski, the AK commander-in-chief, in a report to his men in the field in 1943, ordered them to kill Jews sheltering in the forests, whom he labelled "bandits." He was referring to Jewish partisans operating in the forests of eastern Poland, who had no option but to raid villages for food, and if necessary to use force if the peasants didn't part with it willingly. Whenever NSZ Polish fascist bands and even certain AK renegade units came across groups of Jews in the forests they would try to disarm and kill them. Paradoxically, the Polish nationalist NSZ was as intent on killing Jews as Germans.

A number of surviving Jewish fighters from the Warsaw ghetto uprising the previous year, as well as others who had emerged from hiding, seized this opportunity to join their compatriots in their momentous struggle. All these young men asked for was a weapon so they could fight shoulder-to-shoulder with their allies against their common enemy and avenge their families. Although the AK didn't as a rule accept Jews into its ranks, during the uprising they were somewhat tolerated in certain units, depending on the attitudes of their commanding officers. The much smaller socialist AL (Armia Ludowa) or People's Army, which more readily accepted Jews into its ranks, made common cause with the AK and fought alongside them during the uprising, but had previously acted independently and were otherwise ideologically opposed to them. Sadly, most of the Jews taking part in the uprising were killed in the fighting that ensued. Ironically, they died as Poles, not daring to divulge their Jewish origin.

Not long after the uprising began, the Red Army reached the east bank of the Vistula, and there they halted. Although poised to cross the river, the Russians made no move. Had my sister and I stayed behind in Anin, we would have been freed in a matter of weeks. For us, freedom lay just across the Vistula, but well beyond our reach. Our impulsive trip to Warsaw would turn out to be premature and an unfortunate mistake, a nightmare that was to prolong the war for us by almost another six months, six months of going in daily fear for our lives. I was not destined to celebrate my Bar Mitzvah, after all, undergoing a baptism of fire instead. And having been cut off from my safe-house, I had no prospect to replace *Pani* Gozdzialska: such people were difficult to locate. The uprising also spread to Praga, but it never amounted to much and only lasted a short time, with the Red Army arriving there by early September, as we later discovered.

Stalin's decision not to press on with the offensive beyond the Vistula was essentially political, to enable the Germans to put down the uprising that was staged by Polish patriots who were opposed to the Russians. The rising, as I mentioned, was authorised by the Polish government in London, which was considered reactionary by the Kremlin. The official Russian explanation for holding back was that the troops were exhausted after the breathtaking offensive that had begun more than two months earlier, in June 1944. By now their advance had lost its momentum, and they needed time to bring up reinforcements before the next big push. On the other hand, if their only aim was to see the uprising crushed, they needed to stall no more than a few weeks. And surely they didn't need months to regroup and bring up supplies.

Perhaps the real reason was that Stalin wanted the British and Americans, after Normandy, to lessen the pressure on his forces, as so far the Red Army had borne the brunt of the fighting. We shall never know the whole truth. What is certain is that Stalin's regrettable decision to halt the advance was to prolong the war considerably, resulting in numerous casualties.

Meanwhile, all around our apartment block in Wola, more intense fighting erupted in the following days. There was close combat and determined attacks against the German pockets still holding out. As Luftwaffe Stuka dive-bombers appeared in the skies with their screaming sirens, it became too dangerous to remain in the apartment, so we ran for cover into the internal corridor or the basement, together with the other occupants of the block. Bombs whistled before they fell, exploding all around. Our apartment block shook and the windows rattled, but luckily there was no direct hit. The shelter was crammed full of people, and nobody cared who we were. In all that chaos, no one paid attention to us, or noticed that we didn't belong in the building or thought we might be Jews; there was a strong feeling of solidarity at this time. It wasn't so unusual to see strangers in a shelter—others had also found themselves cut off from their homes by the sudden outbreak of fighting, or they may have come from nearby bombed-out buildings to seek shelter. The atmosphere in the basement was friendly; morale was good and most of the people were in high spirits, joking and putting on a brave face. However, some were so afraid that they kept praying constantly, repeating "Mother of Mercy" and so on. Old women made the sign of the cross after every loud explosion; others kept cursing the Swabians (Germans). The more optimistic among them, especially the men, felt sure it would all end in a decisive Polish victory. "Soon it will be over. With the Russians so near, the uprising can't last," they confidently predicted. As the sporadic aerial bombardment stopped, we returned to the apartment, which had its window-panes blown out. Shards of glass were strewn all over the place. Wala and I helped *Pani* Piatkowska clear up the mess until we next had to run for cover at the next loud cry of, "Everyone to the basement, to the cellar!"

At night the sky was illuminated by burning buildings and German searchlight beams. Long chains of tracer bullets streaked through the night sky, coming from German anti-aircraft batteries positioned somewhere outside Warsaw. They must have been directing their fire at the RAF planes that came over by night to drop supplies to the insurgents. It is significant that there had been no such Allied support held out to the embattled defenders during the Warsaw ghetto uprising earlier, when the doomed and poorly-armed inhabitants rose up against much greater odds. Perhaps it would have made little difference to the outcome, but a show of support would at least have demonstrated Allied concern for the fighters and sent the right message to Hitler. Any visible act of support by the Allied Powers would have given heart to those lost in despair.

Some German units that had previously retreated, now realising that the Red Army had halted its advance and was not poised to cross the Vistula, started to come back, bringing up reinforcements, including heavy armour and turning on the people of Warsaw with savage vengeance. The situation, which had looked so hopeful only days before, had now taken a distinct turn for the worse. Our initial euphoria was short lived, and evaporated completely as the Germans started to regain the initiative. We would again be forced to hide our identity and go in fear of our lives, not only because we were Jews, but because of the uprising as well. My sister started to reproach herself for having brought me to Warsaw.

As luck would have it, we found ourselves in the worst possible locality: as the district of Wola was on the western approaches to Warsaw, it took the German forces no more than a week to reach our vicinity. It was in Wola that some of the worst revenge atrocities against the civilian population took place. We were sheltering in a block of flats opposite what had once been a Jewish hospital and was now a hospital for the general population. It was marked with a large red cross, and we hoped we would be protected from bombardment by its proximity, but it made no difference whatsoever. The Nazis didn't respect any international conventions. In fact, they later shot many of the injured and set the Wola hospital ablaze, with the patients inside.

During the course of the fighting, the Germans began to use a frightening new weapon, the sound of which we hadn't heard before. It was a heavy rocket-launcher that could fire up to six projectiles. At first it made a whining and cranking noise, as if the motor was winding up before firing, and then there was a piercing shriek and moments later the thunderous explosion. It was aptly named "*Krowa*" (bellowing cow) on account of the sound it made. It was in fact called *Nebelwerfer,* or fog-thrower, by the Germans. There was now fierce house-to-house fighting all around us.

On one occasion, someone shouted hysterically, "German tanks, German tanks!" Peering out of a window, I saw a pair of Panzer tanks position themselves at the top of our street with their gun turrets rotating menacingly from side to side, looking for a target. We quickly made for the inner landing, where we thought it safer. The defenders opened up with everything they had from behind their barricades, which had been hastily constructed from overturned trams and torn-up paving slabs. Others hurled Molotov cocktails—bottles filled with kerosene— out of apartment windows at the German armour in the street below. We were now crouching, crammed in with others, at the bottom of the staircase. In a show of bravado, someone was hanging out of a window on an upper floor and relaying a running commentary on the progress of the fighting to those inside on the upper stories. This in turn was relayed all the way down the stairway. A loud cheer went up and spread through the building as someone shouted excitedly, "A German tank's on fire!" It was even rumoured that our forces had managed to capture German tanks and turn them on the enemy. Now and then we heard the terrifying shriek of the *Nebelwerfer,* as someone would shout "*Krowa!*" and everyone braced himself, head between his knees, for the loud explosion to follow. Then someone would shout, "Oh, Jesus, that was close!" One could never know where the projectile would land.

Our building had by this time been badly damaged by the shelling. Deafening explosions were becoming more and more frequent, with debris raining down on us. Our hair was white from the plaster dust that had come down as Wala and I pressed our way down the corridor, to the stairwell then down into the basement. Everyone scurried to and fro in the smoke-filled building, seeking shelter wherever we thought we might be safer, but soon the basement and the entire building became unsafe as the block was hit with incendiary shells and fires began everywhere. Covered in dust and grit, enveloped in smoke, we ran out into the street as charred timbers and plaster fell from the ceilings, and we got separated from Mrs. Piatkowska. Had we remained in the building, we would most certainly have been buried alive. Wala and I ran from doorway to doorway and house to house, keeping close to the walls. Now and then we paused momentarily to decide on the next objective to aim for before running again. There was firing from all sides, with total mayhem around us. It was difficult to decide where to go. We wanted to get away as far as possible from the buildings which were the target of German tank and artillery fire, so we aimed for a nearby grassy square with trees and bushes, which seemed like a good refuge, clear of the crumbling walls and exploding shrapnel.

We ran in the pouring rain—which was at least a welcome relief from the heat of recent days—sidestepping corpses lying in our path as bullets whistled around us and over our heads with a resounding echo. Bent forward, we made for a mound of earth with a cluster of trees around it. While we were running, a depression in the earth appeared on the sodden path in front of us and we instinctively tumbled down into it, breathing a sigh of relief. When we opened our eyes and regained our breaths, we realised what a terrible mistake we had made: the water-logged pit turned out to be a foxhole and machine-gun nest manned by a unit of resistance fighters. Some of the young men tried to bravely raise a smile; others simply ignored us and carried on shooting through their firing-points at the German positions. The Germans, in turn, were directing their much greater fire-power towards us, and all hell broke loose. My sister and I were terror-stricken. We looked at each other in astonishment and knew we couldn't possibly remain there—we had to get out, and quickly. We were sure these brave and desperate men were about to be overwhelmed and perish to a man, together with us. "Dear God, please don't let us die like this, an anonymous and lonely death," I was thinking. We were terrified at the thought of dying as unknown Poles, buried alive under the ruins of Warsaw. To perish in this way, without a trace, was unthinkable. We had struggled and survived this far; we had to live on to tell the story!

We stayed pinned down, waiting for a lull in the shooting before making a dash for it. I stuck my head out slowly at the first opportunity, when the barrage had somewhat died down, and then we scrambled out of the hole, crouching and half-crawling in the rain and mud, aiming for a row of houses on the opposite side of the green. Some of the houses had flames rising from them; others had smoke billowing out of the windows. While we were running, shooting erupted again and became more intense; we seemed to have run into a hail of bullets, with machine-gun volleys coming from different directions. I was out in front, with Wala following close behind, trying to keep up. Bullets whizzed past us—it was a miracle we weren't hit. Suddenly, several crazed Germans with their sleeves rolled-up appeared out of nowhere. They looked fierce in their steel helmets; their uniforms covered in sweat and grime, with stick-grenades tucked under their belts and *Schmeisser* machine-pistols pointing at us. It seemed we'd been running towards German-held lines. I froze to the ground and quickly threw my hands up before they had time to shout "*Haende hoch*." I was petrified, and my heart pounded wildly. I had not experienced such dark fear since my time in the ghetto and brickyard. I had been in this sort of situation before, with death staring me in the face and my brief life flashing before my eyes. I couldn't believe it was happening to me again.

We got ourselves into this mess simply because of an ill-fated short train-ride to Warsaw. I was never meant to be here at all. Nonetheless, here I was, with my sister, in the same sort of tight spot from which there was no escape, with frenzied Germans levelling their guns at us menacingly. To our utter horror, we were caught by Waffen-SS troops, conspicuous from the twin lightning bolts on their helmets and the death's-head insignia on their uniforms. The task of putting down the uprising had been entrusted to the elite Waffen-SS, and in particular, the responsibility of crushing the resistance in Wola was assigned to the notorious SS-Dirlewanger detachment.

For whatever reason, we were spared, although it was a near thing. The Germans forced us at gunpoint through the ruins to join other captives at an assembly point farther away from the fighting. Any young male prisoners were picked out; those with injuries were particularly likely to be deemed what the Germans called "bandits," and presumably executed. We spent the rest of that day and night under guard in the open, sitting or lying on the ground. Early the next morning we were made to join up with an even larger stream of women, children, and old people in a long column winding its way past the smouldering ruins, not knowing where to. We were escorted by Waffen-SS troops and Ukrainians. The latter, traditional enemies of the Poles, were particularly cruel. Had we fallen into their hands it would have been the end. There were rumours going round of people being burnt on pyres. The deserted streets we passed had been captured from the insurgents. We had to pause here and there while sappers systematically detonated buildings in our path. Walls came crashing to the ground in front of us in a huge cloud of falling debris and dust before our column could proceed further. Other houses were torched with flame-throwers, block by block. The world around us was like an inferno; the smell of acrid smoke and dust stung the eyes and made them water, and all the time that searing August heat bore down on us, with the sun almost obscured by the haze. The elderly and infirm cried out for water, while the young and strong endured in silence. The stench from unburied and bloated corpses lying in the scorching heat, combined with the smell of gunpowder and choking dust, was nauseating.

Strangely enough, in this inferno my sister and I felt somewhat safer, relieved not to be singled out as Jews. I must admit that we even derived a certain *schadenfreude* from seeing Poles treated like Jews, driven like cattle through the streets the way Jews had been herded, beaten down and hardly saying a word. We were now in the same plight as all the other inhabitants of Warsaw, as they too were now snaking their way out of their hometown in a long line, stripped of their wealth and possessions, carrying only what they had on their person. Some carried bundles and sacks on their backs, but we had absolutely nothing to carry. This was so reminiscent of when we had first been evicted from our home and forced into the crowded ghetto more than two years before. How ironic. For the first time we were equal, suffering not as Jews but as Poles. Being part of the wider population and sharing the same fate as the other inhabitants gave us a measure of security, and in this fiery hell, no one would think of pointing an accusing finger at a Jew. Poles now also had a taste of what it was like to be at the receiving end of Nazi brutality and retribution.

Hungry, thirsty, and suffering from exhaustion, we continued to be herded along the rubble-strewn streets without knowing our destination or fate. As we passed through a certain neighbourhood, we noticed that the streets were littered with leaflets. The escorting soldiers warned us that it was *verboten* to pick them up, pointing to the sky to intimate that they were dropped from the air by "enemy aircraft." Wala warned me to obey, but as usual curiosity got the better of me, and when I thought the soldier near us was distracted, I couldn't resist picking one up. The bold headline had caught my eye. The leaflet, printed in Polish, shocked us to the core. We couldn't believe what we were reading; coming at a time like this the leaflet's message was particularly hurtful:

CITIZENS OF WARSAW!
We are fighting for a
FREE POLAND
A Poland without Germans, Russians and Jews

A Poland without Jews! We were horrified—what were we, if not Poles? More recently, or at least since the Ghetto and Warsaw uprisings, we thought that Poles and Jews were in this together, confronting the same cruel enemy. But we must have been wrong. Coming at a time like this, this note was the final betrayal. We feared that when the Nazis were gone the danger for us would remain. Was this the beginning of the New Poland that Bolek Piatkowski had promised us? Wala quickly threw away the leaflet without reading the rest. What we'd seen was enough. This was the Poles' darkest hour. The country was bleeding and Warsaw was dying, with the capital levelled to the ground and its inhabitants killed by the thousands. And yet, its chauvinistic leaders considered it imperative to vilify the Jews at this time, though they were fully aware that Polish Jewry was no more and that their dream of a Poland without Jews had already come true. The leaflets were scattered over a wide area that was in German hands, now that the inhabitants had been driven out. The way they lay scattered on the ground, the leaflets could not have been dispersed by hand, nor blown about by the wind. They could have only rained down from above. Since the Home Army had no planes, these must have been dropped from the RAF aircraft flown by Polish aircrews that came over almost nightly to drop supplies. It was inconceivable that at this grave hour the anti-Semitic Polish "old guard" in London should consider Polish Jews their implacable enemies, alongside the Germans and Russians.

Eventually, we reached a large open area outside Warsaw where we were ordered into a massive barbed-wire enclosure together with thousands of other evacuees from Warsaw. We were penned in on all sides by barbed-wire entanglements thrown across a grassy field against a hillside. There we were formed into different groups, reminiscent of a medieval field of battle, with columns of people constantly marshalled about. Men were segregated from women and children and put into different enclosures. I was just thirteen, and still boyish enough to be left with my sister among the women while the Germans looked for any young men who may have been involved in the uprising. We were kept in this vast field without food and drink. People were desperate, and cried out for water. The Germans didn't understand any Polish, or perhaps they simply didn't want to. Women and children learned to beg for water in German. "*Wasser bitte, Wasser bitte*," they pleaded. Eventually water arrived by army tanker. It was hot and humid, and the people had gone without water for many, many hours. Some had fainted, overcome with heat exhaustion. When the tanker finally approached, there was a mad rush to get to it. Some got trampled in the rush. The more stoic among the prisoners tried to restrain the others, shouting, "*Polacy! Polacy!*" But listening to this appealing to their patriotism as Poles, restraining themselves, was easier said than done, when they were going almost insane with thirst in that heat.

Additional prisoners were continuously herded into the stockade. Wala and I tried to keep as near as possible to the makeshift gate, looking for an opportunity to escape. As the barrier was lifted to let yet another column of people in, pushing and jostling broke out, and in the commotion Wala seized the chance and pushed me forward, past the gate. I made a dash for the nearby bushes for cover, hoping she would follow, but she was forced back and didn't manage to make it past the gate. I panicked at the thought of being separated from my sister again. In the mêlée I lost sight of her, and I waited there, forlornly looking towards the mass of people in the enclosure, hoping to catch a glimpse of her and praying that she would somehow manage to escape. Fortunately, the next day the Germans started to release women with children, and luckily Wala had managed to place herself amongst them. I could see her as she slipped past the gate holding a "borrowed" child in her arms. Some women with two or more children would lend them to total strangers to enable them to get away—some people were like that during the war. Again we were very fortunate, as most of the young men and women were transported to the Reich for forced labour. Had Wala been taken away, I don't know if I would have been able to survive on my own.

Meanwhile, it took the Germans just two months to put down the uprising, ruthlessly driving out the Warsaw population and razing the city to the ground, as expressly ordered by Hitler, with the details entrusted to Reichsfürer-SS Himmler. And when it was all over, Himmler apparently reported back to Hitler, "Warsaw has ceased to exist." The uprising, it transpired, was a tragic blunder, and had been doomed from the start. Were it not for the uprising, the Russians would not have halted on the Vistula. They apparently had orders to advance beyond Warsaw, and with the Germans in headlong retreat, there was little to stop them. The ill-advised Polish decision to rise up at this time had changed the situation completely. As a result, the Russians decided to break off their offensive, thereby prolonging the war considerably. This catastrophe resulted in incalculable loss of life. Apart from the terrible carnage in Warsaw, the situation enabled the Nazis to operate their death camps in Poland for several more months.

SYG Archives
People escorted out of Warsaw under armed guard during the uprising.

CHAPTER 14

Shelter at a Police Colony

My sister and I, weakened and totally exhausted, just drifted aimlessly after we were freed, not knowing or caring where we went so long as it was as far as possible from the Warsaw inferno. We were penniless, with nowhere to go and no one to turn to for help. We just trudged from field to field and farmstead to farmstead that day, getting the same brush-off from surly farmers wherever we went. Glancing over our shoulders, back towards the capital, we could see a huge pall of black smoke suspended in the sky above the blazing city like a giant mushroom, with a hazy pink glow below it. Although it was a fine sunny day, the sun was almost blotted out. We could see in the distance terrifying Stuka dive-bombers in action over the capital with their screaming sirens, repeatedly diving in and out, pulverising whatever parts of the city were still holding out. We found out later that by the time it was over, more than 200,000 people had been killed, mostly non-combatants, out of a population of just over a million, with thousands more wounded.

We realised just how fortunate we were to have come through unscathed, apart from some minor scratches, particularly as we had been caught in the heat of battle by crazed SS-Dirlewanger troops. This ragtag SS brigade consisted of convicts largely recruited from German prisons. They were in the main hardened criminals who had earlier committed terrible atrocities when stationed in Russia. Based on information obtained later, the Poles estimated that the Dirlewanger brigade, named after its commander, who was one of Hitler's favourite officers, in an orgy of savagery against the civilian population killed between forty and fifty thousand innocent people within a matter of days in our district of Wola and nearby Ochota alone. They were assisted in their brutality by the Kaminski brigade, consisting of Lithuanians and Ukrainians who had switched to the German side. The Dirlewanger thugs were withdrawn by the German high command after the carnage in Wola, perhaps because the riff-raff had indulged in rape and pillage. To Nazi logic it was quite acceptable to kill thousands of innocent civilians, *aber Ordnung muss sein*—but Germanic order and iron discipline must prevail.

Those who survived the uprising and were not deported to Germany tried to find shelter with relatives and friends outside of Warsaw. Later on, evacuees were sent to a selection camp at Pruszków, outside Warsaw, where they were segregated. The young and fit were sent to Germany for forced labour, the elderly, as well as women with children, were released. Unlike the others, we had no relatives or friends to turn to for help or accommodation. We were as we stood, with only the grimy clothes on our backs, and nothing to live on. The only thing I still had and held onto at all cost was my birth certificate and the vital "magic glue." But unfortunately Wala had never had her stolen identity papers replaced after her miraculous escape from the clutches of the Gestapo. This would immediately put her under suspicion in the event of a random identity check in the street, but now at least she had a more plausible explanation for what had happened to them: they were "destroyed or lost during the uprising."

We trekked from place to place like the eternal Wandering Jew—was this perhaps what Wanda in Anin had meant by, "Jews are doomed to wander the earth for their sins until Judgment Day"? And all the time the oppressive sun kept beating down—it was a particularly hot August that year. We looked for shelter along the way, living on what we could find in the fields. My sister could have taken on temporary work as a farm-hand or domestic helper were it not for me. She was prepared to forego pay in exchange for a roof over our heads, but for two of us it was difficult. Food was in short supply, and nobody wanted an extra mouth to feed, even on a farm. At least we now had a good excuse for being homeless, as there were so many other displaced people from Warsaw. But I was the problem, and a burden to Wala. This preyed on my mind: I didn't like to be a strain on my sister. We needed to quickly find a place where I could be kept out of sight, or perhaps work as a farm-boy, which would have provided good cover for me. But that seemed impossible for a young boy: farmers and villagers were a curious lot, not very welcoming and very suspicious of strangers.

Just as our situation seemed utterly hopeless, Wala had a brainwave. She vaguely remembered that Bolek Piatkowski, who had so kindly offered us refuge in his home, had mentioned that he had a summer-house near a lake in some sort of holiday colony. It may have been in the vicinity of Błonie, she thought, but I cannot be sure of the name now. I do know it was some distance west of the capital. The Piatkowskis had sent their children there for the summer vacation for safety in the event of an uprising, which they must have been anticipating. We trudged along slowly for a couple of days until we finally reached the place. We were very surprised to discover that it was indeed a holiday colony, and was specifically meant for Polish policemen, of all people, who either owned or had the use of these holiday chalets. They were all identical log cabins built around a pond, off the beaten track, in an isolated picturesque setting surrounded by pine trees.

It immediately dawned on us that from our point of view the place would be ideal for us. If we could only stay there, it would provide us with excellent cover. The safest places were often right inside the lion's den! The Polish police collaborated with the Gestapo, insofar as Jews were concerned, and the general population held no great affection for the Polish "Blue" police—not because of their hostile attitude to Jews, but because they were corrupt and served the enemy. Here, we thought, we would be way beyond suspicion; it would never occur to anyone to go looking for Jews inside a police colony. Wala started to ask around for the Piatkowski cabin, which we soon located. Three of the Piatkowski children were there: the eldest, a boy, who was a little older than I, and his two younger sisters. Their mother, whom we had last seen in Warsaw, had not so far appeared. We had gotten separated from her during the turmoil when we'd fled the blazing building. My sister tried to reassure the anxious children that their mother would return safely, as women were slowly being released, and the children had seen Wala in their Warsaw home, so they didn't consider her a stranger, and were calmed by her. We really thought that now we had it made. If only we could remain in the relative safety of the colony, with Wala helping to look after the children, we would be all right. The people in the colony were largely made up of wives and families of Warsaw policemen, with their husbands presumably caught up in the uprising and thus trapped in the capital.

The next morning an off-duty policeman dressed in civvies who was staying in an adjoining chalet started to look in my direction as I was playing in a sandpit with other children, all of them younger than me. Although I didn't look my age, I was a little too old to play in a sandpit, but I wanted to befriend the children, blend in, and play with them, so as not to stand out. I became aware that the man was observing me—it had to be me he was interested in, as he must have known the other children. Hinting that I needed to go to the lavatory, I left the others and I ran inside the cabin. In a panic, I quickly reached for the glue and ran to the toilet to take the necessary precaution.

Afterwards, I decided not to rejoin the other children, and remained indoors, as Wala had meanwhile left the colony to try to get a little food from a farm. It was a hot afternoon and the windows were wide open. After a while, the policeman came over, put his head through, and began to fire questions at me: what was my name, from where had I come, how was I connected with Bolek Piatkowski, and so on. I had to think quickly; this time I had no story prepared. I went on to explain that Wala and I had been sent by Bolek, who had joined the uprising, to take care of his children, and that we had been bombed out of his home. Surprisingly, he didn't ask about my relationship to Wala, and I didn't say she was my sister. If we were ever asked, our plan was to say that she was my cousin; this would help to explain the family resemblance. Before I had time to answer all of his questions, he cut me off and accused me of being Jewish! He was obviously not going to be convinced by any of my explanations. I was stunned; he never even gave me a chance to explain. He quickly hurried around the corner to the front door and barged in, making straight for me. Without too much ado, he pulled my trousers down with one firm tug. Having taken a good look, he said, "There is no place here for a *Żydek*!" and then vanished as quickly as he had come. I was shocked. He had, it seemed, detected that I was circumcised in spite of the disguise which had worked so well until then!

I remained indoors, at my wits' end, impatient for Wala to come back so we could run away together. When my sister finally turned up, I was beside myself as I tried to explain what had happened, and burst into tears, feeling guilty that I had let her down so badly. The episode demonstrated once more that I was a liability and a danger to her. I knew that I was a burden, and it was this that brought on the tears. I was not one to cry easily, but I felt responsible for endangering my sister, who would have done anything for me, come hell or high water. I would have preferred to go away somewhere and not come back rather than harm her in any way.

We immediately decided to make a run for it, but before we could do so, the policeman came back, having noticed that Wala had meanwhile returned. He again barged into the cabin without knocking, and he immediately accused her outright of harbouring a "Jew-boy." Pointing at me, he raised his voice and blurted out crudely, "He may not have had the 'ritual slash' but he's a Żydek just the same. You must be getting well paid for this one. Who is he, the son of a Warsaw physician or some big-shot lawyer? How much are the Yids paying you?," he sneered.

Wala, seeing that he'd gone in the wrong direction, found the confidence to pile abuse on him in the best Polish tradition. "*Psiakrew, skurwysynie*"—Dog's blood, you son of a whore!, she began. "Are you out of your mind? The boy is my brother, and how dare you call me a bleeding Jew!" The bluster was deliberate, as no Jew should have had the audacity to address any Pole in this way, let alone a police officer. The "Navy-Blue" calmed down a little, but still wouldn't let go, insisting that "the lad is Jewish." He claimed that certain lapsed Jews didn't practice circumcision. At long last, he turned and made for the door, without saying what his intentions were.

Luckily, it had never occurred to the blockhead that we might be brother and sister. Apart from the hair colouring, there was a strong family resemblance. With his mind firmly fixed on the money, he had failed to make the connection. He was so cocksure that he never asked to see our documents. He was only interested in Wala, because he thought there was money involved. My sister had no documents anymore, and as we had no pay-off money to offer we were afraid he wouldn't hesitate to hand me over to the Gestapo. We immediately abandoned the colony and the Piatkowski children, without even saying goodbye, in case the policeman grasped the situation. I was the first to slip away, followed by my sister a little while later. She knew in which direction I would head, and she caught up with me when she was able to leave. The children must have been bewildered when they got back inside to find we were gone. We felt terrible about deserting them in this way; their parents might not have made it out of Warsaw, and we could have at least helped to take care of them. We felt bad about deserting a loyal friend. On the other hand, we were a source of danger to Bolek's children and perhaps they would be better off without us. We took to the fields once more, and just ran and ran, not daring to look back in case he had sent the Gestapo after us.

While we were fleeing from Błonie, it crossed our mind that the "Blue" must have been a seasoned Warsaw *shmaltzovnik*, and this would not have been his first attempt at blackmail. If he'd simply wanted to turn me in, he could have done so then and there and just dragged me to the police station, or called the Gestapo to come and get me. Instead, he used the tactics of an extortionist, working up towards a bribe by bringing up the subject of money without actually asking for a share of it at this stage. He was sure Wala was not Jewish, and was getting well paid for taking care of me. He merely fired the first shot with the intention of laying his hands on the money and possibly turning me in later or, at best, chasing me off the colony. There was no point in trying to convince him otherwise, the only thing to do in the circumstances was to make a run for it. It was a real shame; we thought we had found the ideal sanctuary which would have afforded us excellent cover from the Gestapo.

We spent the night out in the open in some bushes. By morning we started to walk aimlessly in the oppressive August heat. It hadn't rained since the day we were trapped in the AK foxhole during the uprising. We just trudged along, not knowing or caring where we were heading. We lived on what we could find in the fields and slept out in the open. Finding drinking water became a problem, and we needed it desperately in the intense shimmering heat that rose from the fields and dusty paths. One farmer spared us a little water at the bottom of the pail, as he was watering a pair of cows; otherwise we had to rely on water from cattle troughs in the fields. We drank the frothy, murky water, slurping it from our cupped hands and spitting out the spiky bits of straw and grass. The liquid smelled and tasted of cud ruminants, but it did quench our thirst. It was past the middle of August and harvest time, and the parched fields had turned to light-brown. There were planted fields in our path, so we at least had ears of grain to nibble at, as well as raw potatoes to crunch. As the wheat was ripe, we were able to separate the kernels from the husks quite easily by rubbing the spiky ears between our hands.

My sister walked up to one farmer as he was milking his cow in the barnyard. "Praise Be!," she greeted him, as he eyed us suspiciously. "Please, sir, can you spare a little milk for an undernourished boy?" Wala pointed at me, standing at the farmyard gate. The surly farmer flatly refused. "Young lady," he answered. "I would rather pour it into the gutter than give it to fanciful folk from the big city!" Those driven out of the capital were not very popular with the oblivious peasants, who derived little pride from the uprising and blamed it for the resulting German anger and harsh treatment. The revolt had, no doubt, led to more of their pigs and produce being confiscated to feed the Wehrmacht.

Our situation had now become hopeless. We were utterly exhausted from running, from the ceaseless strain we'd been under ever since the outbreak of the uprising, and from the unbearable heat that went on and on without let-up. We couldn't see any way out of our predicament. Oh God, had we not suffered enough—would this nightmare ever end? Hungry and thirsty in the blistering summer heat, we felt all our energy ebbing away and were getting weaker and weaker by the hour. We were tottering on our feet. My knees eventually gave way, and my legs would no longer carry me. Wala experienced the same, and we dropped to the ground in a field, in the midday heat, with no shade to be had, overcome with exhaustion and with no strength to carry on. The years of struggle had finally taken their toll and pushed us to the limit.

We lost our temper with each other, which had never happened before: my only sister and I had always been close. I don't know what possessed me to start arguing with her: she was seven years older and like a mother to me. I almost blamed her for the mess we were in. We were so tired of the struggle, of running, and even of life; I wanted only to close my eyes and go to sleep. For the first time, we both felt that giving up would be a release. It could be dangerous to fall asleep in this state and in this heat, weakened by hunger and thirst and probably suffering from sunstroke, but we didn't care: all we wanted to do was to lie down and not wake up; we were done for. However, by late afternoon, when the day had cooled somewhat and we'd had a little rest, our instincts for survival took over once more. I remembered that Father had made me promise before we parted that I would never give up, nor forget, come what may. My sister and I both agreed that if we gave up now, all our struggles would have been in vain. We hugged and made up, resolving to persevere as best we could and never to give up the fight. At the very least, we owed it to our parents, who were never far from our thoughts.

We spent the night dozing intermittently, leaning against the outside wall of a barn. During the night I whispered to my sister that I was hungry to the point of starving and that I wanted to sneak inside the farm to see if I could find something to eat, perhaps some nourishing eggs, as I'd heard clucking hens in the evening before they had settled down for the night. Wala, more practical and less impulsive, restrained me: she was afraid I would disturb the farm dog and alert the farmer. We agreed that we'd had enough of the countryside and being chased off farms like stray dogs by unfeeling peasants. We decided to try our luck with the townsfolk instead. Surely one should be able to find a person with a heart to come to one's aid. But which town should we aim for? We had no idea where we were, nor in which direction to go.

Early the next morning, my sister said that during the night Father and Mother had appeared before her in her dreams. Seeing the predicament we were in, Father had said, "Children, be strong, you must promise to never give up." Father had always addressed us as "Children." Wala said that Father had advised her: "Children, you are going the wrong way; you must change direction and head towards Warsaw." Back to Warsaw? That was the very place we had been trying to get away from. But we never failed to take Father's advice, and could not begin now, even though this advice was only a dream. We made an early start and began to trek back in the direction Father had urged us to go. Although we were in the middle of nowhere, we knew in which direction Warsaw lay by the pillar of smoke rising to the sky above the capital. From this we assumed that the insurgents were still holding out, so we kept off the main roads where we could have encountered German patrols and army traffic heading to and from the capital. Hungry, thirsty, and totally drained, we just about managed to trudge along at a snail's pace. Like before, all we had to eat was cereal grain that we picked from the fields. But to our delight, we came across a very welcome brook in our path—or it may have been a spring—that came like a blessing from heaven. We splashed our faces thoroughly and lapped at the water like puppy dogs, together with the animals and birds that gathered there. This brook revived us and probably saved our lives; we must have been suffering from an advanced stage of dehydration since the previous day, without realising or even knowing the meaning of the word. We certainly knew what extreme thirst was like, but had no idea about dehydration and the harm it can do in just a matter of hours. After a good splash all over, we felt refreshed. Though we were reluctant to leave the watering hole and the shade of the bushes, we had to press on. After walking on and off for about another day and a half, we realised that we could not be too far away from Warsaw, judging by the dark column of smoke we were using as a marker. Having plodded along slowly but doggedly, by the middle of the next day we smelled on the gentle breeze the odour of burning, and we thought that this was as near to the hell of Warsaw as we would want to get.

Just then, we noticed a sign along the road pointing in the direction of a place called Włochy. It rang a bell with Wala, and we liked the sound of the place, so we decided to head for it. The name rather amused us: it stands for Italy in Polish, but to us it could have been the Garden of Eden. Perhaps it was a good omen; we fantasized that this was a place where one could knock on any door and ask for a little water and maybe even a slice of bread, and not be turned away.

CHAPTER 15

"Robinson Crusoe"

Włochy was then a sprawling place on the south-western approaches to the capital. There may have been some historical connection with the Napoleonic Polish Legion, which helped the French to capture Rome, as the Polish national anthem refers to. Other than this, the place held no special allure. As the uprising never spread to this area, it escaped destruction. Włochy was at the time the gateway to Warsaw from the west, and any German supplies had to pass through it on the way to Warsaw. Pockets of resistance in the districts of Mokotów and Zoliborz were still holding out in the capital. As a result, Włochy was under strict military control and crawling with Germans—hardly the place for undercover Jews. It wasn't easy for adults to move about without being checked and searched. Wala no longer had her documents, which was certainly a matter of concern, but she had always been able to talk her way out of any dicey situation. She had winning ways with people. Her good "Aryan" looks no doubt helped—they attracted admiring glances and distracted the Germans from further questioning.

My sister and I anxiously scoured the streets, on the lookout for a place to sleep, before dark set in and the curfew began. We passed a lake, and on the water's edge we saw a ramshackle shack with some lean-to wooden huts. This was interesting, we thought. At first the place appeared to be abandoned. "This could suit us fine," my sister said. "Praise be!" she added in greeting, as the door opened and we discovered that the building was inhabited by a solitary man who looked like a down-and-out recluse. Having overcome her initial surprise, she introduced us as homeless evacuees from Warsaw and begged him to consider taking in an orphan whose parents had perished in the uprising. Looking beyond the door, I saw that the room inside appeared stuffy and dank. The floor was just compacted earth, and the stench coming from within was suffocating. Pointing at me, Wala used her powers of persuasion on the man: "Sir, he's a willing lad who would do anything expected of him, and only begs a chance to prove his worth. He would expect little in return

apart from a corner to curl up in and just a bowl of *kasza* and milk a day."
The man hardly spoke, but he sized me up, looking me over from top to
bottom several times, and didn't seem very impressed. I suppose I didn't
look energetic enough, but Wala explained, "That's because he has gone
without food for some time and he's hungry, but he will recover in no
time at all."

"So he was orphaned in the uprising, was he?.," the man asked. Wala
nodded in approval, and went on to explain that we were cousins and
that I had no one to take care of me. The man spat on the floor, cursing
the "Swabians" roundly, and agreed to take me in, on condition that I
was obedient and worked hard. Wala would have to find lodgings elsewhere, but that would not be too difficult for her—I was the problem.

Right away I thought of the man as "Robinson Crusoe." He dressed in
grubby, ill-fitting clothes, had unkempt black hair and an unshaven face,
and was in need of a good wash. He reeked of body odour and *machorka,*
a cheap wartime tobacco. A wild man, I thought, just as I imagined an
island castaway might look. "Crusoe" led me inside and pointed to a corner of the cabin, where I would have to sleep on the dirt floor. He turned
out to be a sullen man with a brusque manner who disliked idle chatter, but there was a good side to him as well, as I discovered during my
time with him. I settled in at the shanty fairly quickly and was allocated
certain duties. "Crusoe" had a vegetable patch on the sloping edge of the
lake, which I learned to tend with him. It was work I liked; I had always
enjoyed digging and gardening. He also owned, or had the use of, a small
patch of grazing land just beyond the town, where I led his goat, which
I called Elżbietka (Lizzy), to pasture. I became a familiar sight, leading
my nanny-goat at the end of a length of string through the streets of
Włochy. It was a bit strange, as Włochy was not a village and there was
no farming community there. The place could best be described as a
working-class outer suburb of Warsaw.

This would turn out to be the ideal cover for me; no one would have
remotely suspected that the scraggly shepherd boy leading his goat to
pasture could possibly be Jewish. "Crusoe" taught me how to look after
the goat and milk her. Lizzy was entirely my responsibility: I brushed
her coat, kept her clean, and did the mucking out. Lizzy became an even
better "milker," as I took good care of her. In return, I enjoyed some of
her nourishing milk, and combined with all of the outdoor work, it soon
toughened me up. Lizzy got used to me slowly and became like a pet to

me. I liked dogs, but had never really cared much for goats—I only liked pure white kids. They made me think of home, and the popular Passover children's story that every child knew: "There was one little goat, one very little goat that my father bought for two Zuzim. . . ."

In time, I did away with the rope altogether. Lizzy was so good that she just followed me obediently like a dog when I led her to graze. I did, however, have to stop the voracious nanny from trying to nibble at anything she picked up along the way, including old shoes, rags, and paper. When I tried to take anything away from her, she didn't like it and would try to butt me in a playful sort of way. Another of my jobs was to cut the ryegrass in the field with a sickle to prepare the hay for winter fodder for Lizzie and the other animals we kept. This was an itchy job I never liked; the coarse grass mixed with thistles lacerated my hands and made them bleed.

As for the animals, we had quite a menagerie: we kept chickens, rabbits, geese, and other livestock. Still another one of my chores was to mix the feed for the geese. "Crusoe" showed me how to force-feed them to fatten them up. Seated on a stool, I held the struggling bird on the floor between my knees, stretching its head and neck upwards. I stuffed the cereal pellets into the poor bird's gullet and helped ease them down by stroking its long neck downwards, while holding the lethal beak closed with the other hand. I thought this rather cruel and asked to be relieved of the task, knowing it made the bird suffer, and "Crusoe" freed me from it. The fowl was not for our consumption, but for sale on the black market. "Crusoe" was a real miser. Having lived the life of a hermit for so long, he loved to hoard money and would never spend any of it.

In spite of the tasks assigned to me, with which I coped well, I was still left with enough time to pursue my own exploits. I knew what my duties were, and aside from them I was left to my own devices. "Crusoe" realised that I was a diligent worker and never took unfair advantage of me. He also didn't insist that I do anything I found repellent, like feed the geese.

I never used or even knew "Robinson Crusoe's" real name, as I always addressed him as *Pan*, Sir. Before the war he had been the local dog-catcher, but some of his other enterprises had sprung up during the war. He was still snaring dogs, but now he made salami sausage out of them! This was one aspect of his enterprise that I would have no part in. I loved dogs too much to do such a thing, and the very idea made me think of Dynguś, who must have run afoul of a dog-catcher like him. A corner of a nearby shed was set aside for curing and drying the canine sausage rings, which would hang from a long pole in the ceiling. "Crusoe" quite happily ate the garlicky salami, but it was mainly intended for regular customers calling at the shanty. As many people suffered from hunger in wartime, some had to resort to eating horseflesh and even dog meat. Although I often went hungry, I could never bring myself to eat it, except at the very beginning before I realised what it was. Once I learned, the mere thought of it made me feel queasy. However, I remember that it was not unlike Polish *kiełbasa;* with the flesh more pungent and chewy, highly-seasoned and heavy on the garlic. One of the few things that amused the glum "Crusoe" and made him chuckle was when I flatly refused to eat any more of the canine salami, preferring to go hungry. He thought me rather spoiled and prissy and liked to tease me about it—it was one of the few things that made him laugh. We had to be entirely self-sufficient, as he would not buy any food; we had to make do with what we raised or produced. The more palatable produce was sold on the black market, except for the odd rabbit, which he set aside for our own consumption on special occasions. These he despatched with a swift chop of the back of his hand to the rabbit's neck while he held the poor creature up by its ears. The roasted white meat tasted delicious, not unlike a honeyed version of roast chicken. There was no running water inside the cabin and no washing facilities, only a bucket and bowl. Our water had to come from the lake. Like my host, I got into the habit of not washing too often. As it was summer, I preferred to wade into the murky waters of the lake. I suppose it couldn't have been too contaminated, as there were small fish there.

The black soil on the edge of the lake was friable and fertile, with a nearby abundant supply of water. It was an excellent spot for our vegetable garden. We also grew tobacco on the allotment, which I'm sure was not legal. It was now late summer, time to harvest the tobacco leaves and hang them up, tied in bunches, from rafters in the shed to dry. This tobacco, called *machorka*, was strong and coarse, but as imported tobacco was unobtainable people rolled *machorka* in newspaper instead.

Some of our activities at the cottage were highly illegal, but war creates shortages which in turn open up opportunities for profiteering. "Crusoe" also had an illicit still for distilling *bimber* (moonshine), a raw type of vodka he made from rye or potatoes, and sold the hooch to the volatile Vlasov men billeted in the town. The "Vlasovtsy" were named after their commanding ex-Russian general, who had switched sides after he was taken prisoner by the Germans. These traitors had joined the German army to fight against the Russians, convinced they would end up on the winning side. When they got drunk on the home-brewed fire-water they called *samogon*, they would go on raping forays, terrorizing the local women. "Crusoe's" still was hardly to blame, though: I watched the liquid vaporize, and the slow, steady drip never amounted to very much at all.

There were Wehrmacht billets in the nearby houses whose dustbins I regularly picked through for something to eat. Rummaging for any remnants, I found scraps of army rations that were more appetizing than the canine salami. Apart from stale hunks of army loaf, I sometimes came across leftover bits of canned sauerkraut with meat, a popular German dish. I scraped the margarine wrappers for any residual fat, and if I was really lucky I found bits of soft tinned cheese. After a while, this practice became too risky, and one day I was chased off for scavenging by a German who aimed his gun in my direction as a warning. This finally persuaded me to change my eating habits, but I would never succumb to eating dog meat.

Adjoining the Wehrmacht quarters, a high-ranking Volksdeutsche lived with his wife and children in an imposing house which I believe had previously belonged to a Jewish family. My curiosity led me to observe this house, from which loud gramophone music kept blaring out. The strains of a German nursery song, called *Mamatschi*, resonated again and again. "*Mamatschi, schenk mir ein Pferdschen, ein Pferdschen aus Paradies*" (Mummy, please buy me a pony, a pony from paradise). The family included several flaxen-haired children, all neatly kitted out in Hitler Jugend uniforms, right down to the smallest. The outfit consisted of a brown shirt with a Sam Browne belt, black velvet shorts, and a swastika armband. To complete the outfit, a small swastika pin was worn in the neckerchief, and each boy had a small dagger. These Nazi whelps got to know me by sight, and as we passed each other in the street the toffee-nosed boys looked down with an air of superiority on the young "Polish vagrant" in his tattered clothes while the girls giggled coyly and I looked aside with downcast eyes. I envied them—not for their Hitler Jugend outfits, impressive though they were, but for their secure and privileged childhood, similar to the one which had been taken away from me. There is no justice in this world, I thought.

German soldiers sometimes went fishing on the nearby lakes the lazy way: they would toss hand grenades into the water from a dinghy. This would stun the fish and bring them to the surface, belly up. I would watch, noticing how as the fish floated on their sides, the odd lucky one would slowly recover from the blast and swim away, to live another day. After the soldiers had collected the best catch and departed, I waded in to retrieve some of the small fry, or rejects torn apart by the blast. I baked them with potatoes on a bonfire in the field while out shepherding Lizzy. The perch was delicious compared to the suspect fare available at the "Crusoe" shack.

It was while poaching on the lake in this manner one day that I befriended Wehrmacht *Gefreite,* or lance-corporal, Ryschard, who would let me go out with him in the boat to help gather in the catch, which was intended for the army canteen. This useful contact would later turn out to be of great benefit to me. Also, being seen with a German helped to allay any suspicion by neighbours, as the sudden appearance of a stranger, even a young boy, invariably invited gossip. The ginger-haired Ryschard even taught me, on our occasional "fishing expedition," how to unscrew the cap from the wooden handle of the stick-grenade, pull the cord which released the catch, and hurl the explosive into the water as far as possible from the boat. The detonation lifted the dinghy, and the resulting wake made it sway from side to side as we tried to steady it with our paddles.

Across the road from the lake there was a small wooded area where Russian deserters to the German side had pitched their tents between the trees and set up camp. These traitors were serving in the German Waffen-SS. Apart from their ethnic language they spoke Russian and also had a smattering of German. They had dark complexions, hailing, no doubt, from one of the Moslem republics of southern Russia. Perhaps they were Chechens or Tatars. Above their tented camp, alongside the swastika flag, fluttered the Star and Crescent. They were lawless horsemen, and it was dangerous for young women to go anywhere near them. Wearing Cossack Persian lamb caps, they rode into Warsaw daily, on carts drawn by small horses from the steppes, with Russian-made machine guns mounted on two-wheeled wooden carriages. Their task was to quell pockets of resistance still holding out in Warsaw and to systematically demolish the city. I mingled with these cutthroats in their encampment as they brought back their daily plunder from Warsaw. They paid little attention to a scamp like me and would sometimes even throw a crust in my direction as they gulped vodka and gorged themselves, sitting cross-legged on the grass, with their rifles propped up in tripods next to them.

"Robinson Crusoe" harboured a desire to accumulate cash, and the war gave him the opportunity to do so, but as I noted he could never bring himself to spend any of it. I suppose he had no need to. After he lived as a recluse for so long, the life must have been ingrained in him. Never slow to miss an opportunity, he recruited local tarts and set up a "social club" in a small room, just big enough for a bed, that he set aside in our shack for the benefit of these uncouth Russian deserters. Now, the war had robbed me of my innocence, and I had had to grow up quickly. My experiences had made me street-wise, and yet in some respects, I was rather naïve. At first, I didn't quite understand what this was all about, but one thing I was certain of was that I wasn't happy about these turncoats being entertained in our dwelling. Thus, I chose to stay away during "business hours," when the guests arrived to be amused. These repulsive men were often drunk and violent, and were in the habit of drawing their Russian "Nagan" revolvers out of their wooden holsters and letting loose a few rounds into the air as a form of merrymaking or letting off steam. Whatever the reason, it frightened the locals.

This enterprise, fortunately, didn't last long; one day the German military police came and declared the *bordello* out of bounds for reasons of hygiene. "Crusoe" was lucky to get away with it this time.

One afternoon in about the middle of September 1944, I began to hear the monotonous drone of heavy bombers in the sky. Looking towards the horizon, I could see planes in the distance, and soon the sky was filled with them. There seemed to be hundreds of aircraft flying in formation, leaving white contrails behind. As they got nearer, it became clear that they didn't look like the Junkers or the other German planes I was familiar with. These were huge, metallic aircraft, glistening in the afternoon sun. Panicky German soldiers ran into the street, stupefied, but no fighters took off to challenge them. They put up heavy flak, artillery fire, at the formations, apparently, as puffs of grey and black smoke were bursting all around the aircraft. Sadly, some planes were hit, and I saw them spin out of control and begin falling from the sky. Soon after, tiny dots appeared under the fuselages of the remaining planes, and then mushroomed into parachutes; the sky was speckled with them. What a marvellous sight, I thought gleefully—Allied paratroopers being dropped by the thousands on Warsaw and Włochy! I jumped up and down out of sheer excitement. The hysterical Germans ordered everyone off the streets and ran into the middle of the road, opening up with everything they had. They were firing Schmeisser sub-machine-guns and even rifles, blazing away vertically into the air, some lying flat on their backs and shooting wildly into the sky. But as the parachutes descended further down, the Germans realised their mistake and ceased shooting. To my dismay, what had looked like parachutists were in fact elongated metal canisters dangling from parachutes. The gleaming metallic-silver aircraft passed overhead, and I was thrilled to find that I was seeing American planes for the first time, and in broad daylight, yet! I waved at them frantically, though they were far too high up for anyone within to see me. What an awe-inspiring sight, I thought, as the ground beneath me shuddered. What awesome might we had on our side. We were not alone after all, and had not been forgotten.

The planes turned out to be B-17 Flying Fortresses of the US Air Force, dropping supplies to the pockets of resistance still holding out in Warsaw six weeks after the uprising started. As the area held by the insurgents was now quite small, the airdrop missed its target by miles. Many parachutes drifted beyond Warsaw. Some landed in Włochy, and a couple even splashed into the lake in front of me. I watched as the Germans opened the canisters, very gingerly at first, no doubt wary of booby-traps. Then with delight the frolicking soldiers pulled out collapsible British Sten-gun parts, reassembled them, and tried them out by pulling back the catch, pointing the unloaded guns at each other, squeezing the trigger, and going click-click!

Apart from weapons, the canisters contained ammunition, medical supplies, army rations, and even bumper bars of American chocolate, which really delighted the Germans and caused much horseplay.

One early evening, a flight of Russian Sturmovik ground-attack fighters swept in low over Włochy in one pass, strafing and bombing as they went. They were no doubt aiming at the Russian traitors' camp in the nearby wooded area. One stray bomb landed right next to our cottage and practically demolished it, sending some of the roof timbers caving in on us. "Crusoe" and I staggered out covered in dust, with him cursing blindly. Apart from being bruised and shaken, fortunately, we were not hurt. Sturmovik planes only carried small bombs. We now had the task of repairing the roof before the severe Polish winter set in.

So what had happened to Wala all this time? My sister, after she'd taken care of me, had managed to find a bed-sitter, and in dire need of some money was lucky to find casual work in the German army kitchens with other local women, peeling potatoes and vegetables as well as cleaning and laundering. There was no other work to be had in Włochy at this time, and she had to earn money to pay for her lodgings. Wala came to see me whenever possible, and sometimes I would go and wait for her until she came out of her place of work. My sister worried about me, or rather about the goings-on I was exposed to at the "Crusoe" dwelling. My education was limited to that of a ragamuffin on the streets, and she was concerned that I was growing into an ignoramus without any formal schooling. I tried to convince her that I was no dunce, and that I was quite happy the way I was, but now that she could afford it, she insisted that I go to a private teacher she had met who gave clandestine lessons at her home, to learn Polish language, arithmetic, and history. Schools had ceased to function, at least in the Warsaw area. The Nazis didn't want the Poles to become educated, as Slavic people were destined to become vassals of the 1,000-Year Reich.

As time had gone on, I had become more and more acclimatized to the "Aryan" side of life, and well used to acting the part of a street urchin. I had become part of the local scene. It would not have occurred to anyone that I was Jewish, and I would not attract undue attention moving about the neighbourhood. The only problem that could arise was if I came into close contact with some astute person for any length of time, a person who might have sensed that I acted evasively at times. How could one explain convincingly what I was doing here, where I had come from, and why I had no parents and family—and lacking parents and family would make the astute person suspicious right away. It was advisable to avoid close contact with people unless it was absolutely necessary. It paid not to be talkative, and to keep any conversation down to a minimum. It would not do to appear too clever, either, and it was essential to never ask questions. A slip of the tongue, or one wrong gesture, would raise eyebrows and possibly give me away. To try to divert the attention of suspicious people, it was a good idea to have contact with Germans, as they would imagine no Jew would dare be so reckless.

From my point of view, I had to choose my contacts with the utmost care. I considered older Wehrmacht men of lower rank to be the safest bet. The ordinary German "Fritz" was less likely to become suspicious or to challenge me, but it was advisable to give any Polish "Navy Blue" a wide berth; they liked to snoop.

I was still friendly with Corporal Ryschard, whom I helped with the "grenade fishing," at the time of the supply drop. He was stationed at the nearby Wehrmacht quarters where I had raided the dustbins for discarded army rations. He was a decent German, and I sensed he had taken a shine to me, perhaps because he felt sorry for the "orphaned street urchin," or perhaps he missed his own family back home. As I was often out on the streets, I frequently saw him walk to and from his quarters, and this was when I would accost him. *"Kamerad, Kamerad, Schokolade?"* Currently it was American milk-chocolate bars, dropped from the sky, that were in circulation in Włochy.

Ryschard knew the occasional Polish word, and I had by then picked up a fair amount of German. Poles had great difficulty learning the language, and vice-versa, but as a Jew I had no such problem, as Yiddish is akin to German. Thus, I had to be careful not to become too chatty and give myself away by mixing in the odd Yiddish word, which is easily done. I had to keep my wits about me at all times. A good knowledge of German could also invite the suspicion of Poles, so when attempting to speak it, I did so with an exaggerated Polish accent. Later on, my Wehrmacht contact Ryschard was to be of far greater benefit to me than all the chocolate and cigarettes that I managed to sponge off him.

My lessons were, at this point, due to begin. I told Wala that I didn't look forward to going to them, as I was fearful of having to make friends with boys who might get suspicious of me. I would have much preferred to just roam around in my spare time, but she wouldn't hear of it and insisted that I go. I began to make good progress, but all too soon, after I'd been attending the class for about two weeks, the teacher began to suspect that I was Jewish. My evasive manner obviously didn't go unnoticed by everyone. One day, during a history lesson about the Crusades, the teacher started to make derogatory remarks about the "chosen people" and so on, watching my reaction at the same time. Her snide remarks went unnoticed by the other pupils, but I could sense they were directed at me.

Partial view of the lake in Włochy where I went fishing with my Wehrmacht 'friend' Ryschard. The water line has since dropped. Crusoe's shack once stood a little but higher up this sloping bank.

Then came the day that after the lesson, she asked me to stay on behind. As soon as the other students had left, she came straight to the point and accused me of being "a cheating little *Żydek*." I was stunned. Coming as it did from a teacher the accusation left me at a loss for words, unable to utter a word in my defence. Poles had a bent for nosing out Jews. I could never, I realized, have pulled the wool over the eyes of someone as astute and intuitive as my teacher. I had always looked up to school teachers with the greatest respect, and hadn't expected her to behave in this way. It threw me completely. After all, it was now past the eleventh hour of the war, and I presented no danger to her. There was no need for her behaviour; she could have found some other excuse to dismiss me without displaying her anti-Jewish sentiments. She made it patently clear that I was not welcome in her home, showed me the door, and told me in no uncertain terms not to come back. If I could be sure the truth would go no further, and that being expelled was to be my only punishment, it would not have mattered greatly, but she knew where I lived, just across the lake, and after she expressed such hostility, my sister and I felt that she could not be trusted and I could not risk remaining where I was. Both my sojourn with "Robinson Crusoe" and my short academic career came to an abrupt end all at once. During the war, one was often faced with the terrible dilemma of when to run and when to stay, and it was important to be able to make a snap decision. We decided it was better to err on the side of caution, and leave. It was a terrible shame, as I had come to feel secure with "Crusoe" and could have safely remained with him until the end of the war were it not for that ghastly teacher.

I often contemplate whether "Crusoe" ever got suspicious of my being Jewish. I rather think not, but I can never be sure and he never let on; he never liked to pry or gossip. He was the type of person who, had he suspected something, would not have confronted me over it, nor turned me away. As a person, he could be both kind and severe. As a proud Pole, he didn't display any fear of the Germans, and I had after all become helpful to him and felt he had gotten to like me. His boorish ways apart, he was a very courageous man and not entirely bereft of principles.

My sister came up with some story as to why I had to leave. "Crusoe" said he was sorry to see me go; so was I. It transpired that the poor man was some time later taken away by the Gestapo, and his entire enterprise on the edge of the lake was demolished. I would like to think that it was not because of me, as it was some time after I left him that he was picked up. Had the Gestapo known about me, they could easily have found me in Włochy. "Crusoe" must have fallen afoul of the Germans for some other reason, which was not surprising, considering some of the stunts he got up to. He hated the Nazis and made no secret of it, and it required little more than a careless remark to be hauled off to a concentration camp, but I think his transgression was rather more serious than that. For his place to be demolished, he may have somehow been connected with the Polish Underground, though I was not aware of any connection while I was with him.

CHAPTER 16

Stefek: Leader of the Gang

It was by sheer coincidence that Renia Nisker, a young Jewish woman from Ostrowiec, happened to be working as a maid in Włochy for a well-to-do Polish family who lived in a big house. Renia "looked good"—that is, very "Polish." She had been acting as the connecting link between the few of us from our hometown moving about the Warsaw area, and all of us reported back to her whenever possible. It was through Renia that Wala made contact with two other mutual friends from Ostrowiec, Marmula Feffer and Hindzia Szerman, both passing for non-Jews with assumed identities, and both in dire need of help. Marmula, who went by the name of Marysia, and Hindzia, whose assumed name I can no longer recall, had been in hiding in Warsaw, but with the outbreak of the uprising, each had lost her shelter and found herself outside the capital, looking for a roof over her head. Their situation had become precarious, as had mine because of my wretched teacher. We had to find shelter urgently; there was no time to lose.

Wala and I combed the area, desperately looking for a place we could share with Marysia and Hindzia. Ultimately, our attention was drawn to a deserted little house on Kolejowa Street, virtually opposite the railway station. It looked like a jerry-built small bungalow, and bore the year 1938 on the elevation above the front door. The house was still unfinished, with its construction apparently interrupted by the war. The place turned out to be a basic structure, consisting of just two small rooms with no electricity or running water, but there was a well with a pump nearby. The dwelling had no glass panes, just boards nailed to the window frames—ideal, from our point of view. The boarded-up windows made the place look unoccupied and would not attract attention or prying eyes. There was a rear door that was partly glazed, and provided at least a little daylight.

We tracked down the owners of the property, who turned out to be a middle-aged couple living in a detached house with a garden. It stood on the same plot of land as the bungalow, but farther from the road. We knocked on the door, and after the customary Praise Be the Lord was exchanged Wala asked the owner for permission to stay in the vacant dwelling on a temporary basis, as we had no roof over our heads. We had no money for rent, but as they appeared to be reasonably prosperous people, Wala offered to do the housework for them in return, and I would keep the garden tidy. Unfortunately, permission was curtly refused, on the grounds that the place was only partly built and not safe for habitation. We suspected this was not the real reason; it may have been because we had no money for rent. Wala got a little irritated and reminded him, as we were about to leave, that as a Pole it was his patriotic duty to help the homeless from Warsaw, as others were doing at this time. Her reprimand fell on deaf ears.

Still, as we could find no other place, this was an opportunity too good to miss. It was decided that there was no other alternative but to try and enlist the help of my German fishing companion, Ryschard. Soon enough, I managed to locate him, and I told him my sister and I had nowhere to live. I went with him to the owner's house, where he gave the owner a stern warning that unless he opened the place up for us he'd see to it that he was on the next transport of *Ostarbeiter* to the Reich! This did the trick immediately. Thereafter, the landlord and his wife looked upon us with fear and distrust. This unavoidable course of action had a double edge to it; if the owner ever got suspicious of us, he would not hesitate to exact his revenge and turn us in. It was a risk we had to take, and it was true that any vacant dwelling was supposed to be made available to the homeless from Warsaw.

This is how Wala and I ended up sharing the cottage with Marysia and Hindzia. Marysia had dark hair with pronounced Jewish features, so she had to remain indoors at all times. We took a big risk sharing with the others, but my good-natured sister would never turn a friend away. The landlord never knew there were others inside the cottage besides the two of us. What made matters worse was that Marysia was visibly pregnant; she had been separated from her husband Mietek, who had been taken prisoner during the uprising and sent for forced labour to Germany.

My sister and I started right away to go to church. It was important to be seen doing this, because of the neighbours and the landlord in particular, who must have borne a grudge against us. Thereafter, we went in constant fear of being denounced by him, should he ever get suspicious of us. People were jittery and spied on their neighbours, afraid of being implicated in harbouring Jews. On Catholic feast-days it was customary to go to Mass. On entering church, I dipped my hand in the holy water. After crossing myself, I bowed and my sister curtsied. Inside the church we tried to remain as inconspicuous as possible by taking a pew at the back, not wishing to go forward to take Communion. I remembered some of the prayers that *Pani* had taught me, but I only just recognized the hymns, so my sister and I moved our lips in unison with the worshippers, turning the pages of the missal when they did, and when the congregants made the sign of the cross, we followed suit. We did our best to mimic them, and when the worshippers dropped to their knees or rose to their feet, we did the same; we parroted their every move. At the same time I looked out of the corner of my eye to see if anyone was watching us. During the sermon we were able to relax.

I had by this time gained more confidence and had no problem passing for a Christian boy, but I could not afford to trust anyone and had to avoid making friends who might have gotten suspicious. However, there was a gang of urchins in my neighbourhood of about my age that I could not avoid. I wanted to join them, but they weren't interested. As luck would have it, the ragamuffins started to accuse me of being a runaway from the ghetto! The scamps began to taunt me, and to my utter horror they yelled after me in an exaggerated, mock Yiddish accent: "*Żydzie do Getta*" (Oi, Jewboy, back to the ghetto). This was for me, and indeed all of us at the cottage, a matter of life and death. I didn't dare tell my sister, hoping the problem would soon go away. I didn't want to cause her any anxiety. This was something I had to resolve for myself, that she could not help me with. I had to put a quick end to this serious accusation before it spread further and was perhaps overheard by the wrong person. What made it so alarming was that the boys knew where I lived, and there was no way of keeping out of their way, as I had to be out and about to "organise" food for the group. The thing to do was to somehow win them over and gain their trust, so I could team up with them. The only way to go about it was to somehow concoct a story that would impress them to such an extent that they would want to be friends with me.

Every boy in the Warsaw area was fired up by the uprising, so I decided to invent a tale about my part in it. The first thing was to get them interested and make them want to listen to me. I told them that I had taken part in the uprising and had been attached to an AK unit, whose commanding officer was "Młot" (Hammer). This was not his real name, I explained; everyone in the Underground had to have an assumed name, so you could not betray your comrades when captured. One bright spark asked what my code name was. I had not thought of that one, and instinctively thought of my dog, Dynguś. I went on to recount how I had been active in the uprising as a runner and ammunition carrier for the AK, until I was cut off from my unit when my district fell into German hands and an early end came to my exploits. Later, I told them, I'd managed to escape from a holding centre, ending up in Włochy. The boys took much pride in the uprising, but so soon after the event they knew little about it, so it wasn't difficult to impress them. Over the next couple of days I tried to gradually relate to them all I knew. What they were really keen to hear were examples of Polish bravery. The boys sat cross-legged on the ground, listening carefully, and eagerly swallowed every word, wanting to hear more and more. I described the street fighting and the different equipment in the arsenal of the AK, with which I was somewhat familiar. Being interested in weaponry, I could identify the equipment on both sides, and imitate the sound they made when fired. I was able to mimic the punctuated rat-tat-tat of the Spandau heavy machine-gun and the sound the Mauser gun made. I told them about the underground army's favourite piece of equipment, dropped from the air in great numbers by the British—the PIAT anti-tank projectile-firing rifle that was most effective in knocking out German Panzers. They were pleasantly surprised to hear that the AK managed to capture German tanks and turn them on the enemy. I also told them about the "*Krowa*," which really made them laugh. They were fascinated by the enemy's miniature robot-tank, the "Goliath," which was packed full of dynamite and which the "Fritzes" directed by remote control against the defenders' pillboxes and barricades. But what really pleased them was when I told them that these infernal robots could be sent off-course by a single well-placed Polish rifle shot!

The boys were very impressed by it all and decided that I could not have known all this unless I was there and had taken part. I had, of course, learned most of this while in Warsaw, following the progress of the fighting and listening to other people's conversations. There were in fact such boys as I pretended to be enlisted by the AK; being small, they were less conspicuous and more suited for crawling through holes in bombed out buildings to relay messages and to carry ammunition. I produced a silver eagle badge out of my pocket, which represented the White Eagle emblem of Free Poland. I had proudly worn it on my beret, I told them, but it was prohibited to display this now, and I put it back in my pocket quickly. They were all keen to touch it. I also recalled songs adopted by the insurgents that became songs of the uprising, like "*Serce w Plecaku*" (My Heart in a Kitbag), which I had learned from Wala, who liked to sing and knew all the popular songs. Soon enough, my stories did the trick, and the boys became envious of me and full of admiration, wishing they had also been there.

As I was the most savvy and resourceful of the children there, I soon took charge of the gang—they had never had a leader before. They now considered me one of them and were happy to follow me. All the taunts stopped, and I would never again have to face accusations of being Jewish from them. True to street-gang tradition they all had nicknames, mainly deriving from the boys' appearances. I hardly knew their real names. There was *Ząbak* (Goofy), who had long incisors, *Dziobak* (Spotty), who had a pock-marked face as a result of chicken-pox, and *Ślimak* (Snail), who had a gammy leg and couldn't run fast, and ironically I was *Żydek* (Jew-boy). They didn't mean any harm by it; every boy had to have a nickname, and they didn't see anything wrong in calling me that. Perhaps they innocently thought the label suited me for some reason other than that they took me for a Jew. At first I thought it best ignored, but the harsh sound of *Żydek* was like a dagger through the heart every time I heard it. But as I was now the leader of the pack, I had the power to discourage any nickname, and certainly this one, and in time they dropped it, calling me simply "Stefek." I now had friends, which I'd never had before. I wanted pals like them to give me the legitimacy and cover I needed—these relationships would be my guarantee of survival. Being part of a gang also helped me to "legitimately" purloin food—which was quite important as I had several mouths to think of. From then on I went unhindered and was not picked on by any street kids. I wore a chain around my neck supporting a large medallion of St. Stefan, my patron saint, I claimed. It was prominently displayed outside my vest, and I hoped this would help to demonstrate my deep Christian devotion.

The one activity I could never join my pals in was swimming in the nearby ponds, as they swam with nothing on. I had to own up to the "fact" that I couldn't swim and that I hated water. "I even dislike washing," I told them. I could not have turned down their challenges indefinitely, but luckily the summer was almost over, and once the weather grew colder there was one less problem to worry about. There was no school, so we were free to roam, foraging for food, pilfering a little here and there: scrumping fruit from orchards, digging up potatoes, and pulling carrots and turnips from the fields. Some of the boys even lifted from market stalls, but I tried not to resort to that, at least not yet, while there were things to be had from gardens.

The boys came from poor homes, and the war imposed even greater hardships on them. Their endeavours helped to sustain their families. At times, we would end up being chased off by farmers with hayforks, having to make our getaway across fields of bindweed and stinging nettles. Poor *Ślimak,* the Snail, was always the one to get caught and given the "prize" of a tanned hide. My face became bronzed and weather-beaten as a result of all the time we spent outdoors. I blended in well with my gang; I sounded like them, adopting their local singsong twang, and looked grimy like them in my tattered clothes. I wore my peaked cap at a jaunty angle and smoked the odd dog-end, which I really hated, in order to appear like a *cwaniak* (artful dodger). The cigarettes we would cadge off Wehrmacht soldiers by holding a hand out, and begging in German-Polish "speak" "*Kamerad, Kamerad, Papierosy.*" Oval-shaped German cigarettes were highly regarded and a valuable trading commodity. I started a small production going, making low-cost cigarettes out of cigarette ends collected off the streets. I trimmed the stained stub-ends with a razor blade, emptied the clean tobacco into a tin, and mixed it with cheaper *machorka* to make it go further. I had a device to inject the blank *gilzy* (filter-tips) with tobacco. Astute smokers used a pin to smoke them to the very end, saving what they could—only Germans discarded long cigarette-ends. Senior officers smoked highly-prized gold-tipped cigarettes, and they could afford to smoke about half of each one, throwing the rest aside. The kids would fight for them in the dust. In wartime, some people would forego food in favour of a smoke. I sold the "recycled" cigarettes on a street corner where people mingled if they had something to sell or exchange. With several mouths to feed, I was only interested in food.

Our place had no electricity, and we had no money for paraffin for the lamp, but fortunately we did have a small cast-iron wood-burning stove inside the hut. There were no windows, but some daylight came through the partly-glazed door. At night lighting could only be provided by candles. These I collected from graves at the local cemetery. This was a secret I never shared with my pals, as they would never have approved of filching from the Catholic cemetery. Stealing food was fair game, but this, I knew, they would have considered a sin. I also made candles from leftover bits of candle-wax, likewise taken from the graveyard. These I melted down and poured it into a wooden mould, before the mixture set, I inserted a thin piece of string for a wick, then poured the rest of the wax on top. My home-made candles were more square-shaped than round, burned rather quickly, and had a tendency to drip and flare up, but they nevertheless went some way to solving our lighting problem. However, fuel for heating and cooking was of great concern, as winter was fast approaching. The only thing we still had for the pot was a small store of potatoes and vegetables, which we had to ration severely, and no meat or stock, with only the odd packet of army-issue margarine, courtesy of Ryschard.

In wartime, the gloomy, harsh winters were the most difficult to endure. The sixth winter of the war was drawing near, and without heating one could barely survive the harsh Polish winter. As time went on, more and more responsibility fell on me to provide for our small band at the cottage, and things got much harder for me. It was unsafe for young adults to go outdoors, and Wala was forced to stop doing odd jobs, making things even more difficult. She had not been able to replace her identity papers, and as she was a young woman she also ran the risk of being rounded up and taken to Germany for forced labour. Besides, my sister was too pretty to be out and about; she would have been in danger from the lawless ex-Russian auxiliaries stationed in the town. I now kept "my band" locked in with a padlock, making the place look unoccupied before setting out on my daily quest in search of food.

Włochy had never had many shops, and those that had existed were now shuttered, as there was no food to be put on the shelves. To buy food, there was only the black market, and farmers in the countryside for those who had the means. Some people lived by bartering their possessions, but we had neither money nor anything to barter with. Coal was unobtainable, since it all went into the German war effort. The cold was setting in early and without heat our frostbitten feet would begin to ache, then swell up and turn blue; this was the first sign: after that you could simply fall asleep and never awaken. Dried cow-pats made for excellent fuel: unlike wood, they burn nice and slow. Others, however, had the same idea, and any cattle dung soon disappeared from the fields. Anyway, when the snows come, cattle are taken under cover. People cut down their trees or collected twigs and brushwood in the countryside. Unlike other places, Włochy never had a ghetto, so there were no empty homes to tear down for firewood. There were plenty in Warsaw, but that was strictly out of bounds.

I noticed that German coal trains passed regularly along the track running parallel with the main road, just across the street from our hut. Pitiable old grannies, bent double with age, could be seen along the railway track, trying to dig up bits of coal and coke from the ground by picking over the soil with sticks. Others tried to eke out some heating fuel from the coal-blackened earth with sieves, separating the slack from the pebbles and dirt. There had to be, I thought, a better way of "requisitioning" some badly needed coal. I observed that coal trains slowed down as they approached Włochy station, but the train didn't stop there. Włochy station was permanently closed, as it led only to Warsaw, which had been totally depopulated and declared out of bounds to civilians. Only German personnel or people with German *Passierscheinen* were allowed into the station. Once past, the train would pick up speed again. I was about to perform a feat which so endeared me to my gang that Stefek would forever become the object of their admiration as a man of derring-do. I ran along the rear of the train, and as it slowed down I jumped on the step of the last wagon and pulled myself up the foothold and over the wagon to where the coal was heaped high. Then, lying on my back, I pushed the coal over the side with my feet as quickly as I could. As the train pulled into the station, I spread-eagled myself flat on the coal so I would not be seen by the sentries at the station. Stealing Third Reich property was tantamount to sabotage, and I risked being shot. Once past the station, I reversed the routine, shoving more of the coal over the side before clambering down as the train made to gather speed. Meanwhile, the rest of the gang ran alongside the track, collecting the coal in sacks, dragging them as they went. Later on, with a blackened face and covered head to toe in coal dust, I shared out the haul and also spared some for the bent-over *babushkas* who had been scratching at the soil with their sticks. The grateful old ladies showered me with blessings in the name of "Sweet Jesus." My new activity went some way towards easing our heating problem. We now had an inexhaustible supply of fuel, courtesy of the Third Reich!

The tiny cottage in Włochy we and our friends sheltered in.
We only had the use of this rear door, everything else having been boarded up.

An additional problem we encountered when winter set in was, surprisingly, drinking water. There was no plumbing or running water in our dwelling, as it was only partly built, but there was a well in the landlord's garden which we had access to. Later on, during hard frosts, this became a problem. Although the hand-pump was lagged with sacking, it was not enough to stop it from freezing up. We stored all the water we could for drinking, cooking, and everyday usage, but we didn't have enough receptacles to store enough water for five people for long. For washing, we melted down snow. Luckily, we had a very basic cesspool lavatory at the cottage, though without the flush mechanism. Fortunately, it never filled up, but the room had a permanent reek to it. I never added to the problem: as I was always out and about, I got into the habit of doing what boys in the country normally did.

Our contact Renia Nisker at some point that winter informed Hindzia that her husband Chanina, from whom she'd gotten separated in Warsaw, had sent a message to her that he was at the nearby Ursus or Pruszków transit camp with other prisoners from the Warsaw uprising. They were transported daily in sealed freight cars through Włochy station to Warsaw, to work on defence fortifications and the clearing of rubble. Hindzia was concerned for her husband, who was in great danger because of his Jewish appearance; his fellow prisoners were antagonistic to him. Hindzia was anxious for him to join us at the cottage, if only a way could be found of getting a message to him to encourage him to escape. We had a suitable hiding place for him in the hut, a small cellar-cum-larder below the floor, with a hinged tilt-up door.

The train carrying the prisoners only stopped at the station for a few brief minutes, with no one allowed on or off. I took it upon myself to try to get a message to Chanina, but I needed an excuse to get into the station, and I didn't know how to go about it. It was "little" Hindzia who came up with the idea of pretending to be a cigarette seller and sneaking in herself. I acquired a shallow wooden box, to which I attached a strap to suspend it from the neck, like a cinema usherette. On the box I placed some hand-rolled cigarettes, as well as empty packets and some boxes of matches, which were not difficult to obtain. As cigarettes were scarce and expensive in wartime, they were sold singly. Assuming her role, Hindzia, being small and petite, attempted to get into the station, but was turned away. A day or two later, I thought I would I try my luck. I made for the station with the tray around my neck and approached the two sentries standing watch. I asked them, pointing at my tray, if they would allow me inside, "to flog a few smokes." The sentries were rather amused by my cheekiness, shrugged their shoulders, and waved me past.

As the train slowly pulled in, I ran alongside it shouting *"Zapałki! Papierosy!"* (Matches! Cigarettes!) for the benefit of any German guards. As I darted from wagon to wagon, I called out in a low voice for "Jan Wójcik," the name Chanina went by. The freight cars were tightly packed with standing prisoners and I could not locate him. There was a big commotion up and down the train as I went: men shouted and begged me to pass on messages they held in their outstretched hands, but I had no way of helping them all. A couple of days later, I repeated the same routine, running alongside the train. This time, however, Jan was near the opening, looking out for me. He had apparently heard me call out for him last time, but had been unable to get near the opening of the tightly packed wagon. He stretched his arm out through the small, barred-over window high up in the wagon's wall, trying to pass me a note. But as I couldn't reach up to it, he dropped it on the platform. I had realized ahead of time that this could be a problem, and had come prepared with Hindzia's note attached to a stick. He was able to reach it. In the shadow I was just about able to make out his face. I knew Chanina; he had been a Jewish policeman in the ghetto. He was a good man, known to help others, and now I was glad to be able to help him.

In Jan's message to his wife he wrote that his situation had become very dicey because his fellow prisoners were hostile to him, and that he could be betrayed to the Germans at any time. The note from his wife that I'd handed to him contained precise directions as to how to find his way to our place should he manage to escape. A few days later, Jan appeared at our door in the middle of the night, overcome with exhaustion, having trudged in the deep snow from Pruszków to Włochy, keeping off the main roads. Thereafter, he remained hidden inside and never ventured out again until the war was at last over. If there was anyone at the door, or any disturbance outside, he and Marysia would dive into the cellar, and in a matter of seconds we would cover the trapdoor with a mat and put a small table on top. I felt proud that I had a hand in helping a desperate man who would have been detected, sooner or later, or denounced to the Germans by his fellow prisoners.

Personally, I now felt ever more confident of surviving the war, even if it were to drag on another year, especially when I was operating with my gang. I even stopped thinking of myself as Jewish. However, by all staying together in the one place, we were all disregarding a basic wartime rule of not endangering one another. In the event of a knock at the door, there would be no escape for any of us. We took a terrible risk by staying together with Chanina, an adult male whose Jewishness was unmistakeable. Tall and handsome though he was, he had very pronounced Semitic features, with a shock of black wavy hair and a prominent nose—almost like the caricature of a stereotypical Jew. On the one hand, I felt more secure than ever when out and about with my gang, but on the other, I felt unsafe inside my own hut. It would have been so much safer to "operate" with just my sister, as we had been before, but we were tired of the long struggle and felt we had reached the end of the line, taking ever-greater risks. There was no way out now; the five of us were comrades in adversity, linked by a common fate, we either all lived together or all went down together.[11]

---

11 Of the Włochy group, Hindzia and Chanina (Jan) Szerman, who changed their family name to

As winter tightened its grip, there was no fruit left in the orchards, and it became increasingly difficult to find food. The ground was covered by a thick blanket of snow and frozen solid beneath it. There was nothing to be had from the fields either, as all had been gathered in before the onset of winter. All I could find were some withered Brussels stalks, devoid of any sprouts, protruding from the windswept, snowy ground. Any potatoes or root vegetables left in the ground would reduce to an inedible mush when thawed out. Our food stock was depleting by the day, and Marysia was of great concern. Being pregnant, she was in need of nourishing food. We had right from the start pooled all our money together; my sister and I never had much, but Hindzia, being a thrifty little business woman, somehow always managed to scrape a few coppers together when required. However, the kitty was now virtually empty, with every grosz or pfennig spent on food. All my previous sources of supply had dried up because of the weather.

We now got very worried about surviving the long winter. Apart from white beets, all we had left stored in the cellar was a small quantity of mouldy potatoes, which we had to ration severely. We ate them with the peels, but after cutting the blight away carefully we didn't have much left. We still had a reasonable stock of sugar beets, which had been plentiful in the fields in late autumn, before they too had beem harvested. We ate the beets raw at times, but mostly we had them cooked, and drank the sweet liquid they were boiled in, until we were well and truly sick of them. Fortunately, my German friend Ryschard still helped out now and then, but not as much as before. It depended on what he could get. There was no more American milk chocolate, dropped from the sky, to be had, but what was more beneficial was that he passed on some army rations whenever he could. Once he came up with some tins of Wehrmacht-issue cheese-spread, most of which I exchanged for bread in the unofficial market to make it go further. I don't really know why he helped the way he did, apart from feeling sorry for the young "orphaned urchin" who often went hungry and was forced to scavenge for food. He

---

Malachi, live in Hadera, Israel, where Chanina became a poultry farmer in a co-operative. He has since passed away. Renia Nisker, who changed her family name to Nir, lives in Tel Aviv. Marmula (Marysia) Feffer lives in Rio de Janeiro, Brazil. She was reunited with her husband Mietek, from whom she had become separated during the Warsaw uprising, after the war. He was taken with other Poles from the uprising to a slave-labour camp in Germany where he survived. He has since died. Fortunately for Marmula, liberation came in the nick of time for a son Kubush (Jacob) to be born.

may have guessed that I had other mouths to feed, besides my sister, but he never asked any awkward questions. He may even have suspected what I was up to—it wouldn't surprise me; Ryschard was no Nazi, and I had always felt he could be trusted.

One day, word spread that a tired old nag had dropped dead in the street. I decided to join the fray, entering the crowd that was stripping the animal of its flesh, but by the time I had managed to get near enough to the carcass with my knife, the scraggy old horse had already been stripped clean. Only the bare ribcage remained. In the free-for-all, I managed to make off with a couple of the horse's ribs, virtually devoid of flesh. In the fracas, I got covered in the horse's blood and dirt. Nevertheless, the ribs produced a nutritious, if watery, consommé, which was a real life-saver. People went hungry if they had nothing of value to sell or to barter with. There were impromptu street bazaars, without stalls or tables, where one could stand and sell, holding up items for sale in their hands, ready to run if need be. I remember one particular very large woman who stood in the market. She wore several layers of clothes, which made her look even bigger than she was, and was wrapped in a large crocheted shawl with fringes in the style of peasant women. She was selling hot soup from a cauldron standing on some bricks and flaming tinder. The appetising, thick soup was always the same, containing *flaki,* or tripe, cut into thin white strands like noodles. Only those who could afford to buy were allowed to stand near the steaming cauldron to warm their hands while they slurped the piping-hot soup out of chipped enamel bowls. I had to make do with just the aroma. The smell was divine!

Rumour had it that there were rich pickings to be had in the Warsaw ruins. The inhabitants of the homes there had been either killed or driven out, and plentiful dried goods had been left in sculleries and cellars. The city had been completely emptied of people and designated a closed military area, with German soldiers manning the defences along the Vistula, facing the Russian lines on the opposite bank. It was forbidden to enter any part of the depopulated city, under pain of death, but by this time I was so desperate that I was prepared to take the risk of going into the obliterated city to look for food. At the barrier checkpoint out of Włochy, on the road leading to Warsaw, I observed that army supply trucks headed in, and the same vehicles returned empty later on in the day. I decided to disregard the danger and try to jump a ride to Warsaw on the back of a German truck. Then I could try to recce out the deserted city for some desperately needed sustenance. If I could only pull this one off, it could save our group from possible starvation.

One early morning, after saying goodbye to my sister, I told her that I had a busy day ahead of me with my gang, and that she should not expect me back early. I took a long detour round the checkpoint barrier where the trucks had to stop for inspection, then rejoined the road further along, where I stayed hidden behind an obstacle near the road, waiting for a slow-moving lorry to appear. Because of the shortage of diesel fuel, some of the German trucks had to resort to a wood-burning system, with the engines adapted to run on timber logs, or rather the gas extracted from the timber. These trucks were easily recognised by the large metal cylinder mounted beside the driver's cab. Luckily, these were very slow to accelerate, and when the right lorry approached, I sneaked up behind, hinged my fingers on the rear tailboard, and hoisted myself onto the truck, below the canvas flap. To my surprise, the lorry was fully-laden with pallets of mortar shells and other munitions which helped to conceal me from the driver in front. As I didn't know the final destination of the vehicle, I decided not to venture too far into the city centre, in case I had to make it back on foot through the ruins.

This foray brought back memories of home; it reminded me of the carefree rides I used to take on the back of *dorożkis* in Ostrowiec, which now seemed so long ago— my life there was a distant memory. I often dreamed of home, about my parents and brothers and the happy times, now long gone. A lot had happened since—it had been five long, miserable years since the war began. I had also changed in that time. I could hardly believe what had become of me; I had grown into a scavenging young wretch who my parents would scarcely have recognised.

The truck wound its way slowly along the meandering path in between heaps of rubble and piles of bricks. When the vehicle reached a certain spot and almost came to a halt because of some obstacle, I quickly lowered myself from the tailboard and darted away to a concealed spot. Looking around myself, I was astounded by the dreadful scene: the once beautiful city was reduced to a scene of utter desolation. From where I stood, all I could see was a vast landscape of empty shells and ruins. I found myself all alone in a wilderness of burnt-out buildings and heaps of rubble as far as the eye could see, totally devoid of people. It was rather eerie; there wasn't a living soul to be seen. A world where silence and desolation reigned. Apart from the odd rat scuttling by in my path, there was no sign of life. I fantasized that I was not only the last Jew left, but also the last human being, reigning over a vast emptiness and crumbling ghost-land, as if after an apocalypse.

Some years later, reading the novel *On the Beach,* by Neville Shute, I imagined it to be like the scene from Warsaw, when I imagined myself the last human left alive after a nuclear blast. It was hard to imagine that these ruins were once part of a beautiful city; all that was visible now were jagged shells of buildings with only their chimneys jutting out. The interiors were gutted. The only sign of life I saw was the oc-casional German military vehicle moving along the winding path where the truck I'd jumped off of had stopped. As I was picking my way through the ruins, I went numb with fear when I spotted a large skeletal dog in the distance, no doubt scavenging for food like me. Although I had always loved dogs, I tried to keep well clear of it so it would not pick up the scent and perhaps latch on to me, leaving me unable to shake him off. The sound of a dog barking could have attracted the attention of any Germans in the immediate vicinity and perhaps even stopped me from getting back onto the lorry. Besides, I had nothing to share with the dog; I was just as hungry.

I knew it was best to look for food in an area that was recaptured by the Germans early on in the uprising, as districts that had held out for any length of time would have no food left, having been stripped bare by the starving population. So I decided to concentrate on the neighbour-hood of Koło, which was nearby and not far from Wola, where my sister and I had been during the uprising about four months before. Koło, which means "wheel" in Polish, was a modern housing estate compris-ing a number of uniform blocks built in a semi-circle—hence the name. Surprisingly, some of the buildings in this area were still standing, and that was why I headed for it. Some of the buildings had suffered consid-erable damage, with only gutted shells remaining. Where it was possible to get inside, I often came across the odd rotting corpse in my path, lying on staircases and in basements. I had become hardened to seeing the dead; it was nothing new to me, but coming across a fully clothed, putrefied body with bony hands, not quite reduced to a total skeleton, with protruding white dentures and sunken eye-sockets staring at me was a bit ghostly, to say the least. The stench was overpowering.

The homes looked as if they had been left by people departing in great haste, with pots on stoves, dishes and broken plates on tables, and everything covered in a thick layer of plaster-dust or debris. Tangled steel girders and wooden beams were hanging from ceilings. In one place, a section of a staircase was left clinging to the wall, with the rest having collapsed, and I could go no further. Chattels, broken furniture, toys, clothing, single shoes, lay strewn about the place. The desolate scene was terribly reminiscent, I thought, of the deserted ghetto back home in Ostrowiec, after the deadly German *Aktzia* had swept through it.

Searching the cellars and larders, I found dried beans, oatmeal, kasza, and the like, still safe to eat if it was inside tin containers and jars that the rats hadn't gotten to first, but I found nothing that would immediately assuage my hunger. I was hoping to find valuables that I could barter for fresh food on the market, but never found anything of value that was small enough to be carried away. In wartime people take their riches with them or bury them in the ground, making them impossible to find. Sifting through every nook, I came across a rather nice, if somewhat large, leather windcheater, which I was to wear all the time, and a navy-blue ski-cap with earflaps that I treasured, as it was fashionable at the time and good for keeping out the cold. I only took clothing that I liked and could wear; otherwise I only took dried food. I found enough of it; I just couldn't carry it all away. I stuffed my pockets and filled socks I had found among the wreckage by stuffing them until they resembled sticks of salami and then tying the ends. I fastened some to my waist; others I hung from my neck and shoulders, leaving them to dangle, in order to keep my hands free. I must have looked very strange indeed.

By late afternoon I started on my way back, making for the same spot where I had jumped off the lorry in the morning, at a point where the road narrows to a sharp bend. I lay there on a pile of rubble, reclining on my back with the sausage-bags beside me, waiting for a slow-moving lorry to appear so I could follow the same routine as in the morning. Despite the weight, with my hands free I just about managed to get off the ground and clamber into the rear of the truck. As the lorry was empty, the canvas flap was rolled up at the back, which made it easier for me to get in. It was also safer now; as it was beginning to get dark, I was less likely to be spotted by the driver. However, being festooned with the bulging sausage-like bags dangling from my shoulders and waist, I found my movement impeded, making it difficult to jump off the lorry when I was near the checkpoint. Thankfully, it all went without a hitch.

Once out of Warsaw, I managed despite the weight to lower myself from the truck before reaching the barrier, thus avoiding the sentries at the checkpoint. From there on, I continued on foot. It would have been too conspicuous to walk loaded down with the sausage-like bags swinging from side to side, so I stopped to hide the hoard under some bricks, to be carried away piecemeal.

We now had a modest source of dried food and oatmeal. Cooked together with the beets and any mouldy vegetables and frozen potatoes we had, this went some way to ease our hunger. I had to keep my exploits secret from my sister, as she would not have allowed them. To explain the sudden appearance of life-saving provisions, the story told at the cottage was that I must have discovered a robbers' cave and been deft enough to steal from the thieves! I said nothing to dispel the notion and it was left at that, for I could not afford to let on. About two weeks later, when our stock started to run low, I had to risk another expedition, going back to more or less the same spot where I had been before. To make things easier, I took away less this time. This modest supply of food became a life-saver, particularly for Marysia, who was now heavily pregnant. The nutritious food undoubtedly helped her condition. However, as her confinement was drawing near, we feared the risk of her having to seek medical help. With her typically Jewish features, this was a disaster waiting to happen that endangered all of us. Time passed slowly while we waited for news about the war. I was still roaming with my gang, except for my forays into Warsaw, which I could not afford to share with them as they were not something that could be done as a team, and I doubt if their situation was as desperate as mine. Otherwise, I was always out on the streets, loitering with my chums, always on the lookout for an opportunity to "organise" food by any means, even resorting to stealing. I got used to that, too.

I now felt ever more confident and no longer fearful of the Germans, but still on guard against certain bad people. The general Polish population had its own problems with the Germans, and in trying to ward off hunger and survive the severe winter, so they appeared to have stopped actively looking for Jews in their midst. In any case, there were hardly any left. They were glad the Germans had gotten rid of them, but their animosity to the absent Jews was so deeply entrenched that they were still obsessed with them in their everyday conversation. Ironically, they now had a commonplace saying they kept repeating: "First the Jews and then us!" By this they referred to the prevailing situation and the harsh treatment meted out by the Germans. In spite of this, which one might have imagined would cause a feeling of kinship, their fixation on the non-existent Jews never really abated. Perhaps it was just their manner of speech. Whether they were in the marketplace or in another place where people gathered, the Poles' gossip invariably turned to Jews. I often had to stand there and listen with my ears pricked up, trying not to show any emotion as they went on to curse the Jews blindly. They blamed them for all their troubles: the collapse of the uprising, the failure of the Russians to come to their aid, and more; and insisted that Jews sided with the Bolsheviks, that Jews were behind the black market, and so on. They were convinced that there was a Jewish conspiracy behind everything, though you would have been hard pressed to find a living Jew—I hadn't come across anyone outside of our group who I would have suspected of being Jewish since I had left Ostrowiec.

CHAPTER 17

A Shaft of Light

The long "no shooting" war was dragging on and on. At least where we were, there was a total stalemate between the two opposing forces facing each other across the River Vistula. Amazingly, it had been five long months since the Russian guns had fallen silent along the Vistula front, just a few kilometres to the east of us. And yet the safety of the Russian line was far beyond our reach. It was now late December: yet another difficult year was drawing to a close. We agonised over this drawn-out war, wondering when hostilities would finally resume and the war would be brought to an end with the defeat of Germany. We knew nothing about the progress of the war elsewhere, or indeed if there was any fighting going on at all. We could only observe the nearby Warsaw front, and so the only thing we were sure of was that in this part of Poland there was a complete lull, apart from the occasional long-distance shell that seemed to travel directly above our cottage with a reverberating echo. Now and then, the Germans hurled these massive shells during the night, from a colossal rail-mounted gun positioned somewhere in our vicinity, towards the Russian lines across the Vistula. The huge cannon produced a tremendous roar when it discharged, sending tremors through Włochy. Jan referred to it as "Fat Bertha" which I thought rather funny.

The Russians never returned fire, and we could not understand the reason behind their inertia—it had us completely baffled. Was the Russian Bear simply hibernating, or had the Red Army been bled white, lying low behind the safety of the Vistula? All this was mulled over in our hut time and time again, and analysed in great detail during the long winter nights. The war was, naturally, our main subject of conversation while we were waiting impatiently for a sign of Russian activity. For months we waited in vain, and at last came to realise that rescue was not going to come in 1944.

Christmas was rapidly approaching, and the mellow tones of "*Stille Nacht, Heilige Nacht*" could be heard emanating from the German quarters. The soldiers were no doubt dreaming of home, of their sweethearts, of celebrating Christmas with their wives and families at their side under the *Weihnachtsbaum*, Christmas tree. The season of goodwill to all men was almost upon us, but there was no evidence of such goodwill here, nor any sign of peace on earth. Still, though there was no sign of an end to hostilities, it was fairly evident that the ordinary Fritz and Hans had had enough of the war and no longer believed in a German victory, and they had also shed some of their former arrogance. They may still have carried the motto *Gott mit Uns* on their belt buckles, but they could no longer claim that God was on their side. They became disillusioned with what they called Hitler's war, hoping for better times to come. As one reflective Wehrmacht song went at the time:

> *Es geht alles vorüber, es geht alles vorbei.*
> *Nach dem Dezember, kommt wieder ein Mai...*
>
> Everything goes on by, and everything comes to pass.
> After every December, there comes again the month of May...

In wartime, the cold, dismal winters were the most difficult to endure, and this was a particularly hard winter. With the end to the war nowhere in sight, it was prudent to carry on demonstrating our Christian devotion by being seen going to church by our neighbours. On Christmas Eve, my sister and I went to Midnight Mass, and earlier in the day I went to see the children's Nativity Play staged in the church hall. I joined in the singing of carols, but there were no treats to be handed out to the children. I was thrilled just the same to see the performance, as I had not experienced any kind of entertainment, live or otherwise, since before the war.

In spite of the war lingering on, we realised that liberation could not be very far away. With this in mind, the adults at the cottage started to chatter in Yiddish, a language they had hitherto suppressed, during the night, in total darkness. It was a diversion and a form of defiance, in our own small way. The language sounded strange in that setting. I had last heard it way back in the ghetto. Huddled together on the floor, in the cold, the others sang wistful Yiddish songs in soft tones well into the small hours. They reminisced about old times and about food. Each in turn described what they most missed and craved, what tasty dish they would order, and what would be the first thing they would do when the war was over. This deliberate act of speaking and chanting in their forbidden language, albeit in a low voice, gave them the satisfaction of having triumphed over the enemy simply by staying alive and having survived thus far. Being alive and speaking in their ancient tongue asserted their faith and their contempt for the Nazis. My sister recalled later that this small act of defiance helped to warm their hearts in the bitter December cold.

A new year was drawing near, and yet there was nothing for us to celebrate, except that we had lived to see it; it had been more than five long, wretched years since the war had begun. The long delay in the resumption of hostilities didn't augur well for my absent family: we had learned that together with the other prisoners from the Ostrowiec labour camp they had been evacuated the previous August, ahead of the Red Army's advance towards the Vistula as the uprising began. We had no way of knowing where they had been taken. We could only assume it was to Germany, and we hoped and prayed they were still alive. We knew that the death factories had stopped operating in Poland, as the country had been emptied of its Jews. Hans Frank, the Nazi overlord of Poland, had as a birthday gift to Hitler declared all of Poland *Judenrein*, cleansed of Jews. Because of the importance of the steel industry to the Nazi war effort, Ostrowiec was one of the last slave labour camps to be maintained in Poland, and was evacuated only in the face of the Russian advance the previous summer, at the same time as they reached the gates of Warsaw, before the uprising had erupted. As a result, my sister and I were hopeful that the family would have a good chance of surviving, as we felt it likely they had still been alive during the evacuation. If only, we thought, Stalin would give the order for the Red Army, poised along the Vistula, to go on the offensive and resume its advance!

The New Year came and went, and we carried on logging the dreary days, dreaming of freedom. Then out of the blue, about two weeks later, we began to hear the unmistakable rumble of distant artillery. Simultaneously the movement of German troops began. Officers were rushing to and fro, yelling out orders as if preparing to evacuate the area. The next morning, on the 16th of January, Corporal Ryschard, my old fishing friend, called unexpectedly at the door to bid us a hasty farewell; I had not seen him out on the streets for some time. He said he was in a rush, and had brought with him two tins of sardines as a goodbye present. He leaked the information that his unit had orders to pull out at short notice, without giving any further information. His parting words were tinged with sadness. Looking sorry for himself, he said: "I wish I could come with you!" Then he turned, and with a wave of the hand he disappeared. This astounded us: was Ryschard perhaps a *Mischling,* a German of Jewish descent? Such men did in fact exist in the Wehrmacht. The Nazis considered those with only one Jewish grandparent as "quarter Jews" and quietly tolerated them in the army as ordinary soldiers, but they were otherwise treated as full Jews, and never decorated. This could perhaps explain his kindness to me. Was he perhaps hinting that he'd known all along that my sister and I were Jewish? He could not know about the others, for he had never set eyes on anyone else in the cottage. He may have suspected that there were others concealed in there, which would account for my constant search for more and more food. If he knew, that could also be the reason he had never asked to come inside, which was an eventuality we had always been terrified of. We shall never know.

Meanwhile the earlier booming of heavy guns had died down, and we couldn't understand the reason for the pause; it was very worrying. Perhaps these were German guns after all, and perhaps the Germans were trying to pre-empt an expected Russian offensive. In that case, the movement of the troops would be just a prelude to another "strategic withdrawal to more defensible lines" as they liked to put it. This seemed to Jan, our "military strategist" at the cottage, the most likely explanation. As a result of his drawn-out plight, Jan had become so fatalistic that he was unable to comprehend that liberation could be at hand, and that this terrible war would eventually come to an end.

To add to the confusion, later that day, newly-arrived mechanized Wehrmacht units in camouflage kit started to dig in all around our area to replace the troops that had earlier retreated, including Ryschard. Well-armed with *Panzerfaust* anti-tank rocket launchers, the formation took up positions on both sides of the road and along the railway track opposite our cottage, as if to prepare for a last stand. If this was indeed what they were planning, we feared that this place would become like a battlefield, with us caught up in the front line. Much too aroused to sleep that night, we waited impatiently for morning to arrive. Towards dawn, after a quiet night, the big guns opened up again, only this time they were getting closer all the time. It was music to our ears! This clearly signalled that the Soviet giant had not been slain after all; he had just stirred from his slumber and was once more on the move! "The Russians are coming!," we kept repeating. We went crazy with excitement, jumping up and down the room, eagerly looking forward to the rapidly unfolding situation.

Unknown to us at the time, the Red Army had in fact begun their great winter offensive several days earlier. We learned that the storm had broken four days before, on 12 January 1945, when the whole Eastern Front had erupted, stretching from the shores of the Baltic Sea in the north to the Carpathian hills in the south. And instead of attacking Warsaw directly, where the Germans were dug in and lay in wait, the legendary General Zhukov's army broke out of the Magnuszew bridgehead on the Vistula, well to the south of Warsaw, and another Russian army group attacked from the upper Vistula in the north and poured through the breech. With their armour smashing through the German defences with such speed and ferocity that the retreats of many German troops were cut off, Warsaw had been bypassed in one huge flanking movement.

I went wild with excitement on realising that the front had indeed opened up, and I just couldn't wait to see our liberators arrive. Being an inquisitive boy, as always, I decided to start out into the countryside, along the railway track, near the road on which any force advancing on Warsaw would have to pass. I was impatient to see the Russian soldiers approach. With hindsight, I see that this was a foolhardy thing to do, but I didn't see it like that at the time—I was too keyed-up by the fast-moving events and never stopped to think. It was late morning as I made my way further and further into the countryside. Along the way, I passed groups of gloomy and dispirited Wehrmacht soldiers, who paid no attention to me. They appeared to be older men, more like home guard reservists than hardened front-line troops. These soldiers were not manning their weapons, but just reclining in ditches beside the road with their anti-tank rocket launchers and ammunition boxes scattered about them in the snow. The men looked downcast and ready to give themselves up, completely unlike the arrogant Wehrmacht I had known and feared. The Germans had their retreat cut off, and they seemed to know it. Their war was as good as over, and fear of the grim prospect of falling into unforgiving Russian hands was written on their faces.

Wednesday, 17 January 1945, was a cold and dismal day with a light fog, but before the day would pass it would turn into a most glittering and unforgettable day for me, without the sun ever breaking through the grey skies. As I ventured farther out, I suddenly thought I could hear something distant. By putting my ear to the ground—a wartime trick I had learned—I could hear what sounded like the remote grinding and screeching of tracked vehicles. I quickly tumbled down a snowy ditch to take cover, and I waited there, scanning the horizon from left to right and back, until the clatter of tank tracks became clearly audible. Looking towards the edge of a wood in the distance, I saw a long gun-barrel slowly emerge from behind a clump of trees. Then the rest of the tank appeared, followed by another, then another. They didn't look like the German Panthers or any of their tanks, which were all marked with the hated black Teutonic Cross that I knew so well. As they drew nearer, I could just barely make out through the freezing mist the Russian markings on the side of the turret. I could scarcely believe my eyes: these were Russian tanks! Russian tanks! "I'm Free!," I thought. "I'm Freeee!"

When the huge tanks drew nearer, the ground below me trembled as their tracks churned up big lumps of ice and snow. I scrambled out of the ditch and ran towards the column of armoured vehicles, waving my arms about wildly. Not knowing the Russian word for it, I kept yelling in Polish, *"Witamy!"* (Welcome, Greetings!), hoping they would understand, as Polish is somewhat akin to Russian. Then I shouted in Russian *"Ya Evrei, Ya Evrei!"* (I'm a Jew, I'm a Jew!) Perhaps it was a reckless thing to do, but I was so excited I just did it in the heat of the moment. I also knew that the Russian people had a reputation for being kind to children, so I was not afraid. These forward infantrymen, who were wearing white camouflage smocks over their olive-brown uniforms, were riding on top of their tanks, with their *Pepesha* automatics at the ready. In that din, the sturdy Russian soldiers couldn't possibly have heard what I was shouting. Anyway, being a Jew was nothing to rave about! But they could clearly see a harmless young boy waving his hands about, in friendly greeting.

In turn, some of the soldiers opened their arms forward, Russian-style, as if to welcome me. Then one of the leading tanks ground to a halt. With the engine left running, belching out black smoke, a soldier offered me a hand and pulled me up onto the deck. I kissed the sheepskin mittens on both his hands, crying, *"Spasiba! Spasiba!"* (Thank you, Thank you!).

The greeting had to be brief, as the *tankista* commander, with his head and shoulders standing tall above the turret, wearing a padded helmet with the chin-strap undone, didn't stand on ceremony. He looked flustered and impatient to get moving. When he'd had enough of my gratitude, he pointed a little red pennant in a forward direction, shouting *"V'peryod! V'peryod!,"* which was the signal for the tank to rev up and advance. The tank then shuddered in its tracks and we all shook as the "war chariot" trundled off, leaving behind it clouds of black diesel smoke. I was riding on a heavy tank bedecked with soldiers; some stood on the turret, clinging to the gun barrel, and others sat on the engine deck where I held on to them, trying my best to stand up. Thus I rode triumphantly atop of one of the first Russian tanks to roll into Włochy, past our cottage. It was a most thrilling experience, as though I personally had a hand in liberating not just Włochy, but all of Poland! Some tanks had the slogan *Za Rodinu, Za Stalina* (For the Motherland, For Stalin) painted on the side of the turret; others had *Na Berlina* (On to Berlin). Oh, how I wished I could ride all the way to Berlin with those jubilant Russian soldiers. This was to be my most unforgettable moment ever—the day my second life began!

There was no shooting here, it was more like a triumphal ride past than a battle; the Germans never fired a shot. The leading Russian tanks simply ignored the stunned, wide-eyed German soldiers lying by the roadside, who offered no resistance. Some held up makeshift white flags of surrender. The Russians just brushed them aside as their armoured vehicles pressed forward. These German prisoners would later be rounded up by second-echelon infantry troops and taken to the rear. The Russian soldiers looked well padded-out in the intense cold: they were wearing quilted jackets and pants, and *valenki*, knee-high felt boots. Each soldier carried his *Pepesha* slung across his chest. This was the familiar stubby sub-machine-gun with the circular magazine and perforated barrel that typified the Red Army. The infantrymen also wore rolled-up blankets across their chests and small rucksacks containing their meagre rations, usually a hunk of stale black bread and dry biscuits, on their backs. The hardy Russian "Ivan" was well-accustomed to hardship, and didn't require much sustenance to keep him going. Every soldier was self-sufficient and used to living off the land, if need be. Russian soldiers were not perhaps as well turned-out as the Wehrmacht, but what was more important was that they were fearless and brave. Some soldiers clearly suffered from injuries, and sported soiled bandages around their heads; but they nevertheless kept going, remaining on active duty. Their ranks comprised many different races, apart from European types: I particularly remember seeing there were also Asian and Mongolian faces. Following the endless tank column came a multitude of small carts drawn by sinewy little horses from the Russian steppes, fully laden with supplies and ammunition. The carts went on for days on end.

As soon as they realised it was safe to come out, my sister and the rest of our group emerged into the open for the first time in a long while, to cheer and welcome the liberators who were now pouring through Włochy. The tanks didn't stop there, but kept on advancing. Significantly, this momentous day, January 17, also happened to be my sister's twenty-first birthday. What a wonderful birthday present this was for her—the gift of freedom, and a life reborn, on her very birthday!

Although long anticipated, liberation came so suddenly that we couldn't believe we had survived. It would take some time to fully sink in. Were we really free? Although we were still in a daze, our thoughts inevitably turned to our family, trusting that they were alive and well—for we could never imagine otherwise. Ever since I was separated from them, my thoughts and dreams were never far away from my parents and brothers, especially now that we were free.

People took to the streets cheering and applauding their liberators, though some Poles welcomed their historical enemy with mixed feelings, which I thought was a bit miserly. The valiant Red Army soldiers acknowledged the crowd by holding their *Pepeshas* aloft, shouting *"Urra, Urra!,"* and some onlookers lining the streets responded with *"Niech Zhiye Krasnaya Armiya"*—Long Live the Red Army. As they rolled past, a special cheer went up for the *Katyushas,* the legendary self-propelled rocket launchers mounted on trucks. These struck fear into German hearts. Nicknamed "Stalin's Organ," on account of the terrifying high-pitched whine they produced when fired, *Katyushas* had a devastating effect on the morale of the Huns. Following the Russian spearhead, units of the Polish People's Army, which had formed in Russia, also passed through Włochy on the way to the capital that now lay in ruins. The Wehrmacht had abandoned Warsaw without a fight, against the Führer's implicit orders, in which he had designated *Festung Warschau* (Fortress Warsaw) to be defended to the last. Had they obeyed his orders, the Wehrmacht soldiers would have been decimated by the avenging Red Army for having laid waste to their country, for their cruel scorched-earth policy, and for the terrible suffering they had inflicted on the Russian people.

Some felt that the time for redress had come, and a short period of retribution was tolerated, if not encouraged, by the Russians. Any Nazis and their collaborators were rounded up; some were made to strip to the waist in the freezing cold to reveal any SS tattoos under their left armpits. Some SS officers discarded their uniforms for those of the Wehrmacht, to try to escape punishment. No quarter was given to those deemed to be SS or Gestapo. Columns of prisoners were later paraded through the streets, escorted by Russian guards with fixed bayonets. Some onlookers spat in their faces, while others even struck out at them. What appeared to be members of the NKVD, the Soviet secret police, also paraded several captives they labelled "collaborators and saboteurs." They lined them up against a wall and simply mowed them down with a burst of *Pepesha* automatic fire in full view of the public. They must have been Russian or Ukrainian traitors who had joined the German side; these were eliminated without too much ado. We had some of them stationed locally, and the Russians similarly showed them no pity. Presumably they had first undergone some form of trial in the field, but I wouldn't be too sure about that—I suppose if they were Russian or Ukrainian that alone would have been enough to condemn them out of hand.

While mingling with the crowd, we carefully scanned the faces of the people milling around to try to spot another Jewish person who might have come out into the open. We were eager to identify with any fellow Jew, to share with them this moment for which we had waited so long, going in daily fear for our lives. On the "Aryan side" one Jew could usually identify another; there was a secret code-word between us, "*Amchu*"—Hebrew for "one of us." My sister and I never managed to pick out another *Amchu*. We realised few would have survived the way we did. It was all over. We had survived, but where would we go from here?

Wrist-watches were considered prized booty by the victorious Russians, so one of the first things they did was to "liberate" them from the Germans, brazenly demanding "*davai chassyi!*"—Hand over your watch! Some soldiers sported a collection of wrist-watches strapped right up their forearms. Buxom Russian girl-soldiers in calf-length boots were a common sight at road intersections, directing military traffic by waving little pennants, gyrating their lithe bodies like prima ballerinas. Another enjoyable distraction were Russian soldiers, men and women, forming circles in the street and performing impromptu Cossack dancing to the music of concertinas and harmonicas as onlookers gathered around them, clapping and cheering, to urge them on.

For us, the first taste of liberty and the initial hours of freedom were heady indeed. However, we didn't want to remain in Włochy for long. We wanted to get away as quickly as possible from Warsaw, which was one big heap of ruins and chaos. It was great to be alive, but our new-found freedom was far too precious to risk forfeiting again. We were afraid the Germans would mount a counter-attack and come back, and were anxious not to repeat the mistake we had made on that fateful day in August almost six months before, when we had impulsively set out from Anin to the centre of Warsaw, ending up on the wrong side of the Vistula.

Russian-Jewish officers, surprised to find Jews still alive, advised us to leave and head east to Lublin for safety. Lublin was further behind the Russian lines, and had been liberated a few months earlier. Soon enough, we managed to locate a friendly high-ranking Jewish officer with a bulging chest full of gleaming medals who we managed to per-suade to transport our small group to Lublin. I'm sure it was against army regulations to convey civilians, but then we were no ordinary ci-vilians. The tall, sturdy, Yiddish-speaking officer readily concurred and promised to arrange transport for us as soon as possible. He said he had come across few Jews ever since he had crossed over with his unit onto Polish soil.

The city of Lublin had been liberated the previous summer, during the Red Army's breathtaking sweep across Byelorussia and into eastern Poland. After its liberation, Lublin became the seat of The Committee of National Liberation. We asked our friendly Russian officer if there was any likelihood of the Fritzes coming back. "*Nyet*," he answered emphati-cally. "Wherever the Red Army marches in, it stays. Not a step back! *Stalin prykazal*"—it was a direct order from Stalin. In spite of these reas-suring words, we were not prepared to take the risk of remaining, and implored the good officer to arrange transport for us to Lublin without further delay. We had no idea, nor could we believe if we'd known, just how decisively the Germans were being beaten. After years of Nazi tyranny, we were still conditioned to look at German might with trepidation and awed fear.

True to his word, one early morning our friendly Russian army-captain drew up outside our place in his American jeep to see us off. He was accompanied by an army truck that was to transport the five of us to Lublin, as promised. Curtains moved aside as curious neighbours were peeping out from behind, with their tongues wagging. A few of the old gossips came out of their homes and gathered in a circle to watch, eyeing their neighbours with suspicion. I can well imagine how the ensuing gossip went:

> Just hark at them there; I always thought there was something strange about them. There was only two of them to begin with; that la-di-da blonde, with that young dodger of hers bringing home the loot. And now there's no less than five of 'em in there, with a lanky *Zhyd*, to boot. Where did he suddenly come from? And did you see that frizzy-haired Jewess waddling about like a duck with that big belly on her! I wonder who's responsible for that? They were installed here by the Fritzes and now they hobnob with the Russkis! *Pani* Zosiu, I tell you, I don't like it one bit. If you ask me, they are a gang of brazen Bolshie spies. And to think this nest of vipers was here all along, right under our very noses. Jesus, Mary! Had the Gestapo come, we would have all been done for, perish the thought! I never did like them, right from the start. My Kazik was right: he kept saying there was something fishy about them in there. I thought so too, Krysiu, that classy blonde was always aloof and kept to herself.

As our lorry departed for Lublin via central Warsaw, there was a tumultuous army of people converging on the devastated city to try and retrieve what they could from their former homes which now lay in ruins, covered by a thick blanket of snow. A wave of feverish activity began as word got round to go *"na szaber,"* Polish slang for plunder. Everyone seemed to be joining in the enterprise. People rummaged through the ruins for any spoils, to carry away anything they could lay their hands on. Their finds were lugged away on pushcarts, old prams, or sledges, or were simply hauled on improvised sledges or even planks of wood in the snow. Few, I should imagine, were actually from Warsaw; many of Warsaw's inhabitants were dead and wounded, others had been carted off to Germany for slave labour, and those who remained alive and in Poland had been scattered around the countryside. Often the true owners of the property, if they managed to return, had to fight off looters to defend the little that remained of their former homes. Amid all this chaos, it was difficult to prove ownership of anything, and inevitably arguments and fights broke out.

Military traffic was impeded along the clogged-up roads by the vast army of people going in both directions, some heading into Warsaw, perhaps not for the first time, with others going in the opposite way, fully laden, lugging away anything worthwhile they could lay their hands on: furniture, old clothing, pots and pans, window frames, and even entire doors, presumably to be used as firewood as there was no coal to be had. This was considered one of the coldest winters of recent years. Everyone seemed to head for the ruined city, some out of curiosity, but mostly to pillage.

Peering out of the truck from beneath the tarpaulin cover at the ragged Warsaw urchins, I thought of my pals. They had to be out there somewhere, scavenging in the ruins. No doubt they were wondering why "Stefek" was nowhere to be seen—where on earth had he disappeared to? It dawned on me that there, but for the grace of God, went I. Had I not been heading for Lublin, I would have been out there with my gang, going "na szaber" and staking my claim on the spoils. Instead, I was on my way to what I hoped would mark the beginning of a different way of life, one in which I would not have to scavenge and steal to eat. Alas, this option was not available to my urchin pals, not for now, anyway. Coming as they did from deprived homes, the future that lay ahead of them would not be much brighter than the time we'd shared. They would have to struggle on until better times, which might never come. I felt guilty for not saying goodbye to my pals, but I could not have faced them now. Ever since the liberation, I had tried my best to keep out of their way. I didn't have the heart to tell them I was a Żydek after all. Had I not owned up, they would have guessed it anyway, seeing distinctly Jewish-looking people coming in and out of our place where previously they had only caught sight of my sister. Perhaps they had also tried to avoid me, for the same reason. There was a certain code, even among street kids, and they would not have understood why I'd had to lie and dupe them. Nor would they have fully appreciated what was at stake when the Germans were around. The boys had gotten to consider me a pal in adversity. We had been through much together and they would no doubt have thought that I should not have doubted their sincerity. But things could have turned out very different, accidentally or otherwise, and had I not taken the course that I had, it could easily have turned out disastrously, not just for me, but for all of us at the cottage.

As we drove along the streets of Warsaw, the pavements on both sides of the road were piled high with bricks and rubble, with only a track snaking through the middle of what had once been the most fashionable thoroughfare of Marszalkowska Street. It was a bumpy ride in the US-built Dodge truck as the army driver tried to negotiate the potholes and obstacles along the way. It looked as if the entire Russian army was moving on American-supplied transport. The Russian-built trucks looked less sturdy and lighter. Heading in a south-easterly direction, we crossed the Vistula on an unstable pontoon bridge which Red Army sappers had hastily thrown across the river next to the once-impressive Poniatowski Bridge, which had lain partly submerged in the water since the retreating Germans had blown it up following the uprising. The progress of our lorry, like all the military traffic, was hampered by the huge army of looters lugging away their spoils. This soon after the liberation and the departure of the Germans, there was a total breakdown in law and order; transportation and services were not functioning, and utter chaos reigned in the Warsaw area.

Heading in an easterly direction, we left the ruins of Warsaw behind us, moving along what seemed like an endless highway leading out of Praga on the right bank of the Vistula. At this point we were near Anin, but there was no question of the Russian driver interrupting his journey. I should have liked very much to have seen *Pani* Gozdzialska again. She would have been relieved to see us in one piece, for she too must have been concerned for our safety ever since we had left her on that fateful Tuesday morning, full of hope and promise, as we departed for central Warsaw about six months earlier, but we had no way of contacting her. We were quite sure, though, that *Pani* and Wanda had come to no harm, as this area was hardly affected by the fighting at all. Few buildings looked damaged as we drove through Praga, on the other side of the Vistula from where we had been. The Red Army had entered this area a few weeks after the Warsaw uprising had begun.

As the countryside we were driving through became rather featureless, we began to feel drowsy; the motion of the lorry lulled us to sleep. After a while, Wala started to hum a current wistful song she liked, "Warsaw, Oh, My Warsaw," a lament for the ruined capital, and the others soon joined in, half asleep from exhaustion and the aftermath of the excitement. The thought crossed my mind as to when I would again return to a restored Warsaw and be reunited with *Pani* Gozdzialska. First, I would want to shower my kindly rescuer with lots of kisses and presents, and then I would resume, with my sister, my sightseeing of the capital, which had been abruptly interrupted by the uprising.

Wala liked to sing. She knew all the latest hit songs, and she followed the first one with the melancholy "Chrysanthemums," which was also popular at the time. And when Jan broke into his favourite "*Ta Ostatnia Niedziela*" (That Last Sunday) in that deep throaty voice of his, we were all wide awake, eagerly looking forward to reaching Lublin, which according to the Russian officer any Jewish survivors were heading for, in search of safety and a little material help. We were destitute; all we had were the shabby clothes on our backs.

CHAPTER 18

Lublin Orphanage

When we reached the centre of Lublin, our lorry stopped in front of a medieval gate and tower, which turned out to be the entrance to the Old Town district. The driver drew up alongside a group of Russian soldiers to ask the way, and they pointed him in a certain direction. A short while later the lorry pulled up outside a building where we noticed people who looked like Jews milling around outside. I had not set eyes on anyone who looked Jewish, outside of our group, since I had escaped from the camp more than two years before. It was in fact the "Jewish House" we'd been looking for. Unlike Ostrowiec, Lublin had the feel of a big town about it. It was a pleasant city with a rich Jewish history. It had been an important centre for Jewish learning, and had produced many distinguished rabbis. Upon arriving there about ten days after our liberation, we immediately turned to the Jewish community for help. Wala and I found accommodation in the former Jewish school and cultural centre called Dom Pereca, or Peretz House, in Czwartek Street in the former Jewish section of Lublin. During the war, the building was apparently used as an isolation hospital, and it was now restored to the Jewish community and converted into a shelter for survivors, many of whom were heading for Lublin. The town didn't suffer any damage during the war, and there was already a semblance of normality about the place, as compared to the chaos that was Warsaw.

Most of the people in Peretz House had enjoyed freedom since the previous summer, when the town had been liberated. The Red Army had, in one massive sweep, recaptured Lublin and Byelorussia, as well as much of Eastern-Poland during the summer of 1944. It was a wide-ranging offensive the Soviets had code-named "Bagration," after a Russian general who had been active in the war against Napoleon. The majority of the young survivors I met had mostly emerged from hiding places, like forests and convents. Concentration camp inmates had not as yet started to come back; they, apart from those freed from nearby Majdanek, still remained to be freed in Germany and Austria.

Majdanek, just outside Lublin, was the first virtually intact Nazi death-camp facility to have fallen into Russian hands, for the Germans had not had time to dismantle it. The Russians released to the world footage taken here, showing for the first time what there was at a death-camp: gas chambers and crematoria, the walking dead, and the piles of tangled skeletal bodies. Apparently, the BBC and the Western press declined to publish the material at the time, claiming it was a Russian stunt. The Western powers' first reaction to the ghastly reports was tinged with scepticism, and they insisted they had to be exaggerated Soviet propaganda. We now know that the callous politicians of these countries knew better. It has been put, rather cynically, that the whole world knew of the Nazi extermination programme, except for the American president and the British government. This attitude prevailed until the Russians liberated Auschwitz, some six months later, on 27 January 1945. By then the truth could no longer be denied.

Some form of Jewish community infrastructure was already functioning in Lublin, so there was someone to whom one could turn for help, and most important there was a soup-kitchen, so one need never go hungry again. Soon after our arrival, I left the shelter and was placed in a *Kinderheim*, or orphanage, in an imposing building on Krakowskie Przedmieście, the most elegant main street of Lublin. I was also enrolled at a local elementary school, which was named for Queen Jadwiga. My sister had meanwhile dropped her assumed wartime name, Wala Matera, and reverted to her true name. Fela came to visit me regularly at the orphanage while she remained at Peretz House. Most of those in charge of our Home were Polish Jews who had fled to Russia at the beginning of the war and had returned to Poland on the heels of the Red Army where they had fled to at the beginning of the war. They were, in the main, socialist or communist sympathisers, which was only natural at the time.

We all had great affinity for the USSR, as epitomized by the father-figure of comrade Stalin, whom we idolised. We were of course unaware of the Stalinist tyranny, information about which later came to light. We remained infinitely indebted to the heroic Red Army for its enormous sacrifices in defeating Germany and rescuing us from the detestable Nazis. The boys and girls at the orphanage—especially the boys—had great affection for the Russian soldiers, and my pride and joy was a Red Army tunic which I wore outside my trousers like a real soldier, with a wide leather belt and red-star buckle, as well as a Siberian *Ushanka*, lambskin cap with earflaps. This was all wheedled out of friendly Russian soldiers who were convalescing at a nearby hospital that we liked to visit. Unlike German soldiers, the Russians were very poor and had no chocolate to give away, only articles of army clothing and souvenirs. These items were rather big on me, but I felt proud wearing them: Red Army insignia was highly prized by us boys.

One day, the boys in the home got very excited and ran out into the street, for word had spread that German prisoners were being paraded through the city streets. The prisoners, mostly officers, looked bedraggled, with downcast eyes. Many had no overcoats on in the freezing cold, although some had fur earmuffs on. These struck us as rather sissy and not very manly. Earmuffs were for women—real men didn't wear them! The earmuffs, made of rabbit fur, must have been a relic from the Russian front. It was hard to believe that these pathetic beings had once been part of the mighty German war machine and arrogant *Herrenvolk,* members of the "Master Race" that had enslaved Europe and tormented us for five long years. I had fun running beside them together with a gang of youths, taunting and shouting obscenities at them, which the escorting guards with their fixed bayonets didn't seem to mind. We followed the long column until we reached the gates of the Majdanek death-camp, about five kilometres from the city centre, where the Germans in their headlong retreat hadn't managed to destroy all the incriminating evidence of genocide. Here the Russians made the captured prisoners witness the cruelties inflicted, and see for themselves the piles of human hair, children's clothes, shoes, and spectacles that had belonged to the victims, and how mass murder was reduced to an industrial process by their fellow Germans. Many thousands of people had died there, mostly Jews but also Poles and Russian prisoners of war. After Majdanek, the Red Army was further spurred on to avenge the crimes committed against their countrymen, and they showed little pity after crossing over the former Polish border onto German soil.

At the orphanage, the children ranged in age from very young ones, who had been sheltered in convents or by Christian families, to adolescents like me. It occurred to me that I was going on fourteen but still had not celebrated my *Bar Mitzvah,* which concerned me a little. I had turned thirteen during the raging Warsaw inferno, and my birthday had never even entered my head. But now that I was free, I wanted to have a *Bar Mitzvah* celebration, like my older brothers had back home. I had this fixed idea in my mind that one could not be fully Jewish without going through this formal ritual. However, there was no question of it now, as all those in charge of the home were non-believers, totally opposed to any form of religious observance.

When I had been passing for a Christian boy, I had often thought it would be so much better to just give up being Jewish, if it were at all possible, but now, having paid the price, I wanted to stay loyal to my faith. At the orphanage we were exposed to Soviet-style indoctrination, as well as Russian language lessons, and taught stirring Red Army songs of valour. We were also subjected to a form of military-style discipline which we didn't object to, as it was like playing soldiers, schooled on the lines of Soviet Pioneer Youth. We marched in step in the middle of the road, four abreast, with backs erect, swinging our arms high, across the chest, from side to side, Red Army style. We sang Russian songs as we went: songs of war and victory as well as Yiddish partisan songs. Surprisingly, at this time the Jewish language was quite acceptable and was even promoted by the communist authorities, but it was later discouraged on Stalin's orders when he had a change of heart.

Because of the war, I had missed out on a lot and had much to catch up on. I was eager to make up for the lost years, and yearned to do all the exciting things youths of my age normally did. I may have been street-smart, but I was quite ignorant in other respects. I had not enjoyed a normal home life and had virtually no schooling throughout the war years. My short childhood had slipped by, and I had grown straight into a teenager. The war and its aftermath had robbed me, apart from my education, of six of the most formative years of my life. For instance, I had only been to the cinema about three times before the war. The first time I'd gone with my parents to see "The Dybbuk," a scary adult film in Yiddish. It was a haunting story about a young woman possessed by a spirit, and I was not meant to understand it. On the other occasions I had gone with my brothers to the *Kino Marzeń*, to see much jollier films. One was a silent Charlie Chaplin film and the other was *Snow White*, which I had enjoyed immensely. I now looked forward to going to the cinema for the first time in six years, and as far as I know there was only one cinema, the Apollo, that was functioning in Lublin at the time. Happily, it was located near the orphanage. There was little choice; they were screening an old pre-war Polish film, "Znachor." It was a story about a quack doctor, and I didn't much care for it, but I very much enjoyed the long newsreel preceding it, with footage from the Russian front.

It was marvellous seeing on-screen for the first time the German army in headlong retreat, back to where it had come from. The commentary described how the victorious Red Army was hammering the Wehrmacht without pause as it pushed deeper and deeper into Germany. It was thrilling to see Cossack cavalry at a gallop, swinging sabres above their heads, furiously charging across snowy fields to the cries of "*Urra! Urra!*" Oh, the sheer joy of seeing Russian armoured vehicles crushing the cowering Fritzes in their ditches! I sat through the performance twice, hiding under the seats between the performances, just to see once more the demoralized Germans running for their lives. It was now February 1945, and the Russians forces had liberated Auschwitz. The newsreel showed army nurses escorting children out of the camp, past the barbed wire fencing, and my ghetto-loft friend, Pesia Balter, was among them. I recognised her right away. It also showed Russian officers inspecting the bales of human hair and the mounds of shoes and spectacles. The Red Army, supported by the Polish army, had by this time liberated all of Poland, and the front had advanced beyond the pre-war Polish-German border.

After the earlier euphoria of the liberation, despondency began to set in when Fela and I realised that we had little to celebrate; our thoughts were with our missing parents and brothers, wondering where they were and worrying about their safety. Ostrowiec had been liberated at about the same time as Warsaw, but there had been no Jews left there. We knew that the concentration camp inmates had been evacuated a few months earlier to Germany, but we tried to take heart from the pace of the Russian advance: Germany would soon be defeated and our family members saved.

The following month, March 1945, Fela returned to our hometown for the first time since the liberation, in search of news of our family. Travelling at that time was not easy: she made her way to Ostrowiec by climbing on and off goods-wagons until she finally got near the place. There she found that a few survivors had started to filter back, mainly those who had been in hiding and or who were liberated in Auschwitz, within Poland. Among them was our cousin Avram Berman, the only relative on our mother's side to have survived. No one had yet returned from Germany, which had not been totally defeated. It was to Germany and Austria that most of the camp inmates had been transported, ahead of the advancing Russians, the previous summer. After the liberation, it was important for survivors to return to their hometowns to look for any surviving relatives. Families had been torn apart, and there was no other way of finding one another. Germany and central Europe were full of homeless refugees on the move—and not only Jews. However, while others had countries to go back to, Jews were not made welcome anywhere, least of all in their countries of origin.

The remnant that made it back to our town decided for reasons of safety to stay together in one house, belonging to Feiga Krongold, on Starakunowska Street. So few in number, they felt vulnerable, wary of their neighbours' resentment of returning survivors. Fortunately, the day Fela returned she decided not to spend the night with the other Jews, as originally planned. She stayed instead in our former factory building, together with Avram and another ex-employee, to protect the little that remained in the building against looters. During that very night, 12 March 1945, armed Poles attacked Feiga Krongold's home, and four Jews were killed and several more wounded. One of the injured was our old friend Hershel Zylberberg, who had helped build the hide-out in the ghetto below the hen-house. The Poles claimed to have come looking for a list of local Poles who had participated in the killing of Jews during the war, which they said the Jews had put together to perhaps inform the authorities. No doubt some had scores to settle, but there never was such a list; the demand was a pretext to come and rob the refugees, and the planned robbery ended in a killing spree. To have struggled to survive a long and terrible war only to die a violent death at the hands of your neighbours was perverse beyond imagination. Even after the horrors of the Holocaust, Poles still couldn't find it in their hearts to tolerate a handful of returning Jews. After the pogrom, Fela returned to Lublin, where I was attending school. If things had gone better for her, I might have joined her there. But in spite of the dangers, most survivors braved it out and stayed on, hoping for relatives to turn up.[12]

After this shocking atrocity, Fela stayed away from Ostrowiec for more than two months until May, after the war in Europe had officially ended.

---

12 In the March 1945 pogrom four surviving members of the community were murdered in Ostrowiec by local Poles and several more wounded, including Hershel Zylberberg, who now lives in Australia. As a key witness, he had to be moved from the local hospital to Krakow, in case those responsible came back to kill him.

I, meanwhile, remained in the orphanage and at the same time attended the co-educational primary school I mentioned earlier, which was situated in Lublin's historic Old-Town district. Though as intelligent and more clued-up than any of my classmates, academically I was behind them, and although I tried hard to catch up I wasn't there long enough to do so. I had lost out on over five years of schooling, but nevertheless managed to go straight into the fourth form and was ready to be passed into the fifth by the end of term. I had meanwhile dropped my wartime name, Stefan Wojs, and was enrolled under my Jewish name. As far as I know, I may have been the only Jewish pupil at this school—for the other children from the orphanage went to another local school—and I never experienced any overt anti-Jewish hostility. In this it was quite unlike my school in pre-war Ostrowiec. Perhaps the better situation was because Lublin was a far more urbane place. However, also a contributing factor was that this headmaster would never have tolerated racist slurs. They were against the law under the communist system, where a person's race or class was of no consequence and religious practices were actively discouraged. I attended Queen Jadwiga for less than five months, leaving before the end of the spring term, as soon as the war officially came to an end. I then returned to my hometown with my sister for the first time since I had left it during those harrowing days of 1943. After Lublin, I never went back to school in Poland.

We celebrated Victory Day in Lublin on 9 May 1945, one day later than in Western Europe. The war in Europe was over, and Nazi barbarism had finally come to an end. To me, the day the war ended was a mere formality. The celebrations, too, came as an anti-climax to me and my sister; we didn't have much to celebrate, having as yet no news of the family. The most momentous day for us had been a few months earlier, on 17 January, the day of our liberation, when the nightmare had finally ended for us. Fela and I didn't have the heart to enjoy ourselves; as far as we were concerned the celebrations would have to wait until we are reunited with our parents. For us, the war was not completely over, for our family was still missing.

The triumphant Red Army celebrated their great victory with much pomp and merriment, but not everyone joined in the jubilation. Although relieved to be liberated from Nazi oppression, most Polish people resented the Red Army's presence in their country and looked upon Russia as their historic enemy. This resentment was made worse by earlier German reports of the massacre at Katyn of thousands of Polish officers in Russian hands, when the Poles had surrendered to them in 1939 in the face of the German onslaught on Poland. The Russians were quick to put the blame on the Nazis for this shocking crime. This claim later turned out to be a monstrous lie, but at the time we were naturally more inclined to believe the Russians—this was all before we knew what a monster Stalin really was.

There was an impressive victory parade held in Lublin. Apart from the military, civic and other institutions also took part. I myself participated in the victory parade, as part of a contingent of the older boys and girls from the orphanage. We were full of admiration for our Russian liberators and proudly marched through the main thoroughfares of Lublin behind the Red Army soldiers who led the parade, their chests festooned with row upon row of gleaming medals. Various organisations and parties representing the workers also paraded, holding up large banners among a sea of red flags, emphasising the nature of the new "democratic" Poland. Buxom girl soldiers with plump rosy-red cheeks formed circles in the streets while their agile male counterparts performed Cossack dances to the music of harmonicas and concertinas, twirling and leaping in the air and slapping their boots. The tumultuous celebrations went on until the early hours, in the best Russian tradition. After the parade was over, there was street dancing, and as there weren't enough young women to go around male soldiers danced together, which seemed a little strange to me—I had never seen men dancing together! There were Russian "bear-hugs" all around and much passing of bottles from hand to hand, as the soldiers consumed prodigious quantities of vodka as only the Russians know how.

At about this time—it could have actually been on May Day, as I recall that there was a holiday atmosphere on the streets—shooting suddenly broke out near our orphanage. As I happened to be out on the street, I was unable to return to the safety of the children's home. The entire area was cordoned off. Apparently some right-wing Home Army men opposed to the Communist regime were holed up in a building, having raided the state bank, and were besieged by the Polish Security Police. Keeping safely out of range, I was able to observe the scene. The stand-off lasted for several hours, and after the gunmen were killed we were allowed back into the orphanage. Although the Poles got their country back from the German enemy, many could not accept a socialist

Poland under Russian domination. All over the country, the army and the Security Police were battling the clandestine Home Army, many of whose members had never laid down their weapons after the Germans were driven out.

After all the euphoria and the celebrations had died down, Fela came to see me at the orphanage to tell me that as the war was officially over, the time had come to return to Ostrowiec. Not knowing what to expect and whether we would find anyone there; she tried to prepare me emotionally for the homecoming. A few days later, Fela took me out of the orphanage, where I had meanwhile made close friends. She also applied for permission to remove me from the state school. We were so impatient to go back to our hometown that we couldn't wait until the school term ended before starting out. At the same time, we were very apprehensive, afraid of what we would find on our return. I had enjoyed Queen Jadwiga immensely; it was my first experience of regular school since before the war. I had begun to make good progress, and the atmosphere in the class was friendly, in a town where I had experienced my first few months of freedom. I was left with many happy memories of Lublin. We packed up our few belongings and set off together on the journey home, longing to be re-united with our parents and brothers and hoping to recapture the pre-war idyllic life we had lived. Though we knew at heart that things could never be the same again. We were not the same, either: we understood that we had changed. Moniek was dead, that much we knew, and a lot had happened since then.

The Jewish orphanage in Lublin was housed in this imposing building.

CHAPTER 19

Shattered Homecoming

By the time Fela and I set out together for Ostrowiec, after the victory celebrations in Lublin were over, some of the first survivors had started to filter back from camps in Germany and the story of our family began to unfold. Witnesses said our parents and three brothers were last seen at Auschwitz, but they could not say what had happened to them later on. The camp prisoners from Ostrowiec who had not been gassed on arrival were split into different groups and taken over a period of time from Auschwitz in Poland to various concentration camps in Germany. Knowing that all the remaining members of my family had passed the initial "selection" at Auschwitz was very encouraging for us. We lived in hope of their safe return.

It was highly emotional returning to my home town. It seemed strange moving about the streets that I knew so well, which were now devoid of German uniforms—I'd never thought I would see it like this again. No Germans, but no Jews either; you could accommodate us all in the one house. Waking up in the morning on familiar ground, not knowing any fear of Germans, seemed out of place, and I had to keep reminding myself that it was no dream. In spite of the relative safety, I didn't like the town any more; all the familiar places and people I knew were gone. Emptied of my family and friends, it was no longer the home it once was. The place looked familiar, yet different, and we had also changed. My sister and I felt ill at ease and vulnerable, as did all those who came back—it would never be the same again. The once clamorous Jewish district, full of life and laughter, was no more. The desolation and emptiness was felt all around. The bustling streets with all their diverse dwellers and amusing characters were gone; an eerie silence reigned. The shops, including my favourite ice-cream parlour, were completely bare or shuttered. Many of the homes were occupied by strangers; others stood empty, having been looted and stripped bare, many with their doors and windows torn out. The heart of Jewish Ostrowiec had fallen into neglect and transformed into a ghost town. Realism began to set in.

My sister and I were all alone. We were left without parents or extended family: our grandparents, uncles, aunts, cousins, and friends were all gone, mostly taken in the first round-up. As they had no families, people liked to visit the cemetery to find comfort and consolation among their dead ancestors. It would not take long for all traces of a Jewish presence to completely disappear. That world was gone, never to return.

The war was over and we had survived, but we now lived in fear of our Polish neighbours—not the same fear, perhaps, but fear all the same. What's more, they knew where to find us: false papers would no longer help, and we were unarmed and defenceless. This was in some ways the most traumatic period for everyone. Apart from the problem of friction with our Gentile neighbours, we, the returning survivors, didn't know what to do with our lives and were unable to continue where we'd left off. Those who came back had to cope with the pain of loss and anguish, of returning destitute to their empty and lonely homes. Some found others living in their houses and could do nothing about it unless they wanted to risk life and limb. Having been to hell and back, they were of course glad to be alive, but at the same time they were bewildered and traumatized, finding themselves bereft of family and with no livelihood. Some felt guilty for having survived; they asked themselves, why me? Only about eighty people, including barely a handful of children, came back, of a community that had once numbered over 10,000 souls, at least 3,000 of them children. Aside from me, there was only one other young boy, Wicek Rozenberg, and a few girls who had survived. Wicek had been sheltered by a Polish family. Significantly fewer boys came through, as Polish families and even convents were reluctant to take in boys.

The ancient synagogue on Starakunowska, and much of the surrounding historic Jewish area, had been razed to the ground. The cemetery had been badly vandalised by Poles after the Germans had departed, and cattle were grazing in it. The headstone of my grandmother Gittel was still in place at this time, but it too was later smashed to pieces. These gravestones, which were of historic interest, were later broken into fragments and used in the construction of the perimeter wall of the new Catholic cemetery outside town, with the engraved Hebrew inscriptions still evident. The Nazis didn't generally take the trouble to destroy ancient monuments; their main goal lay in the physical annihilation of the Jewish people. Poles, on the other hand, wanted to erase all vestiges of a Jewish past and take over the homes and businesses previously owned by Jews. In the past, they had depended on Jewish traders and artisans for most of their daily needs: to sew their clothes, to make their boots, to mend their shoes, and more. They'd even had to rely on a Jewish haberdasher for a length of white ribbon for their daughters' confirmations. All this had now changed.

Some of us undertook the gruesome task of exhuming the remains of some victims and laying them to rest in consecrated ground in the Jewish cemetery, which is a solemn obligation. We knew where certain groups of people had been shot and buried on the spot, having first been made to dig their own graves. This was an unpleasant and distressing task, but it was incumbent on a Jew to do it; respect for the dead plays an important part in Judaism. The Germans had scattered quicklime into the pits where they had buried their victims, and their bodies had by now reduced to a slippery grey-brown mush and bones. When we tried to lift a limb, it came apart from the rest of the body. The stench of decaying human flesh, mixed with the caustic quicklime fumes, was so overpowering that it stung my eyes badly. The odour lingered in my nose and throat and clung to my clothes for many days.

To enrol at my former School No. 5 was out of the question. I would not have been made welcome and would have been subjected to harassment just as I had been in the past, perhaps even more so. This would have been hard to swallow after the Holocaust. Before the war this was our home and we'd had no choice but to tolerate it—that was how it was, and we had learned to live with it. However, post-war anti-Semitism was far more distressing and threatening. Word passed among the Poles that the Jews were coming back, which got them rattled. The attitude of the local people vis-à-vis the Jews turned considerably worse than it had been before the war. After the horrific events that they had witnessed, one would have thought that our Gentile neighbours would have found some sympathy for the surviving remnant, but it was not to be. People were often greeted by former neighbours and acquaintances with an unenthusiastic, "Oh, so you're alive!" The strained pre-war atmosphere, further poisoned by Nazi propaganda, deteriorated even further. In view of what had happened, one would have expected it to have had the opposite effect.

Chanina Szerman, of our "Włochy circle" was aware that a young niece of his was alive, having been sheltered by a local Polish couple.

His brother had entrusted his baby daughter to them to be looked after until the war is over. The elderly couple was childless and had meanwhile grown attached to little Magda, although money had been the initial motivation. Unfortunately, the child's parents did not come back, and the couple refused to give up the child to the uncle. No doubt she would have received a Catholic upbringing without ever knowing her true identity if she'd stayed. Chanina had no money or the time for a court wrangle, and as no family of his had survived, it was time to abandon Poland. He decided that there was no other way but to seize the little girl, who was almost four years old, and have her spirited out of Poland. He asked me to assist him in the plot because as a boy I would appear less conspicuous. I could hardly turn down an ex-comrade in adversity, and felt confident I could live up to the task. In any case, I thought it was the right thing to do under the circumstances. The cloak and dagger aspect of it particularly appealed to me; it brought back memories of wartime intrigue, only this time without the danger, I thought.

I set about my job with a passion. I began by spying on the house and shadowing the couple, which Chanina could not have done, as he was known to them; they would have gotten suspicious and informed the police. I watched the movement of the husband and wife for some days, tailing them and noting when the child was being taken to the park or to church, and so on. I noticed that the husband didn't always join them on the way to church, which was some distance away. When Chanina had wound up his affairs and was ready to abandon town, he decided to carry out the "operation" on a Sunday morning, on a quiet street as his niece was being brought home from church. To have done so before church would have been better, as the streets were quieter, but it would have been too early to catch the train out of town and the police would then have had time to act. We also decided that the most suitable spot would be as they turned a certain corner, where they would not see us approach. As we suddenly came face to face with the woman, she got startled, and in the bustle we wrested the child from her. The woman cursed and screamed hysterically, and the bewildered little girl was crying in Chanina's arms. The woman tried to run after us, but she couldn't keep up and soon gave up. At this point, my job was done and I split from Chanina, promising to meet in "Eretz" as we referred to Palestine at that time. I was afraid the situation could get out of hand and turn nasty—pogroms had been triggered for lesser reasons. I was not really happy doing it, but it had to be done in the best interests of the child and to fulfil what her parents would have wished for her. I doubt if I would have had a hand in it at any other time; this was, after all, a chaotic and lawless period. The young girl could not have remembered her biological parents, and the "foster" couple replaced them. I don't know how long it took for the child to get over the trauma of separation from her "parents" after she was snatched away by strangers in this way. [13]

Chanina's wife Hindzia waited for him along the way, and together they whisked Magda off to the railway station just in time to board a train that would take them from Ostrowiec and ultimately to Germany. Mission accomplished, I now headed for home in the Rynek, where my sister and I were staying, sharing a house with other survivors. I hoped to ride out the storm by staying indoors for the next few days, trusting that the police would not come looking for me. The woman had seen my face and must have known where the Jews stayed; the police certainly did. I shuddered at the thought of having to face the music all on my own, with Chanina having decamped for the American Zone of Germany. I was scared stiff: it would have been ironic had I run into trouble now, after the war, charged with being an accomplice in a kidnapping—or worse to be the cause of a pogrom. Luckily there were no repercussions; presumably the woman never reported the matter to the Polish militia. In the tense post-war atmosphere, Poles were ashamed for their friends and neighbours to know they had helped Jews to survive, lest they be branded what they called "friends of the Jews."

Fela and I made a visit to what had been our home before the war. We approached the place uneasily, worried about what we would find. The house was there, but only the bare walls remained. The factory building was also empty, and totally silent, with none of the hum of machinery that I remembered from my childhood. Upon entering our former home I ran straight to my room, curious to see what I would find, but that too had been looted and stripped bare. No toys, no books, not as much as a page from an exercise book: there was nothing to keep for a memento. Seeing my old home for the first time in almost five years filled me with nostalgia, and memories came flooding back. I just kept going from room to room, expecting to find my parents and brothers there—an

---

13   Magda, the little girl I had a hand in "kidnapping," was taken from Poland to Germany and then on to Palestine. Now Pnina, she lives happily in Israel and is a proud grandmother.

impossible dream. But it was not advisable to stay in the house on our own; it was prudent to return to the town centre and the safety of the "Jewish house" before nightfall. During the day, we kept going back to our old surroundings, walking the rooms, somehow expecting to find our family, vainly hoping to recapture our former idyllic life and lost dreams.

As for the factory, we found out that the heavy machinery was apparently shipped to Germany as the Nazis were pulling out, perhaps by the German custodian originally appointed to oversee our business. The rest had been looted by local people. Fela, together with Avram Berman, attempted to produce confectionery in a small way, as we had no other means of livelihood. Avram had the know-how, having been one of the key people at the factory, but supplies were difficult to obtain and we had no capital to invest. We existed largely on relief parcels shipped from the USA, provided by American-Jewish charities like the Joint. I still recall the jumbo bars of American milk chocolate with hazelnuts, of a size I had never seen before, and tins of corned beef as well as sweet Carnation milk, which were hitherto unheard of. Anything American aroused much interest and curiosity.

One lovely summer afternoon in June 1945, Fela and I were sitting on the grass outside our factory building, enjoying the spring sunshine. Looking into the distance, we suddenly saw a small, frail figure walking unsteady through the orchard towards us. As she got nearer, we realised with incredulous joy that it had to be Mother, as this path led only to our building! We ran to her and embraced her lovingly as tears of happiness run down our faces. It was incredible; we couldn't believe our own eyes. She was different, and yet it was our *mamusia* all right. She was almost unrecognisable, just skin and bone, with hollow eye sockets and sunken cheeks. Her hair was shorn and just beginning to grow back. She still had her concentration camp striped dress on, with only a woollen cardigan on top. We noticed that she had been branded with a blue number, tattooed on her left twig-like arm.

Mother had been liberated by the Russians at Neustadt-Glöwen, in northern Germany, on 2 May 1945, just four weeks earlier. She weighed about thirty kilos, was still very weak, and spoke slowly. Mother was always a tenacious fighter, and wouldn't wait to regain her strength in Germany before setting out on the long and arduous trek home. She told us that she had to get back without delay to be reunited with her beloved husband and children. How she made it back so soon after liberation in her weak state remains a mystery; she never told us the details of her journey. Passenger transport was non-existent in war-torn Europe, and yet she somehow accomplished it. I can only think she did it riding on goods trains and hitching in army trucks which ultimately brought her to Ostrowiec. Mother was thrilled to be reunited with the two of us, but deeply distressed not to find her husband and other three sons waiting for her as well. However, we were still hopeful, as some camps deep inside Germany and Austria were not liberated until after the war ended, and they would not have had enough time to get back to Poland.

Mother said she last saw Father and our three brothers when she was torn away from them on the platform at the Auschwitz town station. Apparently the siding leading to the camp could not accommodate them because of all the incoming transports. Soon after their arrival there in early August 1944, the men and women were separated before being marched towards the main extermination camp at Birkenau, or Auschwitz II, about three kilometres away. This was unusual: normally trains went directly to Auschwitz-Birkenau, passing under the now familiar "Arch of Death" towards a siding where the victims were off-loaded from the freight cars. There they faced an immediate selection as to who would live and who would die; those on the right for the gas and those on the left for slave labour, to die slowly another day.

Mother told us that she had had a remarkable escape and was extremely lucky to be alive. She said Father would be very proud of her when he'd return and hear how she had escaped from virtually inside the gas chamber. After several days at Auschwitz, she had to face another selection by Mengele, known as the "Doctor of Death," who with a casual flick of his finger directed her towards the right, the side destined for immediate gassing. A little while later, she found herself with the other condemned women undressed, in a small anteroom, perhaps an overflow waiting-room, about to enter the gas chamber itself, which was marked "Shower Room." Mother realised she had only minutes to live and nothing to lose. Being small and skinny, she managed to squeeze through a tiny window in the anteroom and escaped, completely naked. It was after dark, but she managed to find her way into the *Frauen Lager*, or women's compound, to mingle with the other female prisoners. Fortunately, some women from our town spotted her and immediately came to her aid by clothing her in "stripes" they had removed from a dead inmate. Mother was at first in *Lager* BIb (Block 16) and later transferred to *Lager* BIa. She somehow managed to avoid any further medical selections, which was incredible for someone of her age—she was forty-eight by then. She endured Auschwitz until January 1945, but her suffering and torment didn't end there. When fleeing ahead of the advancing Russians, the German guards would not abandon any witnesses to be liberated, and so they made the emaciated inmates depart on a "death-march" to Germany.

Starting 18 January 1945, thousands of women near death from starvation were forced to walk, driven relentlessly westward towards the Reich, ahead of the advancing Red Army, who got to Auschwitz nine days later. Mother and the other skeletal prisoners could barely drag their feet along in the snow; they were like the walking dead. It was bitterly cold, and the haggard women were clad only in their striped camp frocks, some with no shoes on, their feet swathed in rags. Any stragglers who couldn't keep up were shot as they fell by the wayside. Others expired along the way from exhaustion, hunger, and the intense cold. Again my mother had a lucky escape and showed tremendous courage and endurance, particularly considering her age. She told us that at one point she had collapsed in the snow, unable to keep up. The German guard didn't bother to shoot her, giving her up for dead like so many others who fell. A little later she somehow managed to raise herself up with the help of other passing prisoners, rejoining the column further on. Linking arms with the other women, she somehow managed to drag herself along. It was Mother's indomitable spirit and will to survive which enabled her to hang on so tenaciously. Recounting her ordeal, she said that only her unwavering belief in being reunited with her husband and children sustained her and gave her the courage and inner strength to go on.

Somewhere along the torturous route, near a railway junction, the prisoners were made to board an evacuation train's open boxcars and shunted about without food, and with only snow to eat or drink. The journey from Auschwitz to Bergen-Belsen took some days, and many more died from hunger and the intense January cold. The dead were simply thrown over the side of the boxcar. As Belsen was an overcrowded, disease-ridden hell that could not accommodate them, they were again transported, this time to Ravensbrück. This was an all-female camp with prisoners from all over Europe, where, unusually, the Jewish inmates were not in the majority. Ravensbrück was a dreadful camp, not as chaotic as Belsen but home to pseudo-medical and degrading sterilisation experiments that were carried out only on Jewish prisoners. Starvation and disease were the main causes of death. Mother endured these incredible hardships and remained at Ravensbrück until she was evacuated once more as the Russians were approaching the camp. She was finally liberated by the Red Army on 2 May 1945, at Neustadt-Glöwen, near Lübeck, on the Baltic coast. The Americans later took this area over from the Russians as part of a border adjustment deal. Many of her fellow inmates died after the liberation as their emaciated bodies could not take in any food—for them, freedom came too late.

A few days after Mother returned to Ostrowiec, more survivors came back from Germany and Austria and brought with them the shattering and painful news we had been dreading, that Father and Izak would not be coming back. We were utterly devastated, and mother could not be consoled. At the same time, we learned that my two other brothers, Leizer and Abram, had most probably survived, as they were seen by witnesses at Gusen, near Mauthausen in Austria, just before the arrival of the Americans. The four had managed to stay together until nearly the end. The witnesses could not bring themselves to tell us the exact circumstances of Father's and Izak's deaths, and we didn't ask. We didn't want to hear the harrowing details; it was painful enough to know that they had almost made it. I just couldn't believe that Father and Izak would not be coming back: we had been through so much together, and had overcome almost every obstacle. Father and Izak must have died an agonizing slow death just days before the Americans entered Gusen. If only Father had known that we were alive and well, the knowledge would at least have eased his pain. Mauthausen and Gusen were regarded as the most monstrous concentration camps of all, and were among the last to be liberated.

Germany surrendered on 7 May 1945, and the war in Europe ended officially the following day. The Swiss Red Cross circulated lists of survivors, on which we were greatly relieved to find the names of Leizer and Abram, which confirmed that my two remaining brothers were indeed alive. They had by then left Austria and were on their way to Italy, hoping to somehow reach British-Mandate Palestine. However, we had no way of getting in touch with them, and they could not have known that Mother and the two of us were alive.

We sorely grieved the loss of my father and brothers; I just couldn't accept they wouldn't come back, and carried on believing they would somehow return. Compared to other families, we were remarkably lucky, as five out of eight of us survived, whereas most families had been wiped out without a trace. While there was a great deal of luck involved, I also give some credit to our tenacity and the effort we put into avoiding the *Aktions* and roundups. It was during those operations that the majority of people were rounded up and dispatched to the death camps. We had refused to give up when others did; we had planned ahead by preparing ingenious hiding places, and we had never let ourselves be duped by Nazi deceit. Father was clear-thinking and possessed good judgment, and this permeated right through the family. Of course, other people had possessed foresight and had put immense effort into their own hiding places, only to be caught and killed; what saved those members of my family who survived was a combination of our efforts and our good fortune.

Our relatives were not so fortunate, and I lost all of my uncles and aunts. Families were large in those days and I had once had many cousins, but only three survived: Franka Fajngold from Kielce, who had lived with us before the war and who had also escaped to the "Aryan" part of Warsaw; her brother Leonek, who had survived the camps, albeit with a withered arm as a result of a German guard pushing him off a scaffold; and lastly Avram Berman, who had hidden in the countryside near our town. Avram was the only relative to survive in Ostrowiec out of my mother's entire family, the Bermans. Apart from us, not a single member of the Katz family survived in their hometown of Zawichost or in any of the places they had resided in.

On 4 July 1946, a shocking pogrom took place in Kielce, the county town of our province, with forty-two Jews hideously done to death and about eighty more injured. Some were shot and others bludgeoned or lynched by the rampaging Polish mob, which was baying for Jewish blood, screaming "Death to the bloodsuckers!" Several of the victims were from Ostrowiec, including Bela Gertner, a beautiful teenage girl who I was fond of. She had been one of the handful of young survivors I had spent time with in Ostrowiec before she had departed for Kielce. Bela was the only member of her entire family to have come through the war. For her to die so young, and so soon after the liberation, was a cruel twist of fate. People complained bitterly, saying, "They are killing us all over again!" The Nazis had many willing accomplices in many countries during the war, but only the Poles were guilty of such crimes after it was over. Bela Gertner had gone to Kielce to join a group involved in *Hachshara*, agricultural training and Kibbutz-style communal living, in readiness for their departure for Eretz Yisrael. Bela often talked about her dreams of starting a new life in a future Jewish homeland. After all the horrors she had endured, she had no intention of remaining in Poland, but the blood-soaked Polish soil claimed her just the same.

The disappearance of an eight-year-old Christian boy, followed by accusations of ritual murder, sparked the pogrom. The whole incident was a complete fabrication. The boy had apparently gone cherry-picking on a farm owned by a relative. When he hadn't returned by a certain time, his father reported him missing to the police and said that he must have been kidnapped by Jews. When the boy ultimately returned home, he said he was forcibly held in the cellar of the "Jew house." He claimed that other Polish boys were also held there against their will, but that he had managed to escape. The boy's father failed to report to the police that his son had returned until the next day. Despite its being known to both the police and the locals that this house on Planty Street never had a cellar, as it was too close to the river, the angry mob was allowed to enter the building, where they went on a rampage. Some of the residents of the house were thrown into the street from the upper windows, for the mob to set about them. Jews were attacked all over town, wherever they could be found. The pogrom even spread to the railway station, where passengers were attacked. The killing orgy lasted the whole of the next day, with onlookers joining in by assaulting and stoning to death any people of Jewish appearance. Some were thrown out of upstairs windows; others were clubbed to death with blunt instruments or shot by Polish soldiers and militia men, who robbed the injured victims as well as the corpses. In all, forty-two Jews were killed with over eighty wounded, some survived by feigning death.[14]

Similar attacks, but on a smaller scale, took place all over Poland. Poles were dismayed at the thought of Jews coming back to reclaim their properties and possessions, which they had meanwhile appropriated,

---

14   A distant cousin, Józio Fajngold, was shot in the face during the Kielce pogrom, and his injury resulted in a stammer he had for many years. Now Joe Feingold, he became an architect and lives in New York.

and this caused resentment which provoked the pogroms. The Poles were well aware that few Jews were ever likely to return—they were witnesses to their destruction. Now the infamous blood-libel started all over again, but with a new twist. In the past, Jews had been accused of using the blood of Christian children for Passover *matzah*; now ignorant people and the odd crackpot priest helped to spread the lie that the weak and undernourished camp survivors needed to imbibe Polish blood to restore them to good health. There were also instances of Jews being pushed out of speeding trains to prevent them from reaching their former homes. It has been estimated that well over a thousand Jews were killed in the pogroms that swept Poland after the war, but the true figure can never be known.

Soon after the liberation, a family friend found herself sitting on a train next to a middle-aged man. Not realising she was Jewish, he pointed to someone further down the carriage who looked like a gaunt concentration camp survivor, and complained to her bitterly that too many of "them" were coming back. "*Piorunie!*" he swore aloud, regretting that the Germans had departed in such haste that they had never set-tled their debt—they still owed him, he said, a sackful of sugar as a re-ward for informing on fifty Jews! He muttered in a way that was meant to be heard by the entire compartment, but no one so much as batted an eyelid. We realised that although the war was over, our new-found freedom was fraught with danger, and that Poland was not the place to rebuild our lives. Anyway, nothing remained to keep the survivors there—everyone who mattered to them was dead or missing. In spite of this, the attitude of the local people towards their Jewish neighbours had not mellowed. To the contrary, the situation had become fraught with danger: as a result of the war many Poles were now armed.

In the aftermath of the Kielce pogrom, the Jews abandoned Os-trowiec and other small towns for the safety of the main cities, like Warsaw and Łódź. But the great majority of the survivors went back to Germany to seek safety in a Displaced Persons' Camp, mostly in the American Zone of Germany, assisted by UNRRA. There they waited for their turn to emigrate, mostly to Palestine and to the West. How ironic that so soon after the war they should feel safer in Germany, the source of their torment, living among the people who were responsible for the Holocaust, than in Poland, the country of their birth. Mother also fled to Germany, but my sister remained in Poland for the time being. I, as I will describe soon, had by this point made my way to England.

Fela had a good reason to remain in Poland: she had met Benjamin Majerczak, an officer in the Polish Army, who had returned with his unit from Russia, having fled there at the beginning of the war from Włocławek in Poland. He had fought all the way from Russia to Poland and then on to Germany. This army had been formed in the Soviet Union during the war, and comprised Polish and Jewish prisoners of war in Russian hands as well as Polish nationals, including Jews who had fled to safety behind the Russian lines. Mother, Fela, and I had earlier decided that we would all head for Palestine and no other place. We felt that we had been pushed around long enough and we only wanted to live in an independent Jewish state, reunited with what remained of the family, thus realising the dream of returning to Zion and helping rebuild our ancestral homeland. Many pledged that never again would we allow ourselves to be led like sheep to the slaughter; hence the solemn slogan "Never Again" was coined at about this time.

Some time later, Capt. Ben Majerczak was demobilized from the Polish army and married my sister in Łódź. After obtaining their exit visas, they set off for Israel in 1948. Ben, an engineer by profession, assisted the newly-formed Israel Defence Forces as a technical adviser. Having served in tanks, he was familiar with the Russian armoured vehicles that Israel acquired via Czechoslovakia, courtesy of the Soviet Union. Subsequently, Ben and Fela had two sons, both born in Israel. My mother also boarded a rickety old steamer in 1947, bound for Palestine. However, the "illegal" boat was intercepted by the Royal Navy off the Palestinian coast and the hapless refugees, all unflinching Holocaust survivors, were forcibly removed from the ship and put in a British detention camp on the island of Cyprus. Mother was incarcerated there until after the State of Israel was declared in May 1948. A month later she finally reached the promised shore, and was at last reunited with three of her living children. Only I was missing—for I was still in England.

My journey to Britain was a gamble: an opportunity had arisen for me to travel there with a transport of orphaned children. I didn't really want to go to England, and leave my mother and sister behind in Poland; not my sister, with whom I had been through so much and to whom I owed my life. But Mother implored me to go while I had the opportunity, to go "where you can acquire some schooling and the good English manners you sorely need" as she liked to say. Although I was apprehensive about separating again, I was happy at the prospect of leaving Poland, where we didn't feel safe. I had no way of knowing what life had in store for me, on my own in a strange land where I didn't speak the language. Anyplace had to be better than post-war Poland, where we no longer fitted in and were not wanted. Ostrowiec, and all of Poland, had become afflicted with anti-Jewish hatred as never before. There was also an ideological struggle for power going on in the country: Pole against Pole, Left against Right, and vice versa, with Jews caught in the middle and held in contempt by all parties.

Standing in front of our former factory building as it looks today: empty and derelict neglected grounds, condemned for demolition to make way for a new development.

AFTER THE INFERNO

These poignant pictures were taken on 11 October 1945 by my cousin Avram Berman. His intention was to commemorate for posterity the third anniversary of the main *Aktion* and deportation. There was much weeping as Kaddish, the prayer for the dead, was recited in unison.

The survivors wearing funereal armbands walking through the desolate streets, past empty and derelict Jewish homes to a memorial service at a mass grave. I am in the foreground, second from left, one of four Ostrowiec children to survive.

Here I'm just to the left of the man on the right with the high boots and legs apart.

CHAPTER 20

Passage to Tower Bridge

In early March 1946, word had reached us in Ostrowiec that a distinguished rabbi from London was on a rescue mission to Poland, going from place to place, trying to locate surviving children to take back with him to England. He risked his life coming to Poland at this time, in his effort to save orphans from danger and to help the very young, who were likely to be lost to Judaism, return to their community and religion. We heard that an attempt had been made on his life by a nationalist Polish gang, with the car he was travelling in fired at in the nearby Kielce area. As a result, the rabbi was forced to cut his journey short and return to Warsaw. As it was too risky for him to travel to the provinces where some of the children were to be found; word spread that any children under the age of fifteen who wished to travel to England should head for Warsaw without delay, and make contact with the English rabbi.

Like most young survivors at the time, I was angry and thirsting for vengeance, and possessed a burning desire to go to what was then Palestine and join in the armed struggle for a Jewish homeland as soon as I was old enough. But there were barriers in the way: the gates of Palestine were closed to us. My mother implored me to accept that for now, I would do better to join the transport of children to London with that "nice English rabbi," as she put it. She also reminded me of my uncle Paul Katz, who had fled to England before the war and sent his postcard from "Hull," and made me promise to look for him and his family. I wanted to believe there would be an opportunity for me to go to Palestine at some later stage. Meanwhile, the situation in Poland was steadily deteriorating, and there were almost daily reports of deadly attacks on Jews up and down the country. Poles were up in arms about their Jewish neighbours, whom they had not expected to return, coming back to reclaim their homes.

Once again, I had to bid my mother a sad farewell, although this time I was secure in the knowledge that the parting was only temporary and that we would reunite in the Land of Israel before long. With this in mind I set off for Warsaw, accompanied by my devoted sister. Upon reaching the devastated capital which we had left a few months earlier, we immediately went to meet Rabbi Dr. Solomon Schonfeld at the Jewish Community Centre. On our arrival, we were greeted by an imposing figure of a man with piercing blue eyes and a red Van Dyke beard, wearing an army uniform that I was not familiar with. The rabbi commanded the respect and admiration of everyone who came into contact with him. Rabbi Schonfeld looked resplendent in what turned out to be the uniform of a British Army chaplain, with a badge of the Tablets of the Law on his officer's cap. The Van Dyke didn't quite go with the uniform, but then he was, as it turned out, neither a chaplain nor in the army. He had apparently adopted the British uniform to protect him from hostile nationalist Poles.

The rabbi spoke no Polish and Fela spoke no English, but we managed to communicate in a mixture of German and Yiddish. Right from the start the rabbi informed us that the transport was now full to capacity; we had gotten there too late! However, the rabbi said, there might still be a chance of joining the transport, as one of the boys on the list was reluctant to leave his mother behind and was considering backing down. If so, I could perhaps take his place, but I would have to be prepared to take on the boy's identity as well, to comply with the sponsorship regulations, and perhaps not to revert to my own name for years to come. I asked the rabbi if there was any chance of my getting to Palestine, as I would rather go there than to England, to join my two older brothers and fight as soon as I was old enough to hold a gun. The rabbi was rather taken aback by what I said. He looked at my sister, who made no comment; she felt the same way. After our experiences in Europe, the only place we wanted to go to was Palestine. The rabbi replied that he would try to help me in that direction, but I must first be prepared to go to England. "From there you will have a better chance of getting to Palestine, as that country is controlled by the British," he said. I'm convinced that he said this simply to lure me away from Poland, where my life was in danger, living as we did in a small town, where the risk was far greater than in the big cities. In the end, I let the good rabbi persuade me, and I agreed to join the transport. On our part, we tried to reassure the rabbi that he could count on me not to let the side down: I would keep the secret. Fela went on to explain that I had all the right credentials, and it would not be too much of a problem for me to live with a false name, as

I had done during the war when I was passing for a non-Jew.

It was now up to the other boy to decide whether he would go or I would take his place. Soon enough, he backed down, deciding he couldn't leave his ailing mother behind in Poland all on her own. It was now time for my sister and me to part. She had to return to Ostrowiec, because we couldn't leave Mother there on her own at a dangerous time like this—there had already been a deadly pogrom in our town. Meanwhile, Mother could not have known what was happening with us in Warsaw, as there was no way of communicating. It was an emotional parting; my sister and I were very close, and she was more like a mother to me, both because of the big difference in age, and because of what we had been through together.

Adolf Bader, the boy whose identity I had to adopt, was sponsored by a London family by the name of Swimer. All the children had to have a sponsor so we wouldn't become charges of the state. Had I not taken the boy's place, it would have been a wasted opportunity. Rabbi Schonfeld didn't always adhere to convention. It was characteristic of the man to bend the rules, if necessary, so as not to miss an opportunity to rescue another boy at a time like this.

Needless to say, I disliked my newly-adopted name, Adolf, and shuddered to think of how I would fare in England with a name like that so soon after the war. Unlike in England, in mainland Europe Adolf was a fairly common name before Hitler; I had a first cousin with that name. However, I knew nothing about the singularly illustrious name of Bader. I was later to discover that it would prove to be a definite plus to share this distinctive name with a national hero, the legendary legless RAF fighter pilot whose name was on everyone's lips at the time. It was ironic that now, in peacetime, I had to live with another assumed name and would not be able to revert back to my true name until years later.

All the children were assembled and housed in a Warsaw synagogue where wooden bunks were hastily erected, turning it into a large dormitory to accommodate more than a hundred boys and girls. The Nożyk Synagogue was the only house of worship and communal property left standing in Warsaw. It had survived destruction because it had been used as stabling by German cavalry officers. I stayed with the assembled group, mostly girls but including some other boys, for several days until all the preparations could be finalised for our passage to the British Isles. I had to start calling myself Adolf with immediate effect. None of the children knew me, so adopting the name now would present less of a problem in the long run, and it would take time for me to get used to it. Having reverted back to Rubin from Stefan only a few months before, I now had to call myself by yet another name—and Adolf was not a very agreeable name to be saddled with.

On the day of departure, we were informed that the first leg of our journey would be by aeroplane. None of us had ever flown before, and the mere thought of it created a lot of excitement, which turned to apprehension and even fear when we were confronted with a huge war plane awaiting us on the tarmac. As we climbed up the step-ladder and boarded the aircraft, some of the smaller children got agitated, wondering what would hold up the large plane in the sky. We were flown from what was then the military airfield Okęcie, just outside Warsaw, in a Russian bomber, sitting tightly packed on the floor of the hollowed-out fuselage. The flight from Warsaw to Danzig, now renamed Gdańsk, was fairly turbulent, and made us all feel rather nauseous. The port of Gdańsk was not operational; we could see a large partly-submerged warship blocking the harbour. This was my first glimpse of the sea. We spent the night in Gdańsk in a large hall, sleeping on the floor. We were due to be transported by lorry the next day to the nearby port of Gdynia, on the Baltic Sea, where we were scheduled to board a Swedish ship the next day. That this wizard of a rabbi managed to arrange all this, at a time when Europe was still in turmoil, amazes me to this day.

Before starting out to a new life in England, it seems I was destined to undergo one last ordeal in Poland. It was already dark and sleeting heavily; the open lorry was tightly packed with standing boys and girls. Along the way, the truck suddenly lurched forwards, then backwards, and we were all thrown against the tailboard. Under the sheer weight of the children it was holding in, the hinged flap at the back burst open in one corner; perhaps the bolt jumped out. As I was standing at the back, right in that corner, I lost my balance and toppled over the side, with my body hanging upside down over the street. One leg was out of the lorry, and my other foot was trapped in the gap, which fortunately prevented me from sliding completely out of the speeding vehicle. I was hanging upside down, with my leg and arms swinging wildly and my head just inches away from the ground, with the rear double-tyres throwing up slush and ice in my face, blinding me completely. The children were screaming hysterically, banging on the roof of the Polish driver's cab for him to stop, but he took his time bringing the vehicle to a complete halt. The driver probably couldn't see what was happening at the rear, but how could he have ignored the children's cries of hysteria? Luckily, I was helped by two alert boys standing next to me, Ludwig Simonsohn and Zygmunt Kulas, who held on to my one trapped foot for dear life, keeping me from falling out of the truck, thus saving my life. Apart from losing one boot in the mishap, I was lucky to get away with just a sprained ankle—a painful hindrance on my momentous journey to freedom, but nothing insurmountable.[15]

I spent that night nursing my swollen ankle while we waited for other groups of children to arrive to join the transport in Gdynia. As I was shod with only one shoe, and it was now the only shoe I owned, someone came up with a spare pair of rubber plimsolls. They were hardly the thing for the Polish weather, but they nevertheless helped to save the day. I much regretted losing my ski-type, lace-up boots, which were the only sizeable post-war acquisition I treasured.

Before boarding the Swedish ship, we were addressed by a Polish official in the departure hall. He made it clear that by opting to leave the country we were effectively renouncing our Polish citizenship, and we would never be able to return to "our motherland." We thought it a bit rich: the fact was that our motherland spurned us, we were not wanted there and that was why we were leaving. Jews had lived in Poland for almost a thousand years, and yet we were not considered "true Poles" and were often looked down upon with disdain and told to go to Palestine. None of us had Polish passports; we all travelled on a block-visa issued by the British Home Office, who sanctioned our entry into Great Britain. Later, I was furnished with a *Titre de Voyage,* a stateless travel document, which enabled me to travel abroad, except to Poland, where the Crown could not afford me any protection even after I had acquired British citizenship.

As a final farewell, a Polish customs officer mounted on a chair next addressed the assembled children. He cautioned us to declare all American dollars and valuables, or suffer the consequences! This ridiculous

---

15 Of the two boys who clung to my leg on the lorry, Zygmunt Kulas immigrated to Israel and fell in battle in the 1973 Yom Kippur War, leaving a wife with two young boys. Zygmunt was a reservist in the tanks and died in an assault on the Golan Heights while operating a bulldozer-tank. Ludwig Simonsohn worked for El-Al Airlines as a technician. He retired to Dorset, where he lives with his wife Cindy. We keep in touch.

warning resulted in spontaneous, if suppressed, giggling by the assembled youngsters. Notwithstanding the terrible events, the prejudiced officials associated Jews, even very young, very poor Jews, with money. All of us, impoverished and mostly orphans, were lucky to have escaped with our bare lives! This is my last memory of Poland. I hardly felt any emotion at the prospect of leaving the country, as I no longer had any sense of belonging to it. Sadly, my experiences there had left an indelible mark and an indifferent attitude towards the country of my birth. However, it must be said that there were some, all too few, honourable and courageous Poles, who swam against the stream and were heroes to those they helped. Personally, I shall remain forever grateful to those who helped me, in particular *Pani* Gozdzialska, whose memory I shall always cherish with affection, the Radziks, and Bronia. Inevitably, war brings out the best and the worst in people, and as far as the Poles at large are concerned there can be no doubt that many welcomed the Nazi persecution of the Jews, from which they benefited materially. A significant number of Poles were involved in criminal activities against Jews, and a small number of outstanding people risked their lives to help, but the vast majority were actively hostile, or at best indifferent to the Jews' fate. I don't relish saying this, but it has to be said—this is how it was.

It was a Friday evening when we walked up the gangplank and boarded the Swedish cargo vessel the SS *Ragne*. We were all very excited at the prospect of sailing to England and turning our backs on our unhappy country with its terrible memories. After embarkation and bunk assignments, Rabbi Schonfeld assembled all the children in the dining-hall to welcome us on board and to deliver a few words in honour of Shabbat. All the chattering stopped abruptly, and a hushed silence descended on the hall. The rabbi then picked out two of the older girls and invited them to light the traditional Friday night candles. The rabbi then made the blessing over the wine and challah loaves, which had been specially baked on board ship, and passed pieces around so that each boy and girl could partake. It was a touching scene that none of us had experienced since our parents had performed it in our own homes so very long ago. Some of the younger children couldn't even remember the rituals, having only recently emerged from convents, and so their significance was entirely lost on them. The Friday night ceremony and the flickering Shabbat candles that I fondly remembered my mother blessing, symbolised for me a new beginning as a Jewish boy. Apart from my very survival, this was my final victory over the Nazis. We were about to sail to freedom, secure in the knowledge that our own Scarlet Pimpernel, in the guise of the rabbi, was with us on board. That night the *Ragne* weighed anchor, cast off, and with one long blast of the foghorn slipped out of the harbour, steering a westerly course for the British Isles.

Rabbi Schonfeld

At first the *Ragne* made slow progress through the Baltic Sea. Seeking the reasons for this, we learned from the seamen on board that so soon after the end of hostilities there was still danger from sunken ships, as well as uncharted mines adrift on the high seas. After our first day at sea, the weather became stormy and we all got rather seasick. None of us had been at sea before. There was only the rabbi on board to look after all one hundred and twenty boisterous, and now rather miserable, youngsters.

Some of the teenage girls, I'm led to believe, had fallen head over heels for the handsome rabbi and were only too happy to assist him in taking care of the young who needed attention. After a couple of days at sea, the weather improved and we quickly recovered. The Swedish freighter chartered by Rabbi Schonfeld carried no cargo except for barrels of salt-herring stored on deck under tarpaulin covers. We soon sniffed these out. After we had recovered from our seasickness we tapped into a barrel and lost no time in tucking into the delicious Swedish salt-herring, a delicacy we were all familiar with: it was the customary accompaniment to black bread and a glass of vodka in our part of the world.

The journey to our adoptive country took a long nine days. This gave us an opportunity to become better acquainted with the formidable rabbi and vice versa, and allowed him to make an effort to introduce us to good English manners and the rules of proper behaviour. The very first words he taught us were: Please; Thank you; So sorry; Excuse me; and How do you do? The latter we kept repeating as we passed each other on deck, using exaggerated accents and bowing our heads! Rabbi Schonfeld was a great Anglophile, and he endeavoured to turn us into instant little *Engländer*. He lost no time in trying to instil us with a strong loyalty to our host country by introducing us to patriotic songs, such as "Rule Britannia," "Land of Hope and Glory," and, of course, "God Save the King," which we sang lustily when we realised it was to be our new national anthem. The rabbi also taught us some jolly songs, such as "Daisy, Daisy" and "Solomon had a Thousand Wives." The latter I don't recall ever hearing again, but I remembered it because of the amusing title, and because the rabbi's name was also Solomon. But the song we all took to easily was "Tipperary": the tune we had heard in Poland and were already familiar with, and now we were learning the words. None of us spoke any English, so we communicated with the rabbi in a mixture of German and Yiddish that only some of the older children could understand, similar to what Fela and I had used when we had first met him. I feel sure that at the time none of us appreciated the significance behind the stirring lyrics that the rabbi wrote phonetically on a blackboard; we simply repeated them parrot-fashion, trying to mimic the accent as best we could.

On the way to England, we interrupted our journey and docked in the port of Trelleborg, at the southernmost tip of Sweden, to take on supplies and unload the barrels of herring, the stock of which had been rapidly dwindling. In stark contrast to the people of the war-torn, cheerless place we had just come from, the friendly Swedes turned out by the hundreds to greet the "mysterious cargo." Unfortunately, we were not allowed to go ashore. Many people gathered at the quayside, waving and cheering for a long time, throwing sweets and gifts on board and then disappearing only to coming back with more. It was a dull and drizzly day, and what struck me most about the young Swedes was how prosperous they all looked, smartly dressed in similar fawn-coloured military-style trench coats with epaulettes. Most were tall and blond, and looked well-fed and cheerful. They had never known war, and it showed in their carefree behaviour. I had never been outside Poland before, but I could quite happily have jumped ship and stayed on in Sweden were it not for my burning desire to go to Palestine, via England. The assembled well-wishers at the dockside waved us off with their handkerchiefs as the *Ragne* pulled away to resume her course. That night we passed through the Kiel Canal, then along the Gothenburg Straits out into the North Sea, heading in a direct line for the British Isles. I tried to visualise what the country would be like. I imagined it to resemble the nineteenth-century society I had read about in children's adventure stories. We wondered if we could expect the same friendly welcome in London that we got in Trelleborg.

Looking back on it, I can see that the youngsters on board were a defiant and rebellious bunch, resentful of authority, and this was particularly true of the boys. Most of us were tough and astute, lacking in education and showing little respect for officialdom. Practically all of us had been orphaned during the war—I was one of the lucky exceptions, to still have a living parent—and were marked by our experiences and angry with the world. But we soon grew fond of our charming rabbi, who taught us to sing and laugh, and who strove to restore our faith in humanity. Only he would command our respect and admiration, both during and after the voyage.

A few of the boys were still in the habit of carrying knives for self-protection, as I had done during the war, and it was even rumoured that some of the bigger boys had revolvers concealed on them. A secret meeting was called by the older boys, and a plot was hatched to take over the boat—for there was only a small crew on board—and force it to change course and head for Palestine, where most of us wanted to go. During the ensuing noisy discussion, some of the boys came out in favour of the idea and others argued against it as being unfair to the younger children on board. Since we had lived through similar experiences, a close bond had formed between the youths and the younger children. I feel sure that some of the other older boys were reckless enough to try carrying out their plan were it not for the rabbi on board. As no consensus was reached, the matter was postponed, but the "mutiny" simmered on. Perhaps it was just a schoolboy fantasy, but it is true that many of us thought this sounded like an excellent idea.

Though I heard about the plot, I was not in on it, as I was not one of the ringleaders. That group comprised the older boys, some of whom had made themselves seem younger to qualify joining the transport. There was even a pregnant young woman on board! Ironically, during the war some of these same youths had been forced to make themselves appear older to qualify for work. The good rabbi got wind of the plot and delivered a stern warning, telling us that anyone found with a weapon on disembarkation would be sent straight back to Poland! This was a fate no one aspired to, and consequently, hoarded daggers and perhaps even a handgun or two ended up at the bottom of the English Channel before the ship docked. One boy, Manes List, sported several knives and made no secret of it—not that he was violent in any way. His behaviour was symptomatic of the life he had led during the war, and I suppose he had to demonstrate that should anyone try to mess with him, he was more than capable of defending himself.[16]

The curiosity and emotion kept mounting as we neared the English coast, and we all grew very excited when land first came into view. It was early morning, 29 March 1946, when we entered the Thames Estuary, and we were all glued to the deck, spellbound, as the Ragne sailed upstream past Tilbury and the London Docks towards Tower Bridge. As we approached the colossal bridge we stood in awe, astonished by its sheer size. Some of the younger children were so alarmed that they began to scream in panic, afraid that the ship was heading straight for the middle of the awesome bridge and would ram into it. Eventually they quieted down, as word passed along deck for everyone to remain calm, for the bridge would part, enabling the ship to pass—this was a wonder

---

16 Manes List went on to the United States. Having missed out on schooling, as we all had, he studied hard at night school and qualified. I understand from a mutual friend that he built up a successful career as a chief oncologist.

previously unheard of! We remained on deck, transfixed, and marvelled at the sight of the wonder-bridge that split itself in the middle to let us sail past, and raised its bascules in salute, as if to welcome us with open arms to our new country, a better future, and freedom from fear.

The *Ragne* steaming past Tower Bridge on 29 March 1946 with the children lined up on deck. This image is published courtesy of Southampton University. Papers of Rabbi Solomon Schonfeld.

CHAPTER 21

Adieu, *Poland: Welcome to Woodberry Down*

Sunday, 29 March 1946, was a beautiful spring day, and we sailed into the Pool of London overwrought with excitement. It was lunchtime when the *Ragne* dropped anchor and tied up right next to Tower Bridge, across the water from the Tower of London. Tower Bridge, a famous London landmark, left a lasting impression on me.

This was an unusual place to land passengers, but then we were no ordinary cargo. Press photographers were there, waiting for the boat to dock, but unlike earlier in Trelleborg, there was no one to cheer for us. Our hopes of receiving the same welcome we'd gotten in Sweden had been in vain. When the landing formalities were complete, we stepped off the gangplank and set foot on English soil for the first time. Waiting at the quayside to welcome us were Rabbi Schonfeld's sprightly assistant Ruth Lunzer and some of the children's sponsors, including Adolf Bader's sponsor, Yechiel Swimer, an Orthodox gentleman from North London. He and his wife had come to greet Adolf and perhaps take him home with them. The couple must have been told by the rabbi that I was not the boy they were expecting; I was aware of their gaze in my direction. Although Mr. Swimer was in effect my sponsor, the idea of foster parents did not appeal to me. Nothing could have replaced my lost family environment and I also felt I was too old to be fostered. I was tempered by the war, and my experiences had taught me self-reliance: I wanted a measure of independence. Anyhow, I much preferred the idea of a hostel and the camaraderie of boys and girls with a shared experience and background.

It took some time to clear all the immigration formalities, and by lunchtime all those not collected by relatives and sponsors were on their way in motor coaches through the empty streets of London—for in those days, streets were deserted on Sundays. We were taken to Woodberry Down, near Manor House in North London. Our new home turned out to be an impressive mansion, situated in leafy surroundings near some reservoirs. This large residence had been converted into a hostel, which was fully equipped to accommodate all of us. Upon our arrival there, nurses in crisp white coats lined up at the entrance to welcome and take care of us and to provide us with any medical attention we needed. Long trestle tables covered with white tablecloths were ready-set for high tea in the atrium. We tucked into a lavish meal, washed down with large quantities of orangeade and other fizzy drinks that we hadn't seen since before the war. Every day, we were to find, we could eat all the bread we wanted—and it was the whitest, softest bread at that; it went very well with the toothsome English jam! I also discovered the delights of after-dinner jelly, which I had not known before, though tea with milk did not go down too well. Tea in Poland is not drunk with milk.

With the sumptuous meal over, we were given a badly needed change of clothes: we were presented with a mountain of second-hand clothes, and we dived in, tossing items we didn't need aside until everyone found something that fitted. Before bedtime, we were reintroduced to the essential tools of hygiene, like toothbrushes, which some of us had forgotten existed. After such an arduous and thrilling day, we fell exhausted but contented into our bunks and slept very soundly indeed. Rabbi Schonfeld had thought of everything and took care of all our needs. Life looked beautiful and promising again, after six years of deprivation and misery. Over the coming weeks, smiles slowly began to return to the children's faces, coupled with the tinge of sadness that would always be there, below the surface.

Over the next few days, we were all interviewed individually to ascertain the type of background we had come from, our plans and wishes for the future, and whether we had any relatives in England. All the details were noted down. It was imperative that we be placed in suitable homes, to make room in the hostel for future survivors from war-torn Europe. Rabbi Schonfeld tried his utmost to place each one of us in a relevant family environment, in accordance with the child's background and preference. As a result of our wartime experiences, most of us were not interested in becoming Orthodox or having any religious constraints imposed on us. No one was coerced into joining a religious family, although that would have been the rabbi's wish. He no doubt hoped that in spite of everything we would come to realise that it was not so bad to have been born a Jew. One thing I'm certain of: none of his *Kinder* will ever forget Rabbi Schonfeld, and we will always remember him with much affection and gratitude.

I told my interviewer that prior to leaving Poland, my mother had made me promise to make every effort to locate my father's brother in England. His name was Paul Katz, he came here from Nazi Germany at the outbreak of war, and he was living in a place called *Huul,* I said. My interviewer insisted that I must be mistaken, as there is no such place in England. Was it perhaps—and here the interviewer pronounced a name that sounded to me like Hal? No, I insisted, it was *Huul,* the way my mother had pronounced it. Enquiries were put into motion with various refugee organisations, but no trace of Paul Katz could be found. Though I didn't realize it at the time, he had come over independently and not with any organization, and his name would therefore not have appeared on any refugee list. It was thought that perhaps he had been interned during the war as an enemy alien and sent to one of the colonies, as many "enemy aliens" were. At the time, I also didn't appreciate the fact that although he had lived in Germany since his youth, my uncle was in fact Polish by birth, and would therefore not have been classed as an enemy alien. Meanwhile, I was to remain at Woodberry Down hostel until my uncle was located.

Classes were organised at the hostel for those waiting to find foster homes, with priority given to teaching us English. We wanted to become better acquainted with the host country, so one of the first things we had to get used to, apart from having to drink milk with tea, was the confusing currency system. We were given weekly pocket money of half-a-crown for spending and transportation. This was a tradition I very much approved of: no one had ever given me money for doing nothing before! On his visits to the hostel, Rabbi Schonfeld was in the habit of greeting his *Kinder* with: "Have you had your *Taschengeld* this week yet?" He would then go on to produce a half-crown coin from his pocket and press it into the boy's or girl's palm. Having some pocket money enabled us to spend many hours travelling around London on trolleybuses, sitting on the front seats of the upper-deck and exploring the great metropolis, and helped us grow acclimated. However, not speaking the language, we were afraid of getting lost, so we carried pieces of paper with our address printed on them. At first the underground was, despite or perhaps because of its novelty, rather daunting, and since being underground meant you saw nothing of the sights, I avoided them. I was spellbound by the sheer size of London, and dazed by all the traffic and the multitude of people. After Poland, it was quite a revelation—it was like a different world. We admired the people tremendously; everyone was so courteous and fair. One was always welcomed, as soon as one crossed the threshold, with: "How would you like a nice cuppa tea?" The most commonly used expressions seemed to be "I'm so sorry," and "I do beg your pardon." People queued patiently and in an orderly manner. In fact, there were queues for everything; we thought it was the national pastime! The reticent British had calm temperaments and were slow to anger, unlike the volatile people in the land we had just come from. We also loved the tall, friendly London policemen with their funny "Charlie Chaplin" helmets, who always smiled and were happy to oblige. They carried no guns or truncheons that we could see, and no one need be afraid of them. The youngsters soon learned to ask the "Bobbies" to help them across a busy road holding hands, just for the fun of it—one would have never held the hand of a Polish policeman; we had avoided and feared them.

Apart from the orderliness and uniformity, what struck me most about London, as compared to Polish towns, was the neatly clipped privet hedges and, as it was early spring, the bare trunks of pollarded plane-trees with their cauliflower-like tops, which looked a bit strange to me. The houses, at least in the suburbs, were all identical one-family homes, row upon row, built of the same exposed red brick, whereas in Poland no two houses were alike. People dressed elegantly—and not only the adults: teenagers also wore smart three-piece suits with ties and starched white collars and cufflinks. That was daily wear, for work! I just couldn't wait to be issued with my first double-breasted "English suit" with waistcoat and long pants, complete with turn-ups and sharp creases—the latter was a must. England was a country full of contrast. For instance, in Europe people wore their festive clothes on Sundays, whereas here it was the other way round: everyone wore their tatty clothes at weekends, saving their best attire for the week.

Some confusion was, of course, caused by the language barrier: one day, soon after my arrival, I was looking with my pals for a public lavatory in the West End of downtown London. We noticed a couple of doorways with the sign CLOSED, and I took this to be the English equivalent of the Polish word *KLOZET*, for water closet. I tried one of the doors, but it being Sunday, the room beyond it was of course closed!

It was a lovely spring that year, and I discovered that contrary to what I had read back home in Poland and had conjured up in my mind, it didn't always rain in England! We boys were in the habit of loitering about the streets in groups, speaking mainly Polish. Passers-by viewed us with curiosity and looked at us askance. No doubt we were "aliens" to them—that's what foreigners were called at the time. As an alien, I would have to report with my Aliens Registration Book to the Hackney police station if I were to change my address, and have the book stamped accordingly. Wearing a motley collection of discarded clothing, my friends and I stood out and attracted attention in the street at a time when everyone else dressed conventionally. London was not a very cosmopolitan place in those days, and almost everyone in the street was English. Sometimes people came up to enquire where we were from, and what we had done during the war. Naturally, we were reluctant to talk. They could not have appreciated what we had undergone, and would have considered it too incredible to believe. We had no wish to be pitied or patronized in any way, but invariably Jewish people felt sorry for us, so they were keen to tell us that they too had had a rough time of it during the war. The Blitz, as they referred to the bombing of London, the terror of the "doodle-bug" flying bomb, the austerity, and food rationing were mentioned often. The shortage of tea, which was severely rationed, was particularly irksome to the British.

The British Jews may have pitied us, but I waited in vain for an invitation to experience a traditional Friday night meal in a family environment. Truth be told, we were looked down on by many in the Anglo-Jewish community, as if we had just stepped off an onion-boat, which I suppose was not that far from the truth. Perhaps their reaction was mainly because we hardly spoke the language, and had no family background to speak of. Having missed out on education, we weren't thought to have much prospect for a good career, either, and as we got older, we were also not considered suitable escorts for their daughters. This problem I myself experienced a few years later, when I was dating a pretty, auburn-haired girl who lived in a nice house on Clapton Common. The young lady and I were very fond of each other, but one day she sent me a "Dear John" letter to say that her parents had forbidden her going out with an alien!

Back at the hostel, there was a large varnished wall-map of England hanging in the common room. I often gazed at it, reading and trying to memorise the different places in the only way I knew, the phonetic Polish way. One day, staring at the wall-map, I came across the name

Hull, high up on the right-hand side of the map. This struck a cord, and I quickly fetched the youth leader. Pointing to the top of the map, I shouted excitedly in Yiddish, "Look, there's *Huul*, that is where my uncle lives!" "Oh, you mean Hull," the leader told me, pointing to the place, "that's pronounced *Hal*." Enquiries were immediately put into effect to trace my uncle in Hull. Again they drew a blank; the Hull Jewish community had no record of a Paul Katz having lived there, and I gave up all hope of ever finding my uncle.

One day, I was sitting with some of my pals on a bench in nearby Finsbury Park when a smartly-dressed gentleman came up and asked in a tactful way where we were from. He spoke in German, which we understood better than English. He took a particular interest in me, as I spoke reasonable German, and went on to enquire whether I had any relatives in England. I told him that I thought I had an uncle in Hull who came from Germany, but he must have gone on to another country as he was nowhere to be found. The gentleman went on to ask which town in Germany my uncle had lived in and I told him it was Halberstadt. "Halberstadt!" he repeated. "What a coincidence! I also come from there." When I told him my uncle's name, he said he knew of a Paul Katz from Halberstadt who lived in a place called Leeds. He made the connection, and this Paul Katz turned out to be my long-lost uncle! A chance meeting in the street had accomplished what the Chief Rabbi's Emergency Council could not, in spite of all its efforts. Hull was the port where my uncle had landed on reaching these shores, and it was from Hull that he had sent the Red Cross postcard that had reached us in Poland early on in the war. He had left Poland long before I was born, and I had never met him before. Uncle Paul, who bore a strong resemblance to my father in appearance, as well as in manner and speech, came to fetch me, and took me back with him to Leeds to stay with his family. He became my legal guardian. For a long time, I could not stop gazing at my uncle, imagining him to be my father.

In Leeds my uncle enrolled me at the Cowper Street School in Chapeltown. As I had lost out on six years of schooling, all of my classmates were about two years younger than me. Officially, of course, the difference was only one year, because of my assumed identity and date of birth. At school I was often greeted by the boys in the playground with two fingers of the one hand pressed against the upper lip, and with the other raised in a Hitler salute, because of my assumed first name. Still, all this was more than offset by my illustrious surname Bader, which had all the boys puzzled. This time, however, I did not have to concoct a story about "Uncle Douglas" (Bader), the legendary Battle of Britain fighter-ace, to come to my aid: it was enough to just share this gallant name, which made all the boys turn green with envy. The name Bader was rare in this country, and they naturally thought there had to be a family connection, which I made no attempt to deny! Although my English was still limited and I couldn't always follow the lesson, I nevertheless came top of the class at spelling. I was able to do this by memorizing difficult words the way I would spell them in phonetic Polish, where every syllable is pronounced, and my photographic memory did the rest. My broken English may have elicited howls of laughter in the classroom, and I was no good at writing essays either, but I always came top at spelling! As a newcomer, I had the classmates and my teacher completely baffled. I attempted to somewhat anglicise the spelling of my name to Adolph, but it didn't help, as it sounds the same and there was only the one Adolf they all knew of! Outside school, I encouraged my friends to call me Adolek, which is the Polish diminutive of Adolf. It was against the law to change one's name, as the process of deed poll had been suspended when Identity Cards were introduced during of the war, and the suspension was still in force.

After school, there was hardly any tuck, or sweet snack foods, to be had during the post-war austerity period; there was only arrowroot to chew. Instead of bottles of pop, there was sarsaparilla and sherbet, an effervescent powder we could mix with water, to drink. It was in Leeds that I first discovered the delights of potato crisps, which I had never tasted before. Crisps were one of the few things not rationed, so I was able to treat myself on my way home from school as I passed Harris's fish shop in the Chapeltown Road. Like all schoolboys, I suppose, I was always ravenous, but I was never able to afford fish 'n chips. There was no chocolate to be had, either, as my aunt kept the ration books, and she naturally utilised the sweets coupons for more essential things, like sugar, jam, and the like.

Occasionally my uncle would take the family—my Aunt Manya, their children Leo (the *Waffelman*, as we had called him!) and Anne, and me, for an outing to nearby Harrogate in his Ford motor car for a day out; this was an adventure to look forward to. Harrogate had once been a smart Victorian spa resort, and we would round off the day by taking tea at the acclaimed Betty's Teashop, served by waitresses in white pinafores trimmed with lace, and matching caps. There were dainty cucumber sandwiches and delicious scones with home-made jam, but no cream—this was banned during the austerity period. After a lovely day, we would head back to Leeds. In those days we often had the road all to ourselves, for few people had cars and petrol was severely rationed.

Unfortunately, I could not remain long with my uncle and aunt, as the immigration quota they had been waiting for came up, enabling them to travel to the United States. My uncle later opened an art gallery in Manhattan, where he prospered. He would come regularly to England on buying trips, and I would meet up with him there and sometimes accompany him to wholesale art dealers in Yorkshire and Lancashire.

In 1955, Aunt Manya and her young daughter Anne, who was born in England during the war, were on a flight from New York to Tel-Aviv, via London. *En route*, the El-Al Constellation strayed unintentionally over the communist Bulgaria border, and its Mig-fighters wantonly shot down what was unmistakably a civilian airliner, killing all the passengers on board. After this tragedy, my uncle was never the same again.

After I left my uncle, my schooling came to an abrupt end again. I was all on my own once more, but this time it didn't matter greatly, except that I had no means of support and would have to start work right away. I was almost sixteen when I returned to London and began working, as an electrician's mate. My first weekly wage packet amounted to thirty shillings, and I had to spend almost half of it on my lodgings. I rented a small unheated attic room with a German refugee couple in St. Kilda's Road, Stoke Newington, at fourteen shillings and six-pence per week— just under seventy-five pence in today's terms. For that sort of money, you got no board and no bathroom facilities, although there was a sink in the room. With public baths on Church Street charging a shilling a time, I couldn't afford too many of those either. I received no financial help from any refugee organisation, nor did I seek any: I only sought assistance with finding a job. I never felt sorry for myself, for I had overcome far greater adversity. To have survived such a war made everything pale in significance. If by the end of the week I was "skint" and couldn't afford the trolleybus fare to my place of work at Dalston Junction; it hardly mattered. I would simply run all the way there. I found work rewarding, and standing on my own two feet gave me a feeling of maturity and independence.

It was now early 1948, and people were concerned by the dramatic events unfolding in Palestine. Britain had earlier agreed to relinquish the Mandate, and the United Nations voted in favour of a partition plan for separate Jewish and Arab states, which the Jews of Palestine accepted and the Arabs rejected. The Jewish population, called the Yishuv, made plans to declare independence as soon as the British would leave the country. Meanwhile there was much bloodshed, with both Jews and Arabs trying to consolidate their positions before the British forces pulled out. Although barred from entering Palestine, some young men managed to get through the blockade to join in the fight, and I felt it was my duty to do the same. It was, after all, where I always dreamed of going, to be reunited with my mother and siblings. As a result of my wartime experiences, I nurtured a strong desire to hold and use a gun, so I decided I would make every effort to somehow get to the Land of Israel. The only way to enter at this point was clandestinely, and naturally priority was given to young men of military age. I was only sixteen.

Although the British had by then decided to pull out of Palestine, they were still severely limiting the entry of refugees languishing in camps in Germany, which I considered very unjust. This was contrary to the promise made under the Balfour Declaration as well as against the principles of the League of Nations Mandate given to Britain with the aim of fostering a national home for Jews in Palestine.

Like many people at the time, I identified with Vladimir Jabotinsky's brand of right-wing Zionism and drawn to the ideals of Betar, the youth section of that party, perhaps because they didn't believe in turning the other cheek and they fought for Jewish independence. They were also active in smuggling survivors into Palestine that no country was willing to take in. Jabotinsky was a visionary, who had tried in the 1930s to raise awareness among Jews of the unfolding danger. He travelled from centre to centre, imploring people to leave in the face of the impending disaster, but not many would listen, as few options were open to them.

I sympathised with Jabotinsky's movement, though I never intended to harm my adoptive country in any way. After all, it was England that gave me asylum when the country I was born in had rejected me. Nonetheless, I felt bitter about survivors of Nazi horrors still languishing in camps in Germany, barred from their ancestral homeland. I suffered for my mother, who longed to be reunited with her surviving children in the

Land of Israel; she had been through enough. Moreover, the Holocaust would not have happened had the Jews had a homeland of their own to go to: Hitler was willing to let us go, at least in the early days, but no country would take us in.

I made my feelings known to certain Zionist circles in North London, the area I lived in, and in due course was introduced to a Viennese-born folk singer who, I was given to understand, had all the right connections. My girlfriend at the time, Miriam Mayer, was herself a refugee from Nazi Germany, hailing from a good Frankfurt family. Miriam introduced me to a refugee couple she knew, and it turned out that the wife remembered me from the Woodberry Down hostel, where she had been a nurse. This couple were very kind to us, as Miriam had no parents either, we were always made welcome in their home. Their modest abode became like a meeting place for refugees. It was there that I first met the song-and-guitar man in question. I told him about myself, and that I was keen to get to Palestine to fight. He said that he couldn't promise anything, but he would try. Before long, a rendezvous had been arranged with a representative from what I believed to be Betar, the youth wing of the Revisionist Party, although he never identified as such and no group was mentioned by name. Betar was associated with the Irgun Zvai Leumi, which was considered a terrorist organisation by the British. The Special Branch kept certain people connected with it under surveillance. It was an open secret that the Palestine Jewish underground had Zionist sympathisers in this country who built up a network to recruit volunteers to their ranks to defend against Arab irregulars in Palestine.

I didn't look on the Irgun fighters as terrorists, as they didn't target civilians and in any case had by then called off their campaign against the British military. The emergency was largely over, with the Irgun now concentrating on the Arab bands who were increasingly staging attacks against Jewish targets in Palestine.

I was instructed to walk up and down outside the entrance to the Turkish Baths at the Imperial Hotel in Russell Square at a given date and time, and someone would approach me. I was to carry a copy of the *Daily Herald* in the left-hand side pocket of my jacket, folded, with the title clearly visible. If no one approached me by a certain time, I was not to hang around but go home and await further instructions. As arranged, a man, short-sighted and middle-aged with thick-rimmed glasses, approached me out of nowhere. I no longer recall the name he gave, if any;

it would not have been his real name in any case, and he never asked me for mine, though I'm sure he knew it. The first thing he said, while pointing at the newspaper sticking out of my pocket was; "I see you also read the Labour paper!" As we slowly walked along the street, he began by asking me where I was from, what my background was, and my family and the war, and, most crucially, why I wanted to volunteer. I was sure he must have known all this from the contact anyway. After we strolled for some time together, with him constantly looking over his shoulder, I got the impression that he was more than satisfied with my credentials. Then he asked, "Have you had any weapons training, with the partisans perhaps?"

"No, I'm afraid not," I replied. "I was never in the partisans, but as a result of the war, I'm familiar with certain weapons and I learned how to throw hand grenades to catch fish." This rather intrigued him, and he asked me to explain. Finally, he enquired how old I was, and I answered, "Seventeen!"

I was actually about six months short of my seventeenth birthday, and he must have twigged that I was trying to make myself seem older than I was. He stopped abruptly, looked me straight in the eye, and said, "If you feel the same way a year from now, when you're eighteen, contact me again, using the same channels, and we will meet in the same place. Maybe we will even have the time to enjoy a Turkish bath together," he quipped, and then departed with the Betar slogan "Hazak v'Ematz!"—Be Strong and of Good Courage! I replied in the same manner. The man vanished down a side street, as quickly as he had appeared.

With my thirst for adventure well and truly thwarted, there was nothing more to be done but try to concentrate on my work and career. I found work rewarding, and standing on my own feet gave me a feeling of maturity and independence. With a burning ambition to succeed and make up for what I had lost, I tried my hand at various jobs in fairly quick succession. At first, as I mentioned, I worked as an electrician's mate, but all I found myself doing was feeding electric cables through conduits all day long, which I found rather boring. Like all boys, I was interested in motorcars, so I switched to car repair work. Again I found myself doing all the donkey work, like cleaning, wire-brushing, and changing brake linings on cars and vans, day in and day out. After that, the Sabbath Observance Society in Middlesex Street, in the East End of London, fixed me up with my next job. This sounded really exciting:

it was to learn diamond polishing with a firm in Holborn Circus, with the promise of advancing to diamond cutting, where the prospects were even better. Unfortunately, Oliver Brothers, of Olvey Diamond Polishing Co., Ltd., went into voluntary liquidation within months and I could not find another job in that field.

One of the first things I did with my earnings was buy the latest Bakelite PYE radio. As this was my first major purchase, saved for out of my wages, it became my most prized possession. I have it to this day; it sits prominently on a shelf in my study. Alas, it no longer works: the valves for it are no longer available.

As I was always interested in the art of printing and design, I next entered the printing industry, beginning as a compositor. At the same time I went to evening classes at the North-Western Polytechnic in the Prince of Wales Road, learning to operate the Linotype, a mechanical type-setting machine for newspaper and book printing. Having a keen eye for design and layout, I also enrolled at the Polytechnic for a course in graphic design. Although keenly interested in my work and good at my job, I encountered along the way the problem of the "closed shop" rule in the printing trade, which was militant at the time. This was to hold me back considerably, because I was a member of the "wrong union," not having served an apprenticeship, as I was too old when I entered the industry. This stopped me from applying for a better job in Fleet Street with one of the national dailies, where the money was much better. Eventually, I came to realise that because of the "closed shop" rule, I had no future in the printing industry either, so I decided to move on again.

I had originally come to England with the intention of going on to what was then Palestine to join my mother, but this turned out to be a forlorn dream, as mentioned earlier, until after the State of Israel was established. By that point, my circumstances had changed for the better, and I didn't feel any urgency after the fighting was over; it had been the cloak-and-dagger aspect of my earlier attempt that had fired my imagination. Anyway, my mother quite rightly wanted me to remain in England where my career prospects were better, and the new Jewish State had meanwhile consolidated its position and did not, I felt, need my help. Over the years, I visited my family as often as I could. The way to travel in those days was by overnight train to Marseilles, changing stations in Paris, and then on by boat to Haifa. As time went on with me remaining in England, I mellowed; my anger abated and I lost my zeal for vengeance.

Unlike many refugees, I never felt uprooted in my adopted country. As soon as I had acquired a rudimentary knowledge of the language I had started to acclimatise well, adapting quickly to life in my new country and determined to learn good English. About five years after my arrival I was able to revert once again to my true name, leaving "Adolf" behind. From the start I made a conscious effort to converse only in English and to forget my native tongue. I chose not to mix in immigrant circles, and made a conscious effort to shed my accent, so that I would not appear any different and would not have to divulge my background. I never spoke to anyone about my experiences, as I wanted to block out the war period and become part of the English scene; I was determined to get on with life and enjoy it to the full. I decided to move from the rather mundane Stamford Hill to the more agreeable surroundings of Bayswater, opposite Hyde Park. I shared a small flat with an English friend, John M., an ex-Barnard Castle public schoolboy, from whom I tried to learn the "English ways" and hopefully some of the social graces. It was John who first introduced me to the wit of Oscar Wilde and the poetry of John Betjeman.

I was attracted to the British way of life, and over the years plunged wholeheartedly into typically English pursuits. At first I tried cricket, then rugby at the Central YMCA. But the sport that appealed to me most was rowing. Perhaps this was for social reasons—it seemed to me like just the thing for an aspiring young Englishman! I was proposed to Auriol Rowing Club at Hammersmith Bridge by two member friends, and after a trial period was initiated as a novice into the club. I have some amusing recollections from those days; I was rather intrigued to know what the senior oarsmen meant by the references to "catching a crab" that often entered into the conversation. I did not like to ask, and draw attention to my ignorance or perhaps my inadequate English. They would not have told me anyway, and finding out for yourself at your own cost was part of the initiation into the sport. To my regret, a few weeks later I discovered what the mysterious phrase meant. There are different ways of catching a crab, the most common of which is when the blade, or oar, fails to strike the water. The first crab I caught was from not keeping in time with the crew. You can also "catch a crab" by not striking the blade deeply enough into the water, so that the blade just skims the surface and jumps out of the rowlock. This is when I was struck hard in my chest and chin by the shaft of the oar, and fell backwards—it wouldn't be the last time! Yet another way one can catch a crab and lose the oar is by striking the blade too deep into the water. In this case, you even risk being thrown clear of the boat, into the "drink," by the force of the fast-moving shell-eight.

'Shooting the bridges' on the Thames with my rowing 'eight' in the Head of the River Race. I am at 'two' at the rear, the last but one.

This became my main sporting and social activity for a number of years. Rowing is a demanding sport, and it took up most of my free time. My pals at the rowing club were by background rather snobbish, as was the entire sport in those days, at least on the Tideway, as we referred to the Thames. My friends were unaware of my background, but may have guessed I wasn't born in England. Still, I am confident that they never knew my religion. They didn't delve, and I never offered any information. What really mattered was one's social status and the way one acquitted oneself. I was by then reasonably well spoken, with my slight continental accent obscured by my mild Yorkshire inflections. This had the young ladies, in particular, rather intrigued. It was a bit of a challenge for me to mix in those circles, so I made a special effort to learn from my friends' conduct, cultivating their upper-middle-class manners. I was able to adjust to the company I was with, a gift I thought I had inherited from my father and cultivated during the war. Perhaps I was still masquerading—old habits die hard! I also anglicised my name, when with my rowing friends, to Robin. It was not a question of denial, but rather of wishing to blend in and not look like an outsider. I mixed in the right circles and attended good parties at weekends, both in London and in the country. I may not have had "tuppence" to rub together, but that hardly mattered, as what was important was the way you conducted yourself. Luckily, conversation was always shallow and not personal, nor did it often touch on politics or religion. My pals at the club came to consider me a good sport, and I never shied away from any challenge. For instance, I could hold my own in any beer-swilling contest—an important attribute in those circles, as was the ability to hold one's drink. It was also important to demonstrate fair play, and a sense of humour was essential; finally, it wouldn't do to swagger or show off in any way; that was looked down on.

During the winter months, we would train after office hours in an indoor tank that simulated rowing, and went on four-mile runs. During long summer evenings we trained on the Tideway, sometimes even after nightfall. Rowing in the dark is an amazing sensation; all you hear in the evening calm is the swishing of blades as the boat cuts silently through the water, and you feel your way rather than see, in rhythm with the boat and crew as you are at no other time. Summer weekends were set-aside for regattas. The Head of the River race and Henley Week were the particular annual events to look forward to, from both a sporting and a social point of view. I first started in a clinker boat, then a shell-four, finally progressing to a shell-eight that I rowed in most of the time. As I'm not heavily built, I rowed at either "Bow" or "Two," at the opposite end from the coxswain, with the heavier blokes in the middle of the boat. The sport is all about skill and stamina, rather than brute force, and I earned the reputation of getting the bit between the teeth and not letting go.

Admittedly, my rowing club was no longer one of the foremost clubs on the Thames at that time—it had enjoyed its heyday in the nineteenth century! However, since then we have boasted a famous member: the fame did not arise from his rowing, but Graham Hill rose to become a Grand Prix racing driver in the sixties, winning the Formula I championship twice. Graham left Auriol at Hammersmith for the more prestigious London Rowing Club at Putney Bridge, whose rowing stripes he wore on his racing helmet. Putney had greater pretensions than Hammersmith Bridge, and the old-boy network in this upper crust sport was very much alive in the fifties and sixties. Regrettably, I had to give it up when I married Michèle, my French-Jewish wife, at the age of thirty-three, as rowing is a demanding sport and takes up too much of one's time. Prior to marrying, although I had a succession of girl friends, I had tried to avoid any lasting attachments. I was waiting until the right girl came along. We subsequently had three talented children: two boys, and a girl in the middle, with each excelling in his or her own field.

As I got older, I had only one abiding regret which pained me. As a result of the war, I was deprived of the opportunity for further study. I should have liked to take up architecture. I am virtually self-taught, and in order to expand my knowledge I would read encyclopaedia volumes from cover to cover, the way people read novels.

However, the lack of a formal education didn't stop me from getting on. Starting in the early seventies, I built up a successful lingerie manufacturing business in the Midlands from scratch, with the initial factory in Sutton-in-Ashfield, and then expanding into plants in Nottingham and Ilkeston in Derbyshire. Right from the start I wanted to concentrate on export to Europe. That was before Britain joined the Common Market, but it was a member of EFTA (European Free Trade). Business was buoyant, with the result that most British firms could not be bothered with exporting—it was too much like hard work, involving paperwork and red tape, at a time when the British were still somewhat suspicious of anything foreign. Later, when business became more difficult due to competition from the Far East, my firm was not affected. I travelled all over Europe on selling trips, often accompanied by my wife Michèle, who was also our chief designer and who spoke French, German, and Dutch. We exhibited at the main international trade fairs in Paris and Düsseldorf, where our knowledge of languages was obviously an advantage. I adopted the original family brand-name of "Amor," thus carrying on the family tradition, albeit in a different field. As I wanted to repay my debt to the country that took me in when my own had rejected me, and besides, because I had always liked a challenge, I applied for the Queen's Award for Export Achievement. My company, Amor Lingerie, easily qualified by exceeding the criteria laid down, having exported more than 80% of our production for more than four consecutive years. However, as the number of awards had to be kept down, to create an exclusive circle of exporting firms to aspire to and to encourage more technological and innovative fields rather than textiles, we lost the award to other companies whose level of export achievement may have been considerably lower. I was naturally disappointed not to win the award; I had been under the impression that it was only a matter of reaching the target. However, I would later have the honour of being presented to Her Majesty, the Queen.

Throughout those active years, as hard as I tried to forget about the war and its effects, it was never far from my thoughts. It undoubtedly left an indelible mark; it shaped my life and fuelled my ambition to succeed and make up for what I had lost. Having worked hard all my life, I promised myself to retire early and travel the world, but I kept putting it off until I finally got round to it at the age of sixty-six. When I decided to dispose of the business, together with the brand-name of Amor and the cherub logo, hoping the name would live on, there was no future in the textile industry for our children to follow. We did, however, make sure that they received the best possible education.

I have not dwelt much on the post-war period, in comparison with my wartime "adventures": the routine proved rather mundane and predictable in this tranquil and cosy land. There is, however, a matter of great importance to medicine that I would like to bring up, as it gave my wife Michèle and me much satisfaction. Soon after we relocated to Nottingham from London for business reasons, Michèle became pregnant with our youngest son, Simon. At the beginning of 1971 a routine blood sample was sent to the laboratory for testing, and they found that her blood serum contained the fairly rare Rhesus antibody-E. After the baby was born, Michèle was asked to donate blood, but as a nursing mother she was not supposed to do so; in spite of that, the doctor took the blood and separated the fluid from the red cells in a centrifuge, keeping the fluid and giving her back the red cells. A sample of my own blood was also taken at the same time.

When all the tests were complete, it was discovered that Michèle's blood serum also contained another extremely rare antibody, which was very valuable to doctors when matching organs for kidney transplants. At the time, there was only one other known person in the world with this antibody, and that person lived in the USA. One doctor remarked jokingly, "We hope you won't be tempted by riches and go to America to sell it!" A sample of the serum was distributed to research centres all over Britain and Europe. This serum was at its most concentrated during pregnancy and for a short time after giving birth. The antibody present in Michèle's blood detected a tissue antigen which had only recently been discovered. The process of tissue typing was therefore more accurate and made transplantation safer. The discovery of this rare and valuable serum would help to successfully match organs for transplantation for hundreds of patients living on artificial kidney machines. Further research also enabled scientists to ultimately reproduce it artificially under laboratory conditions.

I must add that although it was Michèle who donated the blood, it was actually the combination of the two of us that resulted in this special serum. It was my antigen that caused Michèle to produce the antibody which fought against it, thus resulting in this rare serum—a truly joint effort! The team of scientists from the National Blood Transfusion Centre at Sheffield responsible for its discovery, named it after us: Antibody Kz.

The highlight to my time here was on 27 January 2005, when I was chosen to be presented to Her Majesty the Queen at a reception in St. James's Palace to mark Holocaust Memorial Day, on the occasion of the sixtieth anniversary of the liberation of Auschwitz. Having gently taken the gloved royal hand that was proffered, I bowed from the neck down, as practiced at the rehearsal a few days earlier, when we were also instructed to address Her Majesty as Ma'am. Unfortunately, during the actual introduction, the gentleman presenting got my name mixed up with someone else and mistakenly said that I had survived Auschwitz. This threw me completely, as it had been specifically pointed out that royalty speaks first, and that I must only answer questions put to me by Her Majesty. At first I was in a bit of a dilemma, and hesitated momentarily, but then decided this was a mistake I could not ignore. I felt I must disregard protocol, and hoped I would be forgiven for the breach. I addressed the Queen directly by courteously pointing out the mistake, giving my correct name. The Queen, rather amused by it all, smiled demurely, and listened sympathetically. I felt confident that I'd done the right thing. Having got over this hurdle, I breathed a sigh of relief before Her Majesty asked, "And how long have you been in this country?"

"Almost fifty-nine years, Ma'am," I answered.

The Queen appeared rather surprised, and said, "Oh, as long as that?" I nodded my head in agreement.

"And how long were you in Auschwitz?" Her Majesty next enquired.

"I was never in Auschwitz, Ma'am, although my family was." The Queen listened attentively as I went on. "I was rather young, and had I ended up in Auschwitz, I very much doubt if I would have had this great honour." Here I dipped my head slightly, and went on to explain that I had survived by hiding and running and passing for a Christian boy, together with my sister.

"Oh, how very interesting" the Queen remarked, smiling graciously as she slowly moved away towards the next person to be presented.

Soon after her return from the camps in Germany, while we were still in Poland, my mother related her story to us. After that point, it was hardly ever discussed again. When she first reached Israel after her incarceration in Cyprus, she lived with other homeless immigrants under canvas and never complained. She was proud to be living in a Jewish country, reunited with two sons she had been parted from for far too long. They were now safely on an agricultural kibbutz, working hard and trying to catch up on the studies that had been interrupted by five years of war. As for my mother, over the years the sorrow was always there, and the wound could never heal. There was an aching void in her heart and she often regretted the loss of her beloved husband and two strapping young sons. She always damned the Nazis and their minions—if only we'd had our own country, just a few years earlier, she'd say. However, she often looked back with nostalgia to the pre-war years and liked to relate her fond memories of the idyllic life we had led before the war. Like many other survivors, Mother had lost faith in God after the Holocaust, and was in the habit of saying "There has been too much pain and suffering for God to exist." And yet, she remained as Jewish as ever. For instance, she still observed many Jewish customs, like the dietary laws; she could not have done otherwise, for they were ingrained in her.

In the post-war period the Holocaust was simply not discussed, and the silence wasn't broken until the seventies, or even later. I cannot say exactly why this was so, but it seemed that the survivors were an embarrassment to some and even outcasts to others. People didn't know what to make of them, or how to handle them. Being a survivor was almost like being an inferior being to some, and certainly nothing to brag about. In fact, some survivors were rather ashamed of it, and even went as far as having their tattooed numbers removed surgically, as one of my brothers did.

When I first started to write my memoir, I realised that there were gaps about the family that needed to be filled in and pieced together. This was following my escape from the labour camp, when my family was transported to Auschwitz, and their subsequent movements and experiences. My mother could no longer be asked—she had passed away in 1972—and my brother Eliezer had died in 1987. But I managed to persuade my remaining brother, Abram, to recount what had happened to the family after we separated inside the camp in Ostrowiec during those harrowing days in late 1943, after I had made my escape to Warsaw.

Abram began by recounting how the Ostrowiec slave-labour camp was liquidated on 3 August 1944, and my parents and brothers, together with the other camp inmates, were transported by cattle car to Auschwitz, arriving there the next day. It was from him that I learned how our mother was immediately separated from my father and brothers on the platform. After they were parted, my father and brothers didn't know of Mother's fate. The men were marched the last three to four kilometres to the main Auschwitz-Birkenau camp, where they had to pass a "selection," and then were assigned to Block BIIe, known as the Zigeuner Lager. As the "Jewish Camp" was full to overflowing, they were sent instead to the so-called "Gypsy Camp," although Jews were normally kept apart from gypsies as well as other Gentiles. On reaching Birkenau, the four of them had their heads shaven and were tattooed with the infamous blue numbers on their forearms. This was an auspicious sign, because those destined for immediate gassing were not branded with a number. Abram's number was B-4497. They were all given consecutive numbers. There were no names in Auschwitz, only these numbers.

Abram said they watched with grim apprehension the smoking chimneys during the day and the red glow at night, and could smell the distressing stench of burning flesh. He told me he wanted to believe the Germans were only burning bodies of inmates who had died of disease, and that healthy people were not sent to the ovens. My father and three brothers remained at Auschwitz-Birkenau for about ten days, and were greatly relieved when the four of them were taken away with approximately two hundred other prisoners and transported to Świętochłowice in Silesia, to work in a plant where heavy guns were produced. In this camp they suffered extreme hunger, but still there was somewhat more to eat than there had been at Auschwitz. Most important, there were no gas chambers there with smoking chimneys to haunt them day and night.

In January 1945 my father and brothers were again transported, this time out of Świętochłowice to Mauthausen in Austria, arriving there on 29 January 1945. This was a dreadful camp, far worse than Auschwitz. There was little to eat or drink, and inmates were worked to death in the infamous granite quarries, digging out the heavy granite for use in monumental Nazi edifices designed by Hitler's architect, Albert Speer. Prisoners were done to death by being pushed off the quarry cliffs, and some chose to commit suicide instead, by leaping off. Sometimes several prisoners would join hands and plunge together to their gruesome deaths. The SS guards referred to them derisively as "Jewish parachutists."

At Mauthausen, Father and my brothers suffered extreme hunger and thirst. About two weeks later, on 16 February, they were transferred to the Mauthausen sub-camp Gusen, about five kilometres away. Their relief was short-lived, since Gusen had the worst reputation of all. Mauthausen and its sub-camp Gusen were two of the most notorious concentration camps in the history of the Third Reich. Life expectancy was no more than a few weeks. The prisoners perished by being worked to death in 12-hour shifts, or from starvation and savage beatings. As in other camps, the severely emaciated were referred to as "Musulmen," and the man in charge of the prisoners in each barracks was called a Kapo. To save on rations, a sadistic Kapo might wring or snap the scrawny neck of a skeletal prisoner, or put his head under the water tap. The Musulmen were too weak to resist, and it would be over in a matter of seconds.

There were also political prisoners of various nationalities housed in separate barracks, but conditions for the Jews were much worse, and non-Jews were not subject to "selections" for the gas chambers. Jews received less food and bore the brunt of German brutality. The inmates at Gusen slaved in underground work-tunnels hewn out of the rock in the production of armaments, particularly the new Messerschmidt jet-fighter, with which Hitler was still hoping to turn the tide of the war in his favour. The members of my family were attached to different work sections and usually saw each other at night in the barracks, but this would depend on the shift they were assigned. Reveille was at 4 a.m., and soon after they were herded into open railway wagons that moved at walking pace to the subterranean factories, with the guards following on foot. Near the tunnels, the prisoners were ordered out of the wagons and made to run the last few hundred metres into the work tunnels.

Right from the start, my brother Izak realized that he had been as-signed very hard work. He was by far the strongest of the four, but he complained bitterly in Yiddish: *"Es is mir miess arein gefallen"*—I have been dealt a cruel blow. A bad work assignment was like a sentence of death. Leizer, on the other hand, worked with asbestos, producing the Messerschmidt brake pads. Father and Abram both worked in the alu-minium workshop, where the Messerschmidt fighter-plane fuselage was built, but they were on different workbenches.

By about the middle of April 1945; they had been suffering for so long and were so debilitated that they couldn't believe, despite all the obvious signs around them, that the end to their suffering was close. It seemed that the more the German military situation deteriorated the worse camp conditions became. One early morning there was an Allied air raid in the area just as the prisoners had left the boxcars and were being chased into the work tunnels, and beaten en route. It was still dark, and there was a blackout; Father couldn't see well and he fell. The guards punished him for it, beating him mercilessly. That evening after the day shift, when my three brothers returned to the barracks, they were shocked to see how badly he had been beaten. His nose was broken and his spectacles smashed. Father was short-sighted, and could not see without the spectacles.

He had been beaten by a sadistic German Kapo. These were mostly hardened criminals and murderers, transferred from civilian German prisons to serve in the camps. The Kapos had the power of life and death over the inmates, and if a Kapo saw any sign that a prisoner had been beaten, it was like a mark or stamp on his forehead instructing other Kapos to beat him as well and shorten his life. They next broke Father's jaw and teeth, and he couldn't eat what little food there was. As a result, he became so weak that he could no longer report to the *Appellplatz* for work. The prisoners who remained in the block during the day received no food whatsoever; this was the final sentence of death.

The next day, when my brothers returned from their work-shift, they were devastated to find Father lying dead on the ground outside the bar-racks. Their distress was unimaginable. Izak carried Father's withered body, with the help of other skeletal prisoners, to lay him to rest in a shallow grave they scarcely had the strength to dig. It was very distress-ing and agonising for Izak to bury Father. Afterwards, upon entering the barracks, he tearfully uttered the customary Hebrew words spoken

My mother in Israel in 1963. She was always at her happiest when surrounded by her grandchildren.

after a funeral: "Blessed be the True Judge." It was only days before the liberation.

Father's death affected Izak acutely, as it did my two other brothers. The next day, Izak began to complain of abdominal pains and could not stand erect. Two days later, on returning to the barracks after the day shift, Abram found Leizer standing over Izak, grieving. He was dead, lying outside with his head propped up against the side of the barrack. He was just twenty-three years old. Leizer gave Abram Izak's bread ration, which he had hung on to, wanting him to eat it, but he simply could not. Although he was suffering from extreme hunger, he could not eat it after seeing Father and Izak die one after the other. Abram hid the bread inside his striped camp shirt, and when he woke in the morning, it was gone. Someone had taken it. When one is dying of hunger, it requires considerable will-power to save bread for another. It is impossible to describe what extreme hunger is like; unless one has experienced it himself, one can never understand. Starvation, apart from destroying you physically, also leads to human degradation: one loses all sense of dignity and the ability to control one's emotions. It was not like that with my family, we remained totally committed to each other until the very end. Previously, we had somehow managed to pull through together, but Gusen got the better of them, tragically close to rescue.

The day after Izak died, as the arrival of the Americans was imminent, the camp *Kommandant* announced that Jewish prisoners would receive Red Cross food parcels. Predictably, all that Leizer and Abram managed to get was a little condensed milk at the bottom of a can, while the Kapos and German guards stole most of the food. During that same night, as the guards began to melt away, my brothers climbed the camp fence and started to walk towards the nearby Austrian town of Linz. On the way, they met up with an advance unit of the American 11th Armored Division, and the American soldiers gave them some chocolate. The Americans entered the camp the next morning, 5 May 1945. Mauthausen-Gusen was one of the last camps to be liberated by the Allied Forces.

After the camp was liberated, thousands of the walking dead were too weak to be nursed back to health, while others simply died from over-eating, unable after their long ordeal to digest the rich food. The camp *Kommandant* of KZ Mauthausen-Gusen, Franz Ziereis, who was hanged for his crimes after the war, boasted at his trial that he had given his 14-year-old son fifty Jews for target practice as a birthday present. This offers historians an insight into his mentality and helps to illustrate the pathological and bestial instinct of some of the Nazis.

According to the Czech historian Hans Maršalek, the Nazi hierarchy divided the concentration camp system into different categories of ascending severity. Mauthausen-Gusen stood out in the highest category, well above Auschwitz. To this hell were assigned those whom the Nazis deemed to be "the most dangerous and un-reformable criminals and asocials"—like my honourable Father and seemly brothers? What harm did they do to anyone, that they should be branded criminals? It is rather significant that the worst concentration camp facilities were situated in Austria, with thousands of Austrians living in close proximity to them, and that some of the worst Nazi war criminals were also Austrian, starting with Adolf Hitler and Adolf Eichmann, both of whom spent their youths in Linz.

After the liberation, my two surviving brothers made their way from Austria to Italy, where the Palestine Jewish Brigade was being demobilised and repatriated home. With the assistance of the Brigade, my brothers sailed from Bari, in Italy, on the *Princess Kathleen*, reaching the shores of Palestine in November 1945. There they joined an agricultural kibbutz, Givat Hashlosha. Later on, Abram volunteered for the Palmach, the elite striking force of the Haganah, and with the rank of corporal fought with distinction as an army scout and sniper before and during the War of Independence.

Abram was attached to the 5th Regiment of the Harel Brigade, which was then under the command of Itzhak Rabin, the future Prime Minister. Abram was present at Kiryat Anavim when the distinguished American colonel Mickey Marcus was mistakenly shot and killed by a sentry when he approached their post after dark. After battling Arab irregulars, his unit fought to open the road to besieged Jerusalem, taking part in the escort of relief convoys into the city. He also fought in the costly battles for Kastel and Latrun, against the British-officered Jordanian Arab Legion, and took part in the fighting within the Holy City, including Sheikh Jarrah and Katamon. Many Holocaust survivors died fighting along the "Jerusalem Corridor" to lift the siege of the city. The situation was so desperate that newly-arrived Holocaust survivors had to be sent straight from the boats into battle with insufficient training, after simply being given a rifle with a few rounds. The only thing they were not short of was motivation. In the battle of Latrun, they charged up the hill towards the Taggart fortress, defended by the well-armed, British-trained Arab Legion, and fell by the hundreds with the cry on their lips: "Never Again!"

The Palmach was later disbanded and incorporated into the IDF (Israel Defense Force). Abram was transferred south, to participate in "Operation Horev," the winter campaign in the Negev desert against the Egyptians, and took part in the battles for Rafah, Beit Jamal, Abu Agheila, and other places, including the Faluja "pocket" where Col. Gamal Abdul Nasser, the future president of Egypt and his detachment was encircled. Abram was badly wounded in this campaign and demobilised in 1949. He was later recalled to take part in the 1956 Suez Campaign—his last war.

In the fifties he graduated from the Hebrew University of Jerusalem, with a degree in Modern History and Mathematics, and became a lecturer at the Hebrew University. Tragically, he developed a brain tumour in his thirties which left him in a wheelchair for the rest of his life. Mother maintained until her dying day that his condition was a direct result of the ill-treatment and blows to the head he had received as a prisoner at Mauthausen-Gusen. Abram never married, and passed away in 2007.

My brother Leizer, who now used his Hebrew name, Eliezer, was also unlucky: he contracted TB soon after the war and had to have a lung removed, spending a long period recuperating in a sanatorium. This, too, was a consequence of his incarceration and brutal treatment at the hands of the Nazis. He always regretted that he was unable to take part in the struggle for Israel's independence due to his poor health. It was said by his close friends that had he made the army his career he would have reached a high rank. In the fifties, Eliezer excelled in everything he did. He too graduated from the Hebrew University of Jerusalem, where he earned a law degree, and went on to work for the Bank of Israel. He later went into the automotive industry with British-Leyland when Lord Stokes set up a truck assembly plant at the port of Ashdod. Later still, he attained a high position with the state-owned TAAS ordnance industry. Eliezer died of mesothelioma, the asbestos disease, at the age of fifty-seven. The doctors attributed this to the asbestos dust he had been exposed to at the Messerschmidt plant so many years earlier. He was married with two children, Yair and Shlomit.

Eliezer's death, following a long illness, came in 1987. A family friend from Ostrowiec, Leib Żabner, who had also been imprisoned at Mauthausen-Gusen, came to the *shiva*, the house of mourning. It was now more than forty years since the end of the war, and he felt duty-bound to pass on Father's last words, and to give me an exact account of his dying moments, which my brothers had never had the heart to tell me about. I always assumed that Father had died of starvation, but Leib took me aside and recounted how Father had been very weak, sitting on the barrack floor leaning against the bunk. He said to Leib Żabner, "Leib, I sense freedom in the air!" A German Kapo overheard this and ran up to Father, kicking him viciously as he lay on the ground. Żabner related how Father cried out in agony as he was being tortured, "Żabner, you must tell my sons I did not die, I was murdered!" The sadistic Kapo wanted to make sure that my father would not live to see freedom.

מרכז מידע פלמ"ח

תברי הפלמ"ח

כץ אברהם
בן משה וגיטה

נולד ב- פולין
נולד ב- 18/ 7/ 1929
גויס ב- 1947
שרת בפלמ"ח
ב-חטיבת הראל
ב-פל' א'
ב-הגדוד החמישי - "שער הגיא"
תפקיד אחרון: סייר
בהכשרת גבעת השלושה, הנוער העובד
1948-1949
שוחרר ב- 1949
נפטר ב- 24/ 4/ 2007

קורות חיים:
אברהם נולד בפולין ב- 18.7.1929 ועלה לארץ מאיטליה בשנת 1945.
התגייס לפלמ"ח, להכשרת גבעת השלושה, בפלוגה א', בגדוד החמישי של
חטיבת הראל והיה סייר וצלף בדרגת רב-סוראי. ליווה שיירות לירושלים,
השתתף בלחימה על הרחבת הפרוזדור לירושלים ובלחימה בעיר, בקרבות
בשועפס, שיח- ג'ראח, קטמון, המשלט המשותף, בית ג'מאל ובית נטיף וכן
במבצע "חורב", כיבוש עוג'ה אל חפיר, אבו-עגילה ומשלטי רפיח. במבצע
"חורב" נפצע באופן קשה, סבל משיתוק חלקי ומשיתוק מלא והיה מאושפז
במוסד סיעודי עד לפטירתו. היה מורה למתמטיקה משנת 1949 עד
לאשפוזו. אברהם כץ נפטר ב- 24.4.2007. הדברים נמסרו על ידי יעקב
זיידה.

Abram's impressive service record, which I obtained from the Palmach Museum.

Eliezer with Shimon Peres on a visit to his plant at Ashkelon. Peres was Israeli Minister of Defense at the time.

Father was a proud man who would not bend the knee and whose spirit could not be broken. He never lost his dignity, in spite of the sub-human and degrading conditions around him. This rankled the Kapo, and as my father lay on the barrack floor he placed his boot on his throat and slowly squeezed the life out of him. Izak, on returning from the work shift and seeing our father dead, said, "I have no will to live now." Within days, he was also gone, only days before the Americans got to Gusen and Mauthausen.

According to documents my son David obtained from the Red Cross International Tracing Service at Bad Arolsen in Germany in 1992, my father and brothers carried the prisoner category "Jew," and the official cause of death was attributed to "Myocardial weakness and general physical decay." The Red Cross offered to furnish death certificates, but I did not want them; they were based on doctored Nazi records that didn't state the truth. No doubt my father and brothers suffered from the conditions stated, as did most of the starving prisoners, but it's not recorded that my father was in fact brutally murdered by a German Capo in front of witnesses. It still angers me that my father's murderer went unpunished, as did the vast majority of the perpetrators of the Holocaust; justice was never done.

After abandoning Poland in 1946, following the Kielce pogrom, my mother lived in a displaced persons camp at Bad-Reichenhall in Bavaria, awaiting her turn to leave for Palestine. One day, quite by chance, she and some of her friends on a visit to nearby Munich recognised Army Captain Reimund Anton Zwierzyna, the cruel Ostrowiec labour-camp commandant, in the street. He was an Austrian with a Slavic name, and had been a professional soldier in the pre-war Austrian army. The survivors followed him unobserved to his home, and having discovered where he lived alerted the American Military Police, who arrested him as a suspected war criminal. Zwierzyna had been trying to pass himself off as a displaced person, no doubt awaiting his turn to emigrate to the West, like so many other war criminals who were freely allowed into America, Canada, Australia, and other countries. Britain, too, reluctant to repatriate Baltic war criminals to their countries of origin behind the Iron Curtain, lest they be punished, took in many Ukrainian, Latvian, and Lithuanian ex-*Einsatzkommando* killers without screening them for crimes against humanity.

My mother was one of those asked to identify Zwierzyna in Munich before charges could be brought against him by the American occupation forces. Her friends recalled that although the prisoner had changed his appearance somewhat, as he was led towards the identity parade with several others, and before the line-up was complete, my mother picked him out instantly. Not knowing the procedure with identity parades and unable to contain herself, she immediately pointed at him, shouting at the top of her voice, "That's Zwierzyna! That's Zwierzyna!"

Zwierzyna was ultimately extradited from Germany to Poland, and thanks to the post-war Polish government, he was put on trial in Warsaw and found guilty of crimes against humanity. After the sentence was passed in 1948 he was taken to Ostrowiec and hanged on a gallows specially erected on the very site where the slave-labour camp had previously stood, and where he had condemned innocent people to hang. Some former camp inmates travelled to Warsaw to attend the trial to testify against him, but Mother declined to set foot in Poland, saying, "I cannot go back to the place of Jewish martyrdom and tread the very soil that's steeped in Jewish blood."

The perimeter wall of the Catholic cemetery in Ostrowiec, built with broken-up headstones taken from the Jewish cemetery, with the Hebrew inscriptions clearly visible.

There is nothing to record that Jews ever lived in Ostrowiec, apart from this heap of shattered headstones.

My sister Fela, to whom I owe my life many times over, passed away in Israel on 26 December 2008 after a long illness, almost sixty-four years to the day after our liberation from the Nazis. Her husband Ben predeceased her by several years. They left two sons, Moshe and Arik, and six grandchildren. Fela and I were always very close, having been through so much together, and with her passing, I felt strongly that a chapter of my life had come to a close.

***

After all these years, it is still on my conscience that I was never able to trace my rescuer, *Pani* Gozdzialska, while she was alive. I would have liked to express my gratitude for her goodness and moral courage, although I could never have adequately repaid her for what she did. My sister and I never managed to make contact with *Pani* after the war ended. As hard as we tried, we could find no trace of her. Mail from the West was censored in Poland, and letters came back marked "Return to Sender." Travel behind the Iron Curtain was not advisable at the height of the communist era for someone who was born in that country, and the crown could not have offered me any protection in Poland. As a spinster, *Pani* had no relatives we were aware of, apart from Wanda, who was a very sick person. Considering *Pani's* age, she could not have lived for long after the war.

More recently, I went back to Poland twice to renew my efforts and to at least find out what became of my kindly and brave rescuer and to trace any living relative she may have had. I wanted to have her memory honoured at Yad Vashem in Jerusalem, among the righteous, but unfortunately didn't have enough information to enable me to. In order to have her life commemorated there, I hoped to acquire more information from Poland. On my last visit there, I made every effort I could, assisted by our former Polish *au pair,* Maria Mażyntas, who now lives in Gdańsk. Maria spent days in Anin and Warsaw with me, knocking on doors, speaking to elderly people, and searching record offices. Maria carried on with the enquiries herself after I left the country. While I was there, we met with the Anin priest, Marek Doszko, who let us go over the parish register and burial records. The priest was most helpful and even offered to make an announcement from the pulpit in the hope of finding someone old enough to remember the lady, but alas this too was without success. We advertised in the local press and made enquiries at the local libraries where the elderly get together to socialise. We also met with a local historian, Mrs. Wolodzko-Maziarska, who wrote a history of Anin and its inhabitants—we left no stone unturned, but it was all to no avail. As we could find no trace of *Pani* in the parish records, the priest concluded that under the circumstances she could not have been buried within his parish. If there was no money to pay for the burial she would have been buried elsewhere. I shudder to think that *Pani* may have been given a pauper's burial, with no marked grave and no one to attend her funeral, because she was so poor and all alone. May *Pani* be rewarded in heaven among the Righteous of the Nations.

36485397R00194

Made in the USA
Middletown, DE
03 November 2016